HOUSTON BLUE

THE STORY
OF THE
HOUSTON POLICE
DEPARTMENT

HOUSTON BLUE

THE STORY OF THE HOUSTON POLICE DEPARTMENT

MITCHEL P. ROTH AND TOM KENNEDY

Number 8 in the North Texas Crime and Criminal Justice Series

University of North Texas Press

Denton, Texas

10   9   8   7   6   5   4   3   2   1

Permissions:
University of North Texas Press
1155 Union Circle #311336
Denton, TX 76203-5017

The paper used in this book meets the minimum requirements of the American
National Standard for Permanence of Paper for Printed Library Materials,
z39.48.1984. Binding materials have been chosen for durability.

Library of Congress Cataloging-in-Publication Data

Roth, Mitchel P., 1953-
Houston blue : the story of the Houston Police Department / by Mitchel
P. Roth and Tom Kennedy.
p. cm. — (North Texas crime and criminal justice series ; no. 8)
"Back in 2005, the board of the directors of the Houston Police
Officers' Union commissioned Mitchel Roth, Ph.D., and Tom Kennedy to
research and write a book that chronicled the history of the Houston
Police Department and the Houston Police Officers' Union."—Foreword.
Includes bibliographical references.
ISBN 978-1-57441-472-1 (cloth : alk. paper) — ISBN 978-1-57441-482-0
(ebook)
1. Houston (Tex.). Police Dept.—History. 2. Police—Texas—Houston—History. 3. Police—
Labor unions—Texas—Houston—History. 4. Houston Police Officers' Union—History.
5. Houston Police Officers' Association—History. I. Kennedy, Tom, 1946- II. Houston Police
Officers' Union. III. Title. IV. Series: North Texas crime and criminal justice series ; no. 8.
HV8148.H73.R68   2012
363.209764'1411—dc23
2012028654

Houston Blue is Number 8 in the North Texas Crime and Criminal Justice series.

CONTENTS

FOREWORD

Back in 2005, the board of the directors of the Houston Police Officers' Union commissioned Mitchel Roth, Ph.D., and Tom Kennedy to research and write a book that chronicled the history of the Houston Police Department and the Houston Police Officers' Union.

These men have done an outstanding job of documenting the Department's creation and its rich history since the birth of Houston in 1836. Additionally, they also documented the birth and development of the police labor movement in HPD following the establishment of the Houston Police Officers' Association in 1945.

Throughout the history of our department, there have been 64 different individuals who have led the Houston Police Department as we grew from an unknown place in Texas on Buffalo Bayou to the fourth largest city in the United States of America.

Since the founding of the Houston Police Officers' Association through its name change in 1995 to the Houston Police Officers' Union, there have been 29 Union presidents.

Over the past 176 years, the Houston Police Department's stature as a cutting-edge organization is well known throughout the world. Our Department's ability to mature into the highly respected organization it is today is due to the efforts and sacrifices of the thousands of Houston police officers and non-sworn employees who served the city of Houston with honor and distinction.

This book is a historical testament to every Houston police officer who honorably served our city and did their best each day to make the city safe for all who have lived, worked, and raised families here.

This publication is dedicated to the 112 Houston police officers who made the ultimate sacrifice while in the performance of their duties as Houston police officers.

I also want to give a special acknowledgment to the following officers who dedicated themselves to improving working conditions, gaining job protection and promotional rights, as well as contractually guaranteeing wage and benefit improvements that all of us enjoy today.

These officers literally changed the career trajectory for every Houston police officer that serves today.

They are:

Captain Earl Maughmer Jr., Captain "Ham" Ellisor, Lt. Breck Porter, Lt. Frank Murray and Sgt. Julius Knigge, who in 1945 led the founding of the HPOA, then in 1948 gained state civil service rights for HPD officers and established the Houston Police Officers' Pension System.

Officer Robert J. Thomas who in 1979, after surviving near fatal gunshot wounds, was a police labor pioneer who risked his career to lay the groundwork for significant and aggressive reforms in the area of legal protections and rights for HPD officers.

Senior Police Officers Hans Marticiuc and Mark Clark along with Sergeant Tommy Britt who in 1985 gained independent third party arbitration rights for HPD officers, our grievance procedure and Police Officers' Bill of Rights. Then, in 1997, they achieved what was previously believed to be the unattainable goal of obtaining Collective Bargaining Rights through a state authorized Meet-and-Confer statute. Marticiuc became a nationally recognized leader in police union strategies, while Clark established a sophisticated and highly effective lobbying philosophy that continues to well serve Houston officers.

As previously stated, our Department and Union have evolved into highly respected organizations over the years. It is our hope, that through this publication, all of us will gain an even better understanding of the history and hard-fought gains our Department and Union have made since their inception.

May God continue to bless HPD, its officers and non-sworn employees, their families, and the people we have all sworn to protect in this great city of Houston, Texas.

Ray Hunt
President
Houston Police Officers' Union

1

BAGHDAD ON THE BAYOU

Much of the early history of peacekeeping and law enforcement in Houston has been lost to fire, floods and poor record keeping. Not until the 1840s does the dim outline of what would become one of the nation's largest police departments begin to take shape. The earliest references and anecdotes dealing with law enforcement can be traced back to the early 1830s. By most accounts, the origins of Houston policing can be traced back to the efforts of an Anglo settler named John W. Moore in the years leading up to the Republic. Moore was appointed *Alcalde* of the Eastern Province, a position that covered everything from local judge to sheriff.

However, most law enforcement was community-based in this era. In fact, as far back as Anglo Saxon England prior to the Norman Conquest of 1066, community residents were called on to bring local troublemakers to justice in lieu of formal policing. And so it was in Houston almost eight centuries later; when a crime was committed, someone alerted the community and the familiar posse composed of local residents of western lore would set out to bring the malefactor to justice. Typically the suspect would be held in confinement until the arrival of the *Alcalde*, who would conduct the trial and dole out punishment. There was no need for a penitentiary in the 1830s since punishment usually took place immediately after the trial, whether it was physical or financial in nature.

Few of the inhabitants of what would become the fourth largest city in the United States could have predicted the future stature of what in 1836 was barely a clearing on the bayou with several cabins in the woods. In 1833, one early visitor to the "Town of Houston" noted that "it was hard work to find the city in the pine woods" and that when one managed to actually find the site it was little more than "one dugout canoe, a bottle gourd of whiskey and a surveyor's chain and compass and was inhabited by four men with an ordinary camping outfit." When this visitor returned to Harrisburg, he reported "mosquitoes were as large as grasshoppers" and found his companion's attempt to bathe in the bayou cut short by alligators.[1]

Following independence in 1836, the Republic adopted a constitution that would influence the development of local policing in Texas. According to Article 4, Section 10 of the 1836 Constitution of the Texas Republic:

> There shall be appointed for each county, a convenient number of Justices of the Peace, one sheriff, one Coroner, and a sufficient number of Constables, who shall hold their offices for two years, to be elected by the qualified voters of the district or county, as Congress may direct. Justice of the Peace and Sheriffs shall be commissioned by the President {of the Republic].

Many Western historians consider Texas sheriffs as "the first legally qualified sheriffs of the American Far West."[2]

Houston was situated on the "the south side of Buffalo Bayou, at least sixty feet above the water and about one hundred miles from the coast."[3] Founded just two months earlier, on January 1, 1837, and incorporated as the city of Houston on the following June 5, the city, with a sheriff as its first principal peace officer, held its first official election in August of the same summer. Turnout was reportedly low, due in no small part to the voter qualifications of the day, which required anyone voting for aldermen or mayor to be a free white male, citizen of Texas, a resident of Houston for at least six months, and the owner of at least $100 worth of city real estate for at least three months prior to the election.[4]

Houston, from the very beginning, was besieged by extreme weather events that have since made the city famous. In April of that first year, the town was flooded with seemingly endless rain, followed by a hurricane in October that made the bayou rise four feet to the edge of Main Street. The following February, Houston was jolted with its coldest day when temperatures dropped to sixteen degrees below freezing on February 2 and six degrees colder two weeks later. It was indeed a rare sight to see even Galveston Bay covered with ice and the streets of Houston covered with snow and ice.[5]

Weather did little to dampen the spirits of settlers headed to Houston. Early settlers did not just bring libraries, furniture, musical instruments and the odd piano, but their servants and slaves and even the lumber that would be needed to construct their new homes. Despite advertisements for all kinds of wood in "inexhaustible quantities," there was no sawmill and few laborers.

Trained carpenters earned as much as three dollars a day. One individual reported that Houston "seemed to be the focus of immigration" and "houses could not be built near as fast as required, so that quite a large number of linen tents were pitched in every direction over the prairie, which gave the city the appearance of a Methodist camp-ground."[6]

According to one early history, "In the early days, a man's reputation for personal courage, honesty of purpose and a bulldog determination to do his duty" were the requisites of a police officer. It was his personality, and not his ability as a businessman and executive, that counted. The only ability demanded of him was that "he be quick on the draw and expert in the use of his pistol."[7] By all accounts, Houston's first official peace officers fit the bill.

While a number of sources indicate that G. W. Holland, elected constable in 1837, was the city's first law enforcement official, the best evidence suggests that appointment of two constables in 1838 by the city aldermen inaugurated formal law enforcement in Houston.[8] Foreign tourists were apparently impressed by the Texas brand of justice. Mrs. Matilda Charlotte Houston reported in the early 1840s, "The Texan people go on remarkably well with their primitive system of administering justice,"[9] especially when it came to the lynch law that sometimes prevailed in Houston.

Another British tourist named Francis C. Sheridan several years earlier, upon leaving Houston, commented that lynch law "has been as generally vilified as it has been generally successful." He found that seldom "the judgment of the respectable part of a community errs, or that a punishment inflicted by it is disproportional to the crime, and at all events this much can be said of Lynch law, that it has reached murderers, felons, and swindlers *when no other law could.*"[10]

While the British tourist did indeed support draconian punishments in a frontier town, it should also be noted that England used the "bloody code" in the same era that demanded the death penalty for almost 200 different felonies back in the "civilized" British Isles.

Thanks to his success in his earlier stint as *Alcalde*, John W. Moore was elected as the county's first sheriff in 1836. Sworn in to office in February, the new district court convened for the first time by March 20, 1837, with jurors taking their seats "On a log under an arbour of pine bushes."[11] Sheriff Moore then presented three cases. First, the verdict in an assault and battery case resulted in a judgment of guilty and a fine of five dollars. The second case was a charge of murder. Foreshadowing Texas's future reputation for frontier justice, most of the jurors agreed that they probably would have done the same thing under the circumstances and exonerated him. Alas, the third suspect would not be so lucky. Found guilty of larceny, James Adams was ordered to pay restitution of $295 and receive the draconian punishment of thirty-nine lashes on his back, followed by the branding of a "T" (for thief) on the back of his right hand.[12] As was customary in an era before professional law enforcement, the sentence was to be carried out publicly on a Friday night, a message that could not be sent any louder to potential criminals. As was his duty, Sheriff Moore was assigned to carry out the sentence—quite a day's work for a freshly-minted sheriff.[13]

As sheriff, Moore was required to act as tax collector, keeper of the peace, issuer of warrants, hangman and chief executioner. One early account tells of several sympathizers visiting the judge to complain of the harsh conditions of the jail and requesting more hospitable quarters for two condemned men. The judge acquiesced, pronouncing that because of the jail's inhumane conditions, the prisoners should wait no longer. The following headline reported the aftermath: "Merciful Judge once had 2 prisoners Hung Ahead of Time to Save from Cold," "presumably" by Sheriff Moore.

Arriving on the outskirts of Houston in 1837, an unnamed traveler reported that "The Land from Galveston to the city of Houston, or at least such portions of it as are worth having, have been taken by settlers, and I doubt whether an inch of it can be bought for a less sum than at the rate of five dollars an acre."[14] He came upon the city after traveling first to San Jacinto, less than a year removed from the battle that made Texas a republic, before continuing on to Houston from the mouth of Buffalo Bayou. The next stop was in the burgeoning town of Harrisburg, some twenty-five miles to the north (now part of East Houston), extending some distance above his destination. Mr. Anonymous continued his journey, passing Buffalo, better known as "Pokersville" for obvious reasons.

Just four years later, future mayoral candidate Francis R. Lubbock visited Houston by steamboat, but found "So little evidence ... of a landing that we passed by the site." Backing back down the bayou toward the fledgling city, Lubbock and his party "discovered a road or street laid off from the water's edge. Upon landing we found stakes and footprints" and then "a few tents, one of which served as a saloon, and several small houses under construction."[15] So this was Houston entering its first year of existence—several ramshackle shacks and plentiful alcoholic libations, with enough mouths to sip them. Policemen, firemen and the other hallmarks of urban living had yet to be discussed.

There is little doubt that the city was named for the friend of town-founders Augustus C. and John K. Allen and the hero of the Battle of San Jacinto the previous year—Sam Houston. Houston was probably flattered but no doubt remembered that when he was shot in the ankle just months earlier he had to go all the way to New Orleans to find a capable doctor. According to popular lore, the Allen Brothers had ulterior motives for naming the town after Houston. It was most likely part of their campaign to have the town selected as the headquarters of the new republic. In its planning stages, the city was platted in gridiron fashion, a pattern that flourished after Philadelphia. It was supposed that this pattern was best for future commercial greatness, something the Allen Brothers wholeheartedly expected.

By 1840, Houston was laid out on a nine-square-mile grid, with a courthouse in the centre. Together with the other elected officers who included the mayor, a secretary and treasurer, tax collector and constable, city governance had been pretty well established. Ordinances required two aldermen to be elected from each of the four wards. The First Ward was located north of Congress and west of Main Street. The Second Ward was north of Congress and east of Main. The Third Ward was everything to the south of Congress and to the east of Main, while the Fourth Ward was comprised of land south of Congress and west of Main. Later, as the city continued to spread north of Buffalo Bayou the Fifth and Sixth wards were created. Although these political subdivisions were abolished years ago, the terms, according to journalist Ray Miller, "are still used to describe the black ghettos in the area near downtown."[16]

There are few records that have survived from these halcyon days of the late 1830s and the 1840s; much of the city's history and the evolution of law enforcement from this era can be only anecdotally recovered. Outside of his duties, it would seem that most peacekeeping was the jurisdiction of Sheriff John W. Moore and members of a Citizen's Patrol. When Houston was incorporated as a city on June 5, 1837, law enforcement planning was one of the first issues on the table. Little more than two weeks later a committee composed of the town's leading citizens was charged with forming "the citizens into a patrol for procuring order."[17]

Houston citizens became concerned about violent crime at an early juncture. One early visitor called Houston "the greatest sink of dissipation and vice that modern times have known."[18] Probably more hyperbole than fact,

Isaac Batterson (July 10, 1792 – February 19, 1838)

Appointed a member of the local citizens' patrol on June 22, 1837, Isaac Batterson is one of the earliest verifiable members of the Houston Citizens' patrols. He is noted in an entertaining story in a journal kept by an unidentified man in 1837. *Texas in 1837* is considered one of the earliest written accounts of the Republic of Texas. In the journal the anonymous traveler notes his appearance at the home of a "wealthy squire," who points out to his guest that his floor is missing because "it was converted into a raft for this patriotic purpose [assisting the Texas army]." Born in Fairfield, Connecticut, Batterson arrived in Texas in 1834, taking up residence along Buffalo Bayou (now Clinton). He served as justice of the peace of the Second Militia District of Harrisburg County beginning on February 6, 1837, where he was known as "Squire." He apparently spent most of his time in Houston, which was part of his jurisdiction.[19]

by most accounts early Houston was an open freewheeling frontier town with few restraints on misbehavior. As early as September 23, 1837, the *Telegraph and Texas Register* chronicled the fatal shooting of Leman Kelcy by Zadock Hubbard the previous week. Newspaper editor Dr. Francis Moore Jr. lamented, "This is the first individual of this city who has fallen a victim to the disgraceful custom of wearing deadly weapons—a custom which should be denounced and frowned down by every intelligent and respectable community."[20]

Duelling was so conspicuous in the area that one Louis de France emigrated from France to teach fencing in Houston. Houston was not even one month old when the first duel took place, but the duelling instructor and other members of the fencing fraternity were disappointed that duels were typically fought with pistols instead of swords. Francis Moore was one of the loudest critics of the practice and used his newspaper, the *Telegraph*, as a forum to rail against duelling. The following editorial offers the gist of his comments: "We had an affair of honor settled here yesterday, no blood shed however, all was amicably adjusted by merely shooting into WOOD, If all duels were settled by merely shooting at blocks, instead of BLOCKHEADS, the practice would be far more consonant with the dictates of wisdom and justice."[21] Moore's crusade against duelling led to its criminalization in 1839, and by 1840, there were few if any accounts of duelling incidents in Houston, leading to its virtual disappearance from the streets of Houston by 1840.

By 1838, Houston had established itself as a trading centre, which brought with it its share of criminal activity. The previous year a Methodist minister named Littleton Fowler reported finding "much vice, gaming, drunkenness, and profanity" in the frontier town.[22] Public drunkenness, prostitution, gambling and violence accompanied the growth of Houston from frontier village to city-hood.

Due in part to the promotional acumen of the Allen Brothers and other boosters, businessmen and transients alike found Houston and Texas an irresistible destination during the Republic period. But in too many cases recent arrivals became embroiled in criminal activity. One Englishman passing through recounted, "Murder and every other crime is of great frequency in Texas."[23] Another visitor reported that it was not uncommon "to see men passing on the streets with from 2 to 4 pistols belted around them, with the addition of a larger Bowie knife."[24]

According to HPD historian and former archivist Denny Hair, the first death of a Houston peace officer on duty was probably the murder of a Constable Lewis Way on April 19, 1839 [although WPA notes he was appointed constable on January 6, 1840]. One of the city's original constables, he was reportedly stabbed to death by Army veteran Captain Haigler. The *Morning Star* of the following day chronicled the killing, noting that it occurred at a "house of ill repute" run by someone named Nelly. Way was called to the house to confront the former captain who was breaking crockery and making an all around ruckus. Almost immediately, Haigler drew a "sword cane" and fatally stabbed Constable Way through the right breast and lung. Haigler was arrested, but it is not clear what final judgment was rendered. However, there was talk that if the rudimentary court system would not take care of the case, the citizens might take the law into their own hands.[25]

Before the 1830s ended Houston had become a center for vice. One even asserted that in Houston "barrooms were in the ascendancy."[26] Sundays were no exception, with bars, billiard halls, and faro banks operating in full view. According to the November 15, 1839 *Morning Star*, "The extent to which this vice was carried, exceeded all belief. It appeared to be the business of the great mass of people, to collect around these centers of vice and hold their drunken orgies, without seeming to know that the Sabbath was made for more serious purposes, and night for rest. Drinking was reduced to a system and had its own laws and regulations. Nothing was regarded as a greater violation of established etiquette than for one who was going to drink not to invite all within a reasonable distance to partake, so the Texians being entirely a military people not only fought but drank in platoons."[27]

With little in the way of a law enforcement presence, peacekeeping was often handled by militia groups or extra-legal vigilantes—a hallmark of frontier societies. On one occasion a well-armed mob threatened unarmed customers at the Exchange Hotel bar. However, this time the Milam Guards intervened and ended the riot quickly.[28]

By the late 1830s, counterfeit Texas Treasury notes began appearing in Houston.[29] Financial matters would get even worse following a yellow fever outbreak in which 240 out of the city's 2,000 residents perished. Texas currency had soon depreciated to ten cents on the dollar. With rumours of the capitol moving to Austin, merchants in New Orleans cut off credit lines to Houston merchants. Another one of the Texas Republic's most serious problems was the forging of land titles, leading the first Congress of the Republic to pass a law making forgery a capital offense, with the penalty of hanging.

Houston had a theatre, a courthouse and a jail well before building its first church. Houston's first public buildings included a county courthouse and county jail, both erected on the courthouse square at the intersection of Congress and Fannin avenues. The courthouse was not much to look at, or even distinct from other buildings at first glance. But, it was always important for new towns trying to attract business entrepreneurs to advertise various staples of justice and order by noting the availability of a jail. Like most frontier structures, Houston's (and Harris County's) first county courthouse jail was built with logs. Its design had more in common with a medieval dungeon than a model prison. Measuring 24 by 24 feet, the structure was divided into two cells, each 12-foot square.

According to one early Houston resident the jail was "simply a square log box having neither doors nor windows. Access to the jail was through this trap door. A prisoner was taken to the roof by means of a ladder. The ladder was then drawn up and lowered into the jail where two poorly ventilated cells often held more than six men at a time. The prisoner descended and then the ladder was drawn up and the trap shut."[30] More recent scholarship by Ed Blackburn, Jr. suggests that this was probably a fabrication, noting that access was provided to each room by way of a "three-foot planked door, with an iron grated door that opened into a larger room."[31] Further debunking the previous description was the fact that each cell was graced with a pair of small-barred windows.

Before the jail was even completed, the adjoining neighborhood began to fill up with prosperous families who demanded the removal of the odious structure. As the prestigious environs became home to the families of Cornelius Ennis, William Fairfax Gray and their ilk, a successful campaign was launched to replace it. In 1838, the 11th Judicial Court ruled in favor of the litigants and the jail was torn down. The consensus seemed to be that it would be better to lose the jail than the fine families; rather efforts should be directed toward building "both the Court House and jail in some place where the people are not so refined in their ideas."[32]

A new courthouse and jail were later erected on Congress Avenue. These accommodations would suffice until the 1850s, when the old courthouse was demolished and replaced by a two-story brick building. By then a much more "commodious city lock-up" was being used to house county prisoners as well.[33]

Naturally, it was not long after Houston built its first jail that the first escape attempt was made. Near midnight on January 18, 1840, five prisoners who had been industriously boring through the wood floor hit pay dirt, escaping into the typical Saturday crowds. Two days later the *Morning Star* reported, "These five jail birds with a wonderful knowledge of the locality of the best horses in the place, went to Mr. Osborn's stables and stole seven of the finest in the town, mounted and made their ways to parts unknown." While their destinations remain a mystery to this day, those in the know figured they either escaped by way of the "Sabine chute" or hoped to hide out by joining the Union army.[34]

From its inception until the 1840s, the city grew at a snail's pace. According to one local census, in 1839, Houston was the largest town in Texas, with a population of 2,073. Of these, 1,620 were male. This was a typical ratio for most frontier communities.[35] By May 1842, the population registered 3,000 for the first time. Despite the great hoopla surrounding its establishment in 1837, less than one year later legislators and speculators had found the bad weather, mud, mosquitoes and sickness so noisome that rumblings were heard suggesting a move to a more comfortable location. Houston historian David McComb cites as proof a letter from Kelsey H. Douglass to his wife in

December 1837, lamenting that "I find this the most miserable place in the world."[36]

By September 1839, most of the government had moved farther west to Austin, taking with it not only furniture and other possessions but the archives as well. The local newspaper, the *Morning Star*, noted that the new government buildings created for the capitol of the republic stood "desolate and empty."[37] Ever the businessmen, the Allen Brothers quickly put a rental sign on the former capitol building and it was later turned into the Capitol Hotel. It would serve this capacity until 1881 when it was torn down and made into a new hotel. It would eventually fall into the hands of William Marsh Rice, who became one the city's most prominent citizens.[38]

So Houston would witness its first major defeat in its transition toward urbanization, a not insignificant one, having lost the capitol to Austin. Whatever prominence Houston hoped to achieve would have to come from commerce and the industriousness of business entrepreneurs—qualities that Houston has never lacked.

In 1839, Houston witnessed the creation of its first temperance organization. This should not be surprising considering the report by the *Morning Star* in May that described business as "dull and growing duller. Loafers have increased, and are increasing, and ought to be diminished. District Court in session—crimes and criminals are undergoing its scrutiny."[39] That same year saw the appointment [before it became an elected position] of the first city marshal, Thomas Stansbury Jr., and constable, James Waag [Wag].[40]

According to Houston's first city charter, in 1839 the city accepted the responsibility of providing its citizens with a peacekeeping apparatus. First steps were taken the following year by creating the position of city marshal. One historian noted that except for the years of the Civil War "when the regular police was supplemented by a night patrol composed of citizens from each of the city's four wards, police development in Houston, as in other town's of similar size, evolved around the city marshal."[41] Over the next thirty years the city marshal, deputy and several watchmen "remained the mainstay of law enforcement."

As early as May 1840, the Houston City Council took steps to tackle the local crime problem by passing an ordinance making it illegal for individuals "to wear or carry deadly weapons of any description on their body, or in their hands, within the limits of the city." To back this up, a fine of fifty dollars was implemented. Any citizen who brought an offender before the mayor was given a bounty of half of the fine collected. According to the *Morning Star* of

May 18, 1840, anyone who was found drunk within the city limits would be sentenced to thirty days of work on the city streets for a first offense and not less than sixty days for each following offense. Those cited for disturbing the peace would be fined not less than ten dollar and not more than one hundred dollars, and in default of the fine could be forced to work on the streets between ten and thirty days.

By the early 1840s the position of city marshal was well established. City government sanctioned the creation of the marshal's office in 1841. According to city minutes, Daniel Busby was the first elected to the position. He was elected twice more the following two years. In 1842, Busby's duties were expanded to include duties of wharf master, which also offered additional income through the collection of additional fees. According to city council records, by 1843 at least, the city marshal was an elected office and was voted on each year.

On May 10, 1843 the police committee was forced to hold a special session to investigate Marshal Busby, who was accused of "taking dues of the City and appropriating them to his own without making any report." Busby quickly acceded to the request for his resignation. By most accounts this was the first official evidence of a disciplinary action in HPD history. Joseph Waterman was elected to replace Busby and immediately launched an investigation into Busby's graft. In a report to the mayor, Waterman reported that Busby had taken at least $317.52. Due to the complexities of the city's fee systems and the potential for graft and fraud in 1844, the Houston City Council required each newly elected marshal to post a bond or surety of $2,500.

Until the election of I. C. Lord to the first of six terms as city marshal in 1863, there seemed to be a continuous turnover in the position in the 1840s and 1850s. Due to the paucity of records for this time, there is little consensus as to why there was so little stability in the office during this period.

Early Houston newspapers such as the *Telegraph and Texas Register* chronicled the escalating violence of the 1840s. In fact, Houston had a specifically designated duelling ground in the late 1830s. Duelling became a common method of preserving one's reputation or concluding disagreements. During the last years of the Texas Republic arguments were settled with fists, knives and guns. According to historian William Hogan, "More than two thirds of the total numbers of indictments in the district courts [of Texas] were for the crimes of assault and battery, affray, assault with intent to kill, or murder." Despite a conviction rate of sixty percent, most offenders got away with a small fine and paying court costs.[42] Members of the clergy were appalled by the laxity of sentencing, leading Houston Rev. Charles Gillett in June of 1843 to give a sermon lamenting:

> God has said Thou shalt do no murder. This people have reversed the command. I do not here speak of that fashionable mode of taking life, according to an imperious code of self-styled honor. But, I speak of wanton, barbarous outrages, in violation of all law human and divine, which find among this people, not simply apologists, but everywhere bold defenders.[43]

By most accounts the most common crime in 1840s Texas was gambling. Professional gamblers abounded, as did their victims in the frontier settlements. However, the greatest animosity was reserved for thieves. One Texas physician wrote that "the killing of a fellow was looked upon with greater leniency than theft."[44] A frontier ethos existed in Texas and other territories that came down heaviest on horse and cattle thieves. With little in the way of legal peacekeeping, citizens often took the law into their own hands. According to the criminal code of the late 1830s, robbery, burglary and horse theft were capital crimes. Punishment for larceny, depending on the case, usually called for whipping and branding. Despite the punitive code, evidence suggests that there was more bark than bite to the laws. In Houston at least, one editor expressed the local attitude toward draconian punishment:

> The laws that have heretofore been in operation for the punishment of crime, were of so sanguinary a character that they defeated the very object for which they were intended, and criminals were permitted to escape unpunished because those laws were considered too severe.[45]

2

HOUSTON, USA

As German scientist Ferdinand van Roemer approached Houston in 1845, he recorded in his diary, "I found myself on the way to Houston, next to Galveston, the most important city of Texas."[1] However, upon his arrival in the Bayou City, he reported the houses on the city's main street resembled the frame construction Roemer found in Galveston, but "looked somewhat dilapidated and less tidy."[2] Like most cities of this era west of the Mississippi River, the streets were unpaved and the mud seemingly bottomless. Most residents of early Houston could relate to one contemporary account of an unnamed southern city in which a citizen ran out to assist someone buried up to the neck in mud. The victim replied, "No need to worry, I have a horse underneath me."[3]

Roemer saved his greatest accolades for Houston's numerous saloons, which he found in some cases "really magnificent when compared to their surroundings."[4] Even in this early era, Houstonians had a reputation for enjoying a good time, more like New Orleans to the east, than San Antonio in temperament. Roemer found saloons displaying "divers [sic] kinds of firewater," Cognac and brandy the most popular. The German scientist reported that business merchants would leave their shops unattended momentarily "to indulge in a fiery drink in the nearest saloon."[5]

It would seem by Roemer's description that even at the early date of 1846, Houston was already in the process of shedding its frontier existence. Having joined the Union, Houston also linked itself to a rapidly growing economy. According to Roemer, by 1846, the city was already developing a "well-ordered community life and the laws are generally obeyed."[6] Unfortunately his account does not describe the impact of the city's growing law enforcement presence. For the chronicler of Houston policing, this is doubly unfortunate. Except for random newspaper accounts between 1846 and 1853, the only mention in city records related to civil order and peacekeeping is the position of elected aldermen.

One historian noted that as early as April 1846, city leaders authorized a committee to form "a secret police" to assist city officers in maintaining peace and order. But, in reality, these officers were expected to keep track of strangers "of low type character" and any rumors involving the local slave population. This protocol by all accounts was common throughout the South prior to the War Between the States.[7] Following the Civil War secret policemen played a more important role in city crime detection and investigation.

What little is known about Houston peacekeeping between 1844 and 1856 involved the Harris County sheriffs. Five different individuals served in the office during these twelve years. John Fitzgerald, who held the office between 1844 and 1846, was not new to public service, having served as associate justice, similar to the present day office of commissioner, between 1837 and 1840. He also served two stints as city secretary. During the 1840s and 1850s, the sheriff and his men were paid by a fee system, in effect living off the amount of money their department took in.[8]

In June 1846, David Russell became Harris County's fourth sheriff. His two terms spanned the War with Mexico and the California Gold Rush. He was soon joined in public office by City Marshal R. P. Boyce. Between 1850 and 1856, a pair of brothers wore the sheriff's badge. In 1850, former justice of the peace and Alderman James B. Hogan, Jr., another Battle of San Jacinto veteran, became sheriff. His younger brother, Thomas M. Hogan, served as his deputy sheriff until he replaced his brother in 1854, when James exchanged the sheriff's badge for that of the city marshal. Thomas entered Houston police history lore while supervising a public hanging in 1854, when he apparently stood on the trapdoor of the gallows with the condemned man and was about to cut the rope that held it closed when close friends pulled him off it just in time. Both brothers were later buried in the old Founder's Memorial Cemetery on West Dallas and Ballantine. Hogan Street in the city's Fifth Ward was reportedly named after the brothers Hogan.[9]

Although there is a gap in many of the records concerning Houston and its police force in the 1840s and 1850s, there are other measurements available by which to gauge the city, most importantly the national census every ten years. According to the seventh census conducted in 1850, although there were still a substantial number of German immigrants, by the mid century forty-eight percent of the free inhabitants originated from states that would represent the Confederacy in the next decade, while only thirty-three percent represented countries other than the United States. So it would not be a stretch to suggest that Houston was on its way to becoming a thoroughly southern city. But it would take a couple more decades to make the transition from Western frontier burgh to southern city. The 1870 census supports this, noting that sixty-seven percent of the population had been born in the South and only seventeen percent were born outside the States, nearly half the number in the 1850s census.[10]

As a southern society, Houston exhibited a strong orientation toward military service that exists to this day. Prior to the Civil War, a number of local military groups were on display at celebrations to demonstrate their martial prowess in shooting contests and drill competitions while elaborately dressed in their individual colors. Among these units were the Milam Guards, Davis Guards, Washington Light Guard and Turner Rifles. Many of their members were welcomed with open arms into the Confederate Army since they could immediately be put in the field. Without much of a law enforcement presence in town, these units also could be called on like a militia to act in a police capacity during emergencies and civil disorder.

Despite the growing peacekeeping presence in the 1850s, Houston's streets still echoed with cursing, gunshots and a cacophony of drunkenness. According to historian David McComb, "Protection, however, was inconsistent until after the Civil War."[11] In most cases the only law enforcement at night was due to the civic impulse of volunteers and private guards. The results of their efforts were regarded with mixed feelings. According to the August 16, 1860 *Tri-Weekly Telegraph*:

> If the gentleman who have volunteered upon the night police in Houston, and whose services have already been of no little importance in arresting vicious Negroes, would be a little more careful of their fire-arms, and bear in mind that their business is not to shoot cats and dogs ad libitum as they pass about, they would enhance the appreciation of their services in the minds of the people.[12]

One explanation for the slow evolution of a modern police force was the lack of public support. One editor queried rhetorically whether it was worth hiring police officers, paying them "better wages than they could make at hard work, and all for loafing about our streets with big sticks in their hands, hunting in vain for some official duty to perform."[13]

On occasion Houston's citizens were capable of taking the law into their own hands. But, despite the South's well-earned reputation for extra-legal lynchings, only two incidents have been recorded in the city's history. The first occurred in June 1859, when an accused rapist named George White was strung up by a mob. By some accounts the dearth of such lynchings in Houston in the nineteenth century was the respect paid to local law enforcement personnel—sheriffs, city police and marshals.

As Houston stood on the precipice of the 1860s, its police force was a far cry from the reorganized police forces that had developed in the more settled American cities. Cities such as New Orleans, Boston and New York—with much larger populations—had years of experimentation behind them and a much more complicated environment to police in the 1850s. Houston would lag behind for another fifty years while it rose to national prominence.

3

CIVIL WAR, RECONSTRUCTION, AND THE BIRTH OF HPD

Prior to the Civil War there was little if any police patrol in Houston. After nightfall the lack of protection was even more daunting. What little reliable protection existed was the result of local merchants hiring private guards and volunteers to protect their businesses. As Houston and the United States stood on the brink of Civil War in 1860, most evidence suggests that policing was inadequate by all standards.

One of the earliest accounts of a member of HPD killed in the line duty was of the death of Officer C. Foley on March 10, 1860. According to the report in that day's *Tri-Weekly Telegraph*, Foley had been patrolling the market district when accosted by Michael Flock. Upon being hit by the policeman, Flock left the scene only to return shortly after with a shotgun, fatally shooting Foley. Little is known as to the fate of Flock, who was carried off to jail and later tried in court. It would be more than twenty years before another member of the force was killed in the line of duty.[1]

By the early 1860s, Houston's reputation for poor drivers was becoming evident well in advance of the age of the internal combustion engine. One city ordinance demanded, "No person shall drive, or cause to be driven, or ride over any of the bridges faster than a walk." Houston's seeming war between pedestrians and drivers would become a theme that would resonate into the twenty-first century.

At the outbreak of the Civil War, John Proudfoot was city marshal beginning in 1860. His main duties included enforcing the Sabbath prohibition against the sale of liquors. Legislation at the end of 1861 summarized the duties of patrol officers and delegated the duties of the chief of police, than known as the marshal, as well as the patrol officers. The position of marshal fell under the administration of the mayor's office and the police department.

The marshal was expected not only to "preserve peace and good order" but to "arrest, or cause the arrest, with or without process, all persons breaking or threatening to break the peace, and take them before the recorder."

In addition to his various duties, the marshal also served as the keeper of the city prison. Other responsibilities would be familiar to anyone knowledgeable about Southern police strategies, which until the end of the Civil War were predicated on the control of the large slave population. Many historians now consider the slave patrols of the early 1700s as the first real advances in American police development. In 18th century South Carolina, slave patrols consisted of three to five men who were expected to enforce laws against black literacy, trade and gambling. Recent research suggests that these slave patrols were made up of volunteers which often included "men of superior status, not just poor slaveless whites."[2] Like in the aforementioned slave patrols, "Every white male person over eighteen years, residing in the city [of Houston] [was] liable and required to do patrol duty." The mayor, selected one or more patrol officers after the consent of City Council, to patrol each ward. The ward residents recognized as liable for patrol duty were expected to form patrol companies, elect officers and enter into service immediately."[3]

Following the formation of each company, the organizational structure was reported to the mayor. The captain of each company was responsible for the regular patrol of their ward, and the reporting of anyone absent from duty or refusing to serve. A harbinger of the Civil War practice of paying substitutes in both armies, the ordinance allowed "any member of the company" to "procure a substitute to perform his duty" if "acceptable by the captain."[4] After being reported to city authorities, anyone who violated the conditions of patrol duty could be fined up to $3. These fines would be placed in a separate fund to support other patrol purposes.

Despite these advances in policing, in 1861, Houston still lacked most municipal services. Although there were two fire engines, there were still no paid firefighters, no paved streets, no covered sewers, no street lighting and no board of health. Mental illness was treated as an afterthought, with most "lunatics" incarcerated in the county jail or loose on city streets. According to a report by Sheriff George Frazier in January 1861, of the eleven men incarcerated in the county jail, three were insane.[5]

By May of 1862, Sheriff Frazier had been promoted to provost marshal. In response to wartime conditions, the local law enforcement hierarchy was temporarily changed. Frazier was ranked above the sheriff's and marshal's office, and his new duties included enforcing "the new rules of war."[6]

Houston newspapers published a number of notices testifying to the importance of maintaining order through sobriety. On May 24, 1862, for example, Frazier ordered "All owners of Bar Rooms or Drinking Saloons in the County of Harris" to "discontinue the sale of liquor from and after this date and keep all doors to their establishments closed." Any infraction would result in the confiscation and destruction of all of the owner's liquor stock. As a result, by March 1863 whiskey was going for the unheard rate of $20 to $25 per gallon.[7]

Houston's streets were a far cry from earlier days, with bars shuttered and intoxicants in short supply. One newspaper editor noted, "Two things are missing; quinine and street drunkards," formerly a city standard. However, if one observer was to be believed, the ordinance had the desired effect, with police officers "getting gouty for the want of exercise and Justice can now rusticate and 'let their whiskers grow.'"[8]

Later in May, law enforcement tightened its grip on Houston. Ever wary of agent provocateurs and Union spies, the provost marshal's office ruled that any individuals who wanted to leave Harris County were required to obtain a permit from his office. Additionally, any visitors to Houston who were not county residents were expected to register at the provost marshal's office and report their names, occupations and current city lodgings. So, in effect, passports were required "to enter and leave Houston."[9]

Although the closest Civil War military actions to Houston took place in Galveston in December 1862, Houstonians volunteered for the Confederate Army by the hundreds. By some accounts, it was almost impossible to mobilize infantry in Texas at the outbreak of the war since "no Texan walks a yard if he can help it." Another wrote that "a man on foot was but half a man." According one 1862 estimate, *The Weekly Telegraph* suggested that twelve percent of the county population enlisted. One observer claimed that in less than one month "ten companies of over one thousand men were on their way to Houston to be mustered into the service of the Confederate State Army for the war."[10]

On September 9, 1861, Benjamin F. Terry's cavalry regiment that came to prominence as "Terry's Texas Rangers" came to Houston to recruit. One account describes his 104 men "each armed with a double-barrelled shotgun, a six-shooter, and a two-edged knife." Weighing three pounds and stretching twenty-four inches long, the so-called "Texas toothpick" was a force to be reckoned with.[11] However, Terry, formerly a planter from Fort Bend County, would die in the unit's first battle while leading his Rangers at the first Battle of Bull Run in December 1861. Other Confederate units recruited in Houston included the Bayou City Guards, the Gentry Volunteers, the Houston Artillery and the Texas Grays.

In 1916, former Terry's Ranger H. W. Graber recalled the day in 1861 when the Bayou City Guards left Houston for the Virginia campaign, writing, "I happened to be in Houston when this company, marching through the streets of Houston to the railroad depot, were escorted by a cavalry company and a large concourse of citizens" as they prepared to fight Union troops in the east.[12]

During the Civil War, Houston was a hub of action with "military officers galloping on horseback, gaudy uniforms, rattling sabers and general military activities." Large numbers of prisoners, most of whom were military prisoners transported to the city by the Texas and New Orleans Railroad, were brought to the Bayou City and penned up in the large cotton house and yard covering the city block located at Buffalo Bayou and White Oak Bayou.

On September 3, 1863, a city ordinance formalized the establishment of the Houston police force consisting of sixteen men under the control of the mayor and city marshal, but subject to the regulations of the Board of Aldermen. The marshal was expected to have at least three men in each ward between the hours of 9 a.m. and 4 p.m. He was supplied with thirty rattles, which were doled out to each officer.[13]

On May 12, 1864, an ordinance was passed that circumscribed the duties and responsibilities of the "night police," who were expected to be on the job from 11 p.m. to 4 a.m. Harking back to the duties of night watchmen in the Middle Ages, night police were expected to stop and interrogate all individuals "of suspicious demeanor or character" found in public places or in neighborhoods where they had "no right or permission to be." Prior to the end of the Civil War, this most probably applied quite broadly to strangers, transients and blacks. Anticipating the advent of racial profiling, officers were allowed to decide for themselves what constituted an infraction and could take said individuals into custody merely on suspicion.

Houston experienced the growing pains encountered by all towns on their way to becoming cities. Among the greatest lure to new inhabitants was providing an environment of peace and order, where men, women and children could feel safe inside and outside. As such, the city passed ordinances in 1861 that targeted fighting, public intoxication, boisterous activities, "public" prostitution and even what must be construed as either cross-dressing or indecent apparel. The ordinance specifically targeted "all persons who may be found in a public place dressed in any apparel not appropriate to the sex to which they belong."[14] In a similar vein, the *Tri-Weekly Telegraph* reported in 1860 that while Alderman Riordan was making his rounds he arrested "a man in female attire, who gave his name as Stewart" and said he worked as a carpenter and had been employed as such in Houston for a short time. He was remanded to the custody of Marshal John Proudfoot, "who committed him to lockup for further examination.[15]

Obscenity statutes took many forms in the 1860s, outlawing the public display of "any writing, sign, print, caricature, or any other object which may excite scandal or has a tendency to destroy the public peace." [16] It is possible that this ordinance was so strongly worded because of the recent onslaught of the Civil War and its accompanying fears of subversion and public dissent. Within a few years, Northern states would face similar prohibitions under President Lincoln's martial law policies, which could view caricature or political convictions as sedition.

By June 20, 1865, Texas (and Houston) was under the control of Union troops. Military authorities in Houston advised the mayor that, if necessary, they would intervene in municipal affairs to "protect the rights and property of citizens … establish peace and good order … and [would give] all assistance to city authorities in maintaining law and order within the corporate limits.[17] Despite a Houston police presence of only five officers,[18] by most accounts Houston remained relatively orderly during its occupation, and in November 1865, the office of provost marshal was ended.

At the end of the Civil War, the city council authorized an increase in the number of police officers not to exceed forty men.[19] The average police salary of $60 per month "compared favourably" with what Houston laborers and mechanics earned at the time.[20] However, as the city attempted to operate with inadequate financial resources, police officers for a time were paid either "irregularly or in scrip."[21]

The end of the Civil War was followed by more than a decade of violence and lawlessness in Texas, an era known as Reconstruction. As noted, these problems had afflicted Texas even before the Civil War, but Reconstruction would exacerbate the violence. Following the war, accounts of robbery, murder and looting were common. Crime had indeed become a statewide problem.

Galveston, the state's most populous city, was beset by all types of crime—both petty and serious. Houston newspapers also reported widespread crime, but by most accounts law enforcement was better able to control it here than in the port city to the south. The most common type of crime seemed to be theft. No one was exempt. Even the city mayor had his coat stolen one afternoon in January 1866.

Counter to the image of the freewheeling town marshal with little on his plate except for the occasional gunfight, the position of city marshal in Houston was not very glamorous. According to the 1866 City Charter, the marshal was expected to "gather up all goats running at large and after due notice sell the same at public auction."[22] According to Article 182, the marshal was charged with running a public pound. In it he was not only supposed to keep the aforementioned goats, but "all horses, mules, jacks, jennets, cattle, sheep, hogs or geese, found running at large" within the city limits. What's more, after five days these animals would be sold to the public.[23]

Defined as the "chief police officer of the city, under the mayor,"[24] the marshal was expected to attend all City Council meetings, suppress ri-

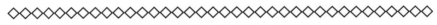

Marshal Isaac Capters "I. C." Lord

I. C. Lord was one of Houston's best known peacekeepers of the nineteenth century. Born in Charleston, South Carolina on November 23, 1827, he moved to Texas with his new wife in 1854, where he would "father sixteen children."[25] During his career Lord served in every capacity of Houston city government and was the only Harris County sheriff to be elected mayor of Houston. After serving several terms as alderman he was elected city marshal in 1863, a position he held until he was appointed interim sheriff in 1866 after the current one, John Proudfoot, mysteriously disappeared, most probably as a result of foul play. Lord returned to city marshal in 1867, but was removed by military authorities.[26] He left public service for a short time and focused on his foundry and sawmill business. In 1874 he returned as commissioner and the following year was elected mayor. In 1879 he returned to the county commissioner's job and the next year became street commissioner.

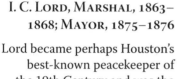

I. C. Lord, Marshal, 1863–1868; Mayor, 1875–1876

Lord became perhaps Houston's best-known peacekeeper of the 19th Century and was the first of only two individuals to first serve as the city's leading law enforcement officer and then, years later, become mayor. He was the first marshal (later identified as police chief) to establish rules governing the conduct of officers. (HPD Museum)

oting and public disorder and arrest lawbreakers, keeping them in the city jail until trial. To assist him, he was allowed to appoint one deputy, "for whose acts and conduct he shall be responsible." The deputy was also imbued with the same power and authority granted the marshal. In 1867–1868, Marshal I. C. Lord was paid $2,000 per year, making him the highest salaried public official under the mayor.

In 1866, Houston's City Charter enumerated a number of duties and protocol that the police force should follow. In order to join the force an individual had to be nominated by the mayor and approved by City Council. Qualifications required U. S. citizenship, residency in the state for at least one year, no criminal record, good health, moral character and sound mind and habits:

> The policeman's exertions must be constantly used for the prevention of crime; he must examine and make himself acquainted with every part of his post, and vigilantly watch every description of person passing his way, and he must, at the utmost of his power, prevent the commission of assaults, and all other breaches of the law. [27]

Article 311 followed on the heels of the Peel philosophy by requiring police to "constantly patrol" their posts unless otherwise directed by the marshal or deputy marshal.

By 1866, the position of city marshal remained an elected office. The rest of the police force was appointed by the mayor following recommendations made to him by the Police Committee. This august group was composed of city aldermen appointed by the mayor. That same year a decision was made to send Marshal I. C. Lord to New Orleans "for the purpose of procuring such information that would facilitate him in the organization of an effective police force."[28]

New Orleans had experimented with policing as early as the late 1700s. Like many other southern cities, it very early developed military-style municipal police forces to handle the large concentration of slaves. To New Orleans' credit, it also "had the first racially integrated municipal police force in the United States [in 1830]."[29]

There is little information concerning Lord's immersion in New Orleans policing. However, it is instructive to examine the New Orleans police force of the late 1860s. In March 1866, two months after Lord was given his instructions, the New Orleans force was purged of most Unionists and turned completely white. In 1867, the city hired its first black policeman since 1830. According to historian Dennis Rousey, this made it "in all likelihood the first American city to desegregate its police force after the Civil War."[30] Houston would hire its first African-American police officers in the 1870s.

As testament to the danger faced by all levels of policing, when Lord returned from New Orleans he was reportedly shot in the head during a "racial disturbance"—an incident "that reflected the hostility and confusion that existed between newly freed slaves and the populace."[31]

When Congress took over Reconstruction from President Andrew Johnson in 1867, Texas was placed completely under the control of Union forces, and the citizens elected Union War veteran Edmund J. Davis the new state governor. He replaced most Houston officials with Union loyalists, including the mayor. Four of the elected aldermen were replaced with "black Union sympathizers." Following the war, Houston became home to a substantial number of freed slaves who took up residence in an area outside the Fourth Ward, an area that became known as "Freedmantown."

Irish-born Thomas H. Scanlan was selected as Houston's new mayor and from the beginning became a symbol of Radical Reconstruction. Regardless of his reputation, during his tenure between 1870 and 1874, he presided over a number of civic accomplishments, including the extension of sidewalks, construction of a market house, completion of a major sewer and road improvements. His administration also welcomed several blacks to City Council and to the police force.[32]

By 1867, the city treasury was virtually bankrupt. In order to meet police salary needs, a police committee recommended asking city merchants to help chip in temporarily in order to retain the current number of officers.

The HPD began to catch up with other professional police forces in the years following the Civil War. In 1867, officers were assigned their own beats within their wards and salaries were increased to $100 per month, indicating that the local business community did indeed rise to the occasion. Officers were equipped with wooden rattles (rattlers), one of the earliest police alarm systems. Rattles were used to summon help when police confronted threatening situations. They came in a variety of incarnations, some were iron weighted and could be wielded like a baton, while others were single or double ratchet. Most were well constructed out of hardwood and when employed made a loud "rat-a-tat" noise when the handle was swung around quickly.[33] Before the telephone and Gamewell call boxes, these instruments were one of the few ways for policemen to communicate with one another at a distance. Once an alarm reached the city courthouse, alarms would be run from there, not unlike the hue and cry of Anglo-Saxon Britain more than 800 years earlier. In order to eliminate hysteria and disorder, a certain protocol had to be followed when it was time to ring the alarm. According to an 1863 ordinance only the "City Marshal, his deputy, or any police officer, shall ring the bell indicating locality [of emergency] by a number of taps corresponding to the number of the ward."

By January of 1867, the city aldermen and mayor had enlarged the police force to nineteen, including the city marshal, the largest number up until that time. But movement was afoot to undo all of this. On May 30, 1868, the *Daily Houston Telegraph* reported the rumor that the "sages in the Board of Aldermen" were to introduce a bill that evening to reduce the police force down to its original number of ten. The report admitted that the city had been relatively calm, but argued that it was because the city had a "sufficient police force." The editor warned that as soon as the force was reduced, pandemonium would return Houston to "those terrible nights, Saturday nights especially, with their din" and would make the city wish for the increased police force.[34]

Houston peacekeeping became even more tenuous in 1867, when Brevet Major General J. J. Reynolds was made military commander of Texas. Almost immediately, he fired Houston's six aldermen and several other officials before setting his sights on the incumbent, I. C. Lord. Reynolds made every attempt to get rid of Lord. The *Houston Daily Times* of September 29, 1868, reported that Lord's only infraction was "his opposition to radicalism" and "his recent spoiling the well planned game of the radicals for a riot in this city has made General Reynolds his eternal enemy."[35] However, the following day Lord was relieved of his duties after "the loyal League Negroes" openly threatened to attack, sack and burn the city. But this threat was turned back after a mob of armed whites came forward to protect the city. Lord was not one to take things lightly and on October 1, the *Houston Daily Times* reported his "determination not to give up until the Board of Aldermen ordered him" to.[36]

A local newspaper editorial from September 30, 1868, lamented "the police are in a quandary. They have two chiefs of police [until Lord stepped aside]." Reynolds had appointed A. K. Taylor as city marshal and ordered Lord removed, but he did not step aside right away. Taylor would resign the following year and be replaced with M. E. Davis, also appointed by Reynolds. Shortly before Christmas on December 22, 1868, the *Daily Telegraph* reported that "the city police have not been paid in city script or greenbacks since October and some of them are in a bad way for bread and meat."

Little progress toward improving peacekeeping in Houston took place during post-Civil War Reconstruction. One citizen approached civil authorities requesting for the army to send a court reporter to "observe and take notes on a city murder trial, claiming that all such trials were 'a mockery and a farce' in Texas."[37]

According to the census of 1870, Houston's population was 9,332, still substantially less than Galveston's. Under Reconstruction, Texas was readmitted into the Union on March 30, 1870. However, due to voting regulations put in place by Reconstruction there were only 898 registered voters—410 white and 488 black. On August 18, 1870, a new city administration by order of Governor E. J. Davis gave the city its "first Negro law-makers"[38] and appointed Thomas M. Scanlan as mayor, the first of two two-year terms.

The early city Police Board or Committee was made up of several aldermen and has been compared to the subsequent Police, Fire, and Health Boards, all of which "were [later] created under the civil service provisions of the 1897

THE MAIN STREET OF HOUSTON IN THE 1870S

The city population was about 10,000, second only to Galveston among cities
in Texas. The recovery from Reconstruction found policing of the Bayou City
"inadequate" with some parts totally neglected, especially at night. The number of
officers on the force fluctuated, depending on city finances. (HPD Museum)

charter." Under a revised code of ordinances, all three committees would be
merged into one board.[39]

According to the original reports by the Police Committee of the Board
of Aldermen, the committee was unanimous in its opinion "that the present police force is wholly inadequate to the growing wants of the city; they
find that while some portions of the City are patrolled by the Police, other
parts are and have been entirely neglected, and left exposed to the raids and
riotings of the lawless."[40] By 1872, the city's population had risen to 10,000.
In response, the committee proposed that the police force be increased to a
total of twenty-one officers, fifteen whites and six blacks.[41]

Despite recent increases in the size of the police department and the public's satisfaction with their performance in February 1873, the mayor and
City Council reduced the department to thirteen members. According to
legislation passed on February 24, it was decided that the city police force

would consist of twelve regular officers and one deputy marshal. For the first time all officers were to be nominated by the Police Committee, rather than the mayor, and elected by City Council.

The United States, as well as Texas, was hit by a nationwide economic recession in 1872 and 1873, so this perhaps explains the reduction of the force. It would be the first of several staff reductions in the 1870s. However, the Houston city treasury was running a deficit for most of the decade. At the 1879 inauguration of Mayor A. J. Burke, the new leader of city government remarked, "We commence a new administration under embarrassing circumstances, burdened with a heavy debt ... an empty treasury and much that ought to be done for the improvement of the city but must remain undone until we are in possession of funds to accomplish these ends."[42]

In the 1870s, local newspapers often offered editorials criticizing the lack of police and their perceived invisibility. On one occasion it was reported that a screaming woman was assaulted in public "but the police were utterly deaf or asleep." The report added, "It is certainly strange that a police force of 23 able-bodied officers can't at least render one of our principals safe to walk in."[43] Nonetheless, by 1878, the force had dwindled to ten officers. Salaries also suffered. In 1878, pay was reduced from $65 to $60 per month. According to several authorities, officers went without pay for almost four months at one point and required City Council to step in and provide subsistence. Between 1878 and 1881, police salaries had plummeted from $60 to $45 a month.[44]

The reduction of police force numbers was common in major Southern cities between 1870 and 1880. In the first in-depth study of a Southern police force, historian Dennis Rousey noted that in eighteen southern cities the ratio of policemen to population had declined in every city except for three. Houston was not included in the study, but its closest competitor Galveston was. It is interesting that of the eighteen major cities cited, Galveston actually had the highest rate of increase, from 9.4 to 13.5 per 10,000, while New Orleans declined from 33.8 to 15.4 per 10,000 residents. Much of the blame for the staff reductions was laid at the feet of City Council members who continued to whittle down police budgets.[45]

Police salaries had always been an issue as well. As early as 1843, Houston enacted legislation that allowed the city marshal to supplement his income through the collection of fees. In this case he received fifty cents for every affidavit filed in justice of the peace courts.[46] Another ordinance was passed in 1861 enhancing his ability to collect fees and soon the position of city marshal, like that of county sheriff, had become a lucrative position. In July 1879, an investigation revealed that that city marshal and recorder were "reaping a golden harvest," noting that during one six-month period he pocketed $3,500 on seven hundred fines.[47]

In 1879, City Council took steps to abolish a reward system that many regarded as a politically motivated fee system. According to the resolution, it was "Resolved: That hereafter there shall be no rewards of money offered for the detection of criminals, incendiaries or other malefactors."[48]

Major changes were in the works for HPD in 1873. One of the most notable was the racial makeup of the new incarnation of the force. There is no real consensus as to when the first black police officer was hired, but there is little doubt that it was sometime in the first half of the 1870s.[49] In fact, at one time during the Reconstruction era the HPD force was evenly split with six white and six black officers, with the white deputy marshal breaking the tie.

Curiously missing from the new provisions was any mention of the city marshal's position. However, this oversight was soon remedied by the current Harris County sheriff. Until the mistake could be officially rectified, Sheriff S. S. Ashe appointed Henry Thompson city marshal and gave him at least a dozen deputy sheriffs until the charter was corrected. When an election did take place in 1874, Thompson won.

4

HOUSTON'S CRIME PROBLEM

Despite a number of strides in upgrading local law enforcement, one local newspaper lamented in 1873, that "at no time in her history, has [Houston] been so immersed in crimes as at the present. The terrors of the blade of the assassin and the bullet of the murder have become a matter of almost daily occurrence."[1]

Citizens had little reason to feel protected by the HPD at this time. In March 1873, a *Daily Houston Telegraph* editorial lamented the fact that officers frequented the barrooms with the same regularity as did private citizens, noting, "It appears that some officers of this city have been in the habit of imbibing too much whiskey ... a policeman who allows himself to get under the influence of ardent spirits should be promptly dismissed from the force."[2]

In 1873, the position of secret policeman was retitled either "special agent" or "detective." The main distinction between regular plainclothes officers and the special agents was that special agents reported directly to the mayor and Police Committee rather than city marshal.[3] In 1875, a resolution passed which solely authorized the mayor to oversee the special agents, with funding provided by a "Secret Service Fund." Curiously, no specific tasks were enumerated for the agents. Most likely, their duties were intelligence-related and might have included the reporting illegal activities by police officers.[4]

With the election of Governor Richard Coke in January 1874, Reconstruction soon ended in Texas. While most of the South still had to contend with depleted treasuries and the collapse of their economic infrastructures, Houston and Texas stood on the brink of unrivalled progress. Physical and commercial expansion was in full gear by the summer of 1874. Improvements included the deepening of Buffalo Bayou, the creation of the Sixth Ward and the inauguration of a new street railway system. Although the new rail system consisted of a streetcar drawn by a mule with the capacity to carry twenty-three people, it is certain that its accident rate could not even approach that of Houston's 21st century light rail. Former Confederate President Jefferson Davis visited the city in June 1875, and while impressed, commented that the "streets are far wider than are or ever will be needed for business." Fortunately his recommendations to narrow the streets "by at least fifteen to twenty feet" never came to fruition.[5]

In late January 1874, the HPD was called on to protect its constituents against epidemic disease. According to the ordinance, police were responsible for prohibiting smallpox victims from entering the city. In addition, the city marshal's duties included having his officers determine which houses contained infected individuals. Once it was ascertained which locations were affected, a guard was to be posted to make sure the individuals did not make contact with healthy citizens.

Despite the end of Reconstruction in May 1874, there were still two black police officers on the force, which was composed of twelve men and a city marshal. Although few records indicate the presence of black police officers in America between 1850 and the 1870s, historians have uncovered black police officers in northern cities beginning in the 1870s and more notably in Midwestern cities such as Chicago and Cincinnati. During the Reconstruction era of the 1870s, one-third of the New Orleans department was African American, as were three out of every five police commissioners.[6] But these advances in the South proved ephemeral. Houston City Directories first began identifying all police officers as well as their race in 1877. The 1877–1878 Directory listed 9 patrolmen, of which two were black.[7] In any case, between 1878 and 1924, there was always at least one, and at most three, black officers on HPD. One historian asserts that none served more than five years in this capacity.[8] Except for the identification of Nathan Davis in 1878 (served 1878–1881),[9] there has been little success in identifying any of these African-American police pioneers.

Initially, black police officers were appointed and referred to as "special officers." They were not paid on par with their white colleagues and were typically assigned to black neighborhoods, a restriction that would still hold well into the twentieth century. It would not be until 1892 that they were given full arrest powers. By most accounts, although they had full arrest powers according to state law previous to 1892, it was departmental policy that a black police officer could not arrest a white offender without the assistance of a white officer. There were few opportunities for promotion outside the position of detective. Blacks were even prohibited from motorcycle patrol duty into the twentieth century.

The year 1889 was a turning point for black Houston police officers when two officers were assigned police badges for the first time. Isaac Hayden received badge No. 119 and Moses Moss badge No. 9.[10] Oscar P. Robinson also broke ground as the first African American to be promoted to special detective. Despite these strides, blacks were underrepresented on the HPD force well into the 1950s.

In the centennial year of 1876, a riot almost broke out after a black voter was arrested for trying to vote for the second time in an election. Various newspapers reported black Houstonians were selling their votes for up to $20 per vote. Regardless of the many attempts at subterfuge by Republican Radicals and Democrats, a new state constitution was ratified in 1876, removing any lasting tinge of Radicalism.

However, any victories against vice and alcohol were far off on the horizon. One harbinger of future municipal progress was uncovered during a survey of temperance, which revealed a membership of 300 teetotallers in a community of 30,000, served by thirty barrooms.[11]

City Council passed legislation in 1876 providing segregated but free schools for children between eight and fourteen years old for the first time. Houston was well on its way to becoming a Southern metropolis, providing free education and a host of cultural activities for the residents.

By the summer of 1878, the manager of the local telegraph company had ordered a telephone to allow citizens the opportunity to converse with friends "a mile distant." Heralding the next century of progress, the Houston Lyceum offered "phonographic entertainment" and in 1879 announced the opening of a library reading room that would be "free to the public." The last Christmas of the decade ended on a high note for local jail inmates, with the *Houston Telegram* reporting that the sheriff "made glad the hearts of the prisoners at the county jail by setting them an excellent dinner and regaling them with plenty of number one eggnog."[12]

It is not hard to figure out how Judge Gustave Cook of the Harris County Criminal District Court would have reacted to the 21st century popular culture that has popularised the phenomenon of the serial killer. In 1879, Cook suggested that the lack of respect accorded peace officers encouraged people to commit crimes, noting that the public made heroes of criminals and did not "sufficiently frown upon crime."[13] However, the American fascination with criminals dates back much earlier. At the time of Cook's writing he was

FIRST "MODERN" HOUSTON POLICE STATION IN 1894

The first city "jail" was actually part of City Hall and Police Court. (HPD Museum)

probably referring to the rise of dime novels that lionized such vile characters as Jesse James and Billy the Kid. Like today, the public could not get enough; newspapers were not much better, using sensationalism and bloodletting to sell papers leading to the journalistic adage, "If it bleeds it leads."

Another phenomenon of the late 1870s that has resonance today was the blaming of rising crime rates on transients and recent immigrants. Echoing the 2006 concern for rising crime in Houston due to the influx of New Orleans refugees in the wake of Hurricane Katrina, one 1873 newspaper suggested that "the permanent citizens of this place are [not] in any way responsible" for Houston's high crime rate. Instead, blame was focused on newcomers: "Like other new cities, and situated in an infant community, we have amongst us a class of reckless adventurers, disreputable characters, worthless vagabonds," who "commit nine-tenths of all the mischief."[14]

Throughout much of their history, Texans have seemed to possess an inherently lax attitude toward law enforcement. When crime was high, it was typical to look elsewhere for explanations—ethnic and racial immigrants were good targets, as were the periodic economic recessions. Others saw rising crime as a result of a post-Civil War malaise, in which a generation came to manhood accustomed to bloodshed and violence. According to an 1874 editorial in the *Houston Daily Telegram*, "During the war, and the occupation of the country by large armies, all moral tone is blunted, and crime of almost every grade is looked upon as innocence."

Still others blamed the opposing political parties, a harbinger of the partisan ugliness that exemplifies 21st century politics. During the Reconstruction era, Democratic newspapers assigned the blame for any black criminality to the Republican constituency and the party of Lincoln. When it came to the attention of the *Houston Daily Telegram* that the *St. Louis Republican* had published a piece stating that crime in Houston under Democrats exceeded that of the former Republicans, the paper responded in kind by blaming the crime on the "corruption left behind by the Republican government."[15] The blame game also encompassed local citizens' displeasure with the incumbent criminal justice system and its ineffective courts. In response, Houstonians began proposing various solutions, ranging from the regulation of liquor sales to limiting the carrying of weapons. Still others proposed the socialization afforded by public education and longer prison sentences.

During the second half of the nineteenth century, a double standard existed in the United States in which certain moral offenses were tolerated as long they did "not threaten the general fabric of society." According to the so-called "Victorian Compromise,"[16] [which coincided with the rule of Britain's Queen Victoria] gambling, prostitution and other related forms of vice and crime were tolerated under the assumption that there was little that could be officially done to eradicate them.

In earlier eras of American history, only married people could legally have sexual relations. Sexual violations such as prostitution and fornication were criminal acts and equated with sin. However, by the early 1800s, the criminal justice system devoted less time to pursuing these behaviors. Recognizing the impossibility of purging immorality from the urban landscape, police focused on more deviant behavior while coexisting with certain "acceptable" forms of vice, such as prostitution and gambling, but with specific limits.

During the 1860s and 1870s, Houston was among the dozens of American cities with districts zoned exclusively for vice. According to minutes of the Board of Aldermen, on May 2, 1879, a motion was made by Houston's city fa-

Perhaps the earliest picture taken of mounted patrol officers in
the Houston Police Department. (HPD Museum)

thers requiring the city marshal to "Strictly enforce Section 3 of an ordinance
entitled 'an ordinance defining Bawdy Houses and to punish the erection or
keeping of the same'; and to do so, more particularly in the neighborhoods
known as 'Johnsons,' and other quarters on Vinegar Hill: Pannell's quarters:
Sam's Quarters on Congress Street and two houses on the east corner of
Congress and Austin Street; also any and all quarters where low Negro dens
of infamy and prostitution are located: and the City Marshal is hereby held
responsible for the Strict and faithful execution of this order."[17]

By the early 1880s, Houston was home to a handful of drug dens. Both the
Houston Daily Sun and the *Daily Post* noted, "The opium den at the corner
of Congress and Caroline Streets is evidently doing a thriving business." As
late as the early twentieth century, Houston still had an area regarded as the
"tenderloin" or "Tin Can Alley." Known to many as the "toughest place in the
South," by 1904 the "Alley" was home to drug dealers and cocaine addicts and

a hive activity for Houston police. Here a 300-pound woman named "Auntie" sold cocaine, which was legal until 1914. In "Schneider's quarters," once a home to thieves and hidden out of sight by the shrubbery of the White Oak Bayou, "cocaine fiends rage at heart's content and no one is disturbed," out of sight, out of mind.[18]

The 1880s witnessed the installation of Houston's first electric arc street-light located on a pole at the corner of Main Street and Preston Avenue. This would be shortly followed by the installation of four more lamps on Main Street. In 1880, Houston's first fifty telephones were installed, but long distance service would not begin until 1895. By the end of 1882, the city was well on its way to prominence offering residents ten railroads, electric lights, telephones, several blocks of stone pavements and eighteen blocks of gravelled streets. Business benefited from a number of these improvements. For example, one bar and billiard saloon owner reported that his lighting bill would be pared down from $168 in one month to $45, thanks to the transition to electric lighting.

Allusions are made to an 1882 "Time Book" at police headquarters (now lost to researchers) in an early history of Houston from 1911.[19] Its pages revealed a police department in transition, consisting of a police chief, a deputy chief and six patrolmen divided into night and day patrols. In December that year six "special policemen" were added to the force to keep the peace during Christmas week.[20] By 1885, two police officers referred to as "cow catchers"[21] were mentioned for the first time. If there was any doubt concerning the cattle problem on the streets of Houston, the mayor's office reported that in October 1885 alone, almost 140 head of cattle were impounded, with 121 redeemed, 11 sold, 2 escaped, 4 unredeemed and 1 that died.[22]

Heralding the city's future ethnic diversity, Houstonians thronged to witness the arrival of the city's first Chinese female resident in 1886. During the 1880s, Houston was visited by the great and lesser lights, but none was better known or better welcomed than former President and Union General Ulysses S. Grant, who passed through on March 29, 1880. At the end of the decade, the city hosted a performance by Edwin Booth as Hamlet; there was little mention of his younger brother John Wilkes's assassination of President Lincoln thirteen years earlier. The decade ended with memorials in honor of the death of Jefferson Davis in December 1889. In striking contrast to the years of Reconstruction that preceded the decade, business was suspended in the city while the flag of the Union flew at half-staff from city hall in honor of the former president of the Confederacy.

During the last decade of the nineteenth century, Houston earned a reputation in some circles as a sophisticated social and commercial center. Looking back from 1929, however, one resident remembered 1890s Houston as best known for its "Light Guard, its citizenship, its rain, mud, mosquitoes, typhoid and malarial fevers."[23] It would take another twenty years for the city to surmount these real problems. By the end of the 1890s Houston claimed to be the largest railroad center south of St. Louis and ranked 75th in population among American cities.

The winter of 1872 was as "cold as Omaha," but it would become a good deal warmer for the city's policemen when they reported to patrol for the first time in their brass-buttoned blue uniforms. In March 1875, the first ordinance making uniforms mandatory was passed. According to the new legislation, officers would be required to wear navy blue uniforms of indigo dye and wool, with pants marked by a white strip sewn down each leg. The frock coat was set off with a short rolling collar and a cap bearing a wreath emblem with the word "Policeman." The officers' hats were furnished by the noted Stetson Hat Company. To distinguish the chief of police, his uniform was a bit more elegant, including a double-breasted frock coat, the waist to extend to the top of the hips and the shirt from within one inch of the knee. The chief must have cut a dashing figure with his two rows of eight police buttons gleaming proudly on his chest, pantaloons with white cords on the outer leg, and a resplendent navy blue cloth cap with a gold embroidered wreath in front bearing the word "Chief" in gold. The deputy chief wore the same uniform as the chief, only differentiated by a cap bearing the words "Deputy Chief" in silver. Each member of the force was expected to purchase his uniform at his own expense within thirty days.

On March 17, 1882, Houston's second police officer was killed in the line of duty. Accounts of the death of Patrolman Richard Snow are sparse. What is known is that he was fatally shot while patrolling the Fifth Ward.[24] According to an account in the March 29, 1882 San Antonio Daily Express, the suspected killer was Henry Campbell, who faced a preliminary hearing for the offense that day and was held without bail.[25]

Houston would not have to wait twenty-two years for the next killing of one of its finest. This time it would be widely covered in the nation's newspapers. The New York Times carried headlines that included "A Policeman Murdered (February 9, 1886)," and the Dallas Morning News reported "Tragedy in the Bayou City (February, 9)." Less than four years after the death of Richard Snow, Officer Henry Williams was called to investigate a fight at a local saloon while on regular patrol in the boisterous Main Street Beat on a busy Saturday night, February 6, 1886. He took part in the arrest of suspect Kyle Terry, who was found in possession of a pistol. After posting bond, Terry was told to appear in court the following Monday, February 8. Arriving early to court, Terry decided to take a walk for another hour before he faced the judge. Walking toward Market Square, he saw Officer Williams standing in the crowd. Terry pulled out his pistol and shot Williams before the officer had a chance to pull his weapon. One witness reported the assailant yell, "I have killed you, you son of a bitch." Williams died from an infected wound. A long-time Houston resident, Williams was survived by a wife and two children.[26]

Due to the "moderate salaries" afforded police officers, a motion in November 1885 was made to have the city pay for officers' uniforms. This motion received little support, due to the fact that "its friends were not out in force sufficient to carry it."[27]

In the fall of 1895, Sidney Porter, later to become better known as the famous short story writer O. Henry, was a young man looking for some direction in what had been a meandering life. Upon arrival in Houston, he was hired as a writer by *The Houston Post* at a salary of fifteen dollars a week. He was assigned to write a column known as "Some Postscripts." During his stint as columnist, Porter created a Houston that closely resembled "a sort of Baghdad-on-the-bayou."[28] His journalism career was cut short in 1896 when he was summoned to Austin to answer charges of embezzlement from a previous job. Porter headed to Austin before thinking better of it and hightailing it for New Orleans and then to Honduras. He voluntarily returned to Austin in 1897 to face trial leading to a conviction and a seven-year prison sentence. Following his early release he would next be heard from as O. Henry. He never returned to Texas.[29]

With the outbreak of the Spanish-American War in April 1898, Houstonians once again proved their martial meddle by enlisting in the various services. Assistant Secretary of the Navy and former New York City Police Commissioner Theodore Roosevelt acknowledged an offer of services from the Houston Yacht Club, and even the Brunner Old Man's Club, made up of Civil War veterans from both sides, who offered to defend the Texan coast from Spanish invasion.

Passing through Houston with his Rough Riders by train, Roosevelt debarked with a number of his "Texas-trained cavalrymen" for a six-hour visit to the Houston. Anyone, especially entertainment-starved soldiers, would

◇◇◇

The Mystery of Marshal Alexander Erickson (Chief 1875, 1892–94)

A number of Houston Police chiefs and marshals also served stints, before and after their terms in Houston, as Harris County sheriff. Among the more mysterious of these individuals was Alexander Erickson (or Albert Erichson, according to author Marj Gurasich).[30] A number of writs and documents are signed Albert Erichson, while newspapers and other sources refer to him as Alex or Alexander Erickson. At least one historian suggests that both are the same individual. Erickson served as city marshal in 1875 and later from 1892 to 1894. He had previously served as county clerk in 1882. Erickson came to prominence during his first stint as marshal when he arrested the well-armed Matt Woodlief, a known criminal "out on bail and looking for trouble." Adhering to the frontier marshal tradition, Erickson was confronted by the desperado on Main Street at "Fox's Corner." Both drew their guns resulting in "one of the most desperate impromptu pistol duels on record." Both were shot and fell wounded to the street before the fight was decided.

Harris County Sheriff's Department historian Marj Gurasich suggests that since Albert Erichson's name is engraved on the cornerstone of the Harris County Courthouse and Jail (built in 1895) that would possibly suggest it was Erickson/Erichson. But, Erichson served one year as sheriff in 1896, the only sheriff to serve only one year. Rumors suggest that he might have committed suicide.

The suicide theory was expounded on by the *Houston Press* in 1932. The newspaper interviewed courthouse janitor Dick Jones, who had begun his duties in 1890 and was still working in the same capacity in 1932 (making him eighty years old at the time). In the article, Jones noted that "One of his most vivid recollections of the old courthouse is the morning during the 1890s when the high sheriff of Harris County shot himself through the head with his six-shooter, in his office on the first floor."[31]

◇◇◇

find plenty to keep themselves busy most nights here. Demonstrating the city's growing diversity by 1899, visitors could choose from the Kalsruhe Beer Garden at Harrisburg or Okasaki Tom Brown's Japanese Restaurant on Congress Avenue before moving on to Stude's Bakery and Coffee Saloon or the Turf Exchange for a nightcap. The more adventurous could move on to the Grand Central Hotel Dining Hall on Washington Avenue for dinner entrees ranging from suckling pig, larded quail and green goose to the more appetizing calf's foot jelly and English plum pudding.

5

THE MARSHAL
BECOMES THE CHIEF

John G. Blackburn was the first head of the Houston Police Department to be referred to as chief of police rather than marshal, signalling another step in Houston's advancement from town to city. Blackburn was born in Mississippi and moved to Marshall, Texas in 1871, where he resided until departing for Houston in 1887 to become a blacksmith for Southern Pacific Shops. For the next eight years he worked in this capacity. In 1895, he formed a partnership with W. F. Black and opened a private blacksmith business. Blackburn entered public service following his election as alderman in the spring of 1898. That December, Mayor Brashear selected Blackburn to fill the vacancy as head of the police department. In 1898, Blackburn was elected city marshal and upon re-election in 1900 took on the sobriquet of "chief of police."[1]

An examination of police rosters over the preceding decade finds no mention of Blackburn except as chief. But this does not preclude that he was unaware of the dangers and challenges faced by the rank and file officer. In the following speech Blackburn outlines a number of themes familiar to policemen in any century:

> There can be no doubt but that the position of a police officer is an honorable and responsible one. Surrounded by dangers, he must, at a moments notice, risk his own life to save that of others. Facing the cold blast of a winter's night or the blazing sun of a summer's day, rain or shine he must patrol his post possessing the strength of a giant and the agility of an athlete, never losing his temper no matter what comes before him, or what position he finds himself in. Calm and collected, he must face danger; close-lipped, open eared, knowing only obedience to law and the command of his superior

POLICE CHIEF JOHN G.
BLACKBURN, DECEMBER
26, 1898–APRIL 8, 1902
(HPD ARCHIVES)

officers. These are but a few of the requirements an ideal police officer should possess.[2]

It is instructive to examine the hierarchy of the HPD under Blackburn. Assisting him was Deputy Chief Henry C. Thompson, who also happened to be "one of the oldest officials in Houston." Prior to his appointment to the position, Thompson headed the Detective Department, where he rose to prominence following his successful pursuit and arrest of several notorious gangs of forgers and counterfeiters, many of whom were sentenced to terms in the state penitentiary. As deputy chief, Thompson ran the department at night. He was assisted by First Sergeant Jack S. Busey, who was responsible for managing the force of night patrolmen and mounted officers.[3]

Daytime police management was entrusted to Second Sergeant Charles Williford, who, according to the police yearbook for 1900, "occupies his official position alone through merit." He was promoted from mounted officer to sergeant the previous year. Williford managed the entire force of daytime police.

Next in the developing bureaucracy of the HPD was Chief Clerk Martin T. Forrest. He was recognized by his peers when elected secretary and treasurer of the City Marshals and Chiefs of Police Association of Texas. Forrest was elected to successive terms in this office. His nighttime counterpart was Night Clerk J. T. Grinstead. Both were responsible for record keeping.[4]

The Detective Branch, while under the supervision of the Police Department, was, according to official policy, "left almost entirely to their own resources and [were] under but few restraints or instructions." They were the only members of the police department who were not required to wear regulation uniforms. John W. Smith and Charles C. Quin were regarded as two of the best detectives. One contemporary described what he thought made a good detective:

> In personal appearance he does not differ from an ordinary individual. Sometimes he is young—sometimes old. Perhaps he is large or small, but whatever his appearance is, he must be possessed of good, sound, common sense. A collegiate education is by no means essential—just a general knowledge of persons and things. He must be able to judge human nature at a glance; be quick of perception, and quick to act; he must form an opinion instantly, and must not waver or be half-hearted in actions; he must pay strict attention to the minutest details, as it is often from these the missing links of great cases are found.[5]

The mounted police force consisted of eight officers, four riding at night and four patrolling by day. Mounted officers typically traveled in pairs, with one pair in the field and the other remaining at the station ready to answer emergency calls. Each pair alternated every two hours. Members of the HPD unit were described in 1900 as being "young or middle aged, of good physique and sit a horse well." Mounted police not only served in a traditional police capacity, but were also required to impound livestock found wandering the city streets. It therefore was important for these officers to be as skilled with the lasso as a nightstick, in order to capture stray cattle and horses roaming city streets in violation of town law. As a result of their efforts, the city's stock pound was usually full of stock that could be sold to produce revenue for the city. In 1899 alone, 977 head of stock were sold for $1,313.75.[6]

By the turn of the twentieth century, HPD officers were still being paid a salary commensurate with the 1860s. A typical work schedule included twelve-hour shifts seven days a week, often more than eighty-four hours a week. Exposed to the worst that society can offer, policemen could expect little assistance in this era if they were too sick to work; pensions and overtime were not even on the table. Catching criminals was the most glamorous part of the job since uniformed police were still expected to clear sidewalks, impound stray livestock, enforce quarantines and remove illegally constructed fences. Despite a population approaching 45,000, the job of policeman held little attraction for most citizens.

Several years before the police professionalism movement was begun by Berkeley, California Police Chief August Vollmer and others, Chief Blackburn attacked a number of features of the political patronage system that held back police innovation in most large cities. In his speech he asserted:

> Political party service, sentiments or affiliations should under no circumstances be part considered a part of the qualifications of an applicant. It is a matter of fact that must be well known to every police official that a politician will never make an efficient, fearless and impartial police officer.[7]

African Americans found many obstacles blocking attempts to enter law enforcement. Nowhere was this truer than in the South. In 1900, American police forces were overwhelmingly white, with blacks making up only three percent of urban police forces. Those African Americans fortunate enough to find employment often faced hostility and were usually assigned to patrol black communities. Few African Americans found success on American police forces until after World War II, with most relegated, like women, to secondary status. By 1907, despite a force of sixty-eight police officers, only one black was employed in such a capacity in HPD.[8]

One of the more curious aspects of the Blackburn regime is that for the first time the number of "colored" officers had been pared down from three to one beginning in 1898. As chief, Blackburn was in command of forty-six men, including two detectives, eight mounted officers, a deputy chief, a chief clerk, a night clerk, a sergeant, a second sergeant and twenty-seven patrolmen. The patrolmen and mounted officers were equally distributed for night and day duties. Having entered a more technological era, each patrolman was expected to report in to the clerk at the police station every hour by telephone while on beat.

Organizationally, Houston was divided into twelve beats, with at least one patrolman on patrol day or night. Four beats crisscrossed the business sector on Main Street. Other beats encompassed Milam, the "tenderloin"[9] section of the Fourth Ward, the resident area of the Fourth Ward and the third, fifth, sixth, first and second wards. Mounted police, who also operated in two shifts, patrolled in pairs, while a pair remained on call at the station for emergencies. Horse patrols alternated every two hours.

When Blackburn attempted to fire an officer, he first demanded a new duty assignment under terms of the city charter. In a legal battle involving another special appointment by the mayor, the policeman eventually received a judgment for back pay. In what became known as the case *City of Houston v. Estes*, patrolman J. A. Estes alleged that he was appointed to the HPD on April 20, 1898 and that "he was duly appointed and qualified as a regular policeman of said city and served as such" until August 11, 1898, when "without fault on his part" Marshal Blackburn fired him "and persistently refused to allow him to perform any further duties as such officer." Estes explained, "That without assigning any reason therefore," Blackburn informed Estes that he need not report for duty any more and that the marshal "would have to let him out."[10]

Estes' argument rested on the fact that he had been appointed by the mayor and approved by City Council as was required by the city charter that became law on May 12, 1897. Therefore, argued Estes, "he could not be removed from office except upon trial before the tribunal provided by the charter for the purpose and upon charges duly presented." Clearly, although Marshal Blackburn would later allege that he was drunk on duty, Estes had not violated any rules and no charges had been put forward to a tribunal. Since the new civil service rules contained in Sections 26 and 26a of the charter protected [except for heads of departments] policemen, firemen and city health officers from being discharged without cause, a jury ruled, on March 4, 1904, that Estes was indeed entitled to recover his salary as a policeman [$75 per month] since his discharge, an amount totalling $1979.98. The city appealed the case but lost and the judgment was affirmed in the officer's favor, ruling he was discharged "without cause by one having no authority to oust him and this in direct contradiction of an explicit charter provision."[11]

As Houston entered the twentieth century, several unforeseen events conspired to push the city into national prominence. The Galveston Hurricane of 1900 (September 8/9) was the nation's greatest natural disaster in terms of loss of life; more than 6,000 residents perished. The destruction of the state's predominate port gave Houston an opportunity to take up much of the slack.

The Houston police bravely faced the aftermath of the deadly natural catastrophe, and by four in the morning of September 9, Deputy Chief Henry C. Thompson had assembled twelve officers and fifty residents and headed for Galveston. Over the ensuing days a number of Houston police would help return order to Galveston.[12] The following year, oil was discovered at Spindletop, one hundred miles away, which would stimulate Houston's industrial and economic growth.

By 1900, criminal identification techniques were considered light years ahead of colonial American techniques such as branding and letter wearing, which identified an individual's criminal tendencies to the public. Among the most revolutionary strategies was the Bertillon system. First used by the police of Paris in 1882, by the following year this system was used to identify forty-nine criminals. Named after its creator, Alphonse Bertillon (1835-1914), the system required the measurement of the width and length of the head, the length of the left, middle, and little fingers; the length of the left foot, forearm, and right ear; the height of the individual, and the measurement of the person while seated from the bench to the top of the head. Other identifying characteristics included scars, birthmarks, eye and hair color, and a description of the nose. The Bertillon system remained popular until the 1890s when fingerprinting replaced it, thus relieving police officers from the arduous identification system it required.[13]

By 1900, HPD had joined the National Identification Bureau but still relied on a variation of the Bertillon system. The department was quite impressed by the system, noting in its 1901 Yearbook that "This great system, though new in this country, and in fact new to the world, has in great measure revolutionized crime as a profession, and has presented the hugest stumbling block ever placed in the way of criminals."[14] However, reality diverged from hyperbole when it came to this system.

During this time, HPD was utilizing the services of the National Identification Bureau located in Chicago. Between 1895 and 1900 the measurements of thousands of criminals were recorded in Chicago. Police departments then would send in measurements of suspects by telegraph or mail.

Houston became one of the first cities in the South to adopt the Dactyloscopic method of identification, better known as fingerprinting. By 1915, few cities in the United States had yet to install this identification system. The HPD, however, adopted the system before Memphis and Atlanta.[15]

The department created its own Identification Department in 1909 under the direction of O. B. Jones. It was not until 1915, that the Houston Identification Division began its rise to national prominence when police Chief Ben S. Davison secured the assistance of W. R. "Bob" Ellis. Widely recognized as one of the country's leading identification experts, Ellis was a colleague of William A. Pinkerton and had served as the sixth vice president of the International Association for Criminal Identification.[16] Bobbie Ellis entered law enforcement with the Hot Springs, Arkansas Police Department in 1907. He gained experience in detective work at various conventions, fairs and reunions. In 1915, he caught the attention of William Pinkerton, head of the Pinkerton National Detective Agency and a member of the Texas Association of Police Chiefs and City Marshals. Pinkerton hired him as an expert for the Panama Pacific International Exposition, which was under the watchful eye of the vaunted detective agency.

Upon taking charge, Ellis proceeded to modernize the department, installing personal indexes to supplement the recent acquisition of a modern fingerprint cabinet. HPD joined important identification networks around the country. It was Ellis' goal to make Houston the clearinghouse for the entire state's fingerprints. Between October 1 and December 31, 1915, of the ninety-eight prisoners examined, the identification department found half had criminal records.

Around 1900, HPD adopted the signal system, which allowed patrolmen on their beats to report by telephone to a clerk at the police station every hour. This would seem onerous today, but it must be remembered that the day and night forces totalled twenty-seven, not including two patrol drivers and a turnkey. According to this system, phones were located over each beat that a patrolman was expected to patrol. The advantage worked both ways; the clerk at the station knew where the officers were each hour and the officer had to diligently keep on the move; should he fail to report on time, his career could be tarnished. Once a crime was reported to the police station, the clerk contacted each officer on the "out" beats and notified them to be on the lookout for certain individuals.

During the first decades of the twentieth century, police work had more responsibilities than most jobs. Still, police officers shared many of the concerns of other wage-earning occupations. Nationwide in the early 1900s, the typical patrolman worked twelve-hour days and was remunerated with low wages. Between 1910 and 1920, policemen began to take an active role in creating labor unions and police organizations. In 1915, two veteran Pittsburgh police officers were inspired to create an organization for the social welfare of police known as the Fraternal Order of Police (FOP). While other police organizations were subsequently created, efforts at unionization lagged far behind.

The year 1901 turned out to be the deadliest year in the history of the HPD up to that point in history. Three officers were killed in two separate incidents between July 30 and December 12. The events leading to the bloodletting began on the evening of July 29, 1901 when John T. Vaughn was arrested by Officer Herman Youngst for discharging his gun through his apartment window. The following day Vaughn, free after posting bail, had a confrontation with Officer William F. Weiss outside of a saloon at the corner of San Jacinto and Congress. A witness reported that Weiss pushed Vaughn's brother. In a flash, John T. Vaughn pulled a pistol from his hip pocket and started shooting, killing Officer Weiss where he stood. Several officers responded to the shooting, chasing and wounding the shooter. Weiss was shot three times and left behind a wife and two children to mourn him. Two of the officers involved in the pursuit of Vaughn would be killed in the line of duty in December.[17]

On December 12, 1901, Officers John C. James and Herman Youngst were killed at 4 p.m. in front of Yaden's Saloon. According to eyewitness Sam Stone: "I was coming down San Jacinto from the Herald office and saw a gang of men on Yaden's corner who seemed to be excited. I saw a buggy start to drive off. I saw Sid Preacher grab a double-barrelled shotgun out of the buggy.... I saw an officer behind a telegraph pole with a six-shooter in his hands" as Preacher said, "Come on you bastard." An exchange of shots between the three men ended with all three mortally wounded.[18]

As usual, little provocation could be found for the carnage. What was known was that a local gambling promoter named Sid Preacher had been arrested the day before by another officer. The officer later recounted a conversation he overheard between the gambler and his attorney. The lawyer, J. E. Brockman, was reportedly overheard telling Preacher, "It's getting to be damn pretty come-off that men are getting arrested every day and thrown into jail without a warrant. You arm yourself with a six-shooter and the next damn policeman who attempts to arrest you without a warrant, shoot his belly off!" When these remarks were reported to Chief Blackburn, a warrant was issued for the arrest of the attorney for the murder of the two officers. At his death Herman Youngst, a Civil War veteran with the 26th Texas Cavalry, was the department's senior officer, with a career spanning twenty-eight

HERMAN YOUNGST   JOHN C. JAMES

DECEMBER 11, 1901

Eighteen-year veteran officer Herman Youngst responded to Detective John C. James, who had just been shot by known gambler Sid Preacher. Youngst was shot in the back and killed after fighting with Preacher, who was able to once again use his double-barrel shotgun. He then used the butt of his gun to make sure Youngst was dead. Within seconds the severely wounded James used his pistol to shoot Preacher three or four times, killing him. (Nelson Zoch)

years. John J. James had only been on the force for a year and left a widow and three children.[19]

Following the deaths of the three officers in the second half of 1901, their widows petitioned City Council for assistance since the murders of their husbands had left them destitute. A sign of the times and the low regard accorded policing, the council awarded each family three months back pay, or $180 per family.[20] This was what a policeman's life was worth a little more than a century ago. Police work was clearly a dangerous profession at the turn of the century. The HPD employed 35 patrolmen and mounted officers in 1901.[21] Of these, eighteen were on duty at night. In 1901, three out of eighteen were killed on night duty; a ratio of one killed for every six on duty.

In 1911, the badges of officers in the Mounted Patrol
were still very prominent. (HPD Museum)

Any officer who had a grievance could bring it to the four commissioners on the Grievance Board. The commissioners were essentially the civil service commissioner and the four aldermen who received the highest number of votes in the previous election. The commission's most important duty, however, was in ruling on the expulsion and reinstatement of officers.

At the close of 1904, HPD employed sixty-two men, exclusive of specials detailed by private persons and organizations. The budget allowance was $65,000, almost $59,000 going toward salaries. Virtually every penny was used that year. Expenditures included food for convicts used for city street-cleaning and ditch digging. Costs for their work came to $3,000, compared to the $10,000 to $15,000 it was estimated it would have cost using free labor.[22] Among the most noteworthy recommendations made by Police Chief George Ellis to Mayor A. L. Jackson at the end of the year was the suggestion to increase the police force so that there would be one patrolman for every 1,000 residents.[23]

With the oil boom of the early 1900s in nearby Humble, Houston grew by leaps and bounds thanks to the economic boom that resulted in the construction of better roads and railroad lines.

HPD uniforms had changed by 1915 and the Department also
had added bloodhounds to the force. (HPD Museum)

In Victorian America, temperance and sexual misconduct drew an increasing attention from government agencies. In Houston, a 1905 municipal
ordinance was approved that forbade flirting or making so-called "goo goo
eyes" under threat of arrest.

The bane of barrooms throughout the nation, Carrie Nation, arrived in
the Bayou City that same year. The hatchet-wielding temperance leader's
first target was appropriately the "Carrie Nation Saloon" in the "bloody Fifth

An Ordinance to Suppress Flirting, aka "Goo-Goo Eyes" (1905)[24]

The so-called "Goo-Goo Eyes" ordinance prescribed penalties for men who made "goo-goo eyes at, or in any other manner look at or make remarks to or concerning, or cough or whistle at, or do any other act to attract the attention of any woman." Its intention was to improve Houston's moral climate. Around the time this law was passed, the *New York Tribune* published a satirical jibe at the ordinance:

> *Just because he made those goo-goo eyes*
> *The copper pinched a chap about his size;*
> > *In defense he said a cinder*
> > *Made him wink his windward winder,*
> *But the girl he winked at called it goo-goo eyes.*
>
> *Just because they make those goo-goo eyes*
> *Western women stare in mild surprise;*
> *Texas law may call it vile,*
> *But New Yorkers only smile—*
> *And they keep right on a-making goo-goo eyes.*

Ward" located on the corner of Wood and Willow streets. Confronting the bartender, Nation reportedly admonished him, "I told you to take my name off that sign two years ago and now I'm here to do it for you." With little warning, but apparently much provocation, Nation shattered a bar mirror with a rock before directing her malevolent intentions on a case of whiskey and a door pane, which she dispatched with several more rocks before whipping out her trademark hatchet. However, before she could create more havoc, she apparently came to a consensus with the barkeep. Despite the $700 in damages, the owners of the bar claimed that the amount of resultant publicity garnered by the episode far exceeded the damages.[25]

6

MURDER WAS IN THE AIR

On August 22, 1910, Houston Police Chief George Ellis resigned, ending an eight-year reign as Houston's top cop. His resignation was unexpected to say the least. By all accounts, Ellis was a popular chief held in high regard by the rank and file. But when he showed up at the police station wearing citizen's clothes that morning, his staff knew something was up. Ellis calmly took off his badge and handed it to Night Chief James Ray, who was on duty conducting morning roll call at the end of his shift. Mayor Rice promptly appointed Assistant Chief Ray to replace Ellis.

Ellis's resignation was not publicly announced until the next day, which one reporter claimed was to forestall a rush on the part of applicants for the position. Mayor Rice was overwhelmed with applications nonetheless. However, reflecting the political climate of the day, the mayor said in response, "There were a good many applicants for the position, none of them being considered. An efficient public service can only be maintained by merited promotions [from within]."[1]

George Ellis had been elected chief in 1902 and re-elected two years later. Once the commission form of government went into effect and police chief became an appointed position, he was kept in office as a "holdover." Ellis previously served a four-year stint as county commissioner, eight years as Harris County sheriff (1886–1894), and four years as clerk of the criminal district court (1895–1899).

Ellis was born in Desoto County, Mississippi on January 29, 1845. He joined the Confederate Army in September 1861 and served until the end of the war. Ellis saw his first action along the Red River and was mustered out in Alexandria, Louisiana. After the war he returned to Houston and found employment as a locomotive fireman on the Texas Central Railroad. He spent the next eleven years with the railroads in a number of capacities. He served stints as hotelier and rancher before entering public office, winning two terms as county commissioner in 1882 and 1884. He won election as sheriff four times between 1886 and 1892.[2] Ellis served as chief of police between 1902 and 1910. Reminiscing in 1938, Ellis recalled his days as chief, when "horse thieves were the public enemies in Houston" and "officers were kept busy breaking up mob fights in saloons" rather than going after the 1930s safe robbers and hijackers. Ellis also noted that when he was chief, the department had but one car, and it was used by the police chief.[3]

During the years of his administration, Ellis had to cope with the familiar complaints about lack of budget and police officers. In his 1906 report to Mayor Rice, Ellis wrote, "There is an urgent necessity for more officers on the force, as the city is growing rapidly, and the residence limits are extending far beyond the former lines." The following year Ellis reported to Mayor Rice, "the force is too small to do justice to this fast growing town. We are below the average of southern cities where conditions are about the same as Houston." An example of HPD's historic under-funding was Ellis' comment that that it would be necessary to buy a new horse for the department "to take the place of one we have, which is old and lame."[4]

An examination of arrest statistics for 1906 and 1907 indicates that public drunkenness was far and away the most common offense, making up more than a quarter of the offenses (2,328) for those two years, when the total number of arrests was 8,078. Arrest records indicate disturbing the peace, fighting, and vagrancy violations accounted for another large cluster of arrests. When it came to serious felonies, the numbers were much lower. Only four counts of rape were reported in the two years; however, it was more probable that this crime was not routinely reported. Dozens of individuals were arrested for either unlawfully carrying or displaying pistols, dirks, and knuckles. Not surprisingly, twenty-six murders and 131 cases of assault to murder were reported in those two years.

By most measurements, Houston in the first decade of the twentieth century had not yet left its frontier roots behind. Violations involving horse theft, gambling, selling livestock on the street, and leaving teams unhitched were far from uncommon. The year 1907 saw a decrease in crime compared to the prior year. Chief Ellis attributed this in part to the new statute closing all saloons at midnight and to stricter enforcement of city and state laws.[5] But even at this early era, some fifty years before the juvenile delinquency hysteria of the 1950s, the police chief reported being alarmed at the number of burglaries committed by boys of "tender age." Ellis was prescient enough to trace this to the lenient treatment accorded minors in the criminal justice system, noting, "These boys are familiar with the laws, and have no fear of arrest." In response, Ellis called for reform measures to handle the rising juvenile crime problem.[6]

Throughout the early 1900s, the shortage of manpower remained the Achilles heel of the department. Although he never explained why he resigned, there is little doubt Ellis had become frustrated at the glacial pace of providing for the undermanned and under-financed force. He reportedly told friends that his twenty-five years of public service was plenty and that "I guess I am entitled to a rest. I like to fish and hunt and I am going to spend an indefinite time at leisure."[7]

Incoming Police Chief James M. Ray had served on the HPD for nineteen years in a variety of capacities, including as assistant police chief under Chiefs Pruitt, Anderson, Blackburn and Ellis. Ray was promoted from day sergeant to night chief after the murder of Deputy Chief William E. Murphy in April 1910. During his almost twenty-year career with the department, Ray developed a reputation as a strict but fair disciplinarian. According to at least one newspaper, "Perhaps no appointment could have been made that would have given more universal satisfaction to the 90-odd members of the department."[8]

Chief Ray wasted no time in telling his constituents and staff that the police force would adhere to an "observation of gentlemanly conduct," noting that if the department was to "maintain its standing in the minds of the residents of this city" each officer would have to "practice all the requisites of a gentleman and an officer." Ray noted that Houston was a "particularly hard city to police" due to "the way it is cut up by the bayous and railway yards," which required a larger police force than a city with less natural advantages would need.

One of Ray's first acts was to create a traffic squad "composed entirely of mounted men from both the day and night shifts." It also was suggested that the four-man force be composed of tall men "which will command respect and attention by their appearance."[9] During its first month of duty, their sole job was to inform pedestrians in a respectful manner what laws they had violated. Arrests were only to be made in flagrant, serious cases.

Local newspapers heralded the results of the first months of the Ray administration, noting the rigid campaign mounted against "drunks and idlers," speed violators and petty offenders. Prior to the new administration, it had been customary for patrolmen to escort inebriated individuals to the end of

WILLIAM E. MURPHY

The moustachioed gentleman in the black hat in the center of the front row is
Deputy Chief William E. Murphy, the highest-ranking officer to die in the line
of duty. He was shot to death on April 1, 1910 by ex-officer Earl McFarland,
the frowning man, also with a moustache, who is standing over Murphy's right
shoulder. Murphy had fired McFarland, who still held a grudge. Although caught
with "the smoking gun," McFarland claimed self defense and a Galveston jury
set him free. The man sitting to Murphy's left in the wide-brimmed hat is Police
Chief George Ellis, the last elected chief in HPD history. (HPD Museum)

their beats and then allow them to depart once they promised to go directly
home. Individuals would only be arrested when they refused to move onto
another officer's beat once the original officer's beat was over. Although this
custom did indeed keep drunks on the move, apparently it did not keep them
off the streets. Ray told reporters that the "only place for a drunk was in the
'runaround' at the police station."[10]

POLICE CHIEF JAMES M. RAY,
1910-1911 (HPD MUSEUM)

By the second decade of the twentieth century, the concept of the "vice dis-trict" had become an accepted feature of many American cities, including Houston. Sometimes referred to as the "tenderloin" or "the block," it was here that a city's gambling halls, rough and tumble saloons and bawdy houses were open night and day, 365 days a year. In most cases a well-worn relation-ship between law enforcement and vice entrepreneurs led to an accommo-dation with the police and the God-fearing public. While most of these vice districts evolved outside of the law over the years, a number of cities actually zoned these districts by law. However, change was on the horizon, not just in Houston, but throughout the country as Progressive reformers[11] directed their efforts at a nation undergoing political, social, and economic transfor-mation, as well as legislating morality.

Prostitutes had worked the streets of the Bayou City since its founding in 1836. Disorderly houses and taverns were historically grouped together just off the main downtown area near Buffalo Bayou and the central market. Until the early 1900s, this locale was referred to as "The Hollow." Earlier at-tempts at regulation and restriction backfired when many of these houses of ill repute moved into residential and commercial neighborhoods. In 1908, the city responded to complaints by passing an ordinance establishing a mu-nicipal vice district on Buffalo Bayou west of the town center in an undeveloped part of the city. The following year authorities followed up by applying Jim Crow segregation laws to brothels.[12]

When James Ray became police chief in 1910, he had to contend with the problem of "how long should a police officer be allowed to remain in the red light district?" Police chiefs around the country were themselves deliberating on similar issues. Cities like Denver advocated switching beats "in the unsavoury districts" after two months. However, Chief Ray argued that officers should be placed in these areas continuously asserting "an officer don't [*sic*] begin to be valuable until he has done at least two months' service on his beat. If he is pulled off after he has been there that long then you are losing the benefit of all he has learned." Once an officer becomes familiar with his beat, he "knows the habits of the residents ... knows danger points ... knows the location of fire alarm boxes" as well as "the condition of the streets." As far as the argument that officers would be tempted toward corruption and graft after two months, Ray replied that "the right kinds of men are not going to graft."[13]

It is difficult to project what Ray's legacy might have been as police chief if he had not resigned just one year into his career. However, he would make his mark as an elected justice of the peace of Harris County. He served four successive terms before the Ku Klux Klan forced him out between 1922 and 1924, making his Catholicism an election issue. However, he won his way back on the bench later in 1924 and rose to prominence as an elected official serving another four terms before retiring in 1932. His retirement speech was short and to the point, "I'm tired of listening to other folks' troubles."

E. C. Noble became police chief in August 1912. Among his early successes was the inauguration of a Police School to instruct officers on their duties and the rights of citizens, when and how to make arrests and how to treat those arrested. One month after taking over, he installed the Police Mounted Traffic Squad, whose members were expected to handle traffic issues on Main and other principal city streets. At the same time, he recognized "how important and necessary it is for a well-organized Police Department to have the very best and modern equipment," such as automobiles and motorcycles. He was particularly impressed by the Gamewell System that allowed the department to keep track of men on their beats. However, one of HPD's biggest problems was the condition of its main station and jail.

Noble described the current city jail as "bad, inconvenient and hard to keep in a sanitary condition." What's more, the force was unable to even keep a police matron "on account of no provision or room being made for women to spend their time in at the station."[14] Noble had much foresight, supporting the need for the department to operate under civil service rules and regulations. He also asserted that officers should be given a graduated pay scale that gave men entering the HPD "something to look forward to" besides his base salary.[15]

Demonstrating the ever-increasing diversity of the city, the year-end lists of city ordinance violations are worth noting. Of the 969 arrests, more than half were traffic-related. More than 100 individuals were arrested for loitering in and around houses of prostitution, while twenty were arrested for violating the "Goo-Goo Eyes" ordinance. At least one other was arrested for wearing the clothes of the opposite sex.

The Houston Police Department was well represented at the 20th annual meeting of the International Association of Chiefs of Police (IACP) held in the nation's capital from June 9 to 13, 1916. When it came to discussing the outlawing of prostitution, HPD Chief Ben S. Davison described, "I am in Houston, Texas, a long ways from here. We have a large population of a little more than 150,000 people. We have the restricted or red light district. The identical system is in vogue in my city, as outlined there by the chief from Savannah."[16]

Davison proceeded to compare Houston's prostitution situation with that of Dallas, which had a population almost twice that of his city. He reported that Dallas abolished its red light district several years earlier and as a result prostitutes from Dallas "came to my town, or they went to Fort Worth or San Antonio, or else they spread over the city [of Dallas]."[17] Davison was attempting to make the point that there was nothing to be gained by moving them from one area to another. He admitted that he could "not defend" prostitution but saw merit in regulating it as many cities of this era did. In the days of the Mann Act and various moral crusades, Davison made sense when he said prostitution "has been with us since the days of Babylon, and my opinion is, the only way to do it is to regulate it." Davison continued his tirade, "We had some fool of a man, I will call him that after they abolished the district in Dallas, he attempted to abolish it in Houston. He sought an injunction—he enjoined me as head of police—he enjoined proprietors of red-light houses—men who rented to the women, and what was the result. The very moment this injunction was applied for, the women in the district went to the men, and they got them out, sneaked them out at night."[18]

In 1915, Chief Davison made a number of recommendations that included the establishment of substations in the various wards, the ownership of all horses for mounted officers; an increase in the number of patrolmen and the installation of additional police patrol boxes. The chief could proudly point to a number of accomplishments that resulted from his recommended adoptions, including the reduction of a police officer's day's work from twelve to eight hours, the establishment of a municipal farm, the maintenance of a pack of bloodhounds—which he noted had "a wonderful moral effect alone, especially among the Negro race"—and the remodelling and updating of the police station.

Davison also established a permanent exchange with all large cities that used the Bertillon and Fingerprint System, including the Identification Bureau at Fort Leavenworth, which was part of the U.S. Justice Department and the repository for copies of criminal records. The department's Bertillon operator was paid $1,200 per year, almost $300 more than the average patrolman's salary. Bertillon operator Bob Ellis reported that he had established a permanent exchange with the Berkeley Police Department in California, where records of all important criminals of the western United States were filed. By the following years he set up exchanges with penal institutions at Sing Sing, N.Y. and Atlanta, Georgia as well. In his final tally for 1915, of the ninety-seven prisoners he examined in 1915, forty-eight were identified as having criminal records and eleven he was unable to identify. During that year he sent 407 combined fingerprint and Bertillon files to other departments.

Murder was in the air in Houston in 1910. Between January 1 and April 1, there were fourteen reported murders (including two suicides). In March alone there were two murder-suicides as well as the unsolved mass murder of three adults and two babies. In a rhetorical flourish, the *Houston Chronicle* asked, "Is Houston suffering a 'psychological moment,' is there any reason for it all?" *The Houston Post* likewise chimed in about the city's murder problem, noting in an article on April 4 titled "The Murder Record for Three Months":

January and February in Houston proved a necropolis, with March a veritable morgue. April began with bloodletting. From old men to prattling babies murder had shown no choice, the slaughter has entered the nursery. Guns have smoked, knives have flashed and blood has been cheap, and Houston has shuddered under it all. Jealousy, vindictiveness, revenge and every phase of passion have been given free rein and the carnage has been bountiful.

None of these murders shook the Bayou City like the killing of Deputy Police Chief William E. Murphy by HPD patrolman Earl McFarlane on the night of April's Fool 1910.[20]

That Friday night started out like any other for Deputy Chief Murphy. Arriving at the Acme Restaurant at 904 Preston, he proceeded to have dinner and a shoeshine. Finishing shortly after 9 p.m., he started rolling a cigarette. As he began to get up from his stool, he was fatally struck by one slug from a .45 caliber pistol. The gunshot entered Murphy's right arm four inches below the shoulder, before continuing into his chest and lung area, severing a vital artery and filling his lungs with blood. He was probably dead by the time he hit the floor.

Witnesses reported that there was little doubt who fired the mortal shot, for most had seen former HPD Police Officer Earl McFarland enter the restaurant through the front door and approach the chief from behind. As Murphy began to rise from the stool, McFarland fired. Murphy could only say "Oh God" before taking a step and falling to the floor. To this day Murphy is the highest ranking member of HPD to die in the line of duty.

Murphy entered the working world as a driver of a horse-drawn cab, or "hack", in Galveston. During this time he began a friendship with future heavyweight boxing champion and native Galvestonian Jack Johnson. Murphy began his law enforcement career on the Galveston Police Department. Known as "Billy" to his friends during his eight years of service, he became the Galveston department's first patrol wagon driver in 1889. He also served several years as a detective on the force. He left for Houston in 1899 and joined HPD as a detective in 1902. He held this position until 1907 when he "received the distinction of becoming the first Deputy Chief appointed rather than elected."

According to his biographer, Jim Dewey, he was well respected but somewhat of a "disciplinarian." Mayor Rice was quoted in *The Post* on April 2, "The killing of Mr. Murphy removes from the police department one of its best men. He was an able officer and one who had no fear. The city is confronted with a condition of affairs that must be remedied and that can not be done until the courts enforce the laws strictly."

An Ordinance Colonizing and Segregating Houses of Ill-Fame, and Assignation Houses; Regulating the Same and Prescribing Penalties (1908)[19]

WHEREAS, The City of Houston is authorized by its charter to colonize and segregate houses of ill-fame, and to regulate same, and

WHEREAS, At the present time such houses are scattered throughout the body of the City, and in many cases in residence sections and in the neighborhood of the public schools, thereby constituting a menace to public order and decency, to the sanctity of the home and to the moral welfare of the young;

Therefore, Be It Ordained by the City Council of the City of Houston:

Section I. From and after the final passage of this ordinance it shall be unlawful for any public prostitute or woman abandoned to lewdness to occupy, inhabit, live or sleep in any house, room or closet situated without the limits of the City of Houston, ...

Sec. II. That it shall be unlawful for any person or persons, whether agent or owner, to rent, lease or hire any house, building or room to any woman, or girl, notoriously abandoned to lewdness, or for immoral purposes ...

Sec. III. That public prostitutes.... Are forbidden to stand upon the sidewalks in front or near premises they may occupy, or at the alleyway, door or gate of such premises, or to occupy the steps thereof, or to accost, call or stop any person passing by ...

Sec. IV. That it shall not be lawful for any lewd woman to frequent any coffee house, saloon or bar room and to drink herein.

Sec. V. That it shall be unlawful for any parties or party to establish or carry on a house of prostitution ...

McFarlane became acquainted with Murphy while serving under him as a night patrolman. By all accounts there was no enmity between the two until McFarlane left the department. According to interviews conducted with Murphy's grandchildren in 2004, Murphy fired McFarlane after he was caught "stealing a wagonload of goods." Subsequently, McFarlane was employed as a special officer for the Houston Electric Company. According to his grandson, Jim Dewey, Mayor Rice did not revoke his peace officer commission until after he shot Murphy.

Bad blood festered between Murphy and McFarlane after his termination and on several occasions they nearly swapped lead except for the intervention of others. Several weeks before his death, Murphy recounted to a reporter for the *Houston Chronicle* several instances in which he believed McFarlane had set him up for assassination. So, few were surprised when he was ultimately ambushed.

McFarlane had altercations with other HPD officers in the weeks leading up to the fatal shooting. Police officers Felts, Wagner and Schults all recounted confrontations with the former officer. Around this time, Chief of Detectives William Kessler was wounded in the right hand in a fracas with McFarlane, requiring the amputation of his little finger. This incident took place in a Main Street cigar store as the two grappled over McFarlane's revolver. Despite a grand jury indictment for assault to murder, McFarlane remained free prior to the Murphy killing.

After McFarlane fired the fatal round, he walked out of the restaurant gun still in hand. Two police officers soon apprehended him without incident and took him to police headquarters. News of the killing traveled quickly, and within a half hour a crowd formed outside the eatery.

With Police Chief George Ellis out of town on a hunting trip, Chief of Detectives William Kessler, a recent McFarlane victim himself and acting chief, sent Officers Lubbock and Little to bring Ellis back to town. Meanwhile, McFarlane was transferred to the county jail where he was interviewed by several reporters. But, his only explanation of the shooting was that he had "Nothing further than that I am sorry it happened," and "I had to do it to defend myself."

Earl McFarlane went on trial for murder in the death of William Murphy on February 15, 1911. The trial was held in Galveston, Murphy's hometown. Ultimately, the jury would be composed of six whites, six blacks and no women. According to a *Houston Chronicle* report in 2004, Texas was one of the few states to prohibit women from serving on juries into the 1950s. What was probably just as surprising was the role of black jurors in deciding the fate of a white man. The consensus of the lawyers on the case was that "Never before to their knowledge in this section of the State, was a jury composed of half white and half black who were empanelled to pass judgement on a white man's life or liberty." From the start McFarlane pled not guilty. Among the dozens of witnesses registered to testify in the case were seventeen members of the HPD, including Chief of Detectives William Kessler.

At least nine witnesses testified that on more than one occasion they had heard the deceased deputy chief threaten the life of the defendant. One sworn witness reported that Murphy said, "The first time I lay eyes on McFarland I'm going to kill him." Others reported that Murphy had told them that, "if he [McFarlane] doesn't leave town I'm going to kill him," or that whoever killed McFarlane "would be promoted and given the best job on the force."

Although the state argued that Murphy was killed without having a chance to defend himself, the youngest witness, fourteen-year-old Barney Young, reported hearing someone in the Acme Restaurant say "Drop that gun!" before noticing Murphy reach in his back pocket as the shot was fired. Other witnesses said they had taken cover before McFarlane fired and thus did not see the entire incident. Like in the trial of O. J. Simpson, McFarlane's veritable dream team of lawyers ruled the day and in the end their "charm and cleverness" prevailed, and despite the defendant's refusal to take the stand, the jury came back in four hours with a verdict of not guilty.

In the end, McFarlane vanished into obscurity. Other questions remained unanswered. Chief Ellis resigned shortly after the trial without testifying or making a "definitive public statement on the case." Ellis and several other HPD members also had been friends with McFarlane's brothers, who had been peace officers and public servants in Southeast Texas, including one, L. R. "Len" McFarlane, who was a deputy U.S. marshal. Chief Murphy was killed in a similar fashion to the eight line-of-duty deaths that preceded his, all "involving an angry citizen, a saloon—or both" just outside Houston's central business district.

Chief Murphy left behind a wife and three children to mourn him. In a 2004 interview, Murphy's grandson, James E. Dewey, recounted a story from his youth that is probably familiar to other young families left behind by murdered police officers. Dewey remembered one day when his grandmother was closing up her home preparing to move in with her father. But, not before showing her grandson a trunk in the shed, which she set down in the backyard. He could tell his grandmother was upset, and "when she opened the trunk, he remembers looking inside and seeing an old police uniform."

The grandson saw dried blood on the front of the uniform, and his grandmother explained that it was the uniform Chief Murphy was wearing the night he was killed. She then proceeded to make a small fire and burn the bloody attire. According to Murphy's great-grandson (and James E. Dewey's son), Jim Dewey, who chronicled the event in a Masters' thesis at the University of Houston, this was "her way of bringing closure to the incident and her pain."

"Bason and Brock will arrest you,
Payton and Boone will take you down,
The Judge will sentence you,
And you Sugarland bound."

—Huddy "Leadbelly" Ledbetter

Over its first one hundred years, the HPD came into contact with the famous and infamous, but it is doubtful that anyone could match up with the visit by the illusionist and escape-artist Harry Houdini in January 1916. Houdini had already conducted exhibitions in Fort Worth and Dallas before arriving in Houston. His exhibition was scheduled to take place at 2 p.m. on top of the Houston Chronicle building, which at one hundred feet was nearly twice as high as his previous public displays. According to the script, the Houston police chief was to place a straitjacket on Houdini before suspending him from the top of the building. The January 27, 1916 *Houston Chronicle* featured Houdini hanging by his feet as he began his successful escape from the straitjacket strapped on him by the HPD. In 1923, he would return and repeat several stunts. But this time it would be a new police chief—Tom Goodson and the captain of detectives, Tom Shelley—lacing up the magician. No matter who it was—the results were the same as seven years earlier, an escape from the Chronicle building in two and half minutes.[21]

Huddy Ledbetter, aka 'Leadbelly'

Arrested for murder in 1917 and pardoned in 1925, Huddy Ledbetter, nicknamed "Leadbelly," for his role as "lead man" in convict gangs while a state prisoner in the Sugarland cotton fields, earned a reputation as a brawler and musician during his short stint on the streets of Houston.[22]

T. K. "Kirk" Irwin, former HPD chief of detectives, recalled, "I remember a great big fellow. Always played guitar and sang when you'd take him in. Some of the boys would see him on the street and pick him up just to hear him make up songs."[23]

Leadbelly is probably best remembered for the song "Midnight Special." He did not write the whole song but added certain parts to it and helped popularize it later on.[24] One stanza that he always included in his version, *"Bason and Brock will arrest you, Payton and Boone will take you down, And you Sugarland bound,"* referred to A. W. Brock who was chief of police during his days in Houston. Payton and Boone referred to two city detectives—George Payton and Johnnie Boone—who usually worked the black sections of town.[25] Since Leadbelly spent little of his life in Houston, it is still unclear exactly when he wrote these stanzas and the only indicator is the careers of the HPD members mentioned in the song.

In 1916, the United States finally entered the world war that had started in 1914. A number of Houston's Finest flocked to the military. Looking at the lot of the HPD patrolman in that year, one would find that minimum salaries started at $65 per month, with the majority making from $75 to $80. The highest ten salaries were between $100 and $150 per month. According to Superintendent Davison, "Since the adoption of the rules of the Civil Service Commission by the City of Houston the Department of Police," the force was gaining a better quality of candidates than in times past. In furtherance of this trend, Davison moved to increase pay for all levels of police by ten percent.

Between 1900 and 1920, Houston experienced tremendous population growth, from 44,000 to 140,000. A confluence of events led to this progress, beginning with the Galveston hurricane of 1900, which would go a long way toward transforming Houston into the largest city in Texas and an important southern urban center. Numerous businessmen and merchants would relocate to Houston. In 1901 the discovery of oil at Spindletop near Beaumont proved even more significant as other oil discoveries near Houston made it a logical location for the nascent petrochemical empire.

The completion of the deep water ship channel in 1914 also factored significantly in the growth of the city and by 1920 Houston's railroad depot, ship channel and oil industry, together with the boost by the war economy, led to the great construction boom of the 1920s. However, the transition from town to urban center was not easy for everyone as rapid urbanization brought an increase in crime and "social deterioration."

7

THE BLOODIEST DAY

By early 1917, HPD consisted of 159 men headed by two veteran police officers, Superintendent Ben S. Davison and Deputy Superintendent J. E. Dunman. The rest of the force was composed of sixteen detectives, twenty mounted officers, six motorcycle cops and several others on special assignment. Except for one black detective and one black officer, the force was completely white.[1]

According to several police veterans, "For years Houstonians had displayed only modest respect for the police department and had shown little faith in its ability to preserve law and order."[2] It had in fact been only six years since two policemen settled a dispute with a duel on Main Street, leading one observer to note, "It wasn't safe to get in range of the police."

Few Houstonians could have imagined that the hot and rainy dog day of August 23, 1917, would turn into the bloodiest day in the history of the HPD. On that day five Houston police officers lost their lives in what became known as the "Camp Logan Riot." But it was much more than that. This was not the only race-related conflict in America's military history—incidents took place at virtually every camp in the south where black troops were stationed during the early 20th century. But, this was by far the worst event of its kind and remains to this day a record holder of sorts; its aftermath resulted in what is still the largest mutiny and the largest domestic court martial in U.S. Army history. It remains the only race riot in which more whites perished than blacks. In all, sixteen whites were killed, including the five Houston police officers, and close to thirty others suffered violent wounds such as the loss of limbs. No black civilians were killed, and only four troopers of the 24th Infantry died. Of these, two were accidentally shot by other soldiers who may have mistaken them for police officers. A white citizen shot a third soldier who later died in a hospital. The fourth black was Sergeant Vida Henry, the well-respected soldier with an honorable record up until he undertook the leadership of the violent attack on Houston. Henry took his own life.

In seeking locales for the training of its growing number of troops as the United States was entering World War I, the War Department chose the Bayou City as the site for Ellington Field, south of downtown, for the training of army flyers, and Camp Logan, to the northwest and outside the city limits, for National Guard training (now the site of Memorial Park).

City fathers and local leaders of industry were taken aback when they learned that Camp Logan would house the segregated all-black 24th Infantry Division of the 3rd Battalion, better known as the "Buffalo Soldiers." The division had a rich history and had distinguished itself in earlier conflicts. Its soldiers were treated with respect at earlier duty stations and were unaccustomed to the Jim Crow laws so prevalent in the South. Civic leaders, concerned about a potential racial conflict in Houston once they arrived, discreetly but unsuccessfully appealed to Washington, D.C. to reconsider sending African American soldiers to Houston.

The 24th was tasked with guarding and protecting the construction of a "tent camp" that could house up to 44,899 men. But, when these soldiers arrived in time for construction to begin on July 24, 1917, they couldn't even find room and board near their charge and were quartered in nearby neighborhoods.

The genesis of the riot developed along the streetcar line on Washington Street (later Avenue), where the conductors and train operators seriously separated black passengers from their white counterparts. The black soldiers were routinely taunted with derogatory language by local residents as well as white workers in the new camp, creating an exceptionally hostile environment.

The white Army officers in charge of the division were probably aware of HPD's reputation for Jim Crow law enforcement in streetcars, movie houses, lunch counters, schools and restrooms and should have expected trouble on the streetcars and in white-owned businesses downtown. What's more, it was common knowledge that Texas was second only to Georgia in the number of racial lynchings in 1916.

Houston's police officers enforced laws at their own discretion. Local blacks coped with discrimination by assuming what various scholars called "dissembling", described by historian Ronald L. F. Davis as the "psychological ploy in which blacks assumed positions and the appearances of non-confrontation," sometimes feigning irresponsibility and accepting "a demeaning racial etiquette". The soldiers in the Twenty-Fourth were less likely to "dissemble". Many of them believed that by serving their country they had overcome the indignities of Jim Crow and deserved to be treated as equals to whites.

At the time of the riot, a former parks director named Clarence Brock served as police chief. Brock was easy on prostitutes, gambling and liquor despite citizen crusades against them; he also was a laughingstock among the rank and file, following the highly respected previous chief, Ben Davison. The pivotal characters in the scenario to follow were two mounted officers known for their callous mistreatment of black citizens and soldiers—Lee Sparks and his partner, Rufus Daniels. They had a well-earned reputation as two of the "meanest" policemen on the force, while regularly patrolling the all-black San Felipe District. The tall Daniels was referred to as "Daniel Boone" and the smaller, more ominous Sparks, was a so-called "Negro baiter." Sparks's background was documented with descriptions by former Chief Davison, as well as Detective T. A. Binford, who would later serve as sheriff of Harris County for twenty years. Binford was the only wounded Houston officer to survive.

On the morning of August 23, 1917, Sparks and Daniels were on horseback on routine patrol in the San Felipe District. Sparks was spotted by Army Private Alonzo Edwards, who was on a 24-hour pass from Camp Logan, manhandling an African-American woman over some minor offense. Edwards intervened. The two officers arrested both parties and took them to jail, but not before Sparks and Daniels beat the chivalric private on the side of the head with the butt of his six-shooter.

The woman was soon released from jail without charges, but Edwards was held for two days after being charged with interfering with a lawful arrest. Word-of-mouth reports of what happened immediately spread to the camp, prompting a provost marshal (military police officer), Corporal Charles W. Baltimore, to approach Sparks and Daniels to get their version of what happened. Sparks took offense at such interference and struck Baltimore over the head with the barrel of his pistol as well. A violent chase ensued resulting in Baltimore's capture. Even before he was booked for misconduct at 2:40 p.m., the camp of the 24th was alive with exaggerated and distorted stories of the incident. Most accounts portrayed Baltimore as the victim of cold-blooded murder.

With a poorly qualified commander in charge at Camp Logan and a lack of effective civic leadership, there was little that stood in the way of 75 to 100 armed and mutinous black soldiers ready to get even with every police officer they met and any white person who stood in their way. Provost Marshal

OFFICER RUFUS H. DANIELS
(NELSON ZOCH)

Baltimore was instructed to return to camp and downplay the events of the day; all attempts at confining the troops to camp went unheeded. More than 100 soldiers either refused to give up their rifles and ammunition or had taken what they needed to be fully armed and prepared for battle. Their call to arms was enhanced by unfounded rumors that an illusory "white mob" was headed in their direction. Soon the march to downtown was on, with the veteran first sergeant Vida Henry emerging as the leader. As the mob approached downtown, soldiers picked off two innocent white citizens who came out on their porch to find out what the all the clamor was about.

The first two officers to be mortally wounded and killed outright were mounted policemen Ross Patton and W. H. Long, who were following orders to patrol the area "in pairs." Long was on the Gamewell telephone when the rioters spotted the officers, ordered them to halt and opened fire, shooting Patton's horse out from under him. As the two officers sought safety in a nearby house, Patton was shot once in the arm and twice in the leg. He died in a hospital two weeks later.

Almost immediately an oncoming vehicle driven by Houston investment firm president Charles W. Hahl and containing police officers Rufus Daniels, W. C. Wilson, Horace Moody and C. E. Carter diverted the soldiers' atten-

Poor Aim Had Positive Historic Effect

As rioting Camp Logan soldiers passed 1119 Roy, west of downtown, several of them saw a lone light shining in the far reaches of the single room on the second floor. They took aim at the light, shot at it and missed.

More importantly, a better aim might have had a serious effect on three people who made positive impacts on HPD history. The homeowner, Peter Morrison, a Southern Pacific railroad man, had carefully hidden his wife and children in the room. One of the children was in his 20s.

Peter Morrison was the father of future HPD Chief L. D. Morrison Sr., whose son, L. D. Jr., would become a long-time Homicide captain. Morrison also was the great-grandfather of one-time HPD acting Police Chief John Bales, who later grew up in the same house.

"Our house had bullet holes in it from the Camp Logan Riot," Bales recalled in 2004. "The house across the street also had bullet holes in the siding of it."[3]

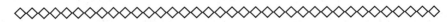

tion. Hahl stopped his car at a point where he and his passengers had just heard the shots being fired at Patton and Long.

Sergeant Henry ordered his men to take cover on the opposite side of the street behind tombstones in a city cemetery at that location. Daniels, literally returning to his and Sparks's earlier arrest scene, charged the entrenched soldiers armed with only his pistol. Henry and his group mowed him down with bullets, killing him instantly. Carter, Wilson and Moody retreated to a garage nearby but Moody exposed their cover when he fired two shots at the soldiers. The soldiers answered with shots of their own, shooting off Moody's leg. He was expected to recover but died when doctors were in the process of amputating his leg.

A few of the men approached Daniels' body and, realizing who he was, battered his face with the butts of their rifles and plunged their bayonets into his body. The rioters had no sooner blown the smoke off the end of their Springfield rifles than they spotted a seven-passenger touring car coming toward them. The driver was eighteen-year-old James E. Lyon, whose vehicle

Horace Moody
(Nelson Zoch)

also contained two white civilians and two Houston police officers, John E. Richardson and Ira Raney. The officers had basically hitched a ride with Lyon because they were anxious "to get into the hot of it." The soldiers disarmed the car's occupants, who got out of the vehicle with their hands up. As one of the soldiers broke the butt of his rifle into two pieces over Richardson's head, Raney and one of the civilians, Eli Smith, ran in different directions. Smith was instantly picked off and Raney was an even easier target, having run in front of the car's headlights. He was shot and died instantly.

The other civilian, Asa Bland, also an eighteen-year-old white, was knocked unconscious by one of the soldiers. Lyon was shot seven times; doctors saved his life when an HPD officer took him to a downtown hospital.

When Ira Raney's body was found, he had been bayoneted and beaten in the head just as Rufus Daniels had been. The scene was bloody. Bland was lying unconscious in the middle of San Felipe and Officer Richardson was nearby pretending he was dead. In another incident, Officer E. G. Meinecke was killed when about forty soldiers opened fire on a vehicle he was in, killing and wounding several white enlisted men.

At this point the soldiers lost their momentum and stopped to talk about what to do next at roughly the eastern edge of the Fourth Ward near a rail-

IRA C. RANEY (NELSON ZOCH)

road track. One group of men wanted to head back to camp, while a second group leaned toward hiding out in the nearby woods or in the homes of black friends. This fork in the road effectively ended the raid since only Henry and a few others still had the burning desire to continue.

Witnesses later told the Army investigators that Henry begged three or four of his close friends who had served with him for many years to shoot him so he wouldn't have to commit suicide. They refused and Henry went off by himself and used his pistol to put a bullet in his head.

District Attorney John Crooker immediately opened his own investigation and a court of inquiry was set up for the primary purpose of allowing citizens to vent their feelings over the violent outbreak. It soon became apparent that the Houston Police Department, led by Chief Brock, failed to respond to the riot with a coordinated plan to stop the rioters and protect civilians.

The Army pressed Southern Pacific Railroad officials into quick enough service to get all the black troops out of Houston on two trains by 9:30 a.m., Saturday, August 25. They were taken to San Antonio and New Mexico to sort out the details of the crimes, taking care to ensure that no Houstonians retaliated in any manner.

The largest domestic court martial in American history resulted in charges of mutiny, rioting and murder against 118 men, 110 of whom were ultimately found guilty of at least one charge (seven were acquitted and one was found mentally incompetent to stand trial). Eighty-two men were found guilty of all charges and twenty-nine were sentenced to be hanged at the first court martial at Fort Sam Houston in San Antonio, this despite the fact that most, if not all, white witnesses could not positively identify the black soldiers at fault.

Justice was swift and without appeal, at least for the soldiers convicted in the first of three courts-martial. Early in the morning of Tuesday, December 11, 1917—not quite four months from the date of the riot—thirteen black soldiers were taken to a remote area of the Alamo City to the specially prepared gallows that were just out of sight of thirteen wooden coffins sitting aside thirteen freshly dug graves. According to Haynes, not a word was spoken and all was over in less than one minute.[4]

Ensuing years saw six other soldiers hanged; the rest went to prison to serve their time. Protests from black leaders, including those from the National Association for the Advancement of Colored People (NAACP) went all the way to three presidents of the United States—Woodrow Wilson, Warren G. Harding and Calvin Coolidge. The NAACP is credited with pressuring these commanders-in-chief to save the lives of the others. By 1930, only a few soldiers were still imprisoned because they either violated parole or had bad conduct records. The last rioter was paroled on April 5, 1938.

The findings of the various investigations of the riots and its causes and effects prominently mentioned the Houston Police Department. Having come from the parks department, Chief Brock was not familiar with policing and lacked the basic training that usually results in earning "the respect of the men." Investigations of the department following the Camp Logan Riot showed Brock's orders were often ignored and mounted officers like Lee Sparks and Rufus Daniels freely used their own policing methods without fear of reprisal.

The funeral for Daniels took place on Sunday, August 26, 1917 at his home on Hussion Street, east of downtown. He is buried in Glenwood Cemetery. Daniels' pallbearers were six Houston police officers. One of them was Lee Sparks.

Sparks went down in history as the mounted patrol officer who provoked the early stages of the riot. Evidence presented at the courts-martial showed that he considered himself to be a self-appointed defender of "the southern way of life." On the very same day Sparks helped carry his partner Rufus Daniels to his final resting place, he shot and killed a black Houstonian named Wallace "Snow" Williams. Two black witnesses testified against Sparks at the trial, contending that they saw it happen. Nevertheless, a jury acquitted Sparks after a one-minute deliberation on October 15, 1917.

The board of inquiry recommended the removal of Chief Brock. Yet that suggestion had no effect since incoming Mayor Joseph C. Hutcheson Jr. kept him in the job throughout his first two-year term.

Sparks was taken off the force, and in early March 1918, while he served as a night watchman for the Texas Oil Company, he shot at two blacks hanging out near a boxcar, severely wounding one of them. The *Houston Press* suggested Sparks could add yet another notch to his gun but he was unable to do so when the wounded man recovered.

Compensation for the survivors of those killed in the riots was slow to come. U.S. Representative Daniel Garrett of Houston continuously pleaded with his colleagues in Congress to help people like Mrs. Pearl Raney, widow of Officer Raney, who was left with eight children to support. Finally in February 1925, Congress awarded $46,000 to compensate the claims of twenty-one riot victims. Ultimately, Mrs. Raney received $3,500 (and a cow), while $2,500 was awarded to Mrs. D. R. Patton, Mrs. Horace Moody and Mrs. E. G. Meinecke. (Rufus Daniels had no surviving wife.)

The riot set Army policy for the future: no black soldiers would be stationed in any rural part of the South. This meant that blacks in the military service were destined to train and serve in remote locations until World War II and thereafter. After a period as a convalescent center, Camp Logan was dismantled by the end of 1918.

8

HPD AND THE KLAN

By 1918, the police department had 176 officers for a city of 153,192. That same year, Mrs. Eva Jane Bacher joined HPD, officially becoming the department's first female police officer. Another woman, Juvenile Officer Ferdie Trichelle, also served. Bacher would be promoted to detective in 1920. The 1918 *Houston City Directory* was the first to include a policewoman—in this case referring to Bacher as "Woman Police." She would be referred to as "Woman Police" the following year as well, although Bacher signed most of her correspondence as "Policewoman." Bacher next appeared as "Woman Detective" in the 1920-21 *Houston City Directory*.

In 1919, the Eighteenth Amendment to the Constitution was ratified and went into effect the following year as the Volstead Act, introducing America to Prohibition. Almost from the beginning, HPD was embroiled with enforcing the federal law. Like modern day police officers tracking drug dealers, early HPD used intuition to capture booze runners. For example, one night in 1920 two motorcycle patrolmen were riding along Sabine Street when they spotted an automobile "with kegs in it." They pulled over the car and found ten kegs containing almost five gallons of moonshine whiskey. The two suspects were charged with violating the federal law. That same week, HPD detectives teamed up with Prohibition agents and raided a house on Wilson Street, where they found a small quantity of wine and whiskey. The tenants Mr. and Mrs. Tomasino operated a grocery store there, but were both arrested; these were little more than pyrrhic victories in a war that could never be won.

Following World War I, HPD issued "citizen's keys" to certain responsible individuals on each block. In the event of a crime they could notify HPD simply by inserting the key into the police call box. When the key was inserted, a lever was tripped which sent a telegraphic message to the police department identifying the location. Keys were issued soon after the boxes were installed between 1917 and 1920. Subsequently forty-one boxes were located

Eva Jane Bacher, the only woman in this picture, was the department's first female detective. In 1917, she graduated from matron status to a badge-carrying officer because of the growing number of wayward girls and a greater need for social services, especially in downtown. When a new chief took office, he didn't like the idea of a policewoman and fired Bacher under a policy that enabled him to do so "for the good of the service." (HPD Museum)

throughout downtown and had permanent keys in them which any citizen could use to report a crime simply by turning the key which opened the box and then pick up the telephone connected to the police department.

Houston was well on its way to prominence in 1920, but there was still plenty of room for frontier style gambling. Motorcycle officers reported arriving at a spot on Leeland Avenue in time to arrest two men readying for their third horse race of the afternoon. According to the police report, they posted a $50 bond for "horse racing in the city limits." The arresting officers reported that a "big crowd of spectators" was on hand to watch the races.

During the 1920s, Houston, like many other cities in the midst of Prohibition and post-war social change, was faced with a rising crime rate. Immigrants, transients, Prohibition and changing social mores led to a certain amount of status anxiety among white Houstonians. Between 1921 and 1925 Houston Police Department arrests rose five-fold, leading to a rampant fear of crime in the Bayou City. In response, Houstonians blamed HPD for lack of enforcement. Fears were compounded by the impact of the automobile on the youth culture and changing societal traditions, as well as by the fear of racial strife on the heels of the Houston Riot of 1917.

The Ku Klux Klan resurfaced nationwide in 1920. That same year, the United Confederate Veterans held their reunion in Houston. Among the attendees was Nathan Bedford Forrest III, the grandson of the post-Civil War Klan organizer. That October, Texas seemed the perfect site to begin recruitment. The new Klan portrayed its incarnation as a "patriotic, ritualistic society". However, this soon proved to be a façade.

By the early 1920s, many of Texas' cities making the transition from small town to city turned in part to the Ku Klux Klan to preserve "the rural minded Texan's conception of true morality."[1] The Klan found a supportive populace in Texas. But when the vigilante activities of the Klan were finally revealed to the public, a growing crescendo of opposition contributed to the organization's decline by the mid-1920s.

Vigilantism is a peculiarly American tradition. Citizens have sporadically taken the law into their own hands throughout the nation's history, beginning with the Regulator movement in 1760s South Carolina.[2] The evolution of these type organizations exemplified "extra-legal" law in which citizens viewed local law enforcement as inadequate or unresponsive to local needs. According to historian Richard Maxwell Brown, there were at least 326 vigilante operations between 1767 and 1904.[3] Operating outside the boundaries of the official criminal justice system, vigilante groups targeted individuals due to their "moral standards," work ethic, vagrancy and dissolute behavior. In 1921, Houston's newspapers published letters from "vigilantes" lamenting the spread of immoral behavior and vice in Houston and Harris County. These letters often contained warnings of tarring and feathering to those caught necking in cars on lovers' lanes. However, "The police publicly admitted they could not halt the parking nor could they discover who was making the threats."[4]

Often those targeted by vigilante groups, including the KKK, would be subjected to violent methods of social control, including flogging, ducking and corporal punishment. The 1920s Klan would sometimes surpass these punishments, embarking on a vigilante campaign in Houston that included castration, beatings and attempted murder.

On one occasion the police received several complaints about a local merchant accused of "insulting several high school girls." When the police did not respond, the local Klan took matters into its own hands by kidnapping, tarring and feathering this individual.[5]

After the re-emergence of the second Ku Klux Klan in 1920, Houston's Sam Houston Klan No. 1 was inaugurated as Texas' first Klan chapter. It initially counted Mayor Oscar J. Holcombe (but he never paid dues nor participated in any Klan activities), Harris County Sheriff T. A. Binford and Police Chief Gordon Murphy among its members. While the mayor resigned soon after its creation, the police chief remained loyal. According to historian Kenneth T. Jackson, Chief Murphy permitted "fellow Knights to tap the telephone wires of Catholics, intercept messages at the telegraph offices, and maintain spies at the city post office."[6]

Houston stalwart Robert Alonzo Welch remembered that in 1921 the KKK initiated close to 2,000 new members in a ceremony on the prairie south of Bellaire. Despite some resistance from elected officials, the Klan's growth continued unabated into 1922. By the end of 1921, the lines had been drawn between the Klan and its protectors in the HPD, the business community and the mayor's office, and the opposition exemplified by several newspaper editors and a coterie of brave local politicians.

In 1923, Murphy resigned, claiming that Mayor Holcombe, in the midst of his election campaign, "had hindered him in the performance of his duties" and that the city had become "infested with crooks, bootleggers, and houses of ill-fame."[7] In early 1923, Holcombe fired several policemen suspected of Klan membership. In response to public opposition, Holcombe said that these men had not been fired; only their positions had been eliminated. In January, Holcombe selected Tom C. Goodson as the new police chief. Throughout all of this, other law enforcement agencies also came under intense scrutiny, particularly the office of County Sheriff T. A. Binford, a known Klan sympathizer.

During the early 1920s, dozens of Houston policemen were initiated into the Klan. At one point the Houston klavern mobilized 5,000 individuals for a local meeting. However, by 1924, declining Klan membership led the local unit to sell its meeting hall to the city of Houston.

One of the more disturbing aspects of 1920s Klan activities in Houston was the collusion of HPD officers with Klan activities. In another incident, the HPD charged a local resident with three counts of indecent exposure. Not waiting for the justice system to take care of the accused Houstonian, KKK members kidnapped and punished the malefactor themselves. In most of the kidnapping cases, the victims usually were reluctant to take part in the investigation.

Both local grand juries and law enforcement failed to act in response to the vigilantes. The grand jury typically identified the kidnappings as "just fistfights," while jurors asserted that the "HPD could not be 'better or more efficient' than it already was."[8]

The *Houston Press* was among the first to publicly speak out against the Klan. In one editorial, the paper inferred that the HPD "was not solving the abductions because it was Klan controlled."[9] The Klan lost any support it might have had from Mayor Holcombe after the abduction, anesthetization and castration of a local black dentist named J. L. Cockrell, who was openly living with a white girl.[10] Tensions between the various factions increased as local newspapers attacked the police, and the Klan and even the mayor became convinced of police/Klan collusion. On May 2, 1921, the *Houston Press* quoted Mayor Holcombe's directive ordering the police to put an end to "gang rule" in the Bayou City. He even threatened to replace the entire police force if it could not do so.[11]

According to one historian, Holcombe's belief in the KKK-police association was "well-founded," as it later turned out that Chief Murphy "was acting on the instructions of [Klan leader] McCall rather than those of elected city officials."[12] Holcombe responded by offering rewards for information about kidnappings and by creating a group of undercover cops to investigate HPD's KKK-related activities. The mayor also offered immunity to any policeman who crossed the blue wall of silence to give evidence.

The national KKK leadership selected Harris County Deputy Sheriff George B. Kimbro as "Kleagle" for Texas. He was given the power to inaugurate chapters throughout the state, including Houston. According to one authority, the Texas organization had become the Klan's most powerful statewide branch. Charles C. Alexander, a leading authority on the Southwestern Klan, asserted that the Houston community regarded the Klan as a way of enforcing law and order.[13] As such, the Klan members were given wide latitude to tap telephones, intercept telegraph messages and place spies in the post offices.

However, after a brief period, Mayor Holcombe and the rest of the city's elite quickly became disillusioned with the Klan. Business leaders agreed, arguing that the Klan was bad for business. On the national level, the Klan became concerned with the sinister image of the Houston chapter. But Klan abductions and beatings continued unabated throughout 1921. During that vigilante-marred year, according to Ahlfield, "the police failed to solve a single vigilante act."[14]

One authority suggests that the HPD did not begin to act on the problem until Mayor Holcombe threatened to replace the police department and its leadership. But in the department's defense, it was next to impossible to arrest suspects when the victims refused to cooperate.

Later testimony by Texas Kleagle Kimbro revealed that the Klan indeed "controlled the Houston police through Police Chief Gordon Murphy,"[15] an accusation supported by an ex-detective who verified Kimbro's allegations during a 1925 trial.

Following a scandal in its leadership, the Klan declined nationwide in the late 1920s and with the onset of the Great Depression in the 1930s, it was little more than a bad memory as Houstonian's grappled with more pressing economic concerns of employment and putting food on the table.

9

THE PROHIBITION ERA

Once Prohibition was legislated into reality with the passage of the 18th Amendment, it dawned on most observers, particularly in law enforcement, that it was virtually unenforceable. Although Prohibition would later be regarded as an unmitigated disaster for providing the opportunity for organized crime to thrive, it was not actually the total disaster that was popularly depicted. Nationwide, the Prohibition era saw a huge decline of public drunkenness; deaths and diseases from alcohol, such as cirrhosis of the liver, declined as well.

Alcohol prohibition had been an issue in Texas since the time of Sam Houston. Prohibitionists were active at state constitutional conventions and elections throughout much of the nineteenth century, with unsuccessful amendments attempted in 1887, 1908 and 1910. Baptists and Methodists were at the forefront of the temperance movement in 1900 and had also helped pass the Sunday saloon closing law in 1866. However, it was virtually impossible to enforce Prohibition along the Gulf Coast, as Galveston became a sanctuary for smugglers. Although anti-vice campaigns had shut down vice sections in Austin, Dallas and Houston in the 1910s, Galveston remained a "sin city" that flaunted its reputation as the "Free State of Galveston" for years.

At the onset of the Roaring Twenties and the Prohibition era, HPD was led by Police Superintendent Searcy Baker and Deputy Superintendent J. E. Dunman. G. J. Lacy was in charge of the Bertillon and Fingerprint System and George H. Iams served as police captain, while Captain of Detectives W. E. Kessler had twenty-six detectives, including one woman, at his disposal. Sergeants totaled six. Other officers included a corporal, desk sergeant and a warrant officer. There were 105 patrolmen; all but three were white. The Motorcycle Squad, still in its infancy, had one officer. Mounted police still predominated with nine officers. The force was rounded out with a vice inspector, a pound keeper, three chauffeurs, a juvenile officer, a humane officer, two traffic police, a special juvenile officer, two engineers, a nurse and a department clerk.

According to the Houston City Directories of the early 1920s, the only recognizable response on the force to Prohibition enforcement was increasing the number of vice investigators from one to four in 1922.

In 1925, the Vice Investigating Squad was composed of three employees, including H. Radke, Eva J. Bacher and E. Berner. According to the department, their duties were "various and their hours irregular," with their targets covering "all classes of men and women." A snapshot of their work can be found in their arrest report for 1925 that reported the arrests of 430 women and 394 men. Shoplifting, juvenile crime, and controlling the spread of sexually transmitted diseases took up much of their time, and liquor cases accounted for only twenty-three arrests.[1]

By 1927, the Vice Squad commanded by Sergeant E. Berner was credited in some corners with reducing the number of disorderly houses but was unable to make much of a dent in the number of bootlegging operations. Like prostitutes, Berner found out that you could force bootleggers out of one neighborhood but they almost invariably moved their operations somewhere else.

In 1923, Thomas C. Goodson began a seven-year stint as Superintendent of Police.[2] He was responsible for a force that totalled 165 officers and the safety of a city population that had reached 200,120. Detective Eva Jane Bacher was designated separately as policewoman rather than detective in the 1923-1924 *Houston City Directory* for that year.[3] Whatever she was called, she was still the only female officer in the HPD.

A clear signal that traffic enforcement had become a major concern was reflected in the 1923 City Directory, which listed twelve motorcycle police, thirty traffic police and only twenty-two mounted police.

HPD experienced a number of changes in the 1920s, most heralding the growth of the city and the increasing professionalization of the department. In 1921 alone, Houston installed its first traffic lights and inaugurated a traffic squad consisting of twenty-two officers to manually run them. In 1922 Houston became the first city in the country to install "a modern interlocked traffic control system" controlling seven street intersections.[4] The title of police chief was changed to superintendent of police. A Police Burial Fund was created at a cost of fifty cents a month per officer. The fund provided $200 to each officer (later increased to $500). On top of these advancements, the city upgraded civil service rules related to police officers.

Traffic continued to monopolize much of HPD's time and manpower, and in 1927 the traffic department began using horses for traffic control and adopted the "ripple system" which alternated red and green lights at downtown corners. But none of these additions could help Houston with insurmountable traffic problems that persist into the 21st century. The experiment with the horses was short-lived. Following the change of administration in 1929 the new police chief, Charles W. McPhail, ordered the mounted police on downtown streets to be placed back on foot and the horses sold at auction.[5] After the abolition of the mounted officers emphasis was placed on the motorcycle force under the leadership of Corporal A. O. Taylor. Taylor set about zoning the city for motorcycle officers to work beats as in other cities. The plan called for overlapping beats and changing routes according to the time of day.

Demonstrating that police work is dangerous no matter the circumstances, HPD mounted officer W. H. Rutland, described as "the cop who always smiled," was killed in 1920 when his gun fell out of the holster as he attempted to put it on in the anteroom of the police station. It discharged, and the round entered his right leg just behind the knee and took an upward trajectory leading to his death.[6]

Just as capable of showing a benevolent side to match their hardened image, HPD officers performed in a vaudeville show for a crowd of several thousand citizens at the City Auditorium during the sixth annual policemen's frolic. In this performance, about one hundred police officers took their places before the footlights of a minstrel skit. Captain J. K. Kuykendall reportedly served as interlocutor, as the "coppers" sprang a bunch of jokes and joined in a bit of harmony and dance." It must have been a scene to behold. Besides the entertainment, it gave Houstonians the chance to see the department's new mounted squad uniforms.[7]

Apparently in the Christmas spirit, on December 24, 1921, a priest known as Father B. Lee was arrested for being drunk and disorderly. Police responding to the scene found the Catholic clergyman sitting barefooted and wearing his surplice in a mud hole in the middle of the street. When he saw the approach of the officers, Father Lee made a run for it. At 300 pounds he managed to run several yards before taking cover behind a three-inch-wide sapling. "In anticipation of the usual frame-up charge," police called in a number of witnesses before taking him into custody. Before being released on bond "the embryo saint" explained that "he was sitting in the mud hole with his alter robes on to cure his corns, as he believed that sitting in a mud hole at midnight was a fine cure for corns." Later reports from Palestine in East Texas indicated his zest for whiskey was well-known. No one was surprised by his arrest. A number of his earlier escapades were recounted in the Houston papers, including the occasion when he stood drunk in front of his home and "tried to kiss everyone who passed, saying he was administering a blessing."[8]

The 1920s proved to be deadly years for the HPD, with thirteen officers succumbing from gunshots and motor vehicle (and other) accidents while in the line of duty. The officers included Johnnie Davidson, Jeter Young, Davie Murdock, J. Clark Etheridge, Pete Corrales, E. C. Chavez, Perry Page Jones, R. Q. Wells, Carl Greene, A. Worth Davis, Oscar Hope, C. F. Thomas and the department's first African-American detective, Ed Jones.

None of these deaths was more controversial than the killing of A. Worth Davis by an African-American suspect. The shooting took place on June 17, 1928, after Davis and his partner made a group of men disperse from a Fourth Ward street corner. One of the men made a mad dash around the corner with Davis hot on his heels. His partner heard several shots fired but did not see the actual shootout. He found his partner bleeding from several fatal gunshots.

Police searched for the suspect and found him at home. Robert Powell was suffering from a gunshot wound to his abdomen. The police had him transferred to Jefferson Davis Hospital. While the wound was not mortal, Powell would ultimately die from the shooting after a lynch mob abducted him and hanged him from a bridge over a gully on the Post Oak Cutoff Road between Westheimer and Katy Road, some eight miles from the city limits. This was Harris County's first lynching in more than half a century.[9]

The city of Houston not only mourned the death of the city detective but the callous and cruel lynching of a suspect before he could face trial. Governor Moody offered a reward for the arrest and conviction of the culprits and posted five Texas Rangers to help with the investigation. Mayor Holcombe placed the entire police force at the disposal of the city district attorney. Just two days later seven men were arrested. Only two faced trial and were acquitted.[10]

By the mid-1920s, civil service changes that were inaugurated in 1914 had wrought tremendous changes for the HPD rank and file. Typical workdays had been cut by a third, from twelve hours to eight hours a day. Salaries had

Officer Worth Davis, shot to death in the line of duty on June 17, 1928. His killer, Robert Powell, also was wounded but later died when he became the only person in history to be lynched for killing a Houston police officer. (Nelson Zoch)

also escalated over the decade despite the shortened hours. According to the 1925 Annual Police Report, the average size of the department was 243 men. Uniformed officers were divided into three eight-hour shifts, with each shift boasting one sergeant, one desk sergeant, one corporal and two station reserves, aside from the regularly allotted mounted and motorcycle officers.[11]

Demonstrating the small-town feel of Houston in the 1920s, the mounted police still carried out tasks more fitting a frontier town. The twenty-four mounted men were tasked with a multitude of duties, including keeping streets free from loose stock, picking them up and impounding them in one of three city pounds. Officers were on call around the clock.

Although the Vice Investigation Squad was responsible for investigating various forms of vice including liquor cases, all members of the force worked jointly to enforce the National Prohibition Law[12] and were often involved in confiscating and destroying illicit liquor and collecting evidence such as stills (once the Federal agents were given the evidence). In 1924, police arrested 371 for gambling violations and 310 for violating Prohibition laws.

Throughout the Roaring 1920s HPD continued to grow and expand its operations. In the late 1920s HPD organized its first police band (1927); saw the

William H. Kegans: HPD's Oldest Cop (1929)

Born on a Harris County ranch near Houston in 1848, Kegans joined HPD in 1890. Except for one year before World War I, the eighty-one-year-old-officer continued to serve the city in uniform as late as 1929 when he was featured in a *Houston Post Dispatch* story.[13]

When he joined, the force only numbered around dozen men who worked twelve-hour shifts. He remembered, "When they put me to work they gave me a badge and told me to get myself a blue suit and a gun. All HPD furnished was the badge and checks for $60 a month. I had to wait a few days to get the suit, but I was able to get the gun right away, because I found a gunsmith who gave me credit, although he charged me fifty cents for the accommodation, until my first pay day. He sold me the gun for $13."

In 1892, Kegans was promoted to the mounted force and given a $15 raise. He remembered traffic was a problem in the 1890s. However, rather than automobiles "the problem was made by hogs and stray cows and horses, and how to keep them off the streets.... I remember one particular bull that was eternally breaking loose and wandering over onto Bremond Square at McKinney and Main to graze."

Hogs were so prevalent he remembered driving a herd of forty of them out of a cemetery where they were busy destroying flowers and rooting up the soft soil. Kegans remembered that "an officer had to be versatile in the early days," noting this was before there were any detectives or traffic police.

installation of automatic traffic control signals (1927), and the installation of the first car radio (1927). At this time KPRC was the only radio station in Houston. When there was a police call all listeners would hear a voice interrupt regular programming to alert officers with police calls. But at this point they did not have the technology in the cars to transmit responses.

As the decade moved to a conclusion, a city ordinance finally repealed the requirement for police officers to carry their weapons under their uniform coats (1928). The department also took steps backward in 1929 when Chief McPhail abolished the position of policewoman, citing the position as "unnecessary." According to his reasoning, since policewomen pretty much did the work of the traditional police matrons, the matron position was adequate for women, with men being more suited to police work. As the 1930s loomed on the horizon, HPD had 330 police officers, 36 police cars and 23 motorcycles.

In the first month of the 1930s, the reorganization of the police force led to far-reaching changes. Under new organization, the HPD created its first homicide squad and automobile theft bureau. Chief Charles W. McPhail, Tom Goodson's successor, appointed Detective Sergeant George Peyton to assume charge of the Homicide Squad and former head of the Vice Squad, Detective Sgt. B. W. Payne, to supervise auto theft. That same month city officials attended the opening of the city's new Northside substation in the 1800 block of Gregg Street. The third of HPD substations, the new facility was described as "roomy," with enough cells to accommodate twenty prisoners at a time. Other offices included one for the desk sergeant and a detective assembly room. During the day, the substation would be manned by four detectives. Two short-call officers were available at night.[14]

Houston's Finest showed off their new summer uniforms on a hot May afternoon, passing in review before the mayor, city fathers and Police Chief McPhail, to the famous drinking song, "A Stein on the Table". Led by Captain James H. Tatum, the first platoon was awarded top honors for best stride and the most regular rhythm. The 215-member force was divided into three groups according to their shifts of duty. A fourth group consisted of auxiliary officers.[15]

In the last few years of Prohibition, arrests for violations of liquor laws plummeted, but it is doubtful that there was much of a decline in related activities. Most probably, Houston police, like other forces around the country, were sick of enforcing the unenforceable and with the gathering clouds of a world war far out on the horizon, other needs seemed more pressing. In the first six months of 1931, Prohibition arrests totalled 223, compared to 102 for the same period the following year.[16] However, not everyone was happy about the way Prohibition was being enforced.

The decline in Prohibition enforcement did not mean that the job of being a Houston police officer was incapable of generating excitement or was

◇◇◇◇◇◇◇◇◇◇◇◇◇◇◇◇◇◇◇◇◇◇◇◇◇◇◇◇◇◇

The 1930 Touchy Furniture Store Robbery[17]

On September 20, 1930, two well-dressed men held up the Touchy Furniture Store at 720 Milam Avenue, making off with more than $300, a significant haul at the outbreak of the Great Depression.

The bandits abducted the store manager T. T. Clark, but safely released him several blocks away. Clark found a telephone and called police with a description of the bandits and their car and, more importantly, the license plate number. Motorcycle officers Edward D. Fitzgerald and W. B. Phares quickly responded to the call from a police box at Dowling and Leeland. Subsequent details were provided by Phares, mortally wounded and bleeding heavily from a gunshot wound to the abdomen.

"As we neared Milam and Anita, we saw an auto parked there with the license number on it. Fitzgerald was the first to alight from his cycle. I followed quickly after and parked my motorcycle. I drew my gun as a man emerged from the automobile. He opened fire at me and the first shot struck me knocking me down to the pavement. I emptied my pistol [.38 caliber] at him and he slumped downward. I did not see Fitzgerald fire and I did not see whether he was shot or not."

Later evidence would suggest that Fitzgerald was shot dead before he could pull his weapon. Phares was then taken to a hospital by a witness. Other key witnesses filled in the rest of the incident and later testified at trial. All agreed that while there were two suspects, there was only one shooter in the car, J. J. Maple. The officers came upon the suspect as they were switching cars. Maple, for some unknown reason, had stayed in the original car, as the other suspect must have gone to get the other vehicle.

Homicide investigators later determined that at least twenty shots had been fired. Fitzgerald was shot and killed at the scene by the gunman, while Phares died from his injuries ten days after the gunfight. Both officers were only twenty-six years old.

The following day police arrested Maple's wife, who led them to the two fugitives. Maple confessed to the shootings and a string of robberies. Maple's partner E. F. Grimes later told officers, "There wasn't a damn bit of reason for him to kill the officers like he did. He could have gotten away like I did if he hadn't been so hard and cold-blooded." Grimes would serve time for the robberies, but was not tried for the murders. Maple was electrocuted in Huntsville for capital murder just sixty-nine days after the crime.

This shootout remains among the most debated in HPD history and led to departmental procedural changes after the deaths of two officers. More importantly, the department made the transition to more powerful weapons, replacing .38 caliber guns with .45 caliber Smith and Wesson revolvers after the bullets failed to penetrate the vehicles of the assailants.

Criticism quickly arose in the aftermath of the shooting as veteran officers complained that police regulations restricted officers to the .38. If they had been using .45s [like the Texas Rangers], the hijacker may not have escaped unscathed and might have been prevented from firing so many shots. The subsequent crime scene investigation, according to HPD historian Nelson Zoch, revealed that "two shots fired by the officers would have struck J. J. Maple had they contained more power."

The bullets that struck the back of Maple's car would have probably hit him in the neck; instead, they bounced harmlessly off the coupe.

any less challenging. What would become one of the most exciting days in Houston police history began outside Springfield, Missouri on a cold winter afternoon in 1932 when ten ill-equipped Missouri police officers prepared to arrest several local youths for auto theft. By the time January 2, 1932 ended, six of the police officers would lie dead and four wounded; a record at that time for police officers killed in one incident. The so-called "Young Brothers Massacre," was carried out on a small rural farm, home to an upstanding family that had been there since before the Civil War. Raised in the Bible Belt by hardworking, God-fearing parents, the two Young brothers, Jennings and Harry, seemed the least likely of killers. The killings resonated throughout the country but the story would not end until Houston police officers had their say.[18]

Two officers maintain the street safety around Houston's City Hall of
the 1920s. (Houston Metropolitan Research Center, Houston Public
Library, Houston, Texas, Litterst-Dixon Collection, MSS-200-382)

In the aftermath of the massacre, the local police force was in complete
chaos, allowing the Young Brothers to make good their escape. Almost 700
miles of two-lane concrete and macadam roads separated Springfield from
Houston. The following morning the *Houston Chronicle* led with the headline "Desperadoes Slay Six Officers in Fight." Few could imagine that the final
chapter of the Young Brothers saga would be written in the Bayou City. Other
Houston papers headlined the shootings as well. The Sunday edition of *The
Houston Post-Dispatch* reported "Gunmen Flee after Slaying Six Cops," and
"Missouri Officers are Mowed Down as House Stormed." Posses lost track of
the killers until officers found their wrecked Ford coupe in Streetman, Texas,
a small village of less than 400 residents 169 miles north of Houston. It just
so happened that the stolen cars found at the Young farm came from Houston, where Harry Young had worked two years while a fugitive from another
crime. At this point the chase shifted to the Houston area where the Youngs
also had several relatives.

Detective Lieutenant Anthony Margiotto was the first HPD official to be
contacted by the Springfield police. Houston officers immediately went on
the lookout for a saleswoman who had recently married Harry Young. The

January 4 *Houston Chronicle* reported, "The officers laid siege Monday morning to a cottage at 1003 Terminal Street but when they entered the place they did not find the Youngs." The residence belonged to Florence Calvert, who was believed to have married the brother just three weeks earlier. The police surrounded the house calling for anyone inside to come out. Detectives entered to find the last morsels of breakfast for two still sitting on the kitchen table. But the only person in the residence was the bride's sister, who was taken into custody. The sister told Detective C. V. "Buster" Kern that Florence had a doctor's appointment that day. Kern immediately rushed to the doctor's office but the woman was nowhere to be found.

Detective Lieutenant Beverly led an attack at a house on Avenue I. *The Houston Post-Dispatch* reported that after firing a tear gas canister into the attic, Detective Kern "mounted a fragile ladder and climbed into the upper story with drawn pistol as he prepared to meet the desperate Missourians."[19] He found the attic empty. However, HPD was closing in on its quarry. On Monday, January 5, a former acquaintance of Harry Young notified officers that he had seen him in the 6500 block of Avenue I. Another former neighbour reported seeing Harry board a bus two blocks away. However, according to the January 5 *Post-Dispatch*, "Like a phantom, the elusive killer from the Ozark hills appeared in another section of Magnolia Park, residents told officers, but a rough search of the vicinity failed to reveal any trace of the ex-convict."[20]

Houston detectives kept a sharp eye on bus stations, highways, the wharf and the airport. Texas Rangers were even detailed to the case by Adjutant-General William Warren Sterling. Guards patrolled the borders as officials tried to decide whether to search all ships. The *Houston Chronicle* described the search as "perhaps the greatest man hunt of Houston's history," reporting, "The waterfront, long considered a stronghold of wanted men had been raked with a fine-tooth comb by 2 a.m. Tuesday without a trace of the desperadoes."

Details are hazy as to how the brothers made it to Houston, but most evidence suggested that they were in the city by six o'clock the morning of January 4. By most accounts both brothers were injured, either from the car wreck or the original shootout. In any case, on January 4, they rented a front-room apartment from a family at 4610 Walker Street in the Eastwood section. It was during the Depression, and the Tomlinsons, like most families, were just trying to get by, even if it meant renting a room in the family house to strangers. The room had been unoccupied for several weeks, so they were more than happy to rent it out. Before turning in that evening, J. F. Tomlinson, as he did most nights, scanned the pages of the day's *Chronicle*. Almost immediately his attention was drawn to the front page headline, "Police Comb Houston for 'Mass Slayers.'"[21] Accompanying the article was a photo of the "hatless" tenant who identified himself as "Claude Walker," aka Harry Young.

Unable to sleep that night, the Tomlinsons decided to wait until morning to contact police. After dropping off his daughter at school Tomlinson went directly to Police Chief Percy Heard's house. Heard was apparently skeptical at first. Reluctant to alert the news media, Heard called his chief of detectives, Kirk Irwin, and nine "select" officers and quickly began coordinating a plan. The team included Heard and Irwin; detective lieutenants, B. W. Payne and Claude Beverly; and detectives W. M. Barrett, Ira Williams, Henry Bradshaw, Bob Martin, George Lathrop and Dave Turner. As they surrounded the Tomlinson home, Lieutenant Anthony Margiotta and Captain Roy Young joined them.

The *Houston Chronicle* took credit for alerting Tomlinson to the presence of the killers, with one editor writing, "Boy delivering Chronicle Began Moves that Ended in Deaths of Slayers."[22] According to one chronicler of the Young Brothers Massacre, the Houston police squad "in their vested suits, white shirts, and ties and, always, the light-colored Stetsons tilted at becoming angles, were clearly Houston's finest."[23] Unlike their counterparts in Springfield, who were armed only with rifles and shotguns, the HPD squad had a sub-machine gun and tear gas bombs.

Heard had Tomlinson walk back to his cottage to make sure his wife was safe. Reporting back that his wife was gone and the two brothers were asleep, Tomlinson prompted Heard to put his plan into action. Unfortunately for historians and Houston police aficionados, the original 1932 records of the "greatest man hunt in the history of Texas" have disappeared from HPD records, just as they have in Springfield, Missouri. Researchers in 1972, seeking to uncover the details of the Houston shootout, were told that the only records of the Young Brothers are a copy of the fingerprints of Jennings Young. Further research turned up the death certificates of the brothers in the Bureau of Vital Statistics of the City of Houston.[24]

The best coverage of the final gunfight was provided by reporters who interviewed participants. The most complete accounts can be found on the pages of the January 5 *Houston Chronicle* and the January 6 *Houston Post-Dispatch*. Most accounts agree that the battle was over in just minutes (the famous gunfight at the OK Corral took only thirty seconds). According to

The decade of the 1920s saw the installation of the first traffic tower in downtown Houston at Main and Capital. It was designed to provide an officer with the ability to direct traffic from the safety of a tower instead of at ground level. HPD quit the practice when an errant vehicle knocked over the tower for the last time. (Houston Metropolitan Research Center, Houston Public Library, Houston, Texas)

the participants, the HPD posse surrounded the cottage with Detectives Stinson and Barrett approaching the back door. Chief Heard, Peyton and Beverly proceeded to the front door where they almost immediately ran into a neighbour who was there looking for work. Officers hustled him away and handcuffed him to a tree as they made their way back into the house and down the hall. While Heard stayed at the front door, Peyton and Beverly "tiptoed" toward the rear bedroom door. When they attempted to move on to the bathroom door attached to the bedroom, they were met with several shots from the bathroom and one coming from the hallway.

Beverly remembered moving with Peyton across the hall to the kitchen door where they "had a view of the rear bedroom and the bathroom door." He reported, "Everything was quiet for a few minutes" and then the "bathroom door opened a few inches and one of the Young brothers peeped out." Beverly fired his sawed-off shotgun. This was followed by four gunshots in the bathroom. Then a voice from the bathroom announced, "We're dead—come on in." Stinson and Barrett followed up with tear gas canisters. No more shots were fired and as the gas cleared and the officers hesitantly moved into the bathroom, they found one brother dead and "the other dying" of self-inflicted gunshot wounds. The brothers apparently had faced each other and shot each other in a suicide pact. Although there are several conflicting accounts of the last battle, the only official records indicate that both brothers died from wounds inflicted by each other.

Despite a reward of at least $300, it appears no one received any money. Chief Heard felt that if anyone deserved it, it was the Tomlinsons. When it came to rewarding any part of it to the HPD, the ever "skeptical Heard" noted that thirteen officers were involved and he would rather "wait till we get it to decide on the cut to be made." He added that whatever they got would probably go to the department's "burial and benefit fund."[25]

10

REORGANIZATION

During Oscar Holcombe's two terms as mayor between 1933 and 1937, he inaugurated several changes for HPD largely regarded as politically motivated. Not the least was his creation of the Department of Public Safety. By making this move, he effectively ended the existence of independent police and fire departments. Holcombe abolished the position of chief of police and imbued the director of public safety, George Woods (his former campaign manager), with the chief's powers and then some. However, Woods stressed, "If anyone calls me chief, they had better take to their heels when they say it."[1]

As public safety director, Woods implemented a number of changes that had long-lasting ramifications for HPD. The egotistical Woods created the position of superintendent of police and appointed Banyon Wylie "B. W." Payne, former captain of detectives, to fill it. In the process, Woods, who claimed that the city budget required it, fired Chief Percy Heard and Captain of Detectives J. K. Irwin. In addition, many high-ranking officers were reduced in rank.[2]

The rapid turnover of HPD chiefs during the 1930s was one of the biggest detriments to the reorganization of the department. During Holcombe's tenure as mayor in the 1930s, he oversaw several bureaucratic advances, including the creation of a Missing Persons Division on November 15, 1934. He also required police matrons to be referred to as "police-women." The following year the Identification Division was in operation 24/7, and a Record Division went into operation.

Following the resignation of George Woods in February 1935, twenty-year HPD veteran "B. W." Payne was appointed acting public safety director as well as "chief of police." Born in Tennessee in 1889, he left farming for police work at the age of twenty-one when he moved to Houston, and he joined HPD three years later in 1915. Celebrating his two decades in policing in 1935, he said, "It is the most fascinating work in the world, and I hope that I

may be able to continue in it the rest of my natural life." And as for his greatest ambition: "To have the most efficient police department in the South."[3]

When Payne first joined the force, there were 12 members of the detective
bureau, compared to 80 when he took over as the top cop two decades later.
The department itself had grown from 140 to 320 officers. Payne remembered fondly the days when the mounted patrolmen were the most prominent members of the force. They had become obsolete by 1935, replaced by
radio-equipped patrol cars that were used for the first time in 1932.[4] Three
new bureaus also had been created during the intervening twenty years, Vice,
Homicide and Auto Theft.

Payne was a good choice for chief, having served stints in a number of capacities over the years. According to one account, he "had taken a hand at everything there was to be done at the police station, except ride motorcycles."[5]
He began as a patrolman working the downtown beat and a year later was
promoted to mounted officer. A year later he was appointed city jailer. Two
years later he made detective, working for the automobile theft bureau. He
held this position for five years before his appointment as sergeant in charge
of the Vice Squad, a position he held for one year. In 1928, he was promoted
to lieutenant of detectives and helped organize the auto theft bureau. During
this period, he was credited with leading investigations that broke up a major
state auto theft ring.

Payne was probably most proud of creating the Houston police school,
although it was discontinued after a year due to retrenchments in the department. The following year Payne was promoted to captain and began a
three-year stint in charge of the homicide bureau. In 1933, Payne took a leave
of absence and went to work in the district attorney's office as a criminal investigator looking into all capital cases.

Among the changes he hoped to implement as chief was the organization
of a separate bureau to investigate robbery by firearms, burglary and theft.
He also hoped to inaugurate a complaint bureau to improve public relations.

In 1935, Payne stressed the importance of increasing the size of the historically undermanned police force. Late that year while serving as acting
public safety director, he announced the necessity of hiring 150 more officers
due to the ongoing threat of labor violence at the Port of Houston. This matter was extremely pressing due to the fact that the longshoreman's contracts
were due to expire at the end of the month. In June 1935, the force had 342
persons on its payroll but only 281 available for actual police duty. If Payne's

HPD's first-ever academy-trained class from 1939 with Mayor Oscar Holcombe (white suit) pictured with the class. Capt. L. D. Morrison Sr. is on the far left, with Police Chief Lawrence C. Brown between him and the mayor. Morrison is known as the father of HPD academic training, whose present-day police academy carries his name. (HPD Museum)

goal was met, the 150 additional recruits would raise the total number of policemen to 431, the largest contingent in HPD history.

A breakdown of the HPD of 1935 had 207 uniformed officers on active duty, including 29 motorcycle officers and 74 plainclothesmen. The remaining 61 persons on the payroll were clerks, garage attendants, elevator boys and 22 elderly school policemen. During the previous year's longshoremen's strike at the port, regular policemen were required to work four extra hours each day, resulting in an overtime cost of $7,500.

Labor conflict was a recurrent problem on Houston's waterfront in the 1930s. In 1936 one observer reported, "It became an annual duty to record some destructive strike on the Houston waterfront."[6] Some saw it as the handiwork of communists while others attributed it to New York labor thugs extorting money from steamship lines.[7] In reality it was symptomatic of the Depression era unrest. The 1935 longshoremen strike was one of the longest and most violent strikes. It began in New Orleans and spread to other Gulf ports and Houston.

In order to suppress the strike, steamship lines hired busloads of strike-breakers from East Texas and positioned them on public wharves. Violence was clearly in the offing as port officials built a fence to protect public property and deputized a special force to police the waterfront under former Texas Ranger Frank Hamer, only a year after his ambush of Bonnie and Clyde in Louisiana at the head of a squad of bounty hunters.[8] His arrival was not well-received by labor leaders who saw him as a hired killer brought in to stop them. Hamer wasn't new to Houston, having been hired to work for Mayor Rice in 1911. According to Hamer's biographer, his first assignment was to help special officers tracking down a gang that killed several HPD officers.[9]

In order to prepare for the looming strike, forty-one "husky trouble shooters" selected from 150 recruits were mobilized for duty along the city dock. According to Chief Payne, half of this group was to be teamed with veteran officers while the other half would work with the "old heads" in patrolling the city. Several of the recruits had been former HPD officers and were allowed to wear their old uniforms in the event of trouble. The others would not wear uniforms but would always be accompanied by current uniformed officers.[10]

If required to serve, they were told they would have to buy their own pistols and pay the $5 fee for a police bond. By October 1935, fifty-six temporary policemen had been selected in the event of waterfront trouble during the scheduled October 11 strike by International Longshoremen (ILA). The general strike at Texas ports was called for on September 26 when the ILA gave notice of a boycott of Texas ports and Lake Charles on ships coming from or destined for New Orleans; in New Orleans, the ILA called for a strike beginning on September 30 and a strike on all vessels beginning October 11.[11]

The strike ended up lasting ten weeks. Violence led to fourteen deaths in Texas and Louisiana during the strike, with many others beaten and much property destroyed. According to the hagiographic biography, *I'm Frank Hamer*, state and city officials arranged for Hamer to lead a special force of twenty ex-Rangers and sheriffs to prevent sabotage and looting. He stayed at the port into the next year and soon joined forces with ex-police chief Roy T. Rogers to open a security guard association; for the next thirteen years, he protected oil fields, refineries, chemical plants, docks and shipping companies from illegal strikes and sabotage.

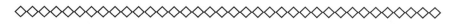

Nazi Crew Mutinies; HPD to the Rescue (1933)[12]

In December 1933, a distress call from the German freighter S. A. Nedenfels embroiled HPD officers in one of their stranger encounters. According to the ship commander, Captain Oetmanns, the crew began to riot after the captain declined their request to authorize a Nazi parade in downtown Houston.

He refused on the grounds it would probably lead to trouble. He discharged the mate who was the most aggressive advocate of the parade. His fellow seamen demonstrated to point of threatening mutiny. In response to the call, a Marine detective led five HPD officers all armed with teargas bombs, sawed off shotguns, and pistols.

They successfully drove the mutineers from the captain's quarters. They left with the dismissed mate. As the police and prisoner strode down the gangplank the crew lined the rail and gave the Nazi salute and sang Deutschland Uber Alles.

In October 1935, Houston Patrolman J. A. Ladd was selected as the first president of the Texas Negro Peace Officers Association (TNPOA). He was one of Houston's six black police officers who created "the first organization of black police officers in the United States."[13] These men were pioneers not only as African American policemen but also as standard bearers for police unionism in general.

African Americans had served on HPD since the 1870s and indeed were a continuous presence since Reconstruction. Regardless where African-American police officers operated in the late nineteenth-century, they were locked into a secondary status and expected to obey certain unwritten rules. Not only were they usually barred from wearing police uniforms and moving up in the police hierarchy, they also were not allowed to arrest whites and were only allowed to patrol black communities.[14] Once Reconstruction ended, black police in most of the South lost their jobs, mainly because their continued presence on police forces reminded too many white Southerners of the former era when "the presence of gun-toting, black law enforcement officers challenged the prevailing notions of white supremacy."[15] By most accounts, Houston's overwhelmingly white police force had little regard for its black counterparts and "did not recognize them as real police officers." Nonetheless, by the end of the 1870s, Houston was one of the few Southern cities that kept African-American police on the force. So despite similar pressures to remove them from the force, Houston remained the only major Southern city with a black officer presence between 1870 and 1926.[16]

Prior to 1921, blacks were only employed on ten Southern city police forces, including Baltimore, Knoxville, Memphis, Wheeling, Tampa and Houston.[17] By 1940, several other cities had joined the ranks as well, but no more than fifty African Americans were employed as police officers in the region. In fact, states with the largest black populations—Mississippi, South Carolina, Louisiana, Georgia and Alabama—still did not employ a black police officer as late as 1940.

By most accounts HPD maintained an unofficial quota of six between 1929 and 1948. The only way a new black officer could be appointed was if one retired or died and needed to be replaced. According to one authority, the only new appointment during the previously cited era was in 1938 when it was necessitated by the accidental death of one of the six. This unofficial quota held until 1948 when thirteen positions were given to black officers "as a payoff for their political support in the city council election of 1946."[18]

On the surface six black police officers still seemed relatively modest; however, compared to the rest of the South's major cities the inclusion of this quota was significant. Only Louisville, Kentucky, in the upper South, had more. Most of Houston's southern counterparts maintained a force with less than three and in some cases no black officers during the 1930s. In fact, the only other cities with an African American presence in the lower South besides Houston during the 1930s were San Antonio, Austin, Galveston, Beaumont and three Florida cities.[19]

At the onset of the twentieth century police work had more responsibilities than other occupations. The typical police officer worked twelve hour days for low wages. Between 1910 and 1920, policemen began to take an active role creating labor unions and police organizations. In 1915, two Pittsburgh police officers created an organization for the social welfare of police known as the Fraternal Order of Police (FOP). But while other police organizations were subsequently created, efforts at unionization lagged behind. What probably sealed the coffin for police unionism more than anything in the early 1900s was the 1919 Boston police strike. Scholars have suggested

An HPD accident investigator attracts a small crowd as he examines the details of
a one-car accident near downtown Houston. (Houston Police Officers Union)

that the strike and its accompanying disorder lost any public support for police reform and set back the police union movement until the 1960s.[20]

So it was in this environment that the Texas Negro Police Officers' Association (TNPOA) created the first black police union in 1935. What perhaps
helped stimulate its creation was the role played by HPD chief Tom Goodson, who in the 1920s campaigned to improve conditions for HPD's "colored" officers while trying to improve the department's strained relationship
with the black community.[21]

After his appointment as chief in 1923, Goodson made it clear that police
brutality would not be tolerated on any level, against any race. Some of his
early actions included suspending a police officer for beating a black Houstonian on a streetcar, appointing nine black officers between 1925 and 1929,
and putting the first two African American officers in uniform.[22]

One of Goodson's biggest supporters was the city's most influential black
newspaper, the *Informer*. The newspaper had been lobbying HPD for a better
relationship with black Houstonians. According to the paper's editor, Clifton

F. Richardson, if the department hired more black officers it would go a long way toward solving the problem. According to Marvin Dulaney, "Richardson's agitation" and the work of the Texas Commission on Interracial Cooperation "resulted in a net increase in the number of black police in Houston from two in 1923 to six by 1931."[23]

By the late 1930s, the number of HPD's African American police had increased but they still were bound by the unwritten codes of yesteryear, as were most other black officers in America. Only black police in New York City and Chicago had the power to arrest whites or move up in the hierarchy.

During the 1930s and 1940s, an uneasy truce existed between Houston's African American community and the mostly white police force, but as Houston historian Cary D. Wintz noted, this relationship proved a "continuing problem" as local black residents reported regular harassment, abuse and sometimes brutality. Local black newspapers such as the *Houston Informer* publicized such incidents, which were blamed on "the caliber of recruits."[24]

In 1938, the newspaper claimed that HPD was made up of mostly "ex-convicts, discarded police officers from other towns, roughnecks, and a few earnest men, green and untrained" in the duties of police work.[25] Black leaders tried to combat police brutality through vocal lobbying for the prosecution of guilty officers and for adding black officers to the force to patrol black neighborhoods. Nonetheless police brutality led to the 1917 Camp Logan Riot and as racial tensions continued into the 1920s, led to the revival of the Ku Klux Klan.

Despite these racial tensions, compared to most large American cities, Houston remained relatively free of large-scale racial violence during the era of segregation. Even the notoriously anti-HPD *Houston Informer* in 1930 noted that "blacks were fortunate to live in a city like Houston where the 'mob' spirit was not rampant."

However, few could argue that even a half century later that the city suffered from inadequate law enforcement, particularly in the black communities, where residents felt more likely to be victimized by excessive force than to be protected from the lawless elements. The ascendance of Lee Brown to police chief in 1982 improved the image of HPD in the black community, which according to Cary D. Wintz was reflected in 1983, when "for the first time in over a decade, the police department was not a major issue in the mayor's election."[26]

In the 1930s, Griffenhagen and Associates, Consultants in Public Administration and Finance, conducted the most detailed review of the Houston Police Department up to that time in its history. The report pulled no punches, but seemed free of political bias. One of its most glaring criticisms regarded the lack of continuity in police leadership. Noting the value of hiring a "well-qualified chief of police," the report found it alarming that between 1921 and 1939 there were nine different chiefs of police—virtually a new one every time there was a city election.

By the end of the decade the HPD organization had a set hierarchy with the chief of police in charge. Although the position of assistant chief of police was established by ordinance, it was not filled. Under the chief was the inspector of police. Next in line, and subject to the orders of the chief and the inspector, was the night chief of police, who was in command between 7 p.m. and 7 a.m. Under him was the senior captain in charge of all uniformed forces who was expected to report to the inspector. The chief of detectives was directly answerable to the chief and was the commander of all detective work except the Vice Division. The lieutenant of detectives oversaw vice and was answerable only to the chief of police.

The Clerical Division was headed by the secretary of police and an acting chief clerk. This position reported directly to the chief as did the supervising technician in charge of the police radio. Other employees were also expected to report to the chief, including detectives acting as special investigators and the police clerk in charge of the missing person's bureau. Toward the end of 1939, HPD had a total roster of 466 individuals, including 297 uniformed officers, some of whom were part-time school police.

During the compilation of the Griffenhagen Report in 1939, several defects in the police organization were brought to the attention of city management. Many of these so-called "defects" were the result of the "rapid increase in the responsibilities thrust upon the department."[27] Particularly troubling was the lack of a unified command over a small number of units. One of the biggest criticisms was levelled at the position of senior captain of police, which at that time had "68 and one half percent of the active force under his supervision." If one took into account the number of jobs directly under his supervision it would include: 1) traffic control; 2) motorcycle escort service; 3) accident investigation; 4) school crossing police; 5) stray animal collection and detention; 6) radio car patrol; 7) foot patrol; 8) lock-up operation; 9) traffic marker location and maintenance; 10) patrol wagon operation; 11) booking of prisoners and traffic violators; and 12) operation of building elevators. The Griffenhagen Report concluded that "the assignment to this supervising officer is one beyond the capacity of any one man when it is considered that in addition to the task of supervision, he is expected to participate actively in policing parades, football games, wrestling matches, and other large assemblies and at the same time, to act as the traffic engineer of the city."[28]

Some Griffenhagen Recommendations Adopted by HPD

- Department divided into five divisions
- Uniform terminology adopted
- Post of Assistant Chief of Police
- Vice Squad changed to Morals Division
- Narcotics Squad combined with Morals Squad
- Uniformed force divided into the Uniform Division and the Accident Prevention Division, each commanded by a Captain of Police
- Work of impounding livestock transferred to Humane Department
- All records except Identification Bureau records combined
- Radio cars conspicuously identified by painting the word "Police" in a prominent place on car
- All cars equipped with two-way radios
- Employment of Traffic Engineer
- Special Detective squads combined and consolidated
- Homicide and Robbery Detail combined
- Promoting detectives from the ranks
- Modern equipment and modus operandi files established in Identification Bureau
- Minimum educational requirements for applicants implemented
- Range of weight in relation to height be narrowed for new patrolmen

From an historical perspective, Houston, as one the pioneering cities as far as modern community policing, was criticized by the Griffenhagen study for its lack of foot patrol, stating, "Except for the foot patrol afforded in the business section by the part-time work of traffic officers, practically none exists in Houston."[29] The report went on to explain that the vast majority of those involved on foot patrol were either older and partly disabled members of the force assigned to railroad stations, bus terminals, public markets and other similar locations.[30]

As far back as 1939, it was obvious to observers that "the presence of a uniformed patrolman on his beat is one of the greatest crime deterrents."[31] Furthermore, said the Griffenhagen study, there are certain duties that cannot be performed by policemen riding in motor vehicles such as "fixed post traffic duty, trying doors of business houses at night, policing large assemblies, guarding against uprisings because of labor troubles"[32] and others.

By the end of the 1930s, HPD was responsible for policing 1,250 miles of streets. From another perspective this meant that Houston had seventy-three square miles of territory that would have to be "divided equally among the existing [twelve] radio cruisers, [with] each car expected to police more than six square miles." In the era of the foot patrol "a hundred men would be required to cover such an area. The assignment of only two [in 1939], even though they were in fast moving vehicles" was not considered adequate coverage.[33]

The Griffenhagen report estimated that to give minimum police protection in the form of once over coverage on each of three tours of duty "twelve radio cars would be expected to cover 3,750 miles."[34] Conservative estimates suggest that officers engaged in this service would consume one third of their time traveling to and from the district for roll call, bringing prisoners to headquarters, making investigations, attending fires, and performing similar duties, which could not possibly be accomplished in this manner effectively.

As the 1930s came to a close, many large cities had already begun painting cruising police cars "a distinctive color" to perhaps making up for the disappearance of the uniformed officer on the foot beat. For example, New York City painted the body of the cars green with the top cream colored, while Cleveland preferred cars painted red, white and blue. Others painted cars white. Houston on the other hand still only identified the cars with the barely prominent identification on two sides of the car. Critics observed that together with the poor street lighting and the cars resembling taxis, it is doubtful that citizens were aware they were receiving any protection at all.[35]

Houston's Mexican population increased five-fold between 1910 and the mid-1920s. Local businessmen led by Fernando Salas and Frank Gibler, a

The Average Age of HPD Officers (1939)

- Regular patrolmen and detectives—43 years old (four over 70, 14 over 60 years)
- Motorcycle officers—36 years old
- Probationary patrolmen—28

former U.S. consul married to a Mexican woman, formed the *Assemblea Mexicana* in 1924. Similar to other self-defense groups that grew up in the 1920s to protect Mexican newcomers in other cities, this organization forced the suspension of one HPD sergeant in 1928 for arresting and jailing a young Mexican injured in an auto accident without medical attention. According to Rosario, "A permissive climate allowed policemen that were so inclined to vent sadistic tendencies by menacing Mexicans.... Police violence in Texas, perhaps more than any other state, kept Mexicans within the web of control" throughout the early decades of the twentieth century.[36]

What's more, Texas remained in the forefront of police homicides at point of arrest. According to one recent monograph, the Mexican government examined cases of Mexican immigrants killed by the police in the United States between 1910 and 1920 and concluded that most incidents occurred in Texas. Texas officials admitted this was true and unfortunately this would continue into the 1920s.[37]

HPD underwent further transformation during the 1930s. Beginning with the creation of the Homicide Division in 1930 and the inauguration of the first in-service police school, offering courses to detectives and uniformed officers, HPD kept up with professional developments in policing. A "Shadow Box" was installed at headquarters where victims and detectives could view prisoners without being observed.

Manuel Crespo: HPD's First Hispanic Officer (1940–1946)[38]

Born in Orense, Spain in 1903, Crespo arrived in Houston in the 1920s. By 1931, he was managing the Mexican Funeral Home on Navigation Street. He soon earned his mortuary license and bought out the owners, renaming the business Crespo Funeral Home.

He left the family business in 1940 while recovering from a skin ailment and was hired by HPD as a detective, earning the distinction as "the city's first Hispanic police officer," according to the Handbook of Texas. In the years leading up to war, Houston's Mexican-American community was reeling from an upsurge in juvenile delinquency and the department was badly in need of Spanish-speaking officers.

However, his hiring as detective led to resentment among the Anglo officers that worked under him. His career was cut short on his own volition. Having arrived home from vacation just six years into his job, he found his desk had been broken into and his records stolen. He quit the next day and returned to the funeral home, where he would remain for the next half century until his death in 1989. His picture is now displayed in the Houston Police Museum.

In 1930, Percy Heard was sworn in as superintendent of police and the department purchased two Thompson submachine guns.[39] The mayor appointed and swore in 425 special officers to be used as reserves in the event of emergency. In 1932, Houston police were baffled when they arrested the famous Siamese Twins Daisy and Violet Hilton, who were appearing at the RKO Majestic Theater, for a traffic violation. Local newspapers had a laugh when the police were unable to determine which twin was driving and how they could arrest one and not the other.[40]

Demonstrating *esprit de corps* in February 1932, Chief Heard and members of the department were congratulated for making cuts in the budget to prevent twenty men from losing their jobs. This was accomplished when every man making more than $100 a month agreed to work five days per month for three months without pay, this after already accepting a fifteen percent pay cut.

By 1935, response time had been reduced from 5.8 to 3.81 minutes. This coincided with a decrease in homicides since the previous year. To control parking downtown, 1,000 meters were purchased. In July 1936, Chief B. W. Payne shook things up when he announced under the new manual of rules and regulations that members of the force would have to be virtual teetotalers. According to the new rules, officers "shall not drink intoxicating liquor while on duty, nor off duty to an extent unfitting them for duty" and "all members [of the department] shall be considered as being on duty at all times." Payne explained that the rules did not actually mean that no officer could drink during off-time, but simply that they should remain sober in the event they were unexpectedly called on to enforce the law in an emergency. He noted that the rule relating to an officer being on duty at all times is merely a reminder of an old police custom which provides that all members of the department are officers twenty-four hours every day if the necessity for enforcing the law arises.[41]

The rule-oriented Payne added another regulation about the same time that prohibited all officers from engaging in religious and political discussions either at headquarters or elsewhere while in duty or uniform. By most accounts, HPD had not printed a book of rules in so many years that a copy of the last one could not be found and no one remembered when it was issued.

Although Payne was considered a "killjoy" by his officers for his numerous rules such as smoking prohibitions and requiring that officers give badge numbers when asked by civilians, both under threat of dismissal or suspension, he did support laws that protected the so-called "forgotten policemen" who walked the beat and did most of the physical labor. Under his direction, these men were no longer allowed [or required] to contribute to the purchase of diamond-studded gold badges or pearl-handled six-shooters every time one of their sergeants made lieutenant or a lieutenant made captain. Although this practice had been banned in 1933, patrolmen were still complaining in the mid-1930s that they felt obligated to contribute to such gifts for fear of losing "prestige with their superiors."[42]

Payne also had the "forgotten men" smiling when he issued a bulletin that examinations would be given to determine promotions when vacancies were available. As one observer commented prior to Payne, "No such examinations were held, and men were often promoted because of their standing both with their superior officers and influential friends on the outside."

In 1936, the Missing Persons Division was established. That same year the Federal Communications Commission named HPD as one of the first five police forces in the United States to be licensed. The following year saw the creation of the Accident Division. By the end of the decade manpower had been increased to 444 officers.

The 1930s would prove particularly deadly for HPD and officers across the United States. The decade that began with the killings of Edward D. Fitzgerald and W. B. Phares and the death of J. D. Landry in 1930 was marked by the subsequent deaths of Harry T. Mereness, R. H. Sullivan, James T. Gambill, Adolph Martial, Marion E. Palmer and George D. Edwards, all cut down in the line of duty while in the prime of life.

11

PERCY HEARD AND
THE WAR YEARS

As the 1930s came to conclusion, city politics were as complicated and acrimonious as ever as a new mayor took office and a new police chief was appointed. L. C. Brown became police chief in January 1939 and almost immediately set about putting his stamp on the force by demoting twenty-six police officers, forcing seven to retire and firing three others. He also closed three police substations and promoted many of the officers that Holcombe had demoted during his administration to their former ranks.[1]

The same year that saw the release of *Gone with the Wind* and *The Wizard of Oz* also saw HPD open its first police training school for new recruits, under the direction of Captain L. D. Morrison. The five-week classes were conducted at the Sam Houston Coliseum. Moving farther away from its roots in patronage politics, the department subjected new recruits to more requirements than simple political party affiliation. In 1939, HPD adopted a military model for screening potential officers. Of the first 362 who passed the initial exam (out of 597), only seventy were selected as recruits and of these only fifty graduated. But due to budgetary constraints, only twenty-four would wear the HPD blue. The remaining twenty-six were put on a waiting list and would be considered for future jobs on the force or as special police officers. One of the questions asked on the written exam was, "Why do you want to be a police officer?" The same question was still on the test seventy years later.

The year America entered World War II started out for the HPD like any other election year—with a new mayor and police chief. With Neal Picket taking office in 1941 as mayor, it was customary to appoint the new police chief or keep the old one. This was typically accomplished with little controversy. But it would not be the case with the selection of former San Antonio Police Chief, thirty-six-year-old Ray Ashworth. Born and educated in Kansas, Ashworth made a name for himself first on the football fields of high

POLICE CHIEF RAY
ASHWORTH, FEBRUARY
18, 1941–APRIL 29, 1942

school and at the Friends University, a Quaker institution. During college he made the all-conference team three times. Ashworth began his career as a patrolman in Wichita, Kansas in 1928—the first college graduate in the department. Within eight years he was promoted to assistant chief. He was next appointed assistant director of the Safety Division of the International Association of Chiefs of Police and moved to Evanston, Illinois at an annual salary of $3,600. From early on he expressed contempt for political patronage, which he demonstrated in his rooting out of politics from the San Antonio Police Department. Ironically, the Houston mayor's selection of Ashworth, a chief from outside the HPD, proved unpopular in local political circles.

However, there were many that approved the move, especially when there were prospects of appointing B. W. Payne as the new chief. Shortly after Pickett's victory over Holcombe in the mayoral election, the *Houston Press* predicted that Pickett would select Payne. Clearly there were a number of Payne-haters in Houston. Several of them wrote letters to Mayor Neal Pickett lashing out against the potential choice of Payne as police chief. Attesting to the low esteem with which he was held in Houston, A. C. T. Thomasen wrote, "[Mayor] Mr. Pickett, I read in the press, that you favor Payne for Police Chief. That can not be true. That you should go to the gammling [*sic*] fraternity for a Police Chief."[2]

In January 1941, members of the Park Place Union signed a petition lob-bying against his selection as chief due to his association "with gamblers and racketeers."[3] Another writer, Alvis F. Day, had been on the police force for less than three years but felt compelled to note that "some of the older men would say that I haven't learned enough to keep my mouth shut," continuing, "The problem of naming our chief of Police I realize is a very difficult one. In solving this problem I feel sure you will consider those who have risk [*sic*] their jobs and have put their whole effort in helping you [win re-election].... Even your opponent who was guilty of everything you charged him with in your campaign would not consider Mr. Payne for the Chief of Police. Cer-tainly if Oscar Holcombe could not use him I don't see how you could even consider him in the face of all the promises you have made to clean up the police department."[4]

Another letter was even more pointed, as the author noted that in 1934, he had been a member of a grand jury that found that when Payne was chief in the 1930s "the preponderance of the evidence accumulated" testified to his "consorting with the big shot gamblers, black and white, with plenty of evidence of payoff."[5]

Still another letter writer noted that during his tenure as police chief, "Mr. Payne knew these rackets [policy gambling] were running in violation of the law and made no effort whatever to suppress it." According to the letter by a J. A. Collier, the policy rackets had continued under the Brown administration and "the Police Department has made it a point to hamper other law investi-gations of the racket." In his revealing letter, Collier noted that:

> I have never seen Brown paid any money nor have I seen [the head of the vice squad] paid any money, but I do have the word of the op-erators of the largest [policy game] in Houston that six companies are paying $500 per month each for police protection, and those statements are corroborated by the fact that the Police Department makes no arrests whatever on the policy writers. If you doubt my word that the policy game is running wide open in Houston with the protection of the police department, I suggest that you walk down on Milam and Prairie Streets and walk into the building and you will observe on the right-hand side several booths, such as are ordinarily found in cafes, and a negro sitting in each one writing policy tickets, and the uniformed officer on the beat is forbidden by instructions from higher-ups to interfere with the writers and if they interfere

with them, they are called on the carpet and transferred to another beat. All in the world that is necessary to break up the policy racket is a Chief of Police who conscientiously wants to break it up.[6]

One of Chief Ashworth's greatest challenges was dealing with the city's seemingly insurmountable traffic problems. He had taught accident prevention in Evanston, Illinois; Wichita, Kansas; and Greenwich, Connecticut in the 1930s and seemed well suited to the job. His contributions to the traffic reorganization in San Francisco, Oakland, Chattanooga, Columbus, Dayton, Cleveland and Atlanta increased his national profile, leading to teaching stints in traffic control at Harvard University, the University of Alabama and Northwestern University.

In 1939, San Antonio Mayor Maury Maverick hired Ashworth as that city's new police chief. The new chief had an almost immediate impact. Reorganizing the force, "he did a lot of things people in the Alamo city had never seen a police chief do,"[7] like firing seventy-five officers because they could not meet physical requirements and setting up raids of local bingo games.

Succeeding Houston Police Chief L. C. Brown, Ashworth was sworn in February 10, 1941. He made waves immediately, telling the force "nobody in Houston was too big to be arrested if he violated the law."[8] He followed up this tenant with a code of ethics that included elimination of political activity from the department. Officers were warned that their only legitimate income should come from their salaries, requiring that all donations and rewards be turned over to the police burial fund.

In May 1941, just three months after taking office, Ashworth launched a crackdown against Houston's gambling rackets. One of his first acts was to convene a meeting with eighty officers to come up with game plan for going after horse race bookies. He formed the officers into twenty-one squads and each was supplied with a bookie location. This strategy paid immediate dividends with the arrest of seventy gamblers. Shortly after these raids Ashworth assembled forty officers and within forty-eight hours busted forty-eight "marble tables."[9] It was not long before the police chief was approached by a representative of the local gambling interests who offered him $1,000 to $1,200 per month to allow the marble tables to resume operation. He rebuffed the offer. However, when one of his own officers approached him with an offer of $500 per week to protect two gambling games "frequented by wealthy women of Houston," Ashworth fired the policeman and raided the two games.

The new chief did not suffer fools lightly. Apprised of citizen complaints that "too many undeserving persons had been given special commissions," he cancelled 341 of the 862 commissions after carefully examining their records. In order to insure that the best qualified individuals held the top posts, he introduced a written test that was used to determine jobs from elevator operators to assistant chiefs.

Ashworth resigned from his job with little fanfare just months after taking charge of the department. A number of sources attribute his leaving to provincial attitudes against his status as an outsider and to Houston politics. According to one editor the "persistent provincial attitude" hampered "Houston's growth as a metropolis."[10] It was felt that Ashworth was under the impression that he was promised more authority than he actually received, with much of his power being nullified by the appointment of two assistant chiefs who had been active in Mayor Pickett's recent campaign. Most observers felt it was no secret that he was disappointed by the failure of the commissioners to "support fully the operation of a non-political police department."[11] Ashworth's actions and method of leaving would lead to great controversy when he tried to return to his position following the end of the war. To all concerned, Ashworth had left to help evacuate the Japanese from the West Coast and defense areas and to supervise the policing of the camps.

As his legacy, Ashworth could point to a number of achievements. During his reign all officers were given one day off each week, all officers were given standardized nickel-plated badges bearing either rank or number. Ashworth also:

- Purchased forty-seven new police cars, doubling the fleet
- Implemented one-man units to cover more area and reduce crime
- Following major departments throughout the country, he required every member of HPD to be fingerprinted for first time (Fifteen were fired for having police records.)
- Created Houston Civilian Auxiliary Police Division.

Ashworth, however, made few friends when he banned the wearing of diamond-studded gold badges, a prohibition that only affected ten high ranking officers.[12] He also issued a bulletin ordering police to use sirens only in case of emergency, effectively ending a long-time precedent which allowed them for escort use. He even threatened to remove all sirens if more cars are obtained by the department, following an example set in San Antonio.[13]

By most accounts, when it was announced that Percy Heard was selected as the new police chief, "There was rejoicing at the police station"[14] where he had distinguished himself in a previous stint as chief between 1930 and 1933. When notified of his selection, one high-ranking officer began singing, "We're back in the saddle again," while another refrained, "I've seen more smiles around here in the last hour than I saw all the past year."[15] Leaving his job as chief special agent of the United Gas Pipe Line Company, Heard promised not to make any major changes.

Percy Heard originally joined the police department in 1917, working his way up from rookie to chief in 1930, when he was appointed by Mayor Monteith to replace the departing Chief Charlie McPhail. Heard came to prominence in 1932, when he participated in the siege of a small house in the East

POLICE CHIEF PERCY HEARD,
AUGUST 1, 1930–MAY 3, 1933;
APRIL 29, 1942–JANUARY 3, 1947

End. It involved the infamous Young Brothers, who had blown into town fresh from killing six Missouri peace officers just four days earlier. He left the force in 1933, and from 1935 to 1942 served in the United Pipeline job. He was forty-eight years old when he regained his old HPD job in 1942. By most accounts he had a laudable record as chief during the 1930s. Several editorials lavished praise on his management style compared to his predecessor. One editor found former Chief Ashworth to be "as cold as a cucumber" and lacking the personality of Heard, who was regarded as "open-and-above board, [and] knows how to treat persons."[16]

Where Chief Ashworth had "little disposition to make friends," Heard was considered more down-to-earth with "no symptoms of his hat being too small." Of course, since Heard was a lifetime resident, he was considered to be "one of us and not a fly-by-night official." As one writer conceded that if he had been a Houstonian, Ashworth "might have been an acceptable chief of police."[17]

Heard's hire paid dividends almost immediately as he crusaded for a larger budget and more officers. During his first month, he added three men to the eight-man Vice Squad and returned the Homicide Squad to its "pre-Ashworth footing." The former chief had dismantled much of the squad, turning over most of its work to the radio dispatchers and the cruising patrolmen. According to this protocol, dispatchers received calls involving murders, assaults and other personal crimes. The initial investigation would then be handled by a uniformed officer rather than the traditional homicide detective. Chief Heard returned to tradition by having the Homicide Squad take its own calls without going through the extra protocol.[18] He also added four men to the squad.

But this was just the beginning. Heard continued to rebuild what Ashworth had dismantled, including the replacement of sirens on police cars. Under Ashworth sirens were ordered removed from all police cars, claiming that "policemen used the sirens to bully their way through traffic." The new chief issued the order after a police car killed two pedestrians.[19]

Beginning in October 1942, all uniformed officers and detectives were awarded a $20 per month pay increase.[20] Exempt from the raise were any high-ranking officials making more than $250 a month. With the loss of so many officers and young men to the war effort, Chief Heard successfully lobbied City Council to increase the maximum age of new officers from thirty-six to forty[21] and to pare down the height requirement two inches from 5-foot-10, with weight proportionate. According to one official, firemen and policemen were "leaving in droves to enter military service or take higher paying defense jobs," resulting in the HPD having more job openings than applicants. New recruits approved by Chief Heard were fast-tracked into immediate service at a starting salary of $125 a month with automatic raises that would bring their salaries up to $170 after seven months. In order to contribute to the war effort, all station chiefs were asked to scour their stations for scrap metal after 8,000 pounds of it were found in the property vault of the city police station and the basement of City Hall.

Less than a year after the bombing of Pearl Harbor, Houston joined the country's other cities in employing "dim outs." By all accounts automobile accidents and crime were less than normal during the first night of wartime dim out. However, officials cautioned that this could be explained by less than normal city traffic and a slower 20-mile-per-hour speed limit. Traffic Captain Carl L. Shuptrine warned that pedestrians would be most at risk during the blackouts and suggested every civilian wear a white handkerchief on their arms or carry one in their hands when crossing streets.[22]

Proving that some things never change, in late 1942 newspapers reported an epidemic of drivers running red lights in downtown Houston, leading to more traffic violations than the previous year. With many mothers and fathers employed in the war industries during the 1940s, a lack of adult supervision at home was reflected in the rise in juvenile delinquency and its attendant problems. Police efforts were directed at gathering places such as pool halls, dance halls, "honky-tonks" and "juke joints." In November 1942, Chief Heard created a four-member special "honky-tonk squad," led by Sergeant J. E. Redden to enforce regulations in "beer places" and pool halls.[23] Any juveniles found in these locations would be turned over to the crime prevention bureau and if there were evidence minors were sold beer; charges would be filed against the proprietors. A Harris County grand jury joined in with "a major investigation of vice and morals,"[24] noting that there were 1,700 spots in Harris County with beer and wine licenses and that of these almost a quarter of them have supplemental permits to stay open after midnight. In one week alone, police arrested more than one hundred individuals for public drunkenness.

Representatives of the City Federated Women's Clubs met before City Council, requesting it adopt several ordinances that they felt would diminish the growing juvenile problem. Included in their suggestions were proposals to eliminate "taxi dance halls," better regulate the hours of operation of dance halls and beer spots, and a recommendation to hire five police women.[25]

Opposition to closing honky-tonks at midnight came mostly from Houston defense workers who frequented these establishments after their midnight shifts. One worker from the Houston Shipbuilding Corporation complained, "Midnight to us is just like 3:30 in the afternoon to day shift men."[26] Others noted that since all other places of amusement were closed when they got off, there were few alternatives for entertainment after their shifts. Responding to the problem of controlling juveniles and sexually transmitted diseases, a chairman speaking for one nightshift grievance committee suggested, "the answer to disease is better medication, and the answer to juvenile delinquency is more parent responsibility."[27]

During the war years Christmas lost most of its lustre as young men died overseas and city blackouts dimmed outdoor yuletide electrical displays.

Gas rationing not only cut energy consumption in the 1940s, but led to a reduction of speeding in the city limits leading one official to claim "night joy riding is considered a thing of the past." Concomitant with less traffic was a drop in parking meter collections.[28]

In 1942, Vice Captain T. B. Morris claimed strict enforcement by the Vice Squad had "caused most street walkers to leave Houston." The Vice Squad attributed much of its success to the practice of arresting street prostitutes and sending them to a venereal disease clinic for examination. This usually involved a stay of at least three days to determine whether they were free of disease. Part of the policy was to try and have this period coincide with the weekends. Captain Morris declared that "Party girls and girls who hang around public dance halls and honky-tonks" were "responsible for 80 percent of the venereal disease in Houston."[29]

One of the greatest advances in police technology was the adoption of police radios. By the 1940s, the HPD radio station was considered one of the best in the country and most police cars were equipped with two-way radios that allowed officers to both receive calls and report back to the central station. Dispatching as many as 1,200 police calls a day, the station first began operation in 1932. In its first year of operation, 30,150 broadcasts were made, including 9,944 calls to cruising patrolmen. During 1941, 438,000 broadcasts were made, including 300,000 to and from police cars. Prior to the introduction of the police radio, cruising police officers called headquarters by telephone every hour and emergency calls were answered by officers at the police station. As a result, it would often take more than half an hour to respond to a crime across town, allowing plenty of time for criminals to get away.[30]

In contrast to the quick emergency 911 process of today, in the 1940s citizen calls for help first went through a switchboard before being transmitted to cruising patrolmen. Officials recognized this "bottleneck" in the system, since calls were first received at the city switchboard before being relayed to the dispatcher's office. In its infancy it took an average of five minutes from the time of the call to the arrival of a police car. However, in the 1930s there were not as many police cars in operation and their districts were much larger. With more cars and smaller districts by the 1940s, the average response time was reduced to one and a half minutes.

During the 1940s, the HPD faced officer shortages due to the enlistment in the armed forces of so many of its young men. To supplement police protection, an auxiliary force of nearly 300 men took up some of the slack. The Auxiliary Police began operation in December 1941 and was considered so efficient that civilian authorities across the nation modeled their forces after Houston's version. Each night a different group went on duty. Most worked from 7 p.m. until midnight two or three days each week. A purely voluntary position, auxiliaries were given their own uniforms by the city beginning in late 1943. The uniform consisted of a navy blue shirt and trousers, black tie and white regulation cap. Auxiliaries were expected to provide their own boots and slickers. However, initially they were decked out in donated HPD uniforms. It was estimated that it cost $2.10 per day to feed and transport each member on duty, with most averaging between 100 and 700 hours of free service since the auxiliary force was first organized in 1941. Auxiliaries commonly were involved in traffic control and emergencies that included storms and fires. [31]

Every night during their existence, a large band of auxiliary policemen from one of the city's four districts descended on the police station after working their full-time jobs elsewhere by day. At 7 p.m. the district captain would assign them their respective duties for the evening. While the majority patrolled in squad cars teamed up with members of the regular force, others were called on to assist the crime prevention bureau, to work in the radio room and to man desks.

Many policemen will admit that they have seen it all, but it is doubtful that any witnessed what Captain T. B. Morris did one hot Friday afternoon in 1942 when he led three officers from the Morals Squad in a raid on a bookie joint. The chase was on through a suite of rooms. Breaking down five doors, the squad found itself in a dentist's office that adjoined the bookie shop. Officers quickly arrested two of the men, who sat "coyly" reading magazines as if they were patients waiting appointments. However, what took the cake was the suspect sitting in the dentist chair. The police waited patiently as the dentist extracted tooth after tooth, before arresting him after the extraction of the fourth tooth. Each suspect was charged with gaming and released on $10 bond, a rather toothless price to pay.[32]

Early May saw the arrival of new police uniforms for the HPD. For the first time in history, the uniforms featured powder blue caps and trousers and

◇◇◇◇◇◇◇◇◇◇◇◇◇◇◇◇◇◇◇◇◇◇◇◇◇◇◇◇◇◇◇◇◇◇◇◇

The Death of Big Dave Turner (1942)

Local newspapers reported the death of noted Houston patrolman "Big Dave" Turner in August of 1942. Born in Magnolia, Texas, he walked several miles to school each day and studied by lamplight in his parents' small farmhouse. Turner moved to Houston at the age of 18 intending for a career in business. He opened a grocery store with his brother, and it was there several years later that the former police chief Tom Goodson ran into the young giant and convinced him to join HPD. At the time of his death, he had been suffering a heart ailment for many years. Turner collapsed as he entered a grocery store with his wife.[33] The fifty-year-old Turner weighed in at more than 240 pounds and was over six feet tall. The *Houston Press* noted that he "had fought gunmen in Houston and against the Kaiser's army at Saint Mihiel" during the First World War. Police Chief Percy Heard remembered joining the force with him as rookies in 1916. Turner had left HPD to enter the service during the late war and returned to duty in 1920. He survived a shooting at a disturbance call in the 1920s after a notebook in his shirt pocket deflected the bullet. He carried the bullet scar to the grave. In 1927, he made detective and served in the capacity of assistant chief and acting chief during various mayoral administrations in the 1930s. From 1939 until his death by heart attack, Turner served as lieutenant of detectives.

navy blue shirts. Each officer was issued two suits and their old uniforms were put to use by the auxiliary policemen.

In June, Houston was just behind Toledo, Ohio in a national ranking of cities with populations more than 250,000 in the reduction of traffic deaths. During the first five months of the year, Houston had reduced its traffic fatalities by forty-six percent. However, the city could hardly rest on its laurels as fatalities began to increase that summer. After the deaths of five Houstonians in late August, Chief Heard announced a campaign against reckless driving. His plan called for more arrests, heavier fines, the jailing of motorists for running red lights, a drive against minor violations, and a publicity campaign in cooperation with the Houston Safety Association. Heard instructed the Homicide Squad to help traffic officers investigate cases of assault by auto and failure to stop and render aid. He also asked the street and bridge department for more traffic lights, stop signs and more painted lanes for pedestrians. During the first day of the safety drive police arrested 110 individuals for various traffic violations.

In August, the *Houston Press* reported that since the Ashworth regime, the number of high-ranking officers had jumped by almost thirty-two percent. Records indicated fifty-four executives on the police payroll for 313 subordinate officers, "a boss for every five and one-half men." Clearly anti-Heard in tone, the article noted that the pre-war organization was better proportioned with forty-one men heading a force of 348, a ratio of one for every eight and a half men. Also noteworthy was the increase in salaries for high-ranking personnel. A number of changes had been implemented under the Heard regime that created the current top-heavy HPD. Chief Ashworth had previously abolished the position of chief of detectives. However, it was resurrected by Heard at a salary of $300 per month. It had been several years since anyone served as inspector of police but Chief Heard hired one at $300 per month. Under Chief L. C. Brown in 1940, there were twelve lieutenants or one less than the current number. At the same time there were fifteen sergeants and three assistants, compared to twenty-eight just two years later.

Women seemed to benefit from the Heard police administration. In 1940, only eight women were employed by the HPD, with three working in the jail, two in the police chief's office and one each in the Missing Person's Bureau, Identification and Traffic divisions. By 1942, the number of women had tripled, with the highest salary paid to supervising policewoman Ruth H. Beem, who earned $200 per month at a time when the average patrolman earned $150 per month. The best explanation for the rise in female employees is the exigencies created by wartime conditions leaving a dearth of male ap-

POLICE CHIEF L. C.
BROWN, JANUARY 9, 1939–
FEBRUARY 14, 1941

plicants. Among the new hires, was Anne K. Porter, who became the department's first female telephone operator. The 1940s were definitely a different era, particularly when it came to gender stereotyping. Lest anyone doubt it, one need look no further than *The Houston Post*, which heralded the new hire by reporting, "A woman Monday will step into a man's shoes at the Houston police station, thereby releasing another man for military service."

Fear of saboteurs and Axis agents had the entire police department on alert during the war's first Halloween. Rumors abounded that German saboteurs were intent on operating under the guise of Halloween pranksters. Because of a partial blackout, authorities were worried that saboteurs would have the upper hand due to the darkness, with their activities obscured by thousands of Halloween fun seekers. In previous years, pranksters damaged tires and other property that was now essential to war industries. This Halloween, any vandalism would be considered an act of sabotage.

The current war hit home in December 1942 when HPD officers and FBI agents teamed up to arrest a German alien who fled along with several others from an Oklahoma internment months earlier. Cornered in a Houston hotel on Milam Street, the special agent in charge of the local FBI office reported, "If he hadn't been considered a potential threat to our national security through espionage and sabotage he wouldn't have been classified as a dangerous enemy alien by the U. S. attorney general."[34]

In November 1942, preparations were made for the adoption of a new city manager form of government. The city manager would have the power to appoint all department heads, subject to the approval of City Council. Chief Heard established a record by continuing to serve the city, the first police chief in the city's history to serve as chief under three different mayors.

As the Houston area became more embroiled in the war effort, the FBI was busy arresting every alien Japanese living freely in the "vital Houston-Galveston industrial area." Assisting the FBI were HPD officers, sheriff's deputies, naval intelligence officers, deputy U. S. Marshals, Texas Rangers and state highway patrolmen. Japanese citizens were arrested as far north as Huntsville in one of the country's most controversial decisions impinging on civil rights. One of those arrested had even fought in the Russo-Japanese War of 1904.[35]

The Lah-de-Dah Burglar

If anyone doubted that the "gentleman burglar" was a thing of the past they would be reassured by the arrest of the so-called "Lah-de-Dah Burglar" in his tent in a patch of woods just west of Kirby Drive. When twenty-one-year old Douglas Fairbanks Bryan was arrested, he was not only in possession of an expensive wardrobe of fifteen suites, but of dozens of books reflecting an eclectic mind. His first request as he was taken to jail was for the officers to let him take a copy of the *Anthology of Light Verse* with him.

The officers acceded to his request. Bryan had escaped from a prison farm where he was serving a ten-year sentence in El Paso for burglary. He had eluded detectives for weeks as he broke into exclusive homes in the South End and River Oaks. During his escapades he would often shave, shower and add to his wardrobe, always maintaining a discrete appearance.

The burglar told detectives that his first stop in each house was usually the kitchen, "where he raided the ice box for milk, fruit, and sweets." Detectives described the dapper bibliophile as "a scholarly looking chap—the kind you find in the laboratories and libraries at college."[36]

Demonstrating the *esprit de corps* of HPD officers, in March 1943 the *Houston Chronicle* featured a photograph captioned, "Former Policemen Stick Together." According to the piece, six former Houston policemen were currently serving together in the Navy, working in a construction battalion on a South Pacific island.[37]

That same month, Police Chief Percy Heard announced a number of changes to the city police administration in the first department shakeup since he took over. According to Heard, these changes were necessary to give him a freehand in running the department. He wanted to get the message across that promotions would only be based on merit. Most prominent were the demotion of Assistant Police Chief Tom Eubanks and the elevation of Captain Millard Weaver to chief inspector. As the new second in command, Weaver would be responsible for leading the HPD when Heard was out of town. Weaver also would continue his duties as police secretary, occupying an office adjacent to Chief Heard. Other changes included the promotions of Captains Carl Shuptrine and L. D. Morrison to police inspectors. Shuptrine was placed in command of all uniformed police and Morrison in charge of the Crime Prevention Bureau, the police school and personnel. Among the demotions and promotions, pay cuts and pay raises, were the new titles bestowed on several officers. Chief of Detectives C. V. "Buster" Kern would now be referred to as inspector of detectives and Captain Bob Davidson, who had recently been placed in charge of the Vice Squad, was promoted to senior captain of detectives. Former assistant chief Eubanks' only duties would be to command the Subversive Investigation Squad.[38]

In order to help the war effort, it was announced in the fall of 1943 that new police uniforms would be missing the last year's light blue pocket flaps due to the shortage of materials.[39]

In April of that year, Chief Heard announced the creation of a "dance hall squad" to enforce dance hall ordinances. The squad was scheduled to include at least two officers and would be consolidated with the honky-tonk squad.[40] With a dearth in prospective male applicants, Heard announced his intention to hire six women to replace the six men who manned the police station's telephone switchboard. Not exactly a statement on gender equity, Heard admitted that "men are hard to get, and we need these six men on the outside." Similar needs led the chief to also hire seven women complaint clerks to free up the seven men for street duty. According to the civil service job description, "applicants should be between 23 and 25 years old" and "have a good telephone voice."

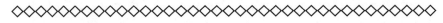

James Davidson: The Consummate Detective

James R. Davidson was considered the consummate detective, earning such monikers as "Sherlock" and "master detective." Davidson left his home in Kansas City, Missouri to enlist in the Army during the First World War. He distinguished himself in combat during the second battle of the Marne and at Verdun. During his seventeen months in France he was constantly in action and during a seventy-nine-day stretch was under fire each day. He was twice wounded in action, noting, "Guess I was too tough for those Germans." Following the war, he returned home and operated a gas station before finding employment in structural steel construction, which brought him to Houston in the 1920s. Unemployed when the Depression hit, Davidson found employment in 1933 as appointed building superintendent for HPD. He was immediately attracted to police work and that same year went to work for the Vice Squad. Over the following decade, he spent stints with both homicide and vice and developed a reputation for his skill at working undercover against gamblers and drug dealers. Davidson conceded, "I don't claim to be a make-up artist, but it was fun milling around those crooks and realizing they had no idea who I was." In February 1943, he was selected to replace T. B. Morris as head of the ten-member Morals Squad.

Policewomen on the force played an integral role in the drive against the so-called "Victory Girls." Three women assigned to the department's crime prevention bureau cooperated with Moral Division officers and military policemen in rounding up girls believed to be less than eighteen years of age who attempted to "entertain" servicemen. Each evening policewomen made the rounds of nightspots such as the U.S.O. Records indicate up to a dozen were arrested each evening. According to Officer Ruth Beem, "Most of the girls express surprise that they are picked up, and saying they consider it their patriotic duty to entertain servicemen."[41]

County safety commission officers came out in favor of appointing women as traffic officers. One member of the Houston-Harris County Safety Association argued "that it does not take an acrobat or a prize fighter to enforce traffic laws." Another committee member expressed admiration for traffic precautions taken in other cities "that are not taken here."[42] He pointed to European cities with a history of hiring women for traffic work, a practice Heard rejected.

In a move to quell the ever-present traffic problems, Heard added ten cruising cars, four sergeants and three traffic investigators to the police force. The ten new cars would be added to the 4 p.m. to midnight shift, bringing the total cars on duty in Houston to thirty during these hours, which was considered the most accident-prone period of the day. At that time there were no plans to add cars to the other two shifts, which stood at fourteen cars between 8 a.m. and 4 p.m. and thirteen from midnight to 8 a.m.

Wartime not only impacted the organization of the police administration, but also criminal activities as well. Police records reveal that although the number of crimes had decreased in the first quarter of 1943, criminals were getting more bang for the buck compared to the previous year. Officials attributed this to the fact that more money was in circulation than ever before.

Due to gas rationing, there was a decrease in car theft but a rise in gasoline theft from parked cars. While there were 4,195 crimes reported compared to 5,583 in the same quarter in 1942, losses were higher at $156,963.49 compared to $136,116.40 the previous year. A number of crimes involved pick pockets preying on defense workers at honky-tonks and nightclubs. Chief Heard recommended that citizens use banks more noting, "There has not been a bank robbery here in many years."[43]

In September 1943, W. B. Cooper became the first policeman to retire under the new police pension plan. The seventy-five-year-old had joined the force in 1907. Over the next thirty-six years Cooper held an array of positions, beginning with patrolman. Between 1911 and 1923, he served as detective and from 1923 to 1930, was the sergeant in charge of the Pawn Shop Division. From 1930 until his retirement, he was in charge of the Property Division. Cooper had not taken a vacation in eleven years, preferring an agreement to give up his vacation time if he was not required to work Sundays. Under the new pension rules, an employee with the city for ten years could retire at sixty. Those with more than ten years were required to retire at sixty-five unless exempted by the city government and those over seventy had to retire. Cooper's pension would pay him $65 per month.

A chapter in HPD history ended with the passing of ninety-five-year-old W. H. Kegans, who earned a reputation as the "Peaceful Peace officer." The son of settlers who came to Texas with Stephen F. Austin, Kegans never fired his weapon on the job during his forty-five years as a police officer. He joined the force as a third class patrolman on Christmas Eve 1890. He remained until he was eighty-six, returning to the same home he had lived in since 1900. He spent a good part of his early career as a mounted officer back when patrolmen were expected to supply their own horses and had to feed and shelter them at their own expense. He worked twelve-hour days on horseback for more than twenty years. When asked why he never became a detective as was customary after several years, Kegans replied that he "never wanted to be [one]."[44]

Every effort was made to suppress rumors during the war years. Newspapers such as the Houston Chronicle even printed full page ads with the boldfaced caption including the following advertisement:

'LOOSE TALK HELPS HITLER'[45]

"Baseless rumors about possible racial troubles are being circulated by loose-tongued, thoughtless people.

There is no plan for any outbreak or riot in the Houston area on Saturday, June 19, or at any other time.

The Police and the Federal authorities have thoroughly investigated every rumor that they can trace, and have found no basis for any of them. A group of well-known white and colored Houstonians on investigation has confirmed these statements.

We urge you – Don't do Hitler's work. Stop circulating rumors which create tenseness and interfere with war production, and attend to your own business.

The colored people of this vicinity are entitled to celebrate their traditional "Juneteenth" holiday Saturday pleasantly and in peace, and the fact they gather for their customary celebrations on that day is no evidence of any intention on their part to create a disturbance. Law enforcement authorities are prepared to deal with thoughtless hoodlums, white or colored, who provoke trouble."

DO NOT BE A RUMOR MONGER.

The ad was signed by the Mayor, Police Chief, City Manager, and the chairmen of various bi-racial and inter-racial commit- tees and commissions.

Not unlike in post 9/11 America, Houston airports were considered pos- sible targets for America's enemies. As a result, a wartime airport detail was organized to patrol the airport perimeter.

In a day before television and reality shows such as *COPS*, consumers of odd criminal activity could rely on newspapers for "reality" entertainment. One example was the case of a young woman, arrested for being intoxicated in early January 1944. The first thing the police noted was that there was an "unnatural bulge" under the woman's coat, which they then asked her to remove. Despite her initial defiance, she slowly took off the coat, revealing a large white chicken, which "fluttered out on to the floor of the police station." Patrolmen E. H. Bennett and R. B. Howard must have been incredulous, as the woman explained that due to wartime restrictions she was "tired of eat- ing beans so I decided to cook me a chicken for my next meal."[46] It cannot be ascertained what happened to the woman or the chicken, which became the responsibility of the keeper of the property room.

Houston experienced fewer traffic accidents during the war years than in the past. However, deaths and injuries were higher. This seeming anomaly was explained away by Police Inspector Carl Shuptrine, who concluded the decrease in accidents was the result of more people carpooling to save gas. However, the rise in deaths and injuries was probably the result of most cars being older and less dependable.

On January 4, 1944, it was announced that Policewoman Inez Crawford would become HPD's first female lieutenant of police. Crawford joined the force in mid-1941. A graduate of the University of Houston, where she ma- jored in psychology and sociology, she worked for several Community Chest[47] agencies before making the transition to policewoman. With her promotion, Crawford's salary was adjusted from $175 per month to $220. It is also worth noting that male Detective A. W. Rainey was also promoted that year to the same position at the same pay as his female counterpart.[48]

Chief Heard established several police substations while serving under Mayor Monteith between 1930 and 1932. But under the subsequent admin- istration of Oscar Holcombe, these were discontinued when police activities were centered downtown under Police Chief B. W. Payne. In 1939, the West

End substation at North Shepherd and Eli and the Northside substation in the 1800 block of Gregg were closed. In 1944, Chief Heard asked for appropriations to open both.

Over the past five years, the FBI had sporadically used the West End Station for detaining and interrogating suspects; however, at the time of Heard's request, both stations needed extensive renovation. During the war years, cars and tires had become victims of various war shortages. By opening these two substations, it was hoped that officers who made arrests in outlying areas of Houston could forego driving prisoners the three-to-five miles to the central station and lockup several times each day. Opening the stations would save tires, automobiles and gasoline, and relieve the rampant overcrowding at the downtown jail. Both substations each had cells large enough to accommodate thirty prisoners. According to Heard's plan, a lieutenant and a squad of officers would man each station. Both would be kept open twenty-four hours a day and would be dedicated to booking minor offenders from the vicinity. The Magnolia substation at 73rd and Avenue F was left out of the plan since it was considered too far beyond repair.

In late January 1944, City Council approved play increases of $10 per month for all police officers and firefighters earning monthly salaries of less than $300. Having been plagued by a lack of up-to-date automobiles throughout the 1940s, the council tried to make up for it by authorizing the purchase of twenty-seven "new 1942 model cars" for the HPD at a cost of $14,859. However, before giving the go-ahead, City Manager John N. Edy had to mollify council members by assuring them that inexpensive model automobiles which the city customarily bought for city departments were no longer available. The new fleet consisted of fifteen Buicks, five Pontiacs, five Oldsmobiles and two Dodges.

The end of January saw the passing of former Police Chief John Blackburn. Blackburn had been born in Newton County, Mississippi and moved to Marshall, Texas in his youth before spending the next half-century in Houston. Following his career with the HPD, he served as U. S. deputy marshal for several years.[49]

Suggesting the seriousness with which HPD traffic officers took their job in the 1940s, the local newspapers had fun with a story in which County Commissioner Ruth Turrentine, on her way to a luncheon at the Rice Hotel with the mayor and other city officials, was stopped for walking through a red light at Main and Prairie. Turrentine admitted her error and explained that her mind was elsewhere at the time and asked the officer for the ticket.

Worried she would miss the meeting, the officer instead launched into a lecture, which she said he conducted at length. He then asked for identification from the flustered commissioner, who was able to produce a poll tax slip, as she again asked for a ticket. She later explained that "by this time a crowd had gathered. Then he started making out the ticket. Few people can spell Turrentine, but he had more trouble with the name than if it was Egyptian." Too flustered to attend the luncheon, she was so mad she returned home and was conspicuously absent from the meeting.[50]

Long-time police officer Jonathan J. Kuykendall passed away in February 1944 after a lengthy illness. Kuykendall joined the HPD in 1913 as a patrolman. In 1921, he was promoted to captain of traffic at a time when traffic policemen operated on horseback. Six years later he became assistant superintendent of police, a position he held until 1929 when he was promoted to captain. In 1930, Kuykendall was appointed head of the Vice Squad before returning to patrolman in 1933. Four years later he was made senior captain. At his death in 1944, the sixty-four-year-old veteran was serving in his fifth year as sergeant. His thirty-one-year career spanned the days of mounted patrol, Prohibition and the introduction of automobile patrol. Former Mayor Walter E. Monteith remembered him well, stating, "I have never known a man who had a greater sense of duty."[51]

In 1944, *The Houston Post* labeled the police station and jail as "antiquated." It was common for police officers waiting for their shifts after traffic court case to spend several idle hours wandering the hallways—wasted time that could have been used to perhaps peruse a police library, if there were one, or to keep up with the latest strides in crime prevention and detection. Instead, officers drifted in small groups, "visiting the press room" where off-duty reporters could be talked into a game of dominoes. Reporting to the station prior to beginning their beats, it was finally time for assembly and some words from the head officer. This took place in a 15-by-35-foot room with seats for thirty, although there was usually double that number in attendance.

It is probably difficult to imagine a not-so-distant time when there was no place large enough for the police chief to address the entire force. Any officer attending police school was forced to drive across town to City Hall at his own expense. There is no better example of the inadequacy of the facility than the juvenile delinquency offices. Composed of three offices once deemed adequate for a police captain and a captain of detectives, by 1944, sixteen officers were crammed into the three offices in an era of rising concern for juvenile crime. This was, after all, a time when skipping school was considered lawless behaviour, worthy of police attention; thus on some days more than sixty youths were hauled in for "playing hooky." One news reporter suggested that the juveniles "made a shambles of the place because there was no way to control them."[52]

The city jail had been built in 1923. During its next twenty years it always seemed to be under renovation. Thousands of dollars were spent to create more space. In the words of one journalist, "The work has been the result of the fancy of new police chiefs, of which the city has had more than the average police reporter can ascertain without going into the files."[53] Apparently, of all the police, none disliked the current arrangements more than Chief Ray Ashworth during his brief tenure. Ashworth ordered the rearrangement of virtually every office in the five-story building. He soon got around to demanding more rooms for questioning prisoners. As a result, six small 10-by-12-foot rooms, commonly known as "sweatboxes," were constructed. Of these, half had no windows, leading officers to jokingly assert "that 30 minutes inside one of them would make the hardest boiled ex-convict confess to anything, not excepting murder." By 1943, only two offices out of the more than fifteen had been never been "remodeled, switched, or changed."[54]

By the mid-1940s, the jail had come under attack for its overcrowding and obsolescence as a place of confinement. Located at Preston and Caroline, the five-story structure served a city of a half million residents. A typical Saturday night could find more than 200 prisoners crammed into space designed for eighty-eight. In the Jim Crow era, segregation separated black and white women into different quarters. African American women were given six small bunks in a small cell. Sometimes almost two dozen women were detained in this small room. On the other hand, white women were afforded fourteen bunks and when the Vice Squads were active working the streets up to fifty women could be crammed into those fourteen bunks. With such a dearth of space, little thought was given toward separating inmates by classification.

Jail conditions had badly deteriorated by the 1940s as the edifice was built for a Houston with one third the current population. Although it was considered adequate in 1923, little more than twenty years later it boasted a kitchen with only one gas range to prepare hot meals for the entire jail population. According to a five-part series of articles in the *Houston Press* chronicling the jail, "sanitary facilities [were] practically non-existent," with only one toilet for each of the two women's quarters.[55]

Pity the poor prisoners! The city jail resounded with complaints one day in November 1943, when the cook failed to show up on time due to weather conditions, forcing the building superintendent to put on a cooking apron. As a result, prisoners were served a breakfast of syrup, bread and coffee.

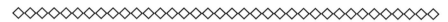

The Mysterious Painting

Sometime in March 1944 a painting, coated with a thick layer of dust, and almost hidden behind a box of tools, a bushel basket and an automobile tire, was discovered in the notorious storeroom of the police station. It turned out the painting was of former Chief of Detectives W. F. Kessler, who had retired after a forty-two-year career. The painting had hung in the police headquarters for years before mysteriously disappearing. No one knew when or how it got to the storeroom. Chief Inspector Millard Weaver, however, remembered asking another inspector to give it to the retired Kessler in 1943. The painting was originally presented to Chief Kessler in 1924 and had cost $150.

Kessler had joined the force in 1896 and reportedly was involved in numerous manhunts and gunfights. His scars were testament to his various encounters, including the loss of one finger in a gun battle. Kessler became chief of detectives in 1910, but resigned three years later to take over the George Smith Detective Agency in Dallas. However, his heart was with the HPD, and he returned to Houston after only several months.

In 1914, he was reappointed chief of detectives under Mayor Ben Campbell. Eight years later he served as acting chief of police for three months. During the remainder of his career he served in a variety of capacities and at his retirement was chief of detectives. According to colleagues, the only time you could find Kessler at the station these days was to catch him collecting his pension check on payday. One reporter noted, "He has a lot of time on his hands, and engages in a red-hot game of dominoes now and then."[56]

12

THE POST-WAR ERA

America has long grappled with juvenile gangs of one sort or another. This has been true throughout a good part of Houston's history. Gang names seemed less sinister in the 1940s when monikers included the Long Hairs, the Black Shirts and the Alley Gang. Most American cities have also endured so-called "juvenile delinquency" problems. Like today, the media often exaggerated the incidence of youth crimes.[1]

During the 1940s, local newspapers filled columns chronicling the large number of crimes by minors and with pleas for curfews to curb juvenile delinquency. *The Houston Post* heralded the use of curfews in 500 American cities as a way of "solving the perplexing problems of teenage life." The newspaper cited a *Parade* magazine article that claimed "curfew is, in part, America's answer to the problem of youth in a country at war." In reality, several city officials noted, there were few figures to support either a decrease or increase in youth crime, explaining that any infraction of a city ordinance was listed as a criminal offense. Hence, children who rode their bikes on sidewalks were committing offenses, as were children who "trespassed" on private property to retrieve a ball that landed there, or shot an air gun on their own lawn but the pellet landed in the next yard. Minors caught smoking cigarettes on the streets were even included in the statistics of law violations.[2]

It was not just the traditional Houston newspapers clamoring for better juvenile control. Houston was home to several African-American newspapers as well. One of the more prominent was the *Negro Labor News*. On March 25, 1944, the newspaper published an editorial captioned, "More Negro Policemen, Stricter Enforcement of Liquor Laws Will Help to Curb Juvenile Delinquency." The article suggested that the increase of delinquency was the result of the number of parents involved in the war effort, either in the armed forces or in defense work. However, what was most edifying about the editorial was its suggestion that "more Negro policemen would go a long way in solving juvenile delinquency."[3]

Black merchants were as befuddled as their white counterparts with how to evict unruly youngsters from their businesses. The popular notion among some members of the black community was that "some white officers take it as a matter of fun to catch a bunch of youngsters shooting dice" and using vulgar language, while "Negro policemen are more interested in curbing this sort of thing than white," and were more willing to chastise the boy or girl and send them home."[4]

One of the year's most bizarre incidents ended on April 24 when the body of a missing African-American male was located in Buffalo Bayou. Detectives P. R. O'Neill and Manuel Crespo lent their help in finding the body of a young man who had drowned in the bayou. When efforts to locate the body failed, thirty-three-year-old Billy Williams Johnson approached the officers and asked if he could try and use his own method in locating the body. The officers granted him permission and he returned a few minutes later holding a shotgun, a loaf of bread and an old shirt. The shirt apparently belonged to the seventeen-year-old victim. Williams threw it in the water then proceeded to walk a short distance downstream where he threw the bread in. The shirt and the bread both drifted to a spot midstream before stopping. The man boarded a leaky skiff and rowed to the location of the shirt and bread and fired his shotgun once into the air. The detectives were astonished when the body of the boy immediately came to the surface. When asked for an explanation for his success, Williams responded, "It always works; it never fails."[5]

In May 1944, Police Chief Percy Heard introduced a civil service ratings system that could be used to determine future promotions or the discharge of personnel. Among the system's criteria were standards such as "cooperation" and "emotional stability." During its first run, all members of the department passed with grades ranging from 74 to 100, with 70 considered passing.[6] However, a number of fire department and HPD representatives deemed the rating system unsuitable for judging "whether a man can stand smoke or whether he has to get out in the street to fight a fire."[7] Others felt that graders played favorites and objected to having the ratings go into their permanent civil service record.

Chief Heard led the campaign for a post-war police station and jail; its estimated cost hovered at just over a million dollars. After attending the annual meeting of the IACP in Dayton, Ohio, Heard returned to Houston intent on building a crime detection laboratory. But he would first have to convince the city manager that considerable costs for equipping the force with a modern laboratory were warranted. After watching a demonstration of a lie detector at the meeting he also was sold on this crime detection tool.[8] (Heard's son Jack, himself a future HPD chief, would become the department's first polygraph operator some years later.)

As the summer heat hovered at 100 degrees in late July 1944, the force celebrated the late arrival of new summer-weight uniforms. Better late than never seemed to be the attitude of police officers, who still donned regular wool winter uniforms into the hottest months of the summer.

On August 16, HPD lost its only woman police lieutenant when Inez Crawford left the force to move to West Texas with her husband. Before joining the force in 1941, she was involved in social work for the Social Hygiene Association of the Community Chest. Crawford earned a BA at the University of Houston, majoring in sociology and minoring in psychology.[9]

Before Harris County's grand jury retired in August, it urged the city to enlarge the HPD and improve the caliber of personnel. Among its suggestions was to give the police chief greater power to select his own personnel, especially division heads, without political interference. Chief Heard might have taken this personally, because he weighed in, replying, "There hasn't been any pressure—political or otherwise—put on me by any human being.... No one has attempted to dictate to me my selection of division heads or my policies."[10] The grand jury asserted that the force needed more black police officers, citing several embarrassing incidents between police and civilians in black neighborhoods. Also targeted was the lack of Hispanic officers, who were badly needed for the special police squad for the suppression of "juvenile Latin-American gangs."

Police officer R. J. Clark received some unwanted attention when the *Houston Press* featured his three-year-old son immobilized by his father's handcuffs on his ankles. Apparently little Robbie Clark was playing at home and came across an extra pair of his father's handcuffs that he then tried on. Unable to find a key to take them off, Mrs. Clark called the station, and three hours later her husband was able to free his son, who said, "Daddy, I won't do that again."

The Houston Police Department made new strides in modernization when the Records Bureau installed Remington Rand Tabulating Equipment to aid in the handling of the avalanche of information in 1945. The addition of this equipment put Houston in the front ranks of the nation's most modern police departments. Information on every case was "interpreted" into a tabulating card through a series of punched holes. According to the HPD, it was possible to sort any sequence of cases "at the amazing speed of 25,200 cases per hour." With the adoption of this system, it was now possible to get up-to-date information on any report not only for HPD, but the FBI, the National Safety Council or other city police departments.

Department officials claimed little skill was required to operate the machines. In simplest terms, a criminal offense was typed up and handed to a card-punching operator. In just moments the operator punched various keys and a card was made out reflecting the case record. For a burglary case, the information included what was burglarized, how the burglar escaped, what was stolen, evidence left at the scene, and any witness descriptions that had been collected. In just a few minutes an officer could use the key cards to determine how many drugstores were burglarized on a particular night, method of break-in, whether cigarette stubs were left behind, and so forth. Officials claimed "the machines [made] it possible to get the maximum efficiency out of the entire department," allowing traffic investigators to determine the most dangerous locations for accidents and even what time of day and day of the week was the most dangerous.

In February, Homicide Lieutenant A. C. Thornton, a twenty-one-year HPD veteran, resigned to go into private business. Filling his place would be George Seber, the son of former police officer George Seber Sr. and the brother of another officer. Seber had been on the force for eighteen years, having joined in 1927. He made detective just three years later. In 1944, Chief Heard sent him to the FBI school for four months where Seber became familiar with the latest scientific and crime-investigation methods. Prior to his promotion, Seber had served as a homicide detective for more than seven years.[11]

Later that month came word that January 1945 had been the most crime-ridden month in the city's history.[12] The chief explained that it was partly due to the lack of officers and the presence of more than 10,000 ex-convicts in the vicinity. Compared to the 2,120 crimes reported that month, the previous January had only 1,520. Heard said, "We need at least 100 additional officers to police the city." The greatest increase in crimes involved auto thefts, which had increased twenty-seven percent over the previous year. The only crime decreases were homicides and burglaries. The FBI also reported that Houston had more Class 1 crimes in 1944 than any of the other nine cities in its population bracket, as well as more of these offenses per officer. FBI records indicated Houston only had 4.3 policemen per square mile, compared to Dallas, which had 6.5. Nevertheless, only Dallas exceeded Houston in homicides in this range.[13]

The inadequate number of police officers became an issue throughout the mid-1940s. One survey indicated that city had only 313 active officers to protect an estimated population of 470,000. Most critics pointed to the rising crime rates plaguing the almost seventy-four-square-mile city. Few citizens were aware that Houston was served by the same number of police officers that protected the city's 350,000 residents in 1936. One editorial suggested, "Many citizens would surely sleep with one eye open if they knew that some nights between midnight and daylight there are only 18 officers cruising the streets."[14]

Chief Heard expressed his intentions in March to set up a scientific crime laboratory, commenting, "By having its own laboratory, the police department will not have to depend on the FBI laboratory in Washington or the state laboratory in Austin." Having had to report to this protocol for years, quite often too much time elapsed before bloodstains and human hairs were examined, allowing criminals time to escape. City Manager John Edy approved a budget of $6,500 for the lab and funds to hire twenty-seven new officers. Also in the budget was $1,000 for a police library. According to Inspector L. D. Morrison Sr. from the Crime Prevention Bureau, he started collecting books in police science two years prior for the library.

One of a parent's greatest fears came true when Chief Heard received word in April 1945, that his son and former Rice University football star Lieutenant William J. Heard was killed in action on Okinawa at the age of twenty-five. He had seen action as a Marine in nearly every Pacific campaign and had been awarded the Bronze Star for meritorious service at Bougainville.[15]

With November came word that "Famed Houston Woman Sleuth" Eva Bacher was ending a half-century of police work. Bacher began her career in Chicago before moving on to Houston. She earned a reputation for arresting up to ten shoplifters in a single day. Bacher claimed she became "infatuated" with police work in the 1880s, when as a thirteen-year-old she took interest in "the rogues gallery, and pictures of crooks that hung in a detective agency." In 1913, she first found work as a house detective for local merchants. Between 1917 and 1929, she was a detective on the Vice Squad and is regarded as the first woman to be hired by the HPD, from which Mayor Walter Monteith dismissed her on an administrative order "for the good of the service" in 1929. Upon her retirement in 1945, she was in her 32nd year as a house detective for Foley Brothers.[16]

An important chapter in the history of the HPD began to take shape in late 1945 when Chief Heard gave his "tacit approval" to the formation of a "Houston Police Association."[17] Coinciding with a grand jury investigation into police mistreatment of prisoners, more than 200 officers signed up for membership that they hoped would be "a united front in combating unfair actions against the individuals or the department as a whole." Plans for such an organization were discussed for some time and, according to most observers, it was expected that 100 percent of the rank and file would join.[18]

One of the biggest challenges facing the HPD following the end of the war was how to reintegrate returning veterans. Questions abounded, the primary one being, "Should officers return to the force in their original positions?" A number of high-ranking officers expected to assume their previous ranks. In early 1946, W. F. Burton, who had been traffic captain when he took military leave in 1942, was offered the position of command of one shift of the Traffic Division. Houston City Council regulations required employers to rehire returning veterans at the same rank and pay as when they left. However, it did not specify that veterans had to be employed in the jobs they left. For example, when Lieutenant L. D. Pyle, formerly a traffic officer, returned to the force he was placed in the capacity of desk sergeant at the city jail although he still held his former rank. So although Burton could return as traffic captain, his new duties would be more in line with a police sergeant in charge of one shift. The newspapers chronicled Burton's indecision as to whether he would return or not, indicating that he was unhappy with his assignment. Ultimately, the conflict was satisfactorily resolved after a meeting with Chief Heard. Burton's swing shift command was considered only a temporary position. Burton was reportedly satisfied with his new supervisory position at the uniform division desk.[19]

Chief Heard expected at least twenty-five returning veterans during the first month of 1946. That same month saw the return of downtown traffic supervision to pre-war conditions, with fifteen new members of the Foot Traffic Squad returning to street corners and red lights with whistles in hand. The addition of another fifteen officers doubled the Foot Traffic Squad at a time when traffic had increased by thirty-five percent since the end of wartime gasoline and tire rationing.

No controversy exemplified the challenge of returning police officers more than the return of former Police Chief Ray Ashworth, who took military leave in May 1942 and expected to return to his high-ranking position when he returned in 1946. According to Mayor Otis Massey and the acting city manager, Ashworth was scheduled to take over the police force on February 1. Almost immediately, city attorneys went to work in order to determine whether the lieutenant colonel was entitled to his old job under the general ordinance of 1940 providing military leaves for city employees. If Ashworth was to receive his old job back, than what would happen to Percy Heard? When City Manager Nagle was asked about this he responded, "I don't know. We can't have two police chiefs."[20]

Ashworth was named chief of police in February 1941. During his tenure he was the highest paid Houston police chief up until that time, earning $6,000 a year. Rumors began to swirl around City Hall as officials grappled with the complexities of this particular case. There was a strong feeling at police headquarters that if Ashworth returned, some of the HPD's top brass would be removed or demoted since they held lesser posts under the original Ashworth administration. By all accounts, Chief Heard was agreeable to stepping down "if it were a fact that Mr. Ashworth stepped down from police chief to enter the army and expected to return." One of the main sticking points was whether Ashworth left the force to join the army or, as Mayor Massey remembered, left the force because he "was sick of his job and went out of here as a civilian and didn't enlist in the army until several months later."[21]

The tension around headquarters was palpable over the next couple of weeks since most assumed there would be an extensive shake-up under Ashworth, who was expected to promote a number of individuals demoted by Chief Heard. Most of the rank and file supported the current chief in the ensuing debate. Meanwhile the mayor ordered Ashworth's service record investigated in order to ascertain whether he went into the army immediately or first took a civilian job. When Ashworth was apprised of this by a reporter, he coolly remarked, "I've been investigated before."[22]

One former assistant city attorney took issue with the city legal department, stating that in his opinion Ashworth "is not entitled to a military leave under the 1940 ordinance." Former city attorney and recently returned veteran Walter Boyd stated, "The 1940 ordinance is invalid as it applies to non-civil service employees." Citing several inconsistencies with the current understanding of the ordinance, Boyd noted that two years after his appointment his first term expired. In order for him to claim legal title to the office, Ashworth would have had to be regularly reappointed when he served two years. Since his term had expired, "he has no claim to the office now." If the city was to award his office back, this would mean that the 1940 City Council had the power to divest future administrations of their right to choose the chief of police and other non-civil service officials.[23]

After several weeks it was still unclear whether Ashworth would receive his old job back. On January 22, 1946, a *Houston Post* story was captioned "Who's Houston's Chief Is Still Police Mystery." That same day Chief Heard asked City Council for a higher budget so he could rehire forty-one officers expected to return from military service. One councilman responded that some men on the force would have to be relieved of duty to make room for the veterans. Heard responded, "All the men now on the force are needed," explaining that "the public expects greater police service." Weekends had become so busy that there were sometimes waiting lists of four and five callers. Heard backed up his argument by noting that the HPD offered the city a ratio of one officer for every 1,000 persons, although the FBI recommended 2:1,000.

A City Council vote for police chief ended in a 3-3 split. Before a final determination over his status could be concluded, it was necessary to wait for Ashworth to be formally discharged from the U.S. Army. With his discharge on February 1, 1946, he had thirty days to formally claim his old job back. Meanwhile, Chief Heard soldiered on, unsure whether he would maintain his position much longer. The city's three newspapers touted the story for weeks, listing the various supporters of both police chiefs. If anything, the debate became a distraction for a department trying to adapt to post-war conditions. The debate finally was resolved when Lieutenant Colonel Ray Ashworth walked into the acting city manager's office in the first week of February and announced that he would not go to court to establish his claim to the job and withdrew his application. Ashworth had won the Bronze Star and was a veteran of six Pacific and European campaigns, including the invasion of Sicily, and enjoyed huge support from the thousands of local veterans. Ashworth had the last word noting, "Had I any reason to suppose such a controversy would arise I would not have made my request."

With the dispute over, HPD next turned its attention to the industrial strife plaguing Houston and the entire country. One of the main concerns was that, with sixty officers assigned to the strike detail, the force was caught shorthanded. It was hoped the returning veterans would narrow the gap as two to three returned to duty each week. In late February, the City Traffic Safety Commission blamed the diversion of one third of the force to strike duty for an escalating crime rate. During the first month of January almost every type of crime increased in Houston with 2,137 criminal offenses reported compared to 1,346 the previous January. Traffic accidents were on the rise as well. The largest increases over the previous year, all up more than 100 percent, were negligent homicide and rape.

Traffic problems continued to plague the Bayou City. According to one survey of 600 cars taken in mid-1946, more than half of them had faulty equipment of one type or another. On his return from a meeting on highway safety in Washington, Chief Heard praised that city's traffic situation, where the public has more transportation alternatives. He also supported more bus service as a remedy for reducing car traffic, a concern that resonates into the 21st century.

In 1946, Houston saw a dramatic rise in capital crimes over the previous year. Eleven murders were reported for June alone, compared to four the previous June. During the year's first six months there were forty-eight murders, compared to thirty-six for the same time period in 1945. Rapes and robberies were also on the increase, while auto theft and burglaries were on the decline.[24]

Only one HPD man in blue died in the line of duty in the decade of the 1940s. Officer Howard B. Hammond was on patrol with his partner T. F. Hambley in Third Ward in the early morning hours of August 18, 1946, when the two officers encountered a raucous crowd outside a cleaning shop. The unruly and perhaps intoxicated members of the group confronted the officers and got into a scuffle with them. As a result, Hammond was shot in the forehead and neck and died on the way to a hospital. Hambley was severely beaten but survived. Hammond's attacker also was dead at the scene, having been shot twice in the stomach and chest.

One of the many strategies to reduce crime and better serve the community included opening the city's first post-war substation. At least four sergeants were required for the Northside station. This was the first time since 1933 that the police department functioned with substations. Chief Heard explained that the new branch stations were not opened sooner due to manpower and material shortages. Unlike the central station, substations were not meant to function as an independent unit, requiring food to be brought in from the central station three times each day. Identification through fingerprinting and photographs was centralized downtown.

In August came news that the HPD had hired its first policewoman since the departure of Inez Crawford in 1944. Policewoman Genevieve W. Harts-

field joined the Crime Prevention Bureau, where her job description included mostly welfare and social welfare work.[25] Described in the characteristic jargon of the 1940s as a "petite green-eyed blonde,"[26] the supervisor
of five policewomen was now responsible mostly for cases involving women
and children.

One issue that pops up on occasion in the 21st century is the hiring of
police officers for part-time outside employment. In 1946, this issue became
public when a number of officers made it known that they thought that the
process of handing out "spare-time police jobs" was unfair, especially since
Chief Heard had taken office. Heard decreed that police officers in uniform
could not work in night spots and dance halls as bouncers. He broadened
the prohibition to include barring officers in or out of uniform from working
at establishments that were the scenes of rowdy behavior. When reporters
queried as to why one specific high-ranking officer was often assigned to
society weddings and social functions, Heard responded, "They ask for him.
If they asked for any other member of the force I'd assign him there instead."
Officers had suggested that outside employment should be rotated among
all officers using the roster, a system used by motorcycle officers. Under that
system, funeral homes paid officers to escort funeral processions. By resort-
ing to personnel rosters, each officer got an opportunity to escort processions at $5 a procession.[27]

By 1946, the HPD maintained a file of more than 300,000 fingerprints. The
collection of fingerprints has been vastly aided by the fingerprinting of every
individual connected with civilian defense, war industry and other civil service occupations. During the first half of 1946, Houston had more burglaries, more murders and more petty thefts than any of the ten other American
cities in its population bracket. One explanation was that of these ten cities,
only one (Columbus, Ohio) had less uniformed police officers. On the flip-
side, only one of these cities (Kansas City) had more administrative, non-
uniformed employees.

It is rare for newspapers to lavish positive attention on the city police de-
partment. In late 1946, the president of the International Association of the
Chiefs of Police visited Houston and complimented the HPD for its courtesy.
The *Houston Press* even chimed in when they heard this, saying, "We agree.
Generally speaking, Houston's police force is courteous, efficient and a credit
to the city." The paper opined "What a far cry the erect, generally slender,

conditioned policeman of today is from the cop on the beat when we were young."[28]

Before the year was out a rise in traffic deaths and accidents led the Traffic Safety Commission to urge the city hire 450 more policemen, noting that Houston would need to hire 810 officers to reach the national average of one and one half per 1,000 residents. Currently there were 360 uniformed officers, or .67 per 1,000.[29]

As a mayoral election loomed, the hot topic in police circles was who would become police chief if Oscar Holcombe was elected mayor in November. If anything was certain, it was that Percy Heard would not be chief if Holcombe won. Those under consideration included former chiefs L. C. Brown and B. W. Payne. Heard told colleagues he would be supporting mayoral candidate Holger Jeppeson, whose victory would be Heard's only chance to keep his job.

Coinciding with the mayoral campaign, internationally famous expert on municipal matters and the current safety chief of Milwaukee, Dr. B. L. Corbett, delivered a lecture in Houston where he criticized the selection of police and fire chiefs as political appointees. Noting that Chief Heard "ranks with the best [chiefs] in the country," Corbett asserted that politics impair the operation of police and fire departments.[30]

Opposition to Oscar Holcombe's election was most vociferous from the Holger Jeppeson camp. One campaign manager referred to Holcombe's prior record as mayor between 1926 and 1940, noting the widespread vice problems that plagued the city in those years. Reading from a grand jury report from 1936–37, Robert Eikel noted that the regime of Police Chief Payne "knowingly and wilfully permitted gambling games and open gambling games to be conducted throughout Houston," and that "three or four Texas Rangers accomplished much more than the entire police force of 300 men."[31]

13

AT THE OLD GRAY
FOX'S WHIM

Known as "the Old Gray Fox, Oscar Holcombe would serve as Houston mayor longer than any other man. He began the first of eleven non-consecutive terms in 1921. The prematurely gray and political crafty Oscar Fitzallen Holcombe was born in Mobile, Alabama and lived with his family in San Antonio before moving to Houston in 1906 at age eighteen. He formed his own construction company and ran for mayor for the first time in 1921 at age thirty-two. Holcombe was elected to eleven non-consecutive terms from the 1920s through the 1950s, a record no other mayor has approached.[1]

Holcombe utilized a police officer spoils system like no other Bayou City mayor in history. He manipulated officers as ward heelers during election years and employed only two police chiefs over four consecutive two-year terms until 1929. In his first campaign, Holcombe vowed to reorganize city departments, pave more streets, build new schools and improve the business climate. Policing this more pleasing environment was seldom mentioned in his speeches.

Residential and commercial thoroughfares were widened in Holcombe's early administrations and sewage systems enhanced by extending water and sewer mains. His name was on the cornerstones of the new municipal auditorium, the farmers' market and the branch libraries. A new state law created a countywide navigation district. Since it included more than just Houston, the taxes that paid for it were more fairly distributed—a move very popular with Houstonians. Holcombe claimed this change as one of his most significant achievements. The mayor set up the city offices of city manager and public service commissioner. To facilitate a policy of annexation—the city's land area went from 34.4 to 352 square miles from his first term to his last one—he created the city planning commission. He also created the Hous-

Mayor Oscar Holcombe,
elected to two-year terms in
the following years: 1921, 1923,
1925, 1927, 1933, 1935 1939,
1947, 1949, 1951 and 1955
(The Story Sloane Collection)

ton Independent School District, which began under the auspices of city government.

Holcombe lost his last bid for re-election in 1958 to Lewis Cutrer, primarily due to his stand against integration of public swimming pools. Holcombe claimed that pool segregation would "prevent bloodshed and violence." Holcombe died of pneumonia on June 18, 1968 in Houston, at the age of seventy-nine.

Over most of the Holcombe years, political patronage was the key to getting a job as a Houston police officer. If an officer of any rank supported an opponent, he could be staring a demotion in the face or hitting the streets to find new work. When Holcombe's first term began in 1921, HPD officers were under-paid with no benefits and laughable local civil service "protection." They didn't even have a burial fund until they got together, established one and funded it themselves.

One of Holcombe's police chiefs resigned as a board member of the Community Chest because his boss had an opponent and he was expected to hit the campaign stump every night. The day after the election, the employment line formed outside the office of the winning candidate and many of those in line wanted to become policemen. Their only police training came on the job in the context of making the mayor look good, a practice ripe for corruption.

A December 3, 1928 headline in the *Houston Press* read "'Big Mike' Fired from Police Force Because He Was Monteith Supporter." The *Press* described H. J. "Big Mike" Meinke as a "picturesque character in law enforcement here," a dedicated thirteen-year lieutenant. Big Mike's only alleged sin was "he opposed the Holcombe administration" and actively and openly talked and worked on behalf of successful mayoral candidate, Walter E. Monteith. Not long after Monteith was declared the winner, the Holcombe-backed HPD brass announced Big Mike's indefinite suspension. He learned of it when he began "the dog watch" at 11 p.m. the Saturday of the election.

Meinke willingly granted interviews in which he expressed his belief that seventy-five percent of the department voted for Monteith, and he speculated that Holcombe probably would fire them too. More than three months passed before Monteith's inauguration on April 16. Fifteen days later the new mayor rehired Meinke and restored his $160 monthly paycheck. Big Mike had worked an interim job, a common occurrence for officers fired at the end of one administration and rehired at the beginning of another. Monteith exercised the spoils of the office by hiring Charles W. McPhail, an eleven-year special investigator in the United States Department of Justice, as Houston's new police chief, replacing Tom C. Goodson, Holcombe's chief for seven of his eight years in office.

Few men who made law enforcement a forty-year career experienced as many ups and downs in rank and salary as James Henry Tatum. Devoted to policing duties from the moment he joined HPD in 1915 until his send-off retirement party in 1955, he was outspoken about leadership and often critical of a boss who fired officers at will.

The mayor had the absolute power to move police officers from one rank to another like replaceable pawns. A young patrol officer, a sergeant, lieutenant or captain could be summarily dismissed if he failed to provide campaign support for the winning candidate. From 1915 through 1924, Tatum worked his way up through five different mayors, earning promotion to captain in Holcombe's second term. There were neither civil service examinations nor promotional rankings. Civil service was provided only by a city ordinance that could be changed by motion at the city council table. Tatum earned his promotions the old-fashioned way, with a commanding leadership presence and strong work ethic.

Mayor Monteith occasionally made it known that he liked Tatum's work and attention to the details of traffic enforcement, a clear enough appreciation for Holcombe to reduce Tatum to the rank of patrolman when he de-

Big Mike Meinke was a well-respected Houston police officer beginning in the 1920s. Meinke was fired one time when his only alleged wrongdoing was opposing Mayor Oscar Holcombe in a city election. (The Story Sloane Collection)

feated Monteith in 1933. Other reductions in rank involved another captain, two lieutenants and a sergeant. He also fired a detective lieutenant and two detectives working under Tatum.

Patrolman Tatum was stationed at Franklin and San Jacinto, quite a come-down from the captain's office. Yet by 1937, Tatum was promoted to sergeant. A January 17, 1939 story in *The Houston Post* detailed a decision by Holcombe's public safety director, George Woods, to demote forty-two officers, dismiss three, promote nineteen and make one brand new appointment. Tatum got his old captain's rank back.

Seven detectives were demoted to patrolmen, and their monthly salaries were reduced from $160 to $140. Nineteen officers were transferred from the Motorcycle Squad, which was abolished, to assignments as cruising patrolmen, losing $10 in monthly salary. Seven "were retired by the department." Three African-American officers were dismissed. Others were demoted by at least one rank.[2]

By the 1940s, police service in Houston was dominated by politics, making employment almost totally dependent on officers' affiliations with whichever faction had a hold on the mayor's office.[3] Policemen knew that they were at the mercy of political bosses just like laborers were vulnerable to the manip-

ulation of management. One assertive officer, Earl Maughmer, began working in secret with his fellow officers to set the stage for the organization of a
police association and the writing of a new state civil service law. Maughmer
is credited with doing the actual writing.

"Anyone who worked in a certain campaign would get a certain job as a reward," Maughmer recalled in 1974.[4] "Every two years they would demote the
high-ranking officers, promote those simply because they were friends of the
administration. There would be a fifty percent turnover. A patrolman would
say he wouldn't do (an assignment) because a new administration would be
in and *he* would be the captain."[5]

A new mayor personally selected the head of the Vice Squad and saw that
gambling and prostitution laws were enforced accordingly. Maughmer and
these officers learned that big money controlled Houston elections. Influential groups who contributed money to a winning candidate could dictate the
administrative policies of the police department. Gambling interests were
among these controlling forces, not just in Houston but elsewhere in Texas.

The terms for mayor and city council members (at one time called commissioners) only lasted two years but two-year police job tenure was enough
for many men to go out and work in a mayoral campaign. Oscar Holcombe
took advantage of these job seekers as well as incumbent officers who wanted
to keep their ranks or be promoted. On a moment's notice, the mayor could
commission any individual as an unpaid police officer with a badge and no
uniform. This carried a lot of weight in the wards, where gambling and prostitution were exposed through the 1940s and faced heavier law enforcement
penalties under reform mayors. Truly, the city was "open." The lack of air
conditioning in the 1940s required residents to keep their windows open,
enabling passerby to hear dice games in progress.[6]

Most HPD officers in the 1940s were poorly trained—some without high
school diplomas—but had the physical toughness to maintain order in row-
dier situations with drunks and violent ex-convicts. The department's more
job-secured leaders saw the need to establish a training academy for the development of a more professional department, better salaries and improved
benefits. Yet the mayor controlled every avenue needed to establish professionalism and could easily thwart any cooperative efforts by officers, including pay raise proposals.

As early as 1919, Houston police officers and firefighters, disappointed
with the salary proposals by Mayor A. Earl Amerman, met en masse to draw
up their own ordinance providing a monthly minimum wage of $125 for of-

ficers and firefighters but no city employees. The frustrated police and fire workforces went to Houstonians with a pay raise referendum, but the mayor saw to it that verification of the signatures on the petitions calling for the referendum could not be established by the March 4 election. This referendum gamesmanship surfaced in Houston each time any petition-initiated referendum with no mayoral blessing took place.

The trend reflected what was happening in other big-city police departments across the nation; officers in New York and other big cities had already organized professional associations to gain benefits such as burial insurance and survivors' funds. The New York City Patrolmen's Benevolent Association was founded in 1892, the first of its kind in the nation. Soon thereafter, similar associations were founded in Buffalo, Milwaukee, Pittsburgh and other eastern cities. The Los Angeles Fire and Police Protective League was founded in 1923, placing the LAPD "in the vanguard of progressive police development," especially in the areas of job tenure, education and pay scales.[7]

Education and training did not become buzzwords in Houston until the 1940s. Lieutenant L. D. Morrison Sr., a future chief for whom the Houston Police Academy was later named, was an early progressive who saw the need to have better trained police officers in a growing city. Mayor R. H. Fonville succeeded Holcombe in 1937 and served one two-year term. Fonville commissioned Morrison to visit other departments to learn their up-to-date training methods. In 1938, Morrison developed a new way to select officers to be trained at the downtown Coliseum. The plan was too far advanced and received too much public support for Holcombe to change it once he returned to office after the 1939 election. It was the first time HPD actually sought applicants. About 1,200 men applied and 800 passed "a preliminary IQ-type of test."[8]

Then, Morrison-led police officials selected candidates based on appearance. Eventually, seventy-five cadets went through a sixteen-week police training course. Maughmer was one of the fifty who graduated.

The group went through a commencement exercise at the Texas State Hotel. The new officers saluted their superior officers, walked up the stairs at headquarters instead of taking the elevator and touched their caps with their hands when they stopped motorists. They were positive about alleged violations and addressed motorists with "I'm sorry, sir, you were speeding" instead of asking "You were speeding, weren't you, buddy?" They learned to make up their minds whether or not they were going to give a motorist a ticket before they reached his car to avoid the antagonistic practice of giving a motorist a ticket for his attitude rather than his driving. Each officer earned $90 a month.

Maughmer stayed proud of being a part of his class, saying, "The Class of '39 was head and shoulders above others. We were promoted to sergeants, lieutenants and detectives. We never had a chief out of the group. I think the situation that was here in those days had a lot to do with police attitudes. Most of them wanted to fairly enforce the laws like they were trained to do." Many of them became resentful of political hiring practices. Members of the Class of '39 worked to change the department and steer it away from the graft and corruption resulting from the politics. But Maughmer noted, "If we couldn't change it, we would quit and go to other fields."[9]

Houston could have continued recruitment for the next few years, further infusing the department with better qualified officers had not World War II changed everything, taking many well-qualified young men. Between 1939 and 1948, there was no growth in manpower. Officially, HPD Police Cadet Class No. 1 started in 1948.

14

SECRET LEADERS
AND 1269M

Breckenridge Porter Sr. was the only Houston police lieutenant in history to be thrown out of the Texas Rangers and charged with murder within a relatively short period of time. The storied details of Porter's life were retold around police headquarters throughout the 20th century, always in modest, down-to-earth segments, using the honest-to-goodness modus operandi of the biographic subject. Just as Ranger Porter got the hang of a job that included earning a $2 bounty for each illegal immigrant he captured in the Valley, the issue of his age cropped up.[1]

The Rangers' age requirement was twenty-one; he was barely twenty. Before the state found out, Porter and a partner were assigned to Galveston, where violence frequently broke out in union picket lines at the port. During one near-riot, shots were fired and Porter was left standing with a smoking shotgun in his hands; one man was dead.[2]

The scene investigation revealed that the fatal shot came from Porter's gun or that of his partner. The young Ranger thought long and hard and asked the district attorney to get a grand jury to true bill him so he could have a trial. Standing square, he went on trial for murder and was promptly found not guilty, the state having no evidence to present since there was no ballistics analysis from a shotgun or anything else. Porter's notoriety amounted to little more than a few paragraphs in the Galveston paper that cleared his record. But enough information surfaced to inform headquarters that the successful defendant was too young to hold the job he performed so well. So he dropped out of the Texas Rangers and joined the police department of River Oaks, an incorporated city with its own small, underpaid police force.

Porter drove his own car on patrol and soon met with Mayor Oscar Holcombe while wearing his ROPD uniform. Holcombe hired him on the spot and instructed him to report for work the following evening, saying, "Just

This picture, taken in 1947, symbolizes the creation of Article 1269m, the state
civil service law that provided unprecedented job protection for Houston's police
officers and firefighters. Texas Gov. Buford Jester (seated) is signing "1269m" into
law. Prior to this bill becoming law, the mayor of Houston appointed and fired
any officer or firefighter at will, often basing the decision on whether or not these
individuals supported him on Election Day. The primary backer of the effort was
the Houston Police Officers Association, formed in 1945. The Association had many
strong leaders, especially Breck Porter, standing over Jester's left shoulder. Other
HPOA leaders present for the historic signing were, left to right, T. C. Christian,
John Irwin and (at the far right) Red Squyers. (Houston Police Officers Union)

wear the uniform you're wearing now."[3] The next day Porter became the first
Houstonian to work for two police departments on the same day. The officer
took pride in his work and looked forward to a long HPD career until 1937,
when a new mayor, R. H. Fonville, fired the young officer without warning.
Porter was living "a hand-to-mouth existence" and later told younger officers
that the sudden dismissal scared the hell out of him.[4]

The River Oaks department easily accepted him back, his old captain telling him, "Okay, come back here and report for duty tomorrow and wear your
Houston uniform."[5] Many of Porter's colleagues went back to driving buses,

managing grocery stores or repairing automobiles. Later, numerous fellow Homicide officers would testify that this experience inspired Breck Porter to be a leader in establishing state civil service protection for police officers. The strident Porter later told his HPD colleagues, "The new guy (mayor) who came in didn't give a shit about my wife and kids. He was interested in getting his people into the right positions. He fired us without even knowing us."[6]

Porter wanted to form the Houston Police Officers Association, a key step needed to campaign for a state civil service law that protected officers from this kind of shabby treatment. He became a leader among a unique "secret society" whose influence over the Houston Police Department lasted well into the 21st century.

Another leader proved to be Earl Maughmer, a well-respected officer who had initial problems with the six-foot height requirement. The men taking the measurements were picky enough not to give a fraction of an inch when Maughmer *knew* he was six-feet-tall but fell fractions of an inch short when he stood in a boxlike area that was this height. The applicant drew the ire of the recruiter when he went back through the line a second and third time.[7] But the steadfast effort drew the attention of the recruiting director, who said, "Pass him. Anybody who wants to be a policeman that bad is bound to be a good one." The new recruit soon started to rise in the ranks almost immediately after his graduation from the department's renowned Class of '39. He fought the political structure as hard as he fought to measure up to the job's height requirement.[8]

Police officers are by nature unafraid to take steps to help the people they are sworn to protect and defend. Yet many of them in Houston kowtowed to the mayor and the department's higher-ups because they had absolutely no job security. An appeal to the Civil Service Commission did no good. An increasing number of men like Porter and Maughmer became a part of the department before and after World War II. Many of these men became first-time fathers and sought security for their families. They were as yet unschooled in politics but knew they didn't come home from a war for a temporary job.[9]

They soon proved that there was strength in numbers. In secret, a core group of leaders developed who knew if the mayor or his politically motivated brass learned of their effort to establish a police association, they would all be fired. Besides Porter and Maughmer, the other men of courage included H. L. "Ham" Ellisor, Julius Knigge, R. J. Clark, C. D. Taylor, John LeVrier, Shorty Evans and Reno Kirby. Each spent long and distinguished ca-

Earl Maughmer, who retired as an HPD captain, was an early leader in the fight to get Civil Service protection for Houston police officers. The Maughmer name has been a mainstay for generations in HPD. Earl Maughmer was one of the few officers who met in secret to form the strategy that led to the passage of the state civil service law that provided job protection for Houston officers. Another leader was Breck Porter, a legendary Homicide lieutenant for whom a building in the Houston Police Officers Union complex is named. (HPD Archives)

reers in HPD, almost all of them achieving high ranks. They carefully learned the art of politicking in the halls of the State Capitol where they could easily identify with the rural legislators who had deep respect for police officers and cared about job security and their families.[10]

In December 1945, Maughmer, Porter and the others got a charter for a police association after realizing that doctors, lawyers and crafts workers had similar organizations. The group had no communications with the well-established police associations in New York and Los Angeles, and Maughmer speculated that the politicians of the times saw to it that police officers were kept in the dark about wages, hours and civil service laws.[11] Totally in secret and at great risk to their careers, these officers developed the Houston Police Officers Association (HPOA) "out of the clear blue sky to solve [their] own problems." The association was the first of its kind in Texas, officially formed on December 3, 1945. Maughmer recalled:

> There were only about thirteen of us willing to put our name on a charter. We went to Austin and got a charter for a police association for thirteen people and it was viewed somewhat with mistrust. A lot of policemen wouldn't join the association. They were

afraid of political reprisals. Others said it was a labor union and we couldn't get involved in union type activities.[12]

The group had problems convincing many policemen that an association was the only way to make their voice heard without political reprisals while the mayor resented this challenge to his power. The association's charter put the officers in business as a Texas corporation that emphasized unity as the only way out of the politicized predicament and job insecurity. Otis Massey was mayor when HPOA was formed in 1945. In 1947, Oscar Holcombe replaced him and served until 1953 and spent his tenure thwarting the group in every way possible.

The recognized association leaders were Maughmer, Porter and Julius Knigge. Accounts in *The Houston Post* and *Houston Press* identified the other charter committee members of the proposed association to be H. L. "Ham" Ellisor, C. E. Bucker, Frank L. Murray, L. E. De Weese, C. E. Easly, T. C. Christian, G. C. Davis, C. V. "Buster" Kern, J. M. Le Vrier and Charles Woodman. Initially, some other members didn't want their names to be made public for fear of retribution, even dismissal. Others named were Lieutenants Fred Cochran and George Seber and Sergeant Curtis Aaron.[13]

The intimidation factor was high. Mayoral henchmen at City Hall kept track of officers who attended meetings usually held in the courtroom of the old police headquarters on Caroline. Police Chief Percy Heard offered no public encouragement but seemed sympathetic to the cause.[14] Unity was the word. The association published a circular distributed to every officer that said the stated objective of HPOA was to present "a united front in combating unfair actions against the individuals or the department as a whole" and to make public "the true actions, aims and purposes of the Houston Police Department."[15]

The charter language gave no clues about the reform program that the HPOA would undertake in 1946 and 1947, nor its everlasting effects on the lives and benefits of officers. Each member paid a $4 initiation fee and annual dues of the same amount. The money was used to defray the expense of social activities, advertisements and attorney fees when required. The initial group elected Detective Frank Murray president, Earl Maughmer first vice president and Detective Johnny Erwin second vice president.

Murray and each of the leaders were threatened in subtle ways or transferred to the HPD version of Siberia. Some were dismissed or transferred from job to job. Maughmer's duty station prevented him from communicating with other HPOA leaders—he was assigned to guard fire boats in the Houston Ship Channel on the night shift.

The state civil service law known as 1269m came to pass due to an unprecedented alliance between HPOA and Houston firefighters. HFD had unsuccessfully attempted to obtain this measure for four legislative sessions. Maughmer suggested that the two groups present a unified front in the 1947 legislative session and formed the necessary coalition.[16] Maughmer wrote the bill and spent his off days and accumulated vacation time in Austin to lobby for the proposal. Since all officers were supposedly on a 'quota system' back then, each member of the association gave the first HPOA lobbyist one arrest per week to ensure that his quota was maintained.

The rural representatives and senators who dominated the Legislature appreciated police and fire personnel wanting more job security. They were more apt to listen to pleas from officers on the street than the big-city hired guns the mayor sent to Austin "by the busloads."[17] An oft-tainted local ordinance set up a three-member Civil Service Commission that heard appeals of officer firings. The mayor appointed the commissioners and told them what to do, setting the stage for voluminous examples of unfairness. Over many years, mayors, particularly the mercurial Old Gray Fox, plodded through the hypocrisy surrounding the micro-management of the police department with hypocritical dexterity. In one breath, Holcombe—or any mayor—could decry the ineffectiveness of the department, while in another, praise chiefs and officers for their efficiency in the fine art of ward politicking.

Instead of arresting prostitutes and breaking up illegal gambling operations so common in the Bayou City, politically-motivated officers secured pledge cards for the mayor. Nothing more rankled the truly professional officers who avoided open support of candidates for city office. By 1947, Holcombe used his silver-forked tongue, likely not realizing the intensity of the incentive he provided the campaigners for civil service protection. Taking over the familiar office from outgoing Mayor Otis Massey, Holcombe summed up the state of HPD in a January message to City Council, saying: "The police department is woefully inefficient. It is honeycombed with feuds and factionalism. It is without discipline and it is badly undermanned.... The police department is worse than a South American Army."[18]

Holcombe played right into the ever-ready, legislatively-adept hands of the HPOA leaders and their firefighter mentors and the formidable Texas

State Association of Fire Fighters. The TSAFF had succeeded in getting enactment of the first state retirement system for municipal firefighters in 1936. The mayor failed to see the writing on the wall ten years later when the association and the firefighters joined forces with the City-County Employees Union to propose a $40-a-month salary increase for Houston police, firefighters and city employees. City Council rejected the proposal and the coalition turned down a $10-a-month alternative.

The strongly bonded three employee groups generated enough signatures through the initiative referendum process to get an election called on the issue of $40 raises on a June 22, 1946 ballot. Houstonians were not taken in by the mayor's scare tactics of layoffs and reduction in city services. They approved the overall measure by a 7-1 margin. One proviso also assured police and firemen that their salaries could not be reduced without prior voter approval. It marked the first of association-backed proposals over the next sixty-plus years that paid attention to the devil in the detail.

The formation of the HPOA and the referendum success in 1946 caused the TSAFF to realize the police/fire coalition could increase the likelihood of getting state civil service reform for both public safety groups. By the end of 1946, they were together as "brothers" and had a plan. They were helped by accusations against officers brought before the Civil Service Commission and almost always lacking in substance. By the time the 1947 session started, a majority of the department's rank-and-file were dues-paying association members.

The city's lobbying faction continued to use scare tactics, throwing out terms like "union strikes" to discourage new legislation benefiting police officers and firefighters. They cited a 1946 "strike" by city employees who were part of a demand by a 2,600-member group for a twenty-five percent salary increase. When the administration rejected the effort, 650 members of the group went out on strike. They got ready support from 20,000 Houston members of the A. F. L. construction craftsmen, 5,000 of whom marched on City Hall.

After much emotional debate, the Texas House eventually passed a law preventing public employees from collective bargaining or striking. The civil service advocates held steady with this new law since officers consistently rejected strikes and membership in labor organizations. Their brothers in the fire department, who had traditional ties to labor organizations, were the real targets of the proposed amendment. Resolution of the union/strike issue left the question of home rule and political patronage as the two most volatile issues.

Opponents argued that a state civil service law would deprive Houston of control over local affairs as a home rule city. But supporters cited horribly unfair and unprofessional examples of political patronage. The city administration got support from the League of Texas Municipalities (later the Texas Municipal League) as well as the *Houston Chronicle*, which likened the threat to the home rule amendment of the State Constitution to the federal government's encroachment in state affairs.

One of the most horrifying disasters in the history of the Lone Star State helped the association make its case for civil service protection. The bill was pending before the Legislature when the Texas City disaster happened on April 17, 1947, killing nearly 600 people, causing another 2,000 injuries and property losses that numbered $67 million in a small Gulf Coast town of 16,000. All of the town's firemen perished when a ship in the Texas City harbor bearing a cargo of ammonium nitrate fertilizer exploded, setting off a chain reaction of explosions and deadly fires. The governor declared it an emergency situation and policemen and firemen from all over this state went into Texas City. A Houston police lieutenant was placed in charge, directing both police and fire personnel.

"So it proved the point that police officers and firemen were state officers," Maughmer said.[19] It also proved that if a man were injured in one of these situations outside his own immediate jurisdiction, that he could come back and be told he was not qualified to be a policeman and be fired. HPOA arranged for injured patrolmen from Texas City to testify to this fact before the Legislature, a move that provided strength to get the new law enacted.[20]

Assistant City Attorney George Eddy took center stage in the debate process by suggesting that Houston police officers and firefighters wanted "not job security, but job perpetuation without responsibility."[21] In the end, Eddy was no match for HPOA's lead advocate, Representative Carleton Moore of Houston, the House sponsor. Moore argued that political patronage had dominated the department and caused perpetually low morale among the troops. In three conspicuous cases, Moore pointed out that two inspectors of police had been demoted to lieutenant and a third to office clerk.

Moore later recounted that the issue was so highly emotional that a Houston city official physically threatened him. Despite a number of amendments, the Legislature passed a bill that provided Houston's public safety personnel with the protection they were seeking with a requirement for the city to call an election to approve Article 1269m, the number by which the new law would be known. The police and fire personnel went directly to the citizens and easily persuaded them to follow their instincts. Houstonians passed the law by a nearly 6,000-vote margin on January 31, 1948.

The department was still run by high-ranking, politically-appointed police officials. These men and the city administration were opposed to local enactment of 1269m. Oscar Holcombe still had plenty of political maneuvers of his own to use over the next five years.

Safeguards were in place. Earl Maughmer's far-reaching wisdom became readily apparent in the wording of the repeal section of 1269m. It was not by accident that the law required a simple majority of voters to *adopt* the legislation, but required a *majority of the registered voters in the county* to repeal it—a far more difficult political task. The value of the statute was immediately proven by those who had been fired because of their efforts to obtain 1269m. They appealed their dismissals and won. Maughmer, who eventually retired at the rank of captain in 1975, continued his legislative leadership. He also led the effort to enact the first Houston Police Officer's Pension System legislation in the same session that enacted 1269m. That legislation separated Houston officers from the pension system of other city employees.

The new 1269m also granted guaranteed access to the courts as an appeals route for disadvantageous civil service decisions at the initial administrative level. The legislation required state district judges to take preference over other cases on the docket so officers wouldn't have to wait many years before getting justice. Since the law was applicable to officers at all levels, HPOA membership consisted of not just police officers but also sergeants, lieutenants, captains and inspectors (later deputy or assistant chiefs).

The only person not initially included under the law was the police chief. Thus, when he was dismissed, he could not be reduced below the rank he held prior to his appointment. A later amendment to the law gave the chief the same right of appeal to the civil service commission and the district courts. When HPOA became the Houston Police Officers Union in 1995, the organization's constitution was changed so that police chiefs could not be members.

The Old Gray Fox made transfers, created new positions and promoted favorites to desirable positions before the establishment of the new civil service system—all in secrecy. He and his police chief, B. W. Payne, agreed on the changes and clandestinely revealed them to City Controller Roy Oakes, who certified the availability of funds to cover the cost of increased salaries. So there, in the back halls of City Hall, Mayor Holcombe tried to out-fox the system.

Maughmer and other leaders knew that further reform would require more years. It was just a matter of time before Holcombe's political cronies in the department would retire or leave. Meanwhile, political patronage made it possible for a few high-ranking HPD officers to protect gambling and prostitution interests in Houston, considered an "open" city during this period.

Before 1269m, many of the rank-and-file feared demotion or firings if they dared to enforce gambling laws. By policy handed down by Chief Payne, only vice officers enforced these laws and the worst-kept secret was the Vice Division's lax enforcement standards. In a notable 1950 case, a Houston tavern owner made public that she regularly paid officers in order to keep her business operating after hours. Revelations like this one encouraged what Inspector L. D. Morrison Sr. termed "do-right officers." Two of them, Walter Rankin and Aaron Curtis, conducted their own unofficial raids of gambling operations and gathered evidence that led them to expose HPD corruption.[22]

The grand jury investigation of the after-hours tavern operations led Chief Payne to fire Night Chief M. M. Simpson and a subordinate officer, C. C. Devine. Soon after, Payne himself resigned under pressure. Then, in October 1950, Mayor Holcombe appointed a chief far more capable of resisting political pressure than Payne—Inspector Morrison, an education advocate and police academy pioneer.

HPOA also coalesced with reform-oriented lawmakers to get laws passed that banned slot machines, policy games and punch cards, thus undermining the influence of racketeers in local political campaigns. The association saw that police all over Texas would be held to higher standards by supporting a 1956 bill that created the Law Enforcement Standard and Education Commission, a nine-member board that set professional standards for municipal police departments in Texas. The commission was the forerunner of today's TCLE-OSE—the Texas Commission on Law Enforcement Standards and Education.

The association, under Breck Porter's leadership, was instrumental in helping police in Abilene, Austin, Fort Worth, San Antonio, Sweetwater and Waco to form their own associations. Porter and Maughmer also were instrumental in forming the Texas Municipal Police Association (TMPA), the largest police organization in Texas. In 1995, after the HPOA became the Houston Police Officers Union, the Board of Directors named the Union building at 1602 State Street the Breckenridge Porter Building. Maughmer died in 1985 and Porter in 1999.

15

A SERGEANT
BECOMES CHIEF

Police Chief L. D. Morrison Sr. closed the little-used North Side Police Substation at 1814 Gregg when the new headquarters at 61 Riesner opened in March 1952. He also transferred twenty-one officers, three sergeants and one lieutenant from the Motorcycle Squad to the Safety Division, effectively disbanding the "solos" squad.

By May 15, Morrison posted his semi-annual bulletin about politics and the men in blue. The bulletin said that civil service rules prohibited policemen and firemen from taking part in such political activities as making speeches, soliciting votes, passing out literature and writing letters. The rules also protected the men from reprisals for refusing to contribute to political campaigns or to render any political service.

One activity that no law affected was the naturally flowing inter-departmental politicking that posed day-to-day distractions for the chief. Even though some ranking officers were dismissed, demoted or chose to resign, some strong followers of B. W. Payne remained to stir the waters of discontent. Morrison did what chiefs before him had always done—he put his loyalists in influential positions and those not so loyal in out-of-the-way assignments in a growing department that now numbered about 600.

Captain Hobson G. "Buddy" McGill, a man who experienced one of the most checkered careers in HPD history, was promoted to acting night chief on May 20, 1952, making him the No. 3 man in the department. In earning this promotion, McGill jumped like a checker over his previous boss. He was demoted during the next mayoral administration, only to work his way back up the ladder to serve as police chief under a different mayor.[1]

Morrison made improvements in overall professionalism by sending Detective Larry Fultz to the University of Chicago for a police and law enforcement seminar whose purpose was to make case studies of racial violence and

POLICE CHIEF L. D.
MORRISON SR., OCTOBER
11, 1950–SEPTEMBER 1,
1954 (HPD ARCHIVES)

determine the role police played in handling racial disharmony. Fultz earned the reputation as another HPD education advocate along with two other rising stars, Harry Caldwell and Jack Heard, a sergeant with a master's degree.[2]

In late July, Detective A. R. Duncan, representing the Houston Police Officers Association, requested a $45 monthly raise. The response was cold. Holcombe quoted studies of cities with populations between 300,000 and 900,000, finding that Houston ranked twelfth among twenty-nine cities studied, with a monthly pay base of $280 for a forty-hour work week. He said that Oakland, California had a base of $310 and New Orleans $200. City Controller Roy B. Oakes estimated that $45 pay raises would cost taxpayers $3 million a year.

HPD intensified its fight against gambling and other vices and saw reform candidate Roy Hofheinz win the mayor's job in 1953. Taking office in January 1954, Hofheinz soon saw Morrison as a liability but not because of policy decisions or differences in philosophy. The chief experienced an almost constant back pain caused by a slipped disk. Rumors had circulated that he was addicted to pain medication, or "illegal narcotics" prescribed by his personal physician.

Other unfortunate incidents complicated the chief's professional life. A federal grand jury indicted a captain and a detective on charges related to $75,000 worth of missing drugs from police custody. In addition, enough drug cases were in the news involving marijuana seizures and heroin that Houston was beginning to gain national recognition for its growing drug problem.

Morrison's personal problem hurt him the most. Embroiled in a controversy that had reached a point that affected his ability to lead the department, Morrison asked the mayor on July 31, 1954 that his resignation be accepted as chief of police just as soon as a successor could be found and sworn in.

Mayor Hofheinz tried to change the job of police chief to a public safety commissioner, where one commissioner would be over both the police and fire departments and any other form of emergency services. He would be housed outside the police station and serve primarily as an administrator. Oscar Holcombe had called the job "public safety director." In theory, the arrangement provided the mayor with more control over the department. He could appoint an outsider completely loyal to him and have oversight of police and fire. But this time under Hofheinz, City Council shot down the idea.

Discreetly, the mayor's trusted aide, Gould Beech, began questioning likely candidates for chief from within the department. Initially, most City Hall observers felt he would choose one of the inspectors or even a captain. Soon the mayor had immediate access to the news media every day and made a statement to reporters that he couldn't find a chief that met his qualifications, a comment that obviously irritated his high-ranking officers. One of them, Assistant Chief George Seber, told one of the department's more ambitious sergeants that he thought the mayor's men would be calling him over for an interview. It wasn't long before Sergeant Jack Heard—the son of two-time Houston Police Chief Percy Heard—was called in for an interview. The five-year officer was the department's first-ever polygraph operator. He was assigned to work with the so-called "police subversive squad," perceived to be an in-house "snoop group" that dealt with alleged wrongdoings of officers.[3]

Heard was thirty-six years old with a salary of $4,080. The chief's $10,000 salary more than doubled his earnings. He said yes to the appointment on August 28, 1954. The announcement hit the newspapers, radio and television stations immediately, and by Monday morning Police Chief-designate John F. Heard held his first news conference. He was a graduate of Houston's Sam Houston High School and held Bachelors and Masters degrees in public administration from the University of Houston. Hofheinz expressed his belief that Heard had the right qualifications for the job despite being only a sergeant. At thirty-six, he was the same age as his father Percy had been when the elder Heard was first appointed chief during the Great Depression. He was the first and only officer to be promoted directly from sergeant to

Police Chief Jack Heard is pictured with the first four female graduates of the Houston Police Academy. They are, left to right, Addie Jean Smith, Jo Bankston, Mercedes Halvorsen Singleton and Emily Rimmer Vasquez. Only Bankston stayed long enough to earn retirement. (Jo Bankston)

police chief, one giant leap that has drawn criticism and endless discussion over the more than sixty years that have passed since it happened.

Years after his retirement from law enforcement, Heard said many old timers despised his appointment while a younger faction admired his education and professionalism. He eventually earned respect from the older officers.[4]

Several councilmen told reporters they wanted a man of more experience to head the force that was using a steady flow of cadet classes to quickly grow toward a total close to seven hundred policemen. One of them questioned the legality of Heard living in suburban Spring Branch, outside the city limits. Coincidentally, the city soon annexed a section that encompassed Heard's property, although there has never been any ordinance or policy requiring the chief to reside in Houston. Another immediate issue was the fate of outgoing Chief Morrison, a close enough friend of Heard's to have him substitute for him in teaching his UH criminology classes when scheduling conflicts arose.

The council approved Hofheinz' selection and Heard fearlessly took over the reins of the department, proving to be a true pioneer unafraid to institute many "firsts." One of them was dealing with HPD's first former chief entitled by civil service law to serve in the rank he held before his appointment as top cop. Morrison was a popular figure despite the drug-related problem. The mayor wanted him returned to the rank of inspector, even though the four inspector positions were filled. Morrison's education and professional standards became a strong enough HPD tradition that the new police academy that opened February 9, 1981 was named the L. D. Morrison Sr. Police Training Academy. His son, L. D. Jr., served as the HPD Homicide captain for many years. No evidence was ever presented in court that gave the slightest indication that Morrison Sr. was addicted to codeine. He was never charged with any offense or accused of violating any laws.

Heard had a positive nature and refused to admit that "the biggest headache he inherited was the bickering and throat-cutting between pro-Morrison and anti-Morrison cliques in the department." The issue of the two Vice officers charged in connection with drugs missing from police custody took an unexpected turn when they both committed suicide, one after being reinstated by Heard following his acquittal.

In the fall of 1954, Morrison was given vacation leave to testify in the trial of his personal physician, Dr. Julius B. McBride. Dr. McBride faced a twenty-six-count federal indictment in connection with allegedly falsifying records to dispense large amounts of codeine to a patient. A *Houston Press* story alleged that he dispensed it to Morrison for the treatment of a slipped disk and a very painful x-ray burn for two of the years Morrison was chief. A jury found McBride guilty on all counts.[5]

On October 27, 1954, Morrison retired on a disability pension based on the old spinal cord injury but came back to work on Christmas Eve with Heard placing him in charge of a new service division that included the jail, automobile compound, Identification Bureau, Communications Division and all service units. He had a doctor's permit saying he was fit for duty.

A typical HPD Radio Patrol car from the 1950s. Police Chief Jack
Heard eavesdropped on officers' conversations as they filled cars like
this one at the gas pumps at 61 Riesner (HPD Archives)

Jack Heard's first action was to disband the Inter-office Investigative Division
that some officers referred to as "the super cops." The group got the reputation
as the in-house "snoop group," that Heard thought was being mishandled.[6]

Houstonians got to know more personal details about Heard than any
chief since his father. This was due to the fact that he had a young family. A
September 2, 1954 article in the *Houston Press* revealed many facts any police chief of today would consider to be none of anybody's business, including
the amount of his monthly payments for an air conditioner and deep freeze.[7]

Often during the day, the chief opened his door to the hallway, a marked
contrast to L. D. Morrison's tightly closed door. Young patrol officers were
awed by the possibility they could be chief even if they were sergeants with
only five years' experience. They often stopped by for a quick visit. Heard
instituted the practice of allowing certain patrol officers to spend a day with
him, even tagging along if he made a luncheon speech.

The young chief made it a habit to check in with the nearby offices to keep
track of ongoing policing activities and newsworthy events. Often, he would

walk down the third floor hallway to the Homicide Division. Heard found that the best place to learn what officers were really thinking was at the gas pump on the backside of 61 Riesner. He grabbed the phone and pretended he was talking while officers visited one another as they filled up the gas tanks of their patrol cars. The chief was listening, not talking—being nosy with a purpose. Heard learned important information. Two officers were killed on April 30, 1955, when they were checking the beer license of a tavern owner. They had called for help but those who answered were too late. Both men died.[8]

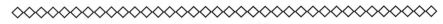

THE 100 CLUB

The city of Houston provided no guarantees of benefits to the surviving spouses and families of officers killed in the line of duty. Many widows wound up taking the oath of poverty, often performing domestic jobs to keep their families afloat. Sometimes the department took care of its own by opening up civilian jobs to widows. By 1920, Houston officers set up a burial fund for themselves by contributing a quarter a month. By modern times, the benefit became $7,500 for funeral expenses in cases of natural or line-of-duty death.

In 1953, a group of civic leaders known for their strong and steady support of police officers took a giant step to provide financial assistance to the survivors of HPD officers slain in the line of duty. They formed what became known as the 100 Club. The founding fathers included prominent citizens Leopold L. Meyer, Ray R. Elliott, R. H. Abercrombie, William A. "Bill" Smith and "Silver Dollar Jim" West. Jack Heard, who would become police chief the following year, became a high-profile cheerleader. The group leaders found one hundred individuals willing to pay annual membership dues of $100 each to start the club.

Initially, the group was known as the Houston Citizens' Traffic Safety Commission. In 1960, the organization officially incorporated as The Hundred Club of Houston. The first HPD officer whose line-of-duty death resulted in a benefit to his survivors was Officer James Thomas Walker, a solo motorcycle officer killed on March 8, 1963, when struck by a speeding motorist. He left a wife and five young children.

One of the first officers honored as "officer of the year" was HPD Officer Walter Rankin, a World War II Navy veteran who joined the department after the war. Rankin was honored for his steadfast and innovative methods for tracking down hit-and-run drivers. Rankin attained the rank of sergeant and went on to become Harry County's Precinct 1 constable and served in this capacity for many years.

The 100 Club has provided a growing number of benefits to the surviving families of each of the brave men and women killed while on duty to protect the citizens of Houston. In 2011, the total number stood at 110 since 1861. The club had more than 26,000 members and extended its policies to providing life-protecting equipment for area Houston area law enforcement agencies. The first gifts were bulletproof vests. Most law enforcement agencies in the Greater Houston area have benefited from gifts of life-protecting equipment, such as vests, radios, specialized equipment for SWAT teams and equipment for bomb squad officers. In excess of $9 million has been provided for life-protecting equipment. The 100 Club has provided scholarships to more than 400 officers to either finish undergraduate work or pursue graduate degrees in Criminal Justice. Survivor benefits were extended to all Harris County law enforcement officers at the federal, state, county and municipal levels. In 1995, the name was changed to The 100 Club of Greater Houston and then to The 100 Club, which now supports 200 law enforcement agencies and 13,000 officers in eighteen counties surrounding counties. On October 2, 2001, The 100 Club Board of Directors unanimously approved extending line of duty death benefits to firefighters killed in the line of duty. In 2006, the Club extended line-of-duty death benefits to all commissioned Texas Department of Public Safety personnel, including Texas Rangers, Texas Parks & Wildlife-commissioned personnel, Texas Department of Criminal Justice institutional personnel and agents of the Texas Alcoholic Beverage Commission. Mary Cooper was the club's first-ever executive director from 1976 until 1994, when the board appointed Rick Hartley to serve in this important leadership capacity. Hartley was a veteran Houston television reporter, the first-ever HPD spokesman in 1976, a Texas Department of Corrections spokesman and returning HPD spokesman under Police Chief Sam Nuchia in 1991 before being named executive director of the 100 Club in 1994. Hartley's leadership and The 100 Club's far-reaching boardroom decisions firmly established the practice of providing $10,000 for the emergency needs of a surviving spouse within twenty-four to forty-eight hours after the tragedy. By 2007, the average gift per family was $300,000. Total gifts exceeded $10 million.[9]

Heard was the first chief to speak regularly before City Council. Right after the two officers were shot and killed, the chief made a statement that he was "sick and tired" of conditions in the department, words that angered some council members. He diplomatically placated them and got to the real point, saying he didn't want the council to accept the low bid for tires on patrol cars because "the tires they have now are of poor quality and there were three police units close to the scene when the officers were killed, but they were sitting on flat tires."[10]

Council then agreed to let the police and fire departments purchase the tires they needed by specific name and grade. It was a great victory for the troops, one made possible by Heard's nosiness and determination.

Many of Heard's sensible ideas directly affected the men on the beat and made them safer and more comfortable. The comfort came when he took the wool out of HPD's summer uniform shirts. Heard instituted a cotton blend for uniforms worn when it was hot outside, which was most days of the year. Heard also abolished the shoulder strap on the Sam Brown belts that were a traditional part of police uniforms. Henceforth, no suspect inclined to wrestle with a police officer would be able to strangle or throw around an officer with a shoulder strap. Heard was the first chief to require helmets for motorcycle (solo) officers, another safety measure, an unpopular rule initially that later became acceptable because of the safety factor.[11]

Sticking to his goal for higher professional standards, the chief made it a rule that solo officers could not smoke cigars while riding. He didn't think it looked professional. He required every officer who was not a detective to wear his uniform every day, saying, "It gave the public an idea of how many policemen they had. In a suit, they could be anybody—a car salesman or a newspaperman."[12]

Lanny Dixon Stephenson
was not only HPD's first
female homicide detective,
she was recognized as the
first in the nation. (Houston
Metropolitan Research Center)

Large "Police" signs were painted on the front and back of every patrol car, thus increasing police visibility.

Instead of holding fast to a bad idea, Heard eliminated it as soon as possible. An obvious case in point was an order resulting from the post-World War II military influence that required officers to salute sergeants, lieutenants, captains, inspectors, assistant chiefs, the chief and the mayor. The brass was expected to return the salute. City Council members would not be saluted because officers didn't recognize them. The idea came from one of the inspectors. Heard cancelled it in less than two weeks after he was named chief.

Houston became the first city in the state to assign an entire police division—one captain and ten detectives—to narcotics work. The *Houston Press* said, "Chief Heard said he considered it so important that he may raise the new narcotics division to the status of a 'bureau' with an inspector in charge." The Narcotics Division was separated from Vice and moved to a separate location and operated directly under the chief. Heard moved Captain J. C. McMahon from Vice to head Narcotics.

In October 1954, Chief Heard studied other big-city police departments in the nation and plainly stated that Houston's force was woefully small. It was a finding often echoed by future chiefs in Houston, each time with the same result—not enough money to fund the right number of cadet classes. At the time of Heard's study, HPD was 600-plus strong, but Boston had 2,478 officers and San Francisco 1,763. The chief said HPD should be twice the size it was. Some council members agreed, but turned their palms up in the air as a way of lamenting the funding shortage.

Heard also unveiled what in that time period was a revolutionary idea—regional substations. Again, the problem was the same—no money. While he couldn't increase the department's size overnight, the young chief put together large cadet classes when he could and was able to decide who carried a badge and who didn't. The losers were the auxiliary police officers; the winners were women. In April 1955, the HPD Auxiliary Police badges and uniforms were changed because Heard wanted to call in all of the old badges. He said that there were only about 600 being worn by regular uniformed police officers, but 1,500 sets of badges assigned to health inspectors, dogcatchers, parking meter attendants, arson investigators, zoo keepers and even politicians. Heard thought the personnel in these areas should have their own badges in order to preserve the dignity of the police badge. Later, state law required the distinction.

Heard wasn't afraid to open the police academy to women. On August 16, 1955, *The Houston Post* pictured four women police trainees and stated that they were a first in HPD history. The four policewomen—the first not to be generally considered "matrons"—were enrolled in "the Houston Police Training school." They were Mrs. Emily Vasquez, Miss Mercedes Halvorsen, Mrs. Jean Smith and Mrs. Jo Bankston, the latter two wives of police officers.

Emily Rimmer Vasquez quit before she was eligible to retire. Mercedes Halvorsen later married Joe Singleton, who became a lieutenant. Addie Jean Smith, wife of Officer R. C. Smith, left HPD after five years. The longest service of the first four policewomen trained at the police training school was that of Jo Bankston, who was married to Officer J. C. Bankston for two years at the time of her selection. Bankston served for thirty years, earning full retirement, the only one of the four to do so. Bankston and the others passed a physical, went through interviews with the head of the academy, actually passed a credit check and had to furnish letters of recommendation from friends and neighbors. "They asked me if my husband would be jealous of me working with a male partner and if he would have objections to a night or evening shift," she said. "How stable was our marriage?"[13]

The "first guinea pigs in the academy" didn't have to climb ropes at the academy and had to wear skirts, not pants. The policewomen earned the same pay as their male counterparts but were initially assigned to Records, the jail or the Juvenile Division. Chief Heard encouraged them with firm but sincere advice: "Always remember you are a police officer, but first you are a woman." He required that policewomen always worked with a male partner, especially when making arrests because he didn't want to put a woman in harm's way.[14]

Change was the HPD way of life under Jack Heard. There was a referendum vote in the city on whether or not the police and firefighters would receive a $45 a month pay raise. It was approved by a margin of 7 to 1.

May 1955 found Jack Heard trumpeting the successful first full year of HPD's using of new technology known as radar—or "the little black box"—to catch speeding vehicles. During that first year, the three-officer radar squad ticketed 4,116 drivers, resulting in fines of $50,000. Not one case was lost in court. The radar guns cost $1,080 apiece and Heard announced plans to buy five more in the coming year.

In yet another "first", Walkie Talkies were used in the police department when Vice Captain J. C. McMahon borrowed two from the Fire Department. Better communications and high technology like radar were badly needed to handle the traffic that moved at higher speeds on the new freeways.

Heard faced new problems with the Gulf Freeway, where vehicles were—in his words—"just running over each other right and left out there." He lined up motorcycle officers everywhere, resulting in a reduction of accidents to almost zero. Heard later said the city "ran out of motorcycles."[15]

New police radios allowed only the calls going to a police car, meaning individual cars no longer had to listen to all citywide cars but just those in the area where they were assigned. Also, a radio signal could be beamed to a police car directly and that car's lights would be connected to the radio, thus allowing the officer to know he had a call when he was out on a traffic stop.

While that technology was helping catch speeders and fight crimes under Chief Heard, City Hall politics were keeping Mayor Roy Hofheinz up late. By August, City Council had tried twice to impeach Hofheinz and remove him from office on grounds he failed to fire some employees in connection with alleged misappropriation of city assets. When council members attempted to carry forth the impeachment proceedings, City Attorney Will Sears told them their actions were unconstitutional.

Also at question on the political side of the impeachment equation were different city charter amendments, one set proposed by the mayor and another by council members. An election on August 16 determined the preference of Houstonians. One week before the charter election Chief Heard refused to serve subpoenas to individuals scheduled to testify at Hofheinz' impeachment trial. In this historical first, Mayor Pro-Tem Matt Wilson insisted that he was the mayor and demanded that Heard act accordingly. However, the chief determined that Hofheinz was still in charge and refused to provide service, referring to a section of the charter that requires the mayor to sign subpoenas like these.

The August 16 vote resulted in a few charter changes but, more significantly, ensured that Hofheinz would stay in office at least until November.

Oscar Holcombe defeated Roy Hofheinz in the 1955 mayoral election. It was typical in that day and time—as it was in later years—for new administrations to change police chiefs. Public support was solidly behind retention of Jack Heard, who was starting to take seriously the advice of up-and-coming HPD Captain Herman B. Short that he had better have a new job outside the HPD when the time came for him to be replaced. The alternative was to be returned to his old rank of sergeant, which paid half the chief's salary, and to be harassed by higher-ranking officers who had worked under him.

Short later said he believed that Heard knew that taking the job of chief of police was a one-way street.[16] Short said the chief served at the will of the mayor and could be fired or asked to resign, a situation Heard recognized when he took the job. "Chief Short was of the opinion that no one should hold the job of chief of police until he was of retirement age or willing for it to be his last duty station within the department," HPD historian Denny Hair wrote. "He should be through with his police career, at least with HPD. In that way, he would be free of politics and could leave at any time and not need the money to keep up his family. He also said that the decisions that are faced by a chief were of such magnitude that returning to the ranks would cause the former chief to be constantly messed with, questioned and asked to second guess his new boss."

Many 1956 City Hall observers, as well as the news media, were curious if Holcombe would return the city to the open days prevalent in his previous administrations. During the heated campaign, Marvin Zindler, the master of ceremonies at a Jaycees luncheon featuring Holcombe, asked the candidate if Houston would become an "open town" as it was in 1949, should he be elected mayor. There was a second question: "Will the present chief of police, Jack Heard, be thrown out like his father in the past, if you are elected."[17]

Holcombe said if elected he would tighten up gambling and booking as much as possible. But he said he would not promise to keep Heard until he carefully weighed the chief's record. Noticeably taking a new stance from his previous administrations, the Old Gray Fox said he thought Heard might stay in his position if he kept out of politics.

Hofheinz lost to Holcombe and the establishment in a city election in which six incumbent City Council members were returned to City Hall. They included Councilman Louie Welch, already an avowed future mayoral candidate. He was one of a few council members wanting Heard to be replaced.

Holcombe told the news media at year's end he would retain Heard as chief "on a trial basis." News reports said the incoming council members had a closed-door meeting with Holcombe to suggest keeping Heard long enough to test his performance under a new administration. The *Houston Chronicle* was in Heard's corner and wrote an editorial telling the council members "that the complaints made to them do not represent any desire to improve the police department or to give Houston better law enforcement and it is to be hoped that they will continue to give support to Heard."[18]

Heard remembered an aside with his new boss: "The conversation was him saying, 'I'm taking everything into consideration as far as you being chief of police until such time that something comes up that would cause me to change my mind.' He meant I would be chief until such time as I blew it."[19]

Heard knew the job better then he did in the initial months when he was still getting his feet wet, and he now felt more secure in it. He withstood complaints from some of the twenty-seven motorcycle officers about his policy requiring them to wear protective helmets. Some said they were going bald. Others said that the helmets were uncomfortable, hot, awkward and embarrassing to wear because they resembled space helmets. Heard said they were purchased for protection. His order stood.

Heard was no micromanager. But Holcombe was accustomed to micromanaging the department in his previous administrations. He summoned his still-youthful chief in July 1956 for an hour-long session that discussed "tightening up the department" with more discipline. He requested a daily report on persons held as long as twenty-four hours without any charges being filed. He soon grew angry with Heard about newspaper stories concerning a suspect involved in an effort to "open up the town." Holcombe was sensitive to the "open city" issue and said he was tired of hearing Chief Heard cry "wolf" when there was no wolf.[20]

On August 6, 1956, Houston newspapers ran stories saying that Police Chief Jack Heard would become an assistant to O. B. Ellis, the head of the Texas Department of Corrections. The assistant director's position paid $2,100 less than the chief's $10,000 annual salary. Legend around Houston was that Holcombe considered himself omnipotent, always the first to know of events long before the public. And he inevitably controlled the lives of literally hundreds of Houstonians during his eleven terms in office.

But the Old Gray Fox, who no longer could operate as the micromanager he was in previous terms, had no idea Heard had accepted the prison system job. As a courtesy, Heard wanted to explain his plans to his boss, catching Holcombe off guard but prompting him to ask, "Who would you recommend to take your place?"

"We went over some individuals," Heard said. "One of the ones I recommended highly was Carl Shuptrine."[21]

Interviews with Heard's top brass began almost immediately. Holcombe or his trusted aides interviewed Inspector W. N. Daut, Inspector Carl Shuptrine, Captain Frank Murray, Captain Jack McMahon, Captain John R. Abernathy, Captain Robert J. Clark, Assistant Chief George Seber, Captain H. G. "Buddy" McGill, Lieutenant H. F. Willis and Lieutenant O. R. Hitt. The mayor said that reports of dissension apparently had been spread by only a very few officers.

Besides Shuptrine (pronounced *SHUP*-trine to rhyme with brine), the group of interviewees included two individuals who would become police chief or acting chief: R. J. Clark, an acting chief for seven months in 1975–76; and Buddy McGill, the chief in 1963–64 (and who Heard demoted from assistant chief to captain for "disgraceful conduct" involving a recently married secretary).

Heard spent sixteen years with the Texas Department of Corrections before returning to Harris County to be elected sheriff in 1972. He lost a runoff for mayor with Kathy Whitmire in 1981 and served a few more years as sheriff before retiring.

In 1956, Jack Heard had scarcely started moving out of his office when Mayor Holcombe announced his successor—Heard's recommendation—Carl Shuptrine.

16

POLITICAL WINDS

By the time Mayor Oscar Holcombe appointed Carl Lester Shuptrine police chief on August 15, 1956, the appointee was in position to achieve a noteworthy Houston policing irony. He was *demoted* in 1947 and *promoted* in 1956—for the same reason: he was non-political. Holcombe promoted police officials for supporting him in 1947 and Shuptrine, then an inspector, was demoted to lieutenant so that a Holcombe supporter would get the higher rank. In 1948 and 1949, the Houston Police Officers Association succeeded in outlawing this practice with the passage of 1269m.

By 1956, the law had solidified rank security and the political winds had shifted 180 degrees. The older and wiser Holcombe, serving what would be his last term, wanted a decidedly non-political police chief to succeed Jack Heard. The factionalism that prevailed in the department when Heard left in August 1956 caused Holcombe to pick someone as far away from either faction as he could get. He and his staff interviewed forty-seven HPD veterans, asking each one to name the person he thought would make the best chief.

Shuptrine, age fifty-one, was the first chief confirmed in an open meeting of the Houston City Council held in the mayor's dining room in the basement level of City Hall. The council members had just agreed to the mayor's choice behind the closed and locked doors of the same room. Usually the vote for approval took place in the council chambers. Mayor Holcombe cited Shuptrine's ability to get along with each HPD faction, evidenced by the fact that his name appeared more often than any other man's among the recommendations from the forty-seven ranking officers interviewed. Shuptrine, a twenty-six-year police veteran, had headed the Uniformed Division and was considered an expert on handling of heavy traffic. The mayor decided on Inspector Shuptrine after inviting him to his home for a meeting. It was the first time Shuptrine had met privately with the mayor.[1]

Silver Dollar Jim

The Houston Police Department of the 1940s and 1950s had no greater friend than an eccentric oilman named James Marion West Jr., who was better known as "Silver Dollar Jim," a nickname attributed to his constant habit of tipping silver dollars everywhere he went, which included many crime scenes with senior police officers. West and his brother and sister inherited $70 million in oil and lumber properties from their father, and multiplied this fortune.

Paunchy and usually sloppily dressed, West tipped as many as twenty-five or thirty silver dollars at a time pulled from the pockets of his tailor-made suits. Notably captured in *Houston: Land of the Big Rich*, by *Houston Post* columnist and editorial page editor George Fuermann, Silver Dollar Jim routinely threw handfuls of silver dollars to the floors of restaurants and watched waiters scramble for them. West loved policing and was actually commissioned a Texas Ranger. He also was known as "Car No. 366" on the HPD radio network when he regularly rode with captains, lieutenants and even sergeants. West most frequently rode with night Lieutenant A. C. Martindale, while freelance photographer Marvin Zindler rode with Sergeant A. T. Cook. West was a common sight at nighttime or early-morning crime scenes. Wherever he went with Martindale, Silver Dollar Jim provided tons of silver dollars for investigating officers. Mayors and police chiefs determined that there was nothing wrong with this practice since no favors were expected in return.

Silver Dollar Jim was known as a policeman at heart, a down-to-earth fellow, not a swellhead. West carried two chrome-plated, ivory-handled 45-caliber automatic pistols under his coat and had numerous radio antennae on many of the forty automobiles he owned. HPD historian Denny G. Hair wrote that West's hobby was patrolling with a select group of officers and helping apprehend suspects. He was an unpaid millionaire volunteer with an eccentric twist that assisted in making arrests with officers in his own car.

On one night in 1952, West was patrolling with Martindale when they rolled up on a burglary in progress in the middle of downtown and shined their lights on a youth armed with a shotgun. Martindale opened the passenger door slightly, drew his own 45-caliber pistol and ordered the suspect to surrender. The suspect opened fire, wounding Martindale in the shoulder. Not fully explained was the fact that Martindale also was shot in both feet. He maintained for a number of years that he accidentally shot himself but years later admitted to Hair that West's gun went off, striking the lieutenant in each foot. He said had these facts come out, West would not have been allowed to ride with the police at a time when West donated money and equipment that HPD could not have gotten otherwise.

Each Christmas the majority of the officers on the night shift received cash presents from West ranging from $10 to $50 apiece. West gifted some of them with new guns and other expensive presents. He never asked a single favor in return.[2] In a 2004 interview, former Police Chief and Harris County Sheriff Jack Heard said Silver Dollar Jim made special arrangements through Heard to pay the way for police chiefs from small towns to attend a police chiefs' conference in Galveston on an anonymous basis.[3]

James Marion "Silver Dollar Jim" West Jr. died on December 18, 1957 at the age of fifty-four. He was buried with a silver dollar in his pocket.[4]

Council members were particularly tough on a regular basis. They had the same attitude as their successors sixty years later. When Shuptrine asked for more money for more manpower, neither the mayor nor the councilmen could ever find enough to provide either one. Heard had done the same thing with the very same results, as did a long list of his predecessors.

One year after he took the reins of the department, Shuptrine fielded heavy criticism for his officers' alleged improper use of firearms as well as the police-supervised practice of marking Houston streets during the day. On the latter count, Councilman George Kesseler took to task the chief, city Traffic Engineer Eugene Maier and the Public Works Department for failing to be coordinated enough to perform the task of marking off traffic lanes at a time when traffic was heavy. Kesseler also demanded that Shuptrine make "a complete report and full explanation" as to what type of training policemen are given in the use of firearms. The councilman referred to a growing number of news reports detailing "some ridiculous horseplay" regarding officers and their sidearms.[5]

"I can't be a bit proud of the lack of discipline that continues to exist in the Houston Police Department," Kesseler was quoted as saying. He specifically referred to two incidents. One involved a police sergeant who shot another officer while they were off duty drinking in a tavern. The other was more celebrated and much funnier. It involved a blank-shooting prank by Lieutenant Larry W. Fultz, who at age thirty-eight became the youngest HPD inspector in history. The event in question saw Fultz load his gun with blanks, confront another officer by calling him a name and firing several rounds at him, all in the presence of the prank's real victim. The scene became legendary because of its realism and dark humor.

Shuptrine quickly advocated a serious traffic study and suggested that motorcycle patrolmen be trained to investigate accidents, opining that this change would be a big help. Then—as in the early 21st Century—people involved in accidents often had to wait a long time before an accident investigator showed up.

Factionalism hurt Chief L. D. Morrison Sr. and ate away at Chief Jack Heard although Heard made generally good impressions on the younger officers on the force and instituted many initiatives that became permanent. Shuptrine stated publicly that every department had different factions that tend to create discord and vowed to do what he could to eliminate them. He soon made a number of captain assignments, proceeded with caution and kept his promise.

This chief had risen in the ranks with the ups and downs of different city administrations and had stayed in the upper ranks in most of his twenty-six years before his promotion. "I told him," Mayor Holcombe said on that first day, "that the running of the Police Department was his job and responsibility. When I don't like the work of a chief, I'll get a new one."[6]

Carl Shuptrine was a religious individual who exercised good judgment without being judgmental. He was the third consecutive Houston chief with more than one college degree and the third to be a teacher.

POLICE CHIEF CARL
SHUPTRINE, AUGUST
16, 1956–APRIL 5, 1963
(HPD ARCHIVES)

Born in the Houston County town of Ratcliff in 1905, Shuptrine was aptly described in a *Houston Chronicle* feature two and a half months into his job as being "a gangling young country schoolmaster who came to the big city" after teaching at such wide spots in the road as Dialville and Alto. He qualified himself for this calling by attending Stephen F. Austin College in Nacogdoches and Southwest State Teachers College in San Marcos, where he earned a bachelor's degree.[7] One of his classmates there, Lyndon Baines Johnson, also shared the same college boarding house table with the chief. Later, when the future president taught school in Houston, he often spent his lunch hour visiting the beat patrolman a block away from where he taught.[8]

Shuptrine gave up being a country school teacher during the Depression when he got a job working at Hughes Tool Co. in Houston, making about $75 a month. One of the apprentice machinists working beside him became a Houston police officer, inspiring Shuptrine to give it a try. In recapping the beginning of his police career, the *Chronicle* said, "He passed the written examination—a fifth grade spelling test—but was rejected because he knew the locations of only a few streets."[9] Undeterred, Shuptrine got a city map, studied it and went back before police interviewers that included Percy Heard, convincing them he was learning all there was to know about Houston.

They hired him in December 1930. He began his career using the same time-honored method chiefs Percy Heard, L. D. Morrison Sr. and Jack Heard did—by patrolling a downtown beat. The officer also spent three years in the Motorcycle Division and liked the nature of the work there until one day in 1937, when Shuptrine ran into a truck as he biked after a speeder at more than seventy miles per hour, miraculously suffering only a broken leg. From that time until the day he died, Shuptrine walked with a limp. His experiences in the Jail Division resulted in the only blemish on his otherwise highly respected record as an officer who rose through the ranks. In 1934, Shuptrine forgot to search a drunk who later stabbed a fellow prisoner with a knife hidden on his person. The department gave him a five-day suspension.[10]

Shuptrine, a deacon and Sunday school teacher at the First Baptist Church, was the first Houston chief to earn a law degree, receiving it in 1943 but never taking the bar exam. He went from Motorcycles to the Vice Squad and the Accident Division and spent a period of time as an investigator for the Harris County District Attorney's Office. Like Morrison and Heard, he strongly believed in educating police officers at the highest possible level. When he was promoted from lieutenant to captain in November 1950, he was placed in charge of the training school.

The new chief took over his $950-per-month job with a reputation for being one of the department's best-informed traffic control experts. More notably, he was considered perhaps the best marksman in HPD despite never having to draw his pistol while on duty. Shuptrine was largely responsible for the development of the target range beneath the Capitol Avenue Bridge, a department tradition until the new academy opened in 1981. The old range was the site of many pranks, given the echoes of pistol shots that often reverberated down Buffalo Bayou on the west side of downtown.

Shuptrine made it clear he in no way tolerated even the hint of an "open city" and didn't face any grand jury investigations of the department. He also didn't grab many headlines. The election of 1957 saw Lewis Cutrer, a former city attorney, become mayor. Cutrer kept Shuptrine as chief since he "has done and is doing an excellent job."[11]

The reputation of the department was good during these years. Bobby Adams joined the department on July 28, 1958 out of Police Cadet Class No. 18. The city was in a slight recession. Those who joined HPD earned $330 a month. The years after World War II and before the Civil Rights demonstrations of the 1960s were peaceful and non-controversial. "It was unheard of for an officer to do anything illegal," Adams said. "They just had a lot of respect in the community." Sergeants were considered "gods" and enforced even the most minor departmental policies. Patrol officers were required to

When the police academy was located at 61 Riesner, just a walk across Buffalo
Bayou from downtown Houston, the Police Academy shooting range was
under a nearby bridge over the bayou. The somewhat muffled shots were
well within earshot of passing downtown motorists. (HPD Museum)

wear their police caps "one hundred percent of the time" or face their sergeant's ire. They constantly faced scrutiny, even while patrolling the back
streets of the city, always poised to don the cap when they saw a car coming
toward them. Despite the hassle, most officers followed the hat rule and were
happy to have a job.[12]

With Houston approaching a population of almost 1 million, Cutrer and
Shuptrine stepped up the pace of the training academy. Between taking office in January 1958 and leaving office in 1964, Mayor Cutrer presented budgets that paid for 650 new officers.

Shuptrine celebrated his fifth year as police chief in August 1961—the longest uninterrupted tenure for a Houston chief of police in thirty-three years.
A *Houston Post* feature by police reporter Jim Criswell enumerated Shup-

trine's numerous achievements, starting with a reorganization of the command staff, which under his predecessors had one lieutenant reporting to another. The chief divided the department into five bureaus, each headed by an inspector. He got City Council to approve an additional inspector, whose job in the reorganization was to run the department at night. Weekend and holiday duty was split between the inspectors and Assistant Chief George Seber "to provide a ranking officer on duty at all times."[13]

Shuptrine likened his leadership method to that of a board of directors. This command staff "board" met three times a week to discuss the age-old big-city policing problem that has never gone away—how to provide services for a fast-growing city with limited city funds. Each inspector would share his plan and personnel changes before making them official, resulting in a smoother operation with less dissention.[14]

Shuptrine contended that Houston was 1,000 men short, but said he would settle for fewer. That year, only fifty-one cadets graduated from the training school and only thirty-seven earned badges the year before. The two largest outputs of new officers took place in 1958 and 1959 when 191 and 179 cadets, respectively, became Houston officers. These increases were planned under Holcombe but came to pass under Cutrer.

Shuptrine accurately predicted that HPD's future problems would be about the same as the present ones: the lack of increase in personnel, the replacement of worn-out police cars, typewriters (now computers) and cameras. He dutifully reported that the department was solving one big headache— the lack of parking for officers—with the purchase of four lots adjacent to Riesner, with two more on the drawing board. Another lot was then under construction between the station and Buffalo Bayou.

The five-year official "score card" for the chief included the following:
- Increased manpower more than fifty percent.
- Started the police dog program.
- Began the sub-station program.
- Beefed up traffic enforcement.
- Increased the number of officers sent to special training schools.
- Increased the amount of in-service training provided officers.
- Modernized the fleet by retiring older vehicles.
- Tripled the radio capacity for the department.
- Redistricted patrol areas and scheduled further redistricting when two new sub-stations are completed.

- Established new regulations with the City Controller's Office to handle stolen property.
- Established a new bonding procedure and control docket for Municipal Courts.
- Formed a planning division, whose first job would be to research the city's traffic problems and find ways of improving traffic conditions.[15]

The chief gave credit to his officers for his three proudest achievements—a decreased murder rate for the past three years, a National Safety Council award for having the fewest traffic fatalities in cities of between 750,000 and 1 million in population, and the curtailment of the policy racket. Most often in the HPD years before 1954, chiefs would come and go with new city administrations. Shuptrine helped to change that practice, at least for the time being. Throughout his tenure Shuptrine was apprehensive that the department would not be increased when the city's annexation program was completed. Holcombe, famous for being the annexation mayor, increased the city's square mileage from 165.2 to 349, more than doubling the land area patrol officers would be required to cover.[16]

By February 1963, the Port of Houston hired Shuptrine as chief security officer, earning $1,000 a month instead of the chief's salary of $1,131. Shuptrine served almost ten years in the job and died in retirement at age sixty-nine.

Houston mayors often inherited their predecessor's chief of police with the idea of keeping him on a trial basis. When Louie Welch became mayor in 1964, the incumbent chief, Hobson G. "Buddy" McGill, immediately went on trial. McGill spent ten months before Mayor Welch reached a verdict that bounced the thirty-four-year veteran back to the inspector's rank to serve out his career.

Lewis Cutrer, who lost to Welch in 1963, selected McGill to succeed *his* inherited chief, Carl Shuptrine, on March 31, 1963. McGill was popular with the troops and had worked his way up the departmental ladder over a policing career that spanned eight mayors beginning with Walter Monteith, a candidate he supported in the 1929 city election. The Depression affected this husky young railroad brakeman, who figured being a policeman would offer better job security. He picked his job by paying $375 for a new motorcycle and joined HPD's distinguished new Motorcycle Squad of forty men, where he spent seven years.[17]

The department was small and it was very common for brothers, cousins or other close kin to ride alongside each other as officers. McGill's teenaged nephew, Jack Renois, borrowed his uncle's machine to learn to ride and soon joined the force. By the time McGill became chief, Renois was the captain in charge of the Narcotics Division. Later, McGill's son Patrick rode motors for years and retired as a detective. The elder McGill made it known to Monteith that he wanted to be a solo motorcycle officer and the mayor made it happen on December 5, 1930, in the days of political patronage and no formal recruiting and academy training, a time in which new officers were not immediately issued a gun and a uniform.[18]

Monteith had known Buddy McGill since he was twelve years old and initially assigned him to guard the Christmas tree at City Hall. Such informalities in the start-up phase of 1930s Houston policing were very common. Soon McGill put together a uniform by obtaining pants here and a shirt there. He got a pistol and officially became a motorcycle officer. Within six years he worked his way up to sergeant and soon became HPD's first motorcycle lieutenant. Even with the rank, he drove a motor after dark with a carbide lamp like miners used, having to strike it to light it up.[19]

McGill didn't recall many details in his "war stories" for the news media when he became chief. *The Houston Post* reported, "McGill is credited with nabbing about eight safecrackers working at their trade." The man spent World War II in the Navy, returned to the force after the war and made captain in 1949 and night police chief in 1952 under Police Chief L. D. Morrison Sr. McGill always felt wronged by accusations that he pulled a crude and vulgar joke on a newlywed secretary during the tenure of Police Chief Jack Heard. He always contended it was a misunderstanding that resulted in Heard demoting him from night chief to captain.[20]

McGill amassed a large number of friends over the years. That coupled with the ability to score high enough to gain a promotion to inspector later in the 1950s caused the people who really counted to understand his predicament under Heard. The blemish eventually became an obscure footnote to Houston police history. He would always be known as a man with a hearty laugh who liked to share jokes. Like many officers and chiefs before him and since, McGill was active with what became known as the Houston Livestock Show and Rodeo.[21]

Scarcely two days passed into McGill's administration before he announced two staff changes over the force of 1,200. The primary promotion—and one destined to have the most profound effect on the history of HPD—made Captain Herman B. Short, head of the Robbery Division, an inspector who would serve as night chief of police. McGill also moved Inspector Weldon Waycott from night chief to a day job as head of the Traffic Bureau, the division second only in size to radio patrol.[22]

These changes set domino effects into motion; promotions begat promotions. Captain H. V. Hickman, head of the Homicide Division, replaced Short in Robbery. Hickman's replacement came from the lieutenant ranks when Lieutenant L. D. Morrison Jr. was promoted to captain and became head of Homicide, an assignment he held for fifteen years—longer than any Homicide captain in history.

Newspaper accounts of McGill's years as chief showed only a few major police-related news stories that caused major concerns from the mayor and citizenry. By April 1964, after Welch had been in office almost four months, the already wavering relationship he had with McGill started to unravel over allegations that the city was too easy on gamblers and that there might be police payoffs involved. Welch got vague, unsatisfying answers to his pointed gambling enforcement questions to McGill. Welch had no confidence in the chief.[23]

Rumors that he planned to dump McGill surfaced by late April during a grand jury investigation of gambling allegations. Further complicating the situation was the fact that the grand jurors got evidence that surfaced largely as a result of Welch's own privately-financed investigation conducted by the Texas Department of Public Safety. The mayor suspected that gambling threatened to give Houston the reputation for being "open" again. He voiced his concerns to McGill, who "pooh-poohed" them.[24]

Upon election to the first of five terms, Mayor Welch received a list of professional gamblers operating in the city. His first order of business was to sit down with McGill and discuss the names on the list. McGill believed these men were just a bunch of tinhorns. Welch later told an interviewer, "I said they were not so tinhorn when they run books as high as half a million dollars on a single local college football game. He pooh-poohed it."[25]

McGill's attitude put his job in jeopardy. Unknown to him, Welch met in February with Governor John Connally, Texas Attorney General Waggoner Carr and Department of Public Safety Director Colonel Homer Garrison to see what could be done. Carr and Garrison agreed to send in some

Cuban President Fidel Castro
was treated to some Texas
barbecue on this April 27, 1959
visit to Houston. HPD officers
were with him to keep an
eye out for trouble. (Houston
Metropolitan Research Center,
Houston Public Library, Houston
Post Collection, RG D0006,1379)

state undercover officers "to check out this gambling." The mayor used an unrestricted $5,000 expense account to underwrite expenses the officers incurred.[26]

The first morning the officers were in Houston, Welch learned that the bookies knew the plan and even where the officers were staying. He believed "somebody had spilled the whole thing." The grand jury found out and subpoenaed Welch and Carr to testify privately in the Memorial area home of a grand juror. The news media were present outside the home and Welch strongly believed the police chief was leaking information. McGill remained defensive.[27]

Two days later the grand jury cleared the department. Its report stated, "We have no reason to doubt the integrity of Police Chief McGill in his offer of cooperation with our investigation."[28] But McGill was still on a hot seat. The mayor simply would not tolerate any officer being susceptible to payoffs. Yet news reports began circulating that Welch and the chief had declared a "truce." Not coincidental was a series of vice and gambling arrests in early May 1964, moves McGill suggested came as the result of a growing number of tips attributed to the grand jury investigation.[29]

There was yet another indication that the route between 61 Riesner and City Hall was becoming a bumpier road. McGill came out against a proposal by the International Association of Chiefs of Police to survey the Houston Police Department's efficiency. Welch and the chief had requested the association to make a preliminary survey, an action that concluded that a more detailed study could lead to improvements. The estimated cost was $30,000. The chief would have none of it. He told the news media he had made several changes in "weak areas" about which he was not specific. He also stated his belief that a higher budget would cure the ills.[30] Uncharacteristically, the mayor had no comment. Already rumors were floating that Welch would name Inspector Herman Short to succeed McGill. The names of Inspector Otto Vahldiek of Radio Patrol and Captain L. D. Morrison Jr. of Homicide also floated about in the news media.[31]

The ever-popular McGill received the support of numerous civic leaders, including businessman Leopold Meyer, one of the four founders of the 100 Club and head of the Houston Crime Commission. A report in the *Forward Times*, a weekly African-American newspaper, also struck a blow in McGill's favor. Publisher Julius Carter said in a story that the investigation was part of a plan to get rid of McGill, who seemed to be popular among *Times* readers. McGill said he now better understood the mayor's points about vice-related cases and placed the Vice Squad directly under his control instead of the joint control of the chief and assistant chief.[32]

The mayor told reporters that the ball was in McGill's court to dispel or confirm rumors about gambling and the lack of enforcement of gaming laws. If Welch had a feeling earlier in 1964 that he didn't like McGill, those feelings intensified by late spring and extended into the fall. Then one day Welch picked up the morning paper that contained a report that greatly embarrassed the mayor in his first term. Twelve federal indictments were returned on September 18, 1964 against alleged gamblers that included seven male defendants who had been on the list Welch supplied McGill at least eight months earlier. With an edge in his voice, Welch reacted by noting that the seven had operated "virtually unmolested for almost two years and with only minor interruptions" for the past six years.[33]

On Monday, September 28, 1964, Welch took three minutes to obtain McGill's resignation in a surprise conference in the mayor's office. Welch told reporters that McGill would return to his inspector's rank over the Traffic Division. Then, he deadpanned, "He'll make a very good traffic inspector." Herman Short's name cropped up immediately as the likely successor to McGill.[34]

"I fired Buddy McGill," Welch said. "I called the chief in and handed him a letter of resignation written on just a regular City of Houston letterhead. And he looked at it and said, 'Nah, I'm not going to sign that letter. Why don't you fire me?' "Buddy was pretty egotistical and he asked why I didn't fire him and my immediate response was, 'You're fired.' He said, 'Why don't you fire me and I said, 'You're fired.' Under state civil service law he could only be placed back as low as he was when he came in. He suggested there was a vacancy (assistant chief) between the two positions (inspector and chief of police) and he would be interested. I told him no way."[35]

Welch put McGill in the Traffic Division because he would do less harm there.[36]

The reaction from some members of the HPD command staff indirectly supported the ousted chief. Three inspectors said they wouldn't have the job of police chief. Probably those inspectors—C. D. Taylor, Weldon Waycott and Otto H. Vahldiek—got the broad hint that another inspector, Herman Short, was odds-on favorite to get the job. Enduring angry council supporters of McGill, Welch stridently named Assistant Chief George Seber as "acting chief" amid speculation that the mayor could keep someone in an acting position for a long time without council approval. Welch grew indignant when the Houston Crime Commission's board of directors took him to task for making the change based on personal reasons. Welch said the accusations were politically inspired.[37]

McGill's list of friends was well publicized. The greatest tribute came October 25, 1964 when more than 1,400 people honored him in the Grand Ballroom of the Rice Hotel. A committee of fifty-eight citizens, chaired by Houston golf champions Jimmy Demaret and Jackie Burke, featured eight leaders who gave testimonials to McGill's time-honored devotion to honest, dedicated law enforcement. They hailed from politics, labor, religion, and state and county law enforcement, as well as city government and HPD. Mayor Welch was not invited. But *Forward Times* publisher Julius Carter termed McGill "tall in the saddle" and presented him with an elaborate western saddle "on behalf of the Negro citizens of Houston." No previous chief got such a celebrated send-off.[38]

17

HERMAN B. SHORT

As a member of the Houston City Council, Louie Welch had a vision of the type of police chief he wanted if he ever became mayor. Welch didn't want an academician or a nice guy. He preferred a squeaky clean, non-political veteran unafraid to strongly enforce laws for all Houstonians.[1]

By the mid-1960s, Welch had support from minority groups, mainly stemming from his strong stand against refusals to serve African-American customers in the City Hall cafeteria. One day in 1961, Councilman Welch became the first Houston public official to sit down with blacks in a public place to share a cup of coffee with them amid booing and catcalls of a crowd outside still favoring Jim Crow laws. Scared by hearing the N-word loudly voiced, the cafeteria's cashier called Welch when she couldn't get an answer from the mayor's telephone to ask him what to do. Not surprisingly, Welch got the vast majority of black votes in the 1961 mayoral election, but lost to incumbent Louis Cutrer.[2]

Welch solidified his instinctive feeling within the next two years that the sixties were going to be a transitional decade for blacks in America. Once elected mayor over Cutrer in 1963, he knew his police chief must be someone who enforced laws without regard to color. In October 1964, the mayor conducted ten days of interviews with six candidates for chief and picked Inspector Herman B. Short, by far the squeakiest and least political of the bunch, a man never involved in anything deemed questionable. Forty years later, Welch said, "Herman was clearly the guy for the job."[3]

Officially appointed October 6, 1964, the forty-six-year-old inspector was described as "a coolly efficient professional" with a personnel file full of commendations and hard-to-get "outstanding performance ratings." One highly respected officer told *The Houston Post*, "If the mayor wants a man to run the police department in finest form, then Short is the man. If the mayor wants a puppet, he's made the wrong choice."[4]

POLICE CHIEF HERMAN B.
SHORT, OCTOBER 7, 1964–
DECEMBER 31, 1973 (LONGEST
TENURED CHIEF IN HPD
HISTORY) (HPD ARCHIVES)

A native of Morgantown, West Virginia, Short came to Houston with his family when he was junior high-aged. He graduated from Milby High School at age sixteen, served in the U. S. Coast Guard for three years as a security officer and became a Houston police officer on December 11, 1945. When Houston swore in Short as its new chief, he only lacked fourteen months to get in the twenty years of service that made him eligible for retirement. Unlike predecessors Heard, Morrison and Shuptrine, Short lacked higher education. Yet everyone knew he was smart and had plenty of common sense.

Short was promoted to detective less than four years after he joined the force. Coincidentally, every time he was promoted to a higher rank, another significant event would soon follow. He got married one day after his promotion to detective (1949) and five years later (1954) when he was promoted to lieutenant, his son Robert was born. He soon became a captain, and on July 16, 1959, he made inspector, the forerunning title to deputy chief. Thrown into this career mix was Short's activism in the Houston Police Officers Association as a supporter of the successful movement to put officers under state civil service laws. Like other officers, Short wanted to be free of the politics that filled police jobs "without much regard for capability or the best man for the best job." As a captain, Short hob-knobbed with some of those politicians, serving on the HPOA's City Hall Committee, always one of the most influential groups in city politics.[5]

Short spent four years in Patrol before serving as detective, lieutenant and captain at various points in the Burglary and Theft and Robbery divisions. He also was burglary and theft investigations instructor at the Police Academy. When he made chief, he was serving as the inspector in charge of the technical services bureau.

Herman Short ran the police department; Louie Welch didn't. Short confirmed as much on June 22, 1976—two and a half years after retiring as chief—in an oral history interview with a Houston Public Library historian. Short said he and Welch had a clear understanding. "What he wanted was an honest, aggressive, professional police department. We had a clear understanding of how law enforcement should be conducted in Houston." That meant not compromising any part of the law or the professional standards of the department or any officer. Furthermore, the law was the same for everyone regardless of their position in life.[6]

Forty-one years after making the Short appointment, Louie Welch, officially the Mayor Emeritus of Houston, said he didn't micromanage anything and only required one policy change from Short—that HPD officers refrain from using the N-word on the police radio. They could use "blacks", "Afros" or "colored"—or be subject to suspension. There were no headlines that day but the mayor was pleased with Short's immediate response, for he had unsuccessfully made the same request of Chief Buddy McGill ten months earlier.

The chief's highest priority was to improve the conditions of a department that was undermanned and under-equipped, a "normal" condition of most law enforcement agencies. The new chief held fast to high hiring standards and was in total agreement with Welch's philosophy to avoid the acceptance of any federal funds, which would result in more federal controls.[7]

America was going through a transition period in which the fight for civil rights for black citizens would be in the news constantly. During this period, HPD consisted primarily of high school-educated white males who generally hailed from three or four Houston neighborhoods or grew up in small country towns. Many were ex-soldiers or men who grew up in the Depression and described themselves as "products of the times" when the N-word was routinely used in a segregated era. African-American Houston officers regularly heard the term used openly.[8]

Short had no racial quotas in his recruiting effort. Those officers involved in the process at the time asserted in retirement that Short tightened up the standards as chief, refusing to consider applicants with two unpaid parking tickets on their record. Bad credit also was an automatic disqualifier. Officers of any color who didn't pay their bills on time quickly got on the chief's bad side. Creditors sent him brief notes that said that "Officer so-in-so hasn't paid his bill from my store for two months and...."[9]

Welch, highly critical of HPD as a councilman, "became our champion when he became mayor," officers from the era later contended. Welch also championed annexation, seeing the city grow from 359.76 to 501.55 square miles during his ten years in office, spurring the need for more officers. Under Short's strict hiring, 1,413 new officers were added, reaching a number still far short of what the city needed.[10]

African-American leaders believed that the department had a racist attitude and never wanted to grow its woeful number of roughly 100 black officers and less than that many Hispanics. The lack of federal control no doubt worked to HPD recruiters' advantage. But Welch later said there was no conscious effort to keep blacks and Hispanics from entering the department. When the department recruited at Texas Tech, Texas A&M and the University of Texas, its recruiters were told that a black man could earn a higher salary in the private sector.[11]

Meanwhile, oil prices were strong and Houston had no problems making its budget with a low tax rate, a fact that strengthened the stand against federal funding. Welch said the city was exempt from the 1964 Civil Rights Act; in fact, by 1965, Houston was not under any federal guidelines whatsoever.[12]

Ten months after Short was named Houston's police chief, a speeding motorist raced at ninety miles an hour along an outer stretch of the Gulf Freeway when suddenly from out of nowhere a white 1963 Chrysler Newport with a hidden siren but no red lights pulled him over. A tall, stern-faced man in a well-pressed business suit emerged, flashed a police badge and told the motorist he was doing 90 in a 60.

"That's just too fast," the suit said. "I'm not going to give you a ticket, but I do want you to slow down and help us prevent accidents." The lucky speeder was skeptical and dared to ask, "What kind of officer are you, anyway?"

"I'm assigned to the chief's office," the man replied.

"But what's your job there?"

"Well," Herman Short said, "I'm the chief of police."

The speeder didn't recognize the daunting figure that arguably every crook in the Bayou City knew well by sight and his growing reputation. He spent twenty-four/seven in an intimidating, no-nonsense mode, always making clear his thoughts with economic word usage and looks that could laser through a subordinate like a finely honed knife through the fresh vegetables the chief grew in the garden on acreage on the far south side. "When he walked down the hall at the station," one veteran officer recalled, "you were scared to look up and you always looked busy. The last thing you wanted was for Herman Short to see you loafing."[13]

A feature story by Harold Scarlett of *The Houston Post* offered a fitting description of Short:

> Now 47 years old, he has the tidy build of a fast heavyweight—a shade under 6 feet, 190 pounds. He has full cheeks, a jaw like a brick, watchful brown eyes and a thin, tight mouth.
>
> He has a boxer's nose that looks slightly crushed and slightly crooked. He looks like the classic detective you can find in any big-city police station—a simple, tough, feet-on-the-desk man.
>
> But he doesn't put his feet on the desk, not nowadays anyway. And Short is not a simple man.... Some fellow officers regard him as a cool, professional, near-perfect police officer.[14]

Short knew Patrol as well as the inter-workings of Robbery, Burglary and Theft and the other investigative divisions. If he didn't know the turf where he hadn't been assigned, he had long-time friends provide candid assessments. He had only a high school education, but with the help of an adept numbers man, George Hogan, his civilian administrator, he successfully put on the table a proposal to purchase two hundred new patrol cars in 1965, a record number in history.

Short also relied on Assistant Chief George Seber's ability to keep people away from him. Seber dealt with every-day interdepartmental human conflicts and troublesome interoffice politics that bogged down the man at the top. No one could do it better. Seber had performed the task for every chief since Jack Heard. In doing so, he virtually eliminated himself from ever being considered for the chief's job.[15]

Short never called regular press conferences or sought center stage when HPD cracked a newsworthy case. He left the publicity to those who worked the case and there were an impressive number of celebrated cases processed by HPD officers, primarily in the Homicide Division. Each of them became the subjects of books, TV movies—or both.[16]

By far the most notable was chronicled in the Thomas Thompson best seller, *Blood and Money*, the intriguing account of Dr. John Hill, a prominent River Oaks plastic surgeon who allegedly killed his wife through medical neglect. Other celebrated cases that were unique to Houston were those involving "the Ice Box Murders," the city's grizzliest unsolved double homicide, and "the Houston Mass Murders," the series of torture murders of teenaged boys masterminded by a person known as "the Candy Man."[17]

Chronologically, what became euphemistically known as the Ice Box Murders was the first of these dramatic murders to happen on Short's watch. On Father's Day, June 20, 1965, Fred and Edwina Rogers were mutilated and dissected, their bodies literally crammed into their refrigerator. *The Ice Box Murders*, a 2003 book based on the case, written by Hugh Gardenier and Martha Gardenier, recapped a scene that was shocking even to jaded officers like C. A. Bullock and L. M. Barta. It was Bullock who discovered the unusual murder scene that featured not one but *two* mutilated bodies in a 1950s model "ice box".

Bullock recalled:

> We came in the kitchen and it just didn't feel right. I don't know why I looked in the refrigerator. For some reason I just opened it. The first thing I saw were hog ribs. I wondered why they were left in the refrigerator to spoil; no, maybe I said, this is a shame, someone is letting a whole bunch of good meat go to waste.

> I started to close the door, and then I looked down, and I saw her head staring up at me. I froze. Then I must have blinked. And she was still there when I looked again. I just slammed the door shut and held it closed for a couple of seconds.

> It could have been a minute that I stood there, and just tried to get my breath. I couldn't believe it. Barta was in the next room and I yelled to him. He came and looked, and he didn't believe it either. Then we both went out the front door pretty fast.[18]

Police Chief Herman Short, center, poses at the graduation of the HPD Bomb Squad on February 26, 1965. Mayor Louie Welch chose Short as a police chief who was a squeaky clean, non-political veteran unafraid to strongly enforce laws for all Houstonians. That's Short's picture on the wall in the classroom. He served nine and a half years, the longest-tenured HPD chief in history. (HPD Archives)

All blood was drained from the bodies and the internal organs removed. The prime suspect was the couple's son, Charles Frederick Rogers, a forty-three-year-old Rice University-educated engineer known to be somewhat of a hermit. HPD issued an all-points bulletin to pick up Rogers. However, he has not been seen since weeks before the macabre discovering.

Although a state district court in Harris County declared Charles Rogers deceased for the purpose of settling the family estate, homicide detectives kept the criminal case open. Some speculated that the CIA hired Rogers to assassinate President John F. Kennedy, but others, such as authors Gardenier, have shot holes in this theory. Lieutenant Breck Porter coordinated the overall homicide investigation, which was later undertaken by Lieutenant Chester Massey, coincidentally born on the same day in 1924 as the infamous suspect.[19] Rogers had an airplane pilot's license and had previously worked in Alaska and Canada. Massey's investigation "turned up with zero."

Dr. Hill was the son-in-law of Ash Robinson, a hardened oil-rich million-aire who doted on his only daughter, Joan, a noted horsewoman. In 1969, Joan Robinson Hill was an apparently healthy thirty-eight-year-old mother of one son, Robert, when she suddenly got seriously ill and died a short time after her husband had her admitted to a suburban hospital. Robinson, later portrayed by Andy Griffith in *Murder in Texas*, a TV mini-series, pressured Harris County prosecutors and a grand jury to indict Hill on the extremely rare charge of murder by neglect. A state district judge later declared a mis-trial in the case when Hill's second wife said from the witness stand that her doctor husband told her he used an infectious syringe to kill Joan Hill.[20]

The plastic surgeon was never tried again. Instead, Robinson took the situation into his own hands, based on the resulting HPD Homicide inves-tigation. Testimony in one criminal and two civil cases tried throughout the 1970s showed that Robinson hired a hit man through a well-known madam. Hill was fatally wounded on September 24, 1972, inside his River Oaks man-sion. Before Homicide detectives Jerry Carpenter and Joe Gamino could nail down the case, the hit man involved, Bobby Wayne Vandiver, was gunned down by police in another Texas city. The madam, Lilla Paulus, received a thirty-five-year sentence for arranging the shooting, and Marcia McKittrick, a long-time prostitute who drove the getaway car, received only a ten-year term when she testified against Paulus and Robinson. Robinson died in 1985, never criminally charged.[21]

The department endured sharp criticism in 1973 with the strange revela-tion of a series of murders of missing boys, aged nine to twenty-one. In all, twenty-seven boys fell victim to "the Candy Man," the nickname given to Dean Corll, a thirty-three-year-old electrician living in the Heights section. Corll got the moniker when he worked with his mother in the candy business and supplied neighborhood youngsters with free samples.[22]

During this tumultuous era of anti-war demonstrations, free love and rampant use of illegal drugs, HPD received an increasing number of miss-ing person reports, viewing most of them as probable runaways. Even the screaming pleas of anxious parents to newspaper and television reporters failed to turn up the violent practices of Corll and two willing teenaged ac-complices, David Owen Brooks and Elmer Wayne Henley, until Henley shot and killed Corll on August 8, 1973.

The details of subsequent events were detailed in Jack Olsen's true crime book, *The Man with the Candy: The Story of the Houston Mass Murders*. The first big scene in the seemingly endless drama unfurled when Channel 2

An unidentified photographer took this photo of President John F. Kennedy on November 21, 1963, the day before he was assassinated in Dallas, 240 miles to the north. The HPD solo motorcycle officers were, left to right, Lynn Maughmer, Dub Nickerson, Terrel Tissue, R. B. Sanford, Sgt. J. D. Black and Roland English. The last officer Kennedy spoke to before boarding Air Force One that day was Pinky Wiggins. "Thank you for protecting me," Kennedy told Wiggins. (Jim Kelley Family)

police reporter Jack Cato allowed Henley to use a car telephone, which was very unique for these earlier times. "Mama, I've killed Dean," the young suspect spoke into the phone as the camera rolled, and Cato had a police story played on every newscast in America. Henley proceeded to detail evidence of what Olsen called a bizarre and brutal story of torture, rape and murder. Two families each lost two sons to Corll's torture murders.[23]

Corll paid Henley $200 "per head" to lure young boys to his house where they could get free alcohol and drugs before Corll forced them into a bedroom designed for torture and murder. Henley subsequently led police to the burial locations of twenty-seven boys, most in Corll's rented Southwest

Houston boatshed. The victims had been sodomized and shot or strangled to death.

Brooks was found guilty of one murder and sentenced to life in prison, while Henley was convicted of six of the murders and sentenced to six ninety-nine-year-terms. His slaying of Corll was considered self-defense.

In November 2008, the Harris County Medical Examiner used new technology to identify yet another Corll victim after going thirty-seven years unable to identify the skeletal remains of fifteen-year-old Randell Lee Harvey. Young Harvey disappeared before he reached home after working at a gas station in the Heights.

Welch and Short regularly discussed the racial protests in Houston and the rest of the nation. Within Short's first year as chief, rioting had taken place in other cities, most notably in the Watts section of Los Angeles. The mayor and the chief believed that Houston's strongest approach was to enforce the laws equally across the board. This meant "moving in" on demonstrators with a potential for violence and making the arrests needed to protect lives and property.[24]

Short reflected on these very trying times in Houston and across America when police almost always incurred the wrath of the black community, especially its activists. Accusations of racism by organizations like the Harris County Council of Organizations didn't surprise Short, who later recalled: "They protested a number of things. They had a lot of demands. With a national movement, there was no end to the demands, the majority of them unrealistic. So the protests were pretty constant. They protested everything—the way the colleges were run, who occupied the positions of authority in colleges and grade schools and everything was being protested just for the sake of being protested, it seemed. I don't think it had any noticeable effect on the officers."[25]

But minorities were afraid of Short's officers. In the sixties, minority suspects began to be more strident in their allegations of police brutality—another condition that followed a national trend. Short handled brutality complaints in business-like fashion, investigating every complaint, asserting his belief that a police department "doesn't leave all its customers as satisfied customers."[26]

Everybody in the department knew Short to be a tough taskmaster and a man of few words. "He saw me in the hall and complimented me and I was so thrilled," said Bobby Adams, a detective who would later serve as Homicide captain. "He was not known for that. It pumped me up that day. I was elated that he even knew who in the hell I was. Normally, in an elevator, it might be just you and him and he wouldn't even speak. I think he was just tough. That was the times and he abided by the feelings of the general community at the time. I have no reason to believe he was a racist. I think he did what he thought was correct for the times. I just don't recall racism under the rank and file. The N-word was used commonly in the early fifties but not in the seventies."[27]

Welch said Chief Short handled minority community problems very well in the *first three years* of his tenure but lacked sensitivity later on. "It was not his problem that we didn't hire blacks," Welch said, "we were just in a period of time when it was difficult to hire them. Blacks didn't want to be policemen. It was a social stigma."[28]

The question of whether Short was a racist chief insensitive toward minorities will go on for years. It didn't help that he was friends with 1968 American Independent Party presidential candidate George Wallace, the former Alabama governor known for his strong segregation stands. Wallace even publicly expressed a desire to have Short as his vice presidential candidate.[29] Short always discouraged such talk.

Those officers who disliked Short quickly learned to respect the chief whose demeanor was polite, somewhat distant, cool and computer-like. One characteristic always stood out as Short's strong suit—he was consistent. When he voiced a policy or issued an order, he stood by it. If he had to repeat it, it was always the same.

Short handled every individual disciplinary action the only way he knew how—man-to-man. He didn't show favoritism, either. A notable example happened when a captain, who had been heavily drinking, was driving near Knapp Chevrolet several blocks from police headquarters and collided with a number of cars on Knapp's lot, fortunately not injuring anyone. Not only was the captain Short's friend, he also was very highly respected within HPD. Short indefinitely suspended him and finally agreed to a two-rank bust that made the captain a detective. Later, this individual overcame his drinking problem and went back up the ranks to lieutenant.[30]

Morale picked up when Short became chief. Retired Deputy Chief Floyd Daigle said, "He was respected because he didn't let the politicians run the police department. If he got it in for you, then he didn't forget and he wouldn't do anything for you. If you were just the run-of-the-mill officer and detective, he was right down the line."[31]

On one occasion Short didn't care for the person who finished No. 1 on the captain's list when there were three openings. Daigle was No. 2 on the

The HPD Honor Guard presents the colors at all memorial services for current and
retired officers. This photo was taken at the September 2006 memorial service for
Senior Police Officer Rodney Johnson, who was shot seven times and killed after taking
an illegal immigrant into custody during a traffic stop. (Mary Pyland Photography)

peg. Three weeks before the list expired and the testing process started over,
the No. 1 and No. 3 on the list persuaded him to meet with Short.

The two other men mentioned to Short that they had talked to a lawyer.
"If you had slapped Herman Short in the face, you couldn't have pissed him
off more," Daigle said. "He got on his phone and called Civil Service. He said,
'Kill those three positions,' which were the captains' positions."[32]

Short didn't undertake any major Command Staff shakeup nor did he
implement any apparent change in the enforcement of gambling laws after
Buddy McGill was fired and demoted. He undertook an objective approach.
He shifted his three inspectors, sending McGill to the traffic bureau, Weldon

Waycott to the radio patrol bureau and C. D. Taylor to the bureau of technical services. Public relations was not Short's strong suit, although he appeared before the representatives of twenty-five black groups, or "Negro organizations," almost immediately after Welch announced his appointment.[33]

The Honor Guard[34]

The Houston Police Department established the first police honor guard in the State of Texas in October 1972, opened to all uniformed officers on a voluntary basis. The Houston Police Honor Guard initially consisted of nineteen police officers under the supervision of Inspector Leroy Mouser and Sergeant Bennie M. Jordy. The first director was Officer James A. Shirley.

Organized under the procedures of military design, its members had to be neat in appearance and conduct themselves according to strict rules and regulations that included regular practice sessions. The Honor Guard's primary functions were to pay the proper respects toward officers killed in the line of duty or who suffered a fatal illness or accidental death. The guard also marched in downtown parades and some outside the city in which it won first place marching awards.

The original twenty Honor Guard members were James A. Shirley (commander), H. V. Hernandez, Harold Smith, Wilbur Robertson, Roy A. Henley, Douglas M. Hudson, Matt Perales, Ruben Garza, Joe Lanza, Bobby D. Hamaker, W. J. Schultea, Gerald A. Anderson, Cooper C. Gilbert, David E. Freytag, Howard Martin, V. A. Rodriguez, D. V. Muskiet Sr., R. L. Johnson, R. W. Zipp and W. G. Gower.

Officer Shirley was commander for seven years until his retirement in January 1979, followed by Officer Douglas M. Hudson. The department reorganized the Honor Guard in April 1979, and it became an appointed group instead of consisting of volunteers. When an ensuing morale problem developed, Deputy Chief B. M. Finch was appointed to supervise the operation, and Hudson returned to reorganize the guard and return it to a voluntary group consisting of twelve members.

In April 1980, Deputy Chief Lester Wunsche took over the direction of the guard and became instrumental in assisting Hudson to include officers from throughout the various divisions. Besides Chief Wunsche and Lieutenant A. J. Januhowski, the Honor Guard personnel consisted of Ceremonies Officer Douglas M. Hudson, two sergeants, eighteen regular members and six alternates.

By 2011, the Houston Police Honor Guard, under the strong leadership of Officer David E. Freytag, acted as the official representatives of the HPD in conducting funeral services for deceased present and retired Houston officers and served as HPD's representatives in parades, special department functions and at funerals for out-of-town officers and civic functions as requested. The Honor Guard provides casket guards at all Houston police officer funerals and a twenty-one-gun salute and sounding of "Taps" for officers killed in the line of duty. Throughout the southern region of Texas, the guard has been requested to conduct funeral services for officers from other police departments who have no honor guard.

Short's early effort at community relations wasn't impressive, a record that came to haunt him as civil unrest grew and the lack of communications with minority groups made his life more complicated. One of the early advocates of opening doors to the minority community was a well-educated lieutenant named Harry Caldwell. Short and Caldwell had polar opposite approaches. Short hated public speaking; Caldwell wrote Short's speeches, while always urging the chief to establish better communication lines.[35]

At Caldwell's insistence, Short named him head of the first-ever Community Relations Division—five men in a little office off the Property Room. Caldwell spent a great deal of his time in the African-American community, which was becoming angrier by the day due to continued enforcement of Jim Crow laws. Many blacks like Albert Blair returned from fighting in World War II only to learn that the color of your skin was a deterrent to being treated like everybody else. Blair never forgot his police academy days when the sergeant in charge called him and the other black in the class aside for an important message: they could not eat in the police cafeteria, even though it was a public building, leased to the department for police personnel. Instead, Blair and fellow black cadets would drink their coffee in the kitchen.[36]

Many American police departments in the mid-1960s still had ideas that spilled over from the 1930s. If a black man used something besides the "Colored Only" water fountain, the law required police to arrest him. Continued enforcement of Jim Crow laws was part of Short's policies, creating the perception that police were racists. "He never was able to break down this concept," Caldwell later said. "Unfortunately, we had persons in the department that were. Herman was a big friend of George Wallace. That didn't help the department's image much in the black community. We did a poor job of establishing meaningful relationships there."[37]

The progress was slow and often unnoticed. Short integrated the police cafeteria without anybody telling him he had to. He seldom cracked a smile and was known to be very nice and business-like. Many around 61 Riesner noticed that he rarely spoke to people riding the elevator. He was exceptional in his management skills—decisive, principled and consistent. Short would "make scenes" to offer help or make sure investigators had everything they needed to make their case. He drove himself to work, one of the few Houston chiefs not to use a commissioned officer or sergeant as a chauffeur. His practice of occasionally cruising the city at night, particularly during his early years as chief, was probably his only unorthodox characteristic.[38]

Never one to take a long lunch, Short usually remained at his desk, the door closed and a sandwich readily available. After lunch he read the newspaper, especially the comics. When John Wayne was in town for the 1968 release of the film, *Hellfighters*, a biographic film of the life of Houston oil field firefighter Red Adair, "Duke" dropped by 61 Riesner to visit the chief. The two hit it off well, laughing and talking about the good guys winning. Wayne had left his toupee at the hotel and out of respect for his image, Short didn't insist on a picture.[39]

He did allow the cameras the day the stars of the television police hit, *Adam 12*, paid him a visit on their national tour of police departments. Actors Kevin McCord and Martin Milner had some fun. Some officers tell the story that the rank-and-file put them up to it, with sources saying that the actors were serious in their conversation with Short. "Chief," one of them asked, "why do you insist that your officers always wear their caps? They don't do that in LAPD—or anywhere else we've been."[40]

Short allegedly rescinded the requirement in a memo the day after the two TV stars left town. This anecdote was just one in a series of accounts about

Louie Welch was mayor in 1970 when HPD got its first helicopters. Mayor Pro Tem Johnny Goyen and Police Chief Herman Short look on as Mayor Welch pins the "wings" on HPD's first helicopter crew. (Louie Welch Family/Homer Harris Photo)

the cap-wearing requirement that was high on Harry Caldwell's regulation list when he became chief in the late 1970s. Caldwell liked to catch hatless officers on traffic stops and used his hat regulation as an intimidation technique. It may have actually been worse in Short's time since officers were required to wear the caps and ties at a time when patrol cars had no air conditioning.

Short's intimidation in another area became an even sorer subject with the men in blue—contributions to the annual United Way Fund. This requirement was in effect until the HPOA complained to Police Chief Pappy Bond in 1976. A 1960s patrol officer said, "Our supervisor called us in and asked if we liked our days off and wanted to continue with our partners. We were asked, 'You like riding with your partner?' or 'You like being off on Friday and Saturday nights?'" HPD often had 100 percent United Way participation—on paper, anyway.

Perhaps nothing showed the human side of Short more than the day in 1970 when he lost his first wife, Nettie Lucille Short, when she was struck and killed by a pickup truck driven by an allegedly drunken driver. Friends described Mrs. Short as being as ebullient as her husband was reserved. She was in the process of taking carrots fresh from the couple's garden to a neighbor across the street. The driver was later cleared of the charges. The chief, married twenty years, changed significantly after the tragedy, although he later married a second time.[41]

Upon retirement, he entered the real estate business under the tutelage of Houston oil multimillionaire R. E. "Bob" Smith and for a time was a partner with conservative political activist Clymer Wright, who in the 1990s led the citywide vote for term limits for city offices. Wright said Short made a fortune in real estate in the years after he was chief. "After his wife was killed," another insider recalled, "he lost interest. It just took everything out of him." He also developed a fondness for the bottle.[42]

Descriptions of Short's later retirement years were a far cry from the legends that developed around him. There was one legend in particular. Depending on the source, the actual Houston representative in the scenario could have been Harris County Sheriff C. V. "Buster" Kern, quite a crime fighter in his day at HPD before seeking the elective office in which he served twenty-four years. The most common recollections have Short meeting a Mafia leader at Hobby Airport to tell him in terse terms that "You and your kind are not welcome in Houston. I want you on the next plane back to New Orleans." The location of the exact round-trip destination might have been New Orleans, Chicago, Las Vegas or New York. The end of the story was always the same: Herman Short succeeded in closing Houston's doors to organized crime.

Short lived his final years out of the public eye. He died of a heart attack on December 28, 1989.[43]

18

CONFLICT AT TEXAS SOUTHERN

Houston's leadership kept violence and damage to neighborhoods and businesses to a minimum when compared to the Watts section of Los Angeles, Detroit and other scenes of rioting during the violent days of the Civil Rights movement. Accounts of what became known as "the TSU Riot" vary in their judgment of HPD and the city administration under Mayor Louie Welch. The number of persons arrested, wounded or killed never approached the toll of other riot-torn cities. Instead, Houston held a rare distinction: More white people than blacks met death in the violence. The only individual to die was a white Houston officer with hardly a month's experience.

A department report detailing the events leading up to the "riot" itself said the groundwork was laid when the TSU Friends of the Student Nonviolent Coordinating Committee formed in October 1966. A "Snick" (SNCC) speaker, James Forman, addressed the subject of "Black Power—A New Religion?" that month, setting the stage for picketers of a campus speech by Mayor Welch on December 13, 1966. Further intervention by members of the W. E. B. DuBois Club—identified by FBI Director J. Edgar Hoover as an alleged Communist front organization—spawned increased discontent and led to demonstrations in March and April 1967.[1] TSU students boycotted classes and left the campus cafeteria in shambles. Wheeler Street, the major campus thoroughfare, enabled gangs to harass motorists, throw rocks at cars and quickly flee.

In May 1967, black leaders from outside generated an atmosphere of racial unrest, particularly around the campus of the predominately African-American, state-supported school in Third Ward. Protesters demonstrated on May 15 and 16 on campus, at the Holmes Road city landfill over a long-promised incinerator, and at Northwood Junior High School on Homestead Road over false rumors of an African-American juvenile being shot by a white man.

On Tuesday, May 16, 1967, Criminal Intelligence Officers R. G. "Bobby" Blaylock and James O. "Bo" Norris were among many officers assigned to monitor the TSU demonstrations. Police arrested twenty-nine people for illegally demonstrating at the Holmes Road site. In a related development, Al Blair and Charles Howard—both long-standing and well-respected African-American officers—reported that potential rioters were bringing large amounts of weapons onto the TSU campus, particularly to one of the men's dormitories. Intelligence also revealed that there were SNCC members agitating students on campus. Blaylock and the other three officers used marked and unmarked police units to monitor these activities.[2]

At about 10:30 p.m. on May 16, an individual identified as Charles Freeman began stirring up a large crowd of students near the Student Activities Building in the center of the campus. The next issue of *Time* magazine, reporting that the rumor was blatantly untrue, said, "About fifty students were gathered in front of the student union when a rumor went through the crowd that a policeman had shot a six-year-old Negro child that day. Someone heaved a watermelon at a police cruiser, and the crowd dispersed to shout the shooting rumor through the campus. It was too late to tell them that the six-year-old was actually a white child wounded by a white boy who was target-shooting."[3]

When officers arrested the individual who tossed the watermelon, they found that he was carrying a pistol. Leaders identified as Charles Freeman, Floyd Henry Nichols, Trazawell Franklin and John Parker continued to agitate the crowd over the alleged shooting. The violence escalated, with some of the students feeling brave enough after dark to shoot at the officers from the windows in the nearby men's dormitory. One of the shots struck Blaylock in the left buttock. Blaylock wasn't seriously hurt and later said, "They never took the bullet out."[4]

Chief Herman Short stationed another several hundred officers around the campus. He and Mayor Welch worked with the residential and business property owners in the area, setting up a plan designed to confine any demonstration and violent outbreak to the campus and not the surrounding neighborhoods. African-American leaders included the Reverend William Lawson, pastor of the Wheeler Avenue Baptist Church and director of the Baptist Student Union on the TSU campus. Accounts from both sides of the issue, forty years after the fact reflect the general lack of communications between Houston blacks and whites of this era.[5]

Earlier, Lawson and two other representatives of campus religious organizations heard about the Holmes Road conflict and went to the scene to maintain peace. The two hundred protesters never reached their destination, having been arrested, placed in paddy wagons and jailed on trespassing charges. Lawson was incarcerated when the TSU situation heated up. Welch ordered his release and saw that he was brought back to campus. Lawson said that he planned to talk to the students but never got to the dorm before shots broke out. The mayor later said that Lawson told Short he thought that the students meant business and that force was needed to restore peace. Lawson steadfastly disagreed with this recollection and always believed the police overreacted.[6]

At 2:20 a.m. on May 17, a group of officers neared the northwest corner of the University Center, lined up along a wall awaiting directions from supervisors. Chief Short directed officers to fire only when fired upon and only above the building or directly at a known source of the gunfire. The rioters in the dormitory were virtual snipers from their roosts above the officers. Reporters Charley Schneider of *The Houston Post* and Nick Gearhardt of KHOU-TV (Channel 11), were with this group of officers. Schneider said there were two officers and a TV newsman in front of him. He said that Officer Louis Kuba was directly behind him with his hand on Schneider's shoulder.[7]

Heavy fire broke out from the dorm. Suddenly, Schneider felt Kuba's hand go limp. Turning, he saw the officer slump backward into Gearhardt's outstretched arms, an expressionless look on his face and blood pouring from his forehead. "There was no riot at TSU. It was war," Schneider reported. An ambulance rushed Kuba to Ben Taub General Hospital, where doctors pronounced him dead at 8:38 a.m. from a bullet wound above his right eye. Kuba was a quiet, easy-going, even-tempered individual only thirty-four days out of HPD Police Cadet Class No. 34. He was only twenty-five years old and the only fatality of the confrontation. One student suffered wounds but recovered and another officer was wounded.

The shooting stopped and officers arrested 489 people. HPD was assisted by the Harris County Sheriff's Department, the District Attorney's Office and the Texas Department of Public Safety. The state charged Douglas Waller, Charles Freeman, Floyd Nichols, Trazawell Franklin and John Parker with inciting a riot and murder. Vice Officer Allen Dale Dugger received a gaping secondary bullet wound to his face, which required over three hundred stitches in three layers. He recovered. One young officer went into hysteria and was treated for shock.

Louis Kuba was one of many officers assigned to what became known as the Texas Southern University Riot on May 17, 1967. HPD officers sealed off the campus when sniper fire from dormitories held about 200 officers at bay for 40 minutes. Officer Kuba was struck in the head by a high-caliber slug and was pronounced dead a short time later. Houston holds the distinction of having the only U. S. riot in which more whites were killed than African Americans. The *only* person killed was Officer Kuba, who was only 34 days out of the academy at the time of his line of duty death. (Nelson Zoch)

In retrospect, African-American leaders such as Bill Lawson called the action an act of "police terrorism" that took place when students were preparing for final exams. "Then somebody discovered Kuba was killed by friendly fire," Lawson said.[8]

From a prosecutorial position, the cases against the alleged riot leaders were difficult to prove. Even though the state felt the five suspects incited the students to riot, there was no testimony that put guns in their hands or showed that they were even on campus when the fatal shot was fired. Firearms analysis of the slug indicated that it was a secondary strike, meaning that it probably ricocheted off something prior to striking Kuba. Thus, the slug was not in very good shape for any positive matching to a particular weapon. To make investigative matters even more problematic, it was not the caliber of any of the weapons recovered from students. Another HPD officer who later rose in the ranks was a few feet away from Kuba thought it was friendly fire. Kuba was shot between the eyes. The shot had to come from somewhere sideways.[9]

Harris County District Attorney Carol Vance got a change of venue to Victoria, ninety miles southwest of Houston, because of excessive publicity.

Vance and his staff were in uncharted waters since it was difficult to prove that the inciting-to-riot charge led to Kuba's murder. The district judge in Victoria refused to allow the jury to consider the state's theory that Charles Freeman was guilty of the assault because he engaged in a riot. Vance believed the state lost when it was not possible to get the riot statute considered as part of the evidence. He officially moved to dismiss the charges against the five defendants in November 1970.

Time reported that Houston police poured more than 3,000 rounds of shotgun and carbine fire into the building. It quoted one officer as saying, "It looked like the Alamo." The national magazine took a negative slant on the story, only quoting SNCC leader F. D. Kirkpatrick as saying "hate" caused the riot—hatred of the school administration, police, Whitey, and every other target of a student's ire on the eve of final exams, which ultimately were held on schedule. *Time* quoted no Houston official. In hindsight, the news was good. Houston got only three paragraphs of coverage, compared to elaborate cover stories about destructive race-related riots in other cities.[10]

Houston survived the fiery Civil Rights period of history without other demonstrations that resulted in higher rates of death and destruction. This record came when the black community often portrayed Herman Short as a "racist" chief, an image that influenced the next three mayoral elections. Louie Welch believed that the wrong combination of fact and fiction caused the negative perception.

Welch's vote totals in the black communities skyrocketed to 94 percent in 1965 and 96 percent in 1967. He was the first mayor to have a well-known African-American on his full-time staff. Al Henry was an administrative assistant whose job included a study of racial attitudes in the city. Henry was part of the division headed by Blair Justice and termed "the human relations department for civil matters." Justice's staff included future Fire Chief and long-time Fire Marshal Eddie Corral and black undercover officers Albert Blair and Charles Howard.[11]

The incident offered a lesson in Houston's race-related politics that lasted more than forty years. They city's black community was spread out and not confined to one neighborhood or ghetto. African-American home ownership represented a higher percentage of the population when compared to other urban cities. "If you own your own home, you're less likely to burn it down to make a point," John Whitmire, a Texas state senator, said in his personal analysis. "We were lucky by geography and had some good leadership."[12]

Lawson never believed the violence had anything to do with Short and credited black leaders with working with the white establishment to thwart acts of violence. Mack Hannah of Standard Savings and Loan and a large insurance company; Hobard Taylor, who owned two or three cab companies; and the Reverend L. H. Simpson, pastor of Pleasant Hill Baptist Church were leaders in these efforts. The Houston Chamber of Commerce leaders included Lawson and the three others in meetings at the Rice Hotel and talked to business leaders about various business issues and community attitudes. They got the message that the city had a thriving economy perceived to be fragile enough that it couldn't stand any blemish from community activism when the city had a thriving port operation and a space center that was the focus of national attention.

The city weathered the latter stages of the Jim Crow storm quietly and effectively. The "Colored Only" restroom signs were discreetly removed from facilities at the courthouse by long-time Tax Assessor-Collector Carl Smith and at City Hall by aides to Mayor Roy Hofheinz. Signs on buses were removed without publicity in 1964. By habit, black people still sat at the back of the bus. Leaders like Lawson believed that Houston's quiet desegregation was a result of the business community having things under control and wanting to keep the economy strong and secure.[13]

Yet the aftermath of desegregation focused on the get-tough policies of Chief Short, detracting from Welch's efforts to thwart the violent attitudes in the wards and zeroing in on the chief of police. Young black activists like future Houston City Attorney Gene Locke and future Congressmen Mickey Leland and Craig Washington developed their strong impressions of Short from stories their elders related to them. Locke served in the administration of Mayor Bob Lanier. Older African-Americans communicated one impression to the future city attorney in his younger years: Houston is a place where you stay in your place. Unless you had reason to be in a predominately white neighborhood, you stayed out and you conducted yourself in a certain way with officers.[14]

There weren't very many African-Americans on the police force—only three or four had high visibility in the black community. Black leaders knew the officers were only allowed to patrol in African-American neighborhoods, where police were held in disdain because they kept you in place, prone

Houston Dispersion

While he served as a high-ranking staff associate to Mayor Louie Welch in the late 1960s, Dr. Blair Justice compiled an exhaustive research project that led to conclusions about "the SEAD Factors of Unrest" in Houston. In the defining chapter of his book, *Violence in the City*, Justice, a one-time distinguished journalist with the *Fort Worth Star-Telegram* and *The Houston Post*, developed SEAD as acronym for the four key factors in his analysis: Spotlight. Expectations. Attitudes. Dispersion.

Justice cited the latter factor, dispersion, as the primary reason why a major violent outbreak never happened in Houston during the turbulent Civil Rights era of the 1960s and 1970s. Before Justice reached his conclusions about dispersion, leaders at City Hall and black communities didn't realize that "the biggest part of the black community is dispersion. They are not together."

Houston African-Americans experienced a unique geographic condition: they lived in several dozen different sections; Houston was—and remained—the largest city in America without zoning. A neighborhood like Acres Homes could exist with its own mom-and-pop storefronts and establish its own set of amenities and businesses, education practices and community traditions.

Justice's findings ran 180 degrees from conditions in such racially troubled areas as Watts in Los Angeles. "We went to a number of riots in the United States, Watts included," Justice said. "They (the people) are stacked on top of each other out there." Not so in Houston, where the 1960s era map identified twenty-seven different sections of the city with significant black populations. Los Angeles was thinly dispersed and prone to uncomfortably hot summer conditions more apt to spawn violence-oriented unrest. "You cannot go to any part of Houston and expect one big demonstration because a lot of people have their own homes now, even in 'the Bottom' (section of Fifth Ward)," Justice said upon years of reflection. "Most of those people in Acres Homes and Sunnyside own their own homes."

Justice could not apply his findings in Houston to the African-American neighborhoods in other American cities because of dispersal. Black communities in many other large cities lacked the number of black-owned businesses Houston had in each of its black neighborhoods. The interests of Third Ward activists didn't jibe with the concerns of their Acres Home counterparts. Thus, the possibility of a mammoth city-wide riot was highly unlikely.

As for the three other "SEAD factors," he found that "Spot-light" and "Expectation" were low. Not since the Camp Logan Riot of 1917 had there been a "spotlight" on Houston as a scene of racial violence. The Expectation factor was low. Houston blacks had very low expectations in terms of better housing, education and economic opportunity. "Attitude"—the "A" in the SEAD analysis—interrelated with Spotlight, Expectation and certainly with Dispersion.

The Justice study showed that the TSU ordeal aroused attitudes in blacks all over the city like never before. After the violence, his polling showed dramatic increases in the number of blacks that felt police were treating them unfairly and that only five percent felt the police chief was doing a good job. Houston's African-American leaders made Herman Short a campaign issue in the four elections following the TSU Riot, a key factor in the 1973 election of Fred Hofheinz as mayor.[15]

toward brutality. There was equal disregard for African-American police officers because they had too little authority.

Blacks felt Short was intimidating, arrogant and intolerant of public protests despite the understanding by politicians, businessmen and minority leaders that changes were taking place across the country. From behind the scenes, these leaders tried to diffuse any escalation of confrontation in Houston. Some officers made sure Civil Rights protesters were victimized while others were quietly helpful in making sure that peaceful demonstrations didn't get out of hand. Unlike the more diverse Houston police force of the late 20th century and beyond, HPD in the sixties was not well-trained or equipped to handle a civil disturbance of the magnitude of TSU.[16] Officers used riot helmets borrowed from other policing agencies, had no bullet-

When U. S. Supreme Court Justice Thurgood Marshall visited Houston in the late 1960s, he was guarded and driven to activities by HPD's Charles "Sideburn" Howard, left, and Al Blair. Blair and Howard were long-time members of the Criminal Intelligence Division. They were part of the intelligence-gathering team that learned that a growing number of TSU students were purchasing guns in the days prior to the TSU Riot. (Al Blair)

proof vests and were armed with their own shotguns or carbines. Many of them used their personal deer rifles. Their understanding of the right to protest in the streets was fuzzy, at best, just like it was in police departments in other parts of the country.[17]

Veteran officers under Chief Short continued to contend long after their retirements that the chief's law enforcement philosophy was very clear to each one of them—if a citizen were committing a law violation or a crime, you put them in jail. It made no difference if they were white or black. In the 1960s, a distinctly high number of service calls came from locations in the Third, Fourth and Fifth wards or from the predominately black Acres Homes section or the public housing projects known as Cuney Homes or Allen Parkway Village.

Earlier in the spring of 1967, protesters threw rocks and glass bottles at automobiles that passed through the campus on Wheeler Avenue, TSU's major east-west thoroughfare. Later in the 1970s, school officials closed Wheeler in order to combat drug deals made easier by the easy access to big crowds of students. Neither school officials nor police resorted to street closings or traffic diversions as ways of thwarting the potentially violent activities of the late-1960s.

Mayor Welch believed the Bayou City was fortunate to have community leaders who worked with him and Blair Justice to take steps to thwart violent conduct before it took seed and sprouted. In the subsequent months the progress Welch made to improve conditions in the African-American community and its relationship with City Hall went out the window. The good communications developed during the "riot" failed to last. Although both Welch and Lawson agreed in later years that it was fortunate that only one person was killed, Welch adhered to his belief that Lawson discreetly suggested that given the students' violent attitude, police had no choice but to go in shooting.

Although not stated in any official report on the riot, many at the scene speculated that friendly fire resulted in the death of Officer Louis Kuba. In *Violence in the City*, Blair Justice wrote, "It was never established where the bullet came from that killed Kuba."[18]

Officers knocked out all nearby outside light globes so they would be harder to spot from the upper stories of the dormitory. Some of those present described it as "like a war zone." Kuba was hit in the middle of the forehead and died instantly. Police had pistols and shotguns and felt the students "wanted to get out of there." Black women in a safety zone cursed the officers. Officers at the scene later recalled that they were so inexperienced in situations like this one that some of them were wearing white shirts, making them easy targets in the dark.[19]

Once the smoke cleared and officers arrested the students and took them downtown in buses, Welch asked that Lawson meet him in Chief Short's office as soon as possible for a private debriefing. But Lawson never openly stated that the police had no alternative but to go in after the students. Welch always believed Lawson felt he would "lose his constituency" if he did so.[20]

The mayor attributed this attitude as pivotal in the community's feelings toward his administration and Herman Short. He was angered but never risked a public confrontation. Henceforth, his relationship with Lawson was always cold.[21]

Instead of appreciating the lack of a huge casualty list, while lamenting the death of a rookie police officer, black leaders undertook a steady flow of criticism of Short and his officers. Cries of racism and brutality became common, obscuring the fact that Houston was the only American city experiencing a one-fatality race "riot".

By nature Short was not a defensive person. He claimed to enforce the law for all Houstonians and maybe he did, in effect. Yet his "negatives" didn't help himself, the department, Mayor Welch or Houston in general.

Instead of Welch earning a legacy for being a strident leader helping African-American citizens, he got more opposition than ever before. It came in the form of an African-American opponent in the 1969 mayoral election, state Representative Curtis Graves, an individual Welch described as running "the most blatantly racial campaign that has been run in Houston, before or since."[22]

Black leaders believed Short failed to show any remorse for the actions of his officers and appeared to justify future use of violence if he thought it necessary. They wanted to see more concern for putting so many innocent people in harm's way. Improved officer training for handling demonstrations didn't take place until Lee Brown became police chief fifteen years after the TSU conflict.

The Carl Hampton Shooting

The second major race-related police event took place on July 26, 1970, on Dowling Street in the Third Ward, the night Carl Hampton, a leader of Peoples Party II—a local affiliate of the Black Panther Party—was shot and killed in an armed confrontation with Houston officers.

Police with shotguns and bayonets lined up on Elgin and Dowling and dispersed a peaceful crowd. Most of the officers stood to the side. A black leader at the scene recalled that some officers used the N-word and "the Billy stick," while others were firm but courteous.

Officer Bobby Blaylock—the man shot in the butt during the TSU Riot—also fired the bullets that killed Carl Hampton about one year later. Blaylock said what many HPD officers believed about the Civil Rights Era in Houston: "If we had not had Herman Short as a chief during the time of TSU and Carl Hampton, if we had had a weak chief, all hell would have broken loose in the town. It would have been like Los Angeles and Detroit. It also took a strong mayor. We had problems like those other cities, but violence wasn't tolerated. We jumped on it quick. Every time something stirred up, we jumped on it quick and that put an end to it."[23]

19

THE SUCCESSOR

The man succeeding the legendary Herman Short as police chief of Houston found it impossible to fill the larger-than-life shoes. One particularly clever HPD soldier said, "You could have chosen Dick Tracy and it wouldn't have worked."[1]

"The man Short elected mayor" picked a flawed successor ill-prepared for the big job on the third floor of 61 Riesner. Mayor Fred Hofheinz was a social liberal whose friends in the department were a few reliable old hands he got to know when his father Roy Hofheinz served two years as mayor in 1954 and 1955 between Oscar Holcombe terms. The second Mayor Hofheinz sincerely wanted to see positive changes in HPD, getting out of the Short school of hiring and moving away from the tough-country-boy approach to policing the growing minority community.

To find the person he thought could create these changes, Hofheinz selected three men to screen any candidate *they* thought would fit the profile in philosophy and temperament. They were retired Inspectors Buddy McGill and C. D. Taylor and current HPD Lieutenant Joe Singleton. Singleton had chauffeured Hofheinz to campaign speaking events and served as his bodyguard. The new mayor felt none of the three men was interested in the job and all could ably screen possible choices.[2]

The empowered triumvirate brought forth the name of Carrol Lynn, who started with three strikes against him. If a modern-day Dick Tracy couldn't ably succeed Herman Short, a captain who had worked under the inspectors his appointment bypassed surely couldn't. To make matters more difficult, Lynn didn't socialize within the department, preferring to go home to a wife and family. Unlike Short, he never played any significant role with the Houston Police Officers Association and wasn't a street cop.

The new chief's efforts to make changes weren't well received. He served eighteen months and never got the full support of the men he was promoted over. He formed SWAT and succeeded in seeing the promotion of the first

219

**POLICE CHIEF CARROL LYNN,
JANUARY 9, 1974–JUNE 28,
1975 (HPD ARCHIVES)**

two black sergeants in the department's history; he also took baby steps toward better communications with the African-American and Hispanic communities and oversaw the hiring of more policewomen. These strides weren't
enough to make persons of color forget Short, the TSU confrontation and
other race-related episodes. But they got HPD headed in a more inclusive
direction. Lynn's lack of support from the inspectors made him appear in-
decisive, and the normal course of human policing dropped him into a fire
of controversy.

Carrol Lynn was living proof that if you were a good test taker with the
right mentor, you could go all the way to the top. Lynn was a carpenter's son
born in a log cabin outside of Pottor, Arkansas, during the Great Depression.
He volunteered for the U.S. Air Force and served in the Korean Conflict before joining his father and mother in Houston, where the economy was far
better than in rural Arkansas and the demand for master carpenters was far
greater. When the radio said you could make three hundred dollars a month
as a Houston officer, Lynn applied and graduated the academy in the fall of
1956. He felt it was a temporary job since he really wanted to be a lawyer.[3]

After spending duties on a three-wheeler and on patrol his first twenty-
seven months as an officer, Lynn received a call from the lieutenant at the

training academy asking if he would come over temporarily to help conduct personnel investigations of the latest applicants. Little did the lieutenant realize at the time that this move would aim Lynn in the direction of the chief's office. The lieutenant was C. D. Taylor. Lynn liked working under Taylor, and it wasn't long before his temporary assignment became permanent. He picked up the fact that Taylor felt HPD needed more African-American and female officers at a time when many in the department felt differently, a lingering Herman Short legacy. Blacks frequently washed out of the academy, while the 5-foot-10 height requirement still prevented most Hispanic entries. The trend reflected recruiting requirements of the times in most departments in the nation: a police officer needed to be big enough to stop and pin down a suspect. Like HPD, many departments hired ex-servicemen and country boys with only high school diplomas or GEDs. Recruiters paid close attention to credit ratings and often got recommendations from the friends and neighbors of applicants. Computers were fifteen or twenty years down the road in 1960, necessitating recruiters like Lynn to travel all over Texas investigating applicants by examining hand-written police records in ledger books.

The department hired ten detectives in one sweep, and Lynn wound up in the Homicide Division as a detective. He stayed just long enough to get on the promotion list for lieutenant twice, the second time with the highest test grade. He made lieutenant in 1965. By this time his mentor, C. D. Taylor, had made inspector and tapped Lynn for the recruiting and selection division.[4]

Taylor picked someone with the same policing traits he had. The inspector came across as a real smart guy—not a smart *aleck.* He was intelligent and widely respected, but was not one to hang around the shop with the guys. Officers from the era described Taylor as especially business-like in academy classes, avoiding "war stories" and sticking to the lessons at hand. Like Lynn, he didn't go into the HPD good ol' boy association.

By the time he took over Recruiting, Lynn thought recruiters had too many hang-ups on little sexually-related things coupled with their reluctance to recruit minorities. So many applicants had been turned down that the number of prospective recruits steadily dwindled. Then Lynn and his staff saw the virtues of Ken Garnett, who had been seriously injured in an automobile accident. Unable to perform patrol duties, the officer became head of the Community Relations Division, serving as the safety officer on a Houston television station's kids' show called "KiTiRiK". KTRK/Channel 13 was getting high viewership with local personality Bunny Orsak portraying the title character, whose name cleverly and strategically contained the station's call letters.

Lynn thought it was a good idea for Garnett to appear on TV and promote HPD. Garnett corralled some television writers that included Dave Ward, later the long-time Channel 13 anchor, and they produced an award-winning spot featuring a police dog rescuing a lost baby in a park.

Recruiting efforts improved in 1966 with thousands of people applying. HPD began recruiting more women and minorities, even setting up recruiting trips to TSU, Prairie View A&M University and some of Houston's predominately black high schools. Reaction was mixed in the department. Like other veterans from the era, Lynn didn't think HPD was racist as a whole but had some individuals with race-related problems. Lynn took the test for captain and scored high and Taylor expanded his duties in the Personnel Division, where Lynn served from 1966 until 1974.

Hofheinz had focused on Short's attitude toward minority groups in both the 1971 and 1973 campaigns and credited this stance with finally putting him in office in the 1973 election. He rallied his coalition of supporters by convincing them that the demographics of Houston were changing. So should HPD. The Houston Police Department was fundamentally white and full of the old southern mentality, one ethnic group policing a multi-ethnic community.[5]

The political attention in Houston had steadily shifted from school board politics to City Hall. Throughout the sixties and early seventies the liberal-versus-conservative battles were fought at Houston School Board meetings. Frequently the issue involved emotional practices that affected black students. Hofheinz focused on these changing political tides and homed in on the real issue. He saw the TSU confrontation and the assassination of Martin Luther King Jr. one year later as turning points.

The new focus solidified in 1969 with the Citizens for Good Schools coalition, which helped elect a school board slate in the Houston Independent School District. CGS thus showed the strength of the black community's desire to assert political influence in Houston. All that interest in the school board election in 1969 flipped and started to focus on the HPD. Hofheinz believed the major reason he was elected mayor in 1973 was that Herman Short was police chief—the villain of the black community, the hero on one side of town and the villain of the other side. He was the symbol of the old way of doing things. The Houston Police Department viewed itself as the protector from black activism whenever it reared its ugly head.[6]

Lynn's First Significant Event

A significant event transpired the first week Lynn was chief that led to the formation of SWAT. A hijacker "mental case" at a grocery store on the east side took a store trainer and eleven young female trainees as hostages. The first lieutenant on the scene volunteered to be taken in lieu of the hostages, but wound up standing in with the others at the point of his own .45-caliber pistol. Lynn arrived and took command of the chaotic scene with news cameras everywhere. A widely respected inspector, B. K. Johnson, also was present and Lynn made his first major decision as chief, putting Johnson in total control. There was no SWAT and Lynn and Johnson actually considered "trading" the chief for the lieutenant. The hostage taker wouldn't have it.

The man arranged to leave with the lieutenant and half of the hostages. He released the others and got a car with a full tank of gas, holding a gun on the driver, Lieutenant W. C. "Hoss" Doss. Johnson and Doss were hunting buddies and knew the roadways out of the area. Doss drove down a rural route that was a dead end. "We'll put some country boys (officers) there," Johnson told Lynn. "These guys can shoot. If they get a clear shot, they'll take him out."

The hijacker took the bait. One shot was fired but didn't hit him. After the arrest, a more reflective police chief decided HPD needed its own SWAT team despite predicted turf problems.[7]

Hofheinz's plan was to replace Short and change HPD. His plan had enough impact over his opponent, Jewish councilman and long-time Houston TV personality Dick Gottlieb, to barely put him into the mayor's office. Since Hofheinz was the victor, the writing was on the wall. Short said he couldn't work under Hofheinz and retired effective December 31, 1973. He had served longer than any other chief in HPD history, nine years and three months.

A City Council of eight white men and one black man confirmed Lynn on January 9, 1974. In the selection process, the new mayor asked tough questions and heard the right answers in a series of five private meetings with

Lynn. He wanted every citizen to be treated fairly, and Lynn convinced the
new mayor he was prepared to meet that challenge and ready to recruit more
minorities and females. Hofheinz' friends wanted him to appoint Harry
Caldwell, noted for an intellectual approach to policing quite the antithesis
of the Short philosophy. Harris County Precinct 1 Constable Walter Rankin
was briefly on the list but never seriously considered. Hofheinz thought about
hiring a fire chief from outside but felt that going the same route for a police
chief would have a negative effect on council members generally advocat-
ing a promote-from-within approach. Ultimately, Hofheinz felt Caldwell was
too controversial but later wished he had appointed him instead of Lynn.[8]

On his first official day in office when the New Year began, Lynn went to
Texas Southern University to meet with black community leaders, welcoming
blacks to apply to HPD and vowing that they would be treated fairly. The words
encouraged blacks and other members of Hofheinz' campaign coalition.

Inspectors who were passed over didn't like working for a captain even
though Lynn ranked high on the inspector promotion list. Hofheinz later
officially placed him at the inspector's rank so he would be able to return to
that pay scale by civil service laws if he left the chief's office before retirement. Lynn had eighteen years and four months when Hofheinz appointed
him. Lynn's first command staff meeting at 61 Riesner wasn't as warm as the
mild January weather outside. He quickly picked up on the coolness in the
air and got the feeling they would have been more accepting of an inspector.[9]

A cold reception from the inspectors was not the only rift early in the honeymoon. Less than a week after his City Council confirmation, Lynn closed
police records to reporters. Previously, the media had access to offense reports, mug shots, confessions and criminal records. The chief had a new interpretation by the city attorney on a state open records law to back him up.

The Creation of SWAT

The Houston Police Department's SWAT team was created in
1974 under Chief Carrol Lynn at a time when HPD's lack of
properly trained men and equipment became apparent. HPD
didn't have a commando team capable of surrounding a building with negotiators capable of speaking with armed and/or
suicidal subjects. Chief Herman B. Short had set up the Tacti-

cal Squad in 1970, which was much more limited in its scope than SWAT would become. Initially, patrol officers considered SWAT grounds for a serious turf battle since these officers heretofore performed all of these dangerous duties when necessary as part of their job.

SWAT got off to a decidedly unsupported and underfunded operation. Practically the only "special weapon" the initial group possessed was a scoped deer rifle the department's designated "sniper" kept in the trunk of a take-home car. Many of the initial "tactics" were drawn up in a SWAT office that previously served as a janitor's closet at 61 Riesner. The first SWAT van was a converted bread truck and one of its first female officers became Houston's first-ever female chief, Elizabeth Watson.

The FBI Academy trained the original team members until the late 1970s when SWAT had its own experienced trainers. Team members were originally expected to run felony arrest warrants and fugitive warrants when not in training. There were four entry teams and one marksman support element, the same concept in place for the next thirty-five years. While the first SWAT officers had to beg or borrow equipment, they did have one built-in advantage from the start—they stayed together as a unit after their most intensive training sessions. The most difficult problem was convincing other officers that SWAT had a special mission.

SWAT's first real test on the streets proved disastrous, yet provided important "lessons learned." In October 1975, three escaped convicts were holed up in an east side house after having taken and released two hostages. The Harris County Organized Crime Unit requested HPD assistance in dealing with the situation. Before SWAT's arrival, HPD Officers Richard Calhoun and Michael J. Lyons climbed in an unlocked back room window while other officers were at the front door. Gaining entry, Calhoun took the lead and was shot in the neck; he died instantly.

SWAT used discarded military teargas that ignited when it hit a floor or wall, catching the house on fire. One of the teargas canisters blew up in an officer's lap and severely burned his legs. In the process, the shotgun he was carrying went off and struck another officer's legs. When the fire was finally extinguished, the bodies of the three convicts were found in the smoky ruins. Both officers recovered.

Lieutenant James E. "Peter" Gunn injected a stronger discipline into the SWAT ranks later in the 1970s. Gunn used every publicity opportunity to accustom the public to having SWAT. He led officers through exercises and drills every morning. In 1978, Gunn sent Sergeants Ronnie Noskrent and Ellis Johnson to learn hostage negotiation at the Springfield, Illinois, police academy known for this type of specialized training. The academy preached, "Let's talk them out instead of blasting them out." SWAT members also learned to rappel out of helicopters at Fort Polk, Louisiana and to use the finer techniques from the FBI and Secret Service academies to secure the inner parameter of visiting dignitaries, training that worked well when presidents visited.

SWAT went through a period in the late 1970s and early 1980s when most situations involved suicides—sometimes "suicide by police." The group began training more negotiators after seeing the advantage of ending confrontations peacefully without gunfire. This methodology developed from police experiences across the nation that found resolution was more effective than entrapment.

The group's heavy equipment included a $250,000 command post, custom built on a large Ford "bob-tail" truck frame. Along with serving as the communication and command center, it carried all equipment not individually assigned to SWAT members. There also was an armored vehicle referred to as the "Big MaMoo," a Dragoon Patroller able to carry twelve officers at speeds up to seventy miles per hour. It had all-wheel drive, a hydraulically operated battering ram and could stop three hits from a 7mm in the same hole. The 100 Club purchased both of these vehicles. SWAT also provided "active shooter" training for all officers.[10]

SWAT grew to become a full-time operation with twenty-four officers, three sergeants, one lieutenant and one captain. It is currently structured in the Tactical Operations Division,

which also includes the Hostage Negotiations Team, the Bomb Squad, the Dive Team and the K9 unit.

◇◇

Lynn immediately ordered the recruitment of more minority officers and policewomen. The department soon promoted the first two black sergeants in the Houston Police Department. Void of much fanfare outside Houston's black news media, the mayor set up a brief swearing-in ceremony on April 12, 1974 for the two new sergeants and twenty-three others. The two first-ever black sergeants were former Major League Baseball player J. C. Hartman and Officer R. C. Humphrey. Lynn heard claims that the troops wouldn't take orders from a black. It was common talk that Lynn and Hofheinz promoted twenty-five sergeants to enable promotions of the two African-Americans. For the time being, Hofheinz was very happy; he was proving to Houston blacks that he meant business.[11]

Lynn laughingly admitted that he wasn't sure of the location of the men's room in his first few days in the chief's office. Finding it was nothing compared to learning from federal officials that Narcotics officers were using illegal wiretapping to develop evidence. He also learned that the Criminal

HPD Police Academy Class No. 67 had a large number of minorities and women in its ranks, a trend established by Police Chief Carrol Lynn, the second man on the right in front of the class picture. (May Walker)

Intelligence Division had secret files on approximately 1,500 Houston civic leaders and politicians, even well-respected black state legislator and future Congresswoman Barbara Jordan. The discovery angered Hofheinz, whose political allies included Jordan.[12]

The files fell into Joe Singleton's bailiwick as head of CID. Singleton's troops operated much like similar divisions in police departments all over the nation—trying to determine the backgrounds of radicals participating in civil rights and anti-war activities.[13] The concern was that some of the more radical individuals would initiate violent acts that endangered large numbers of innocent people.

News media pressure prompted the mayor to take action, especially when word leaked out that CID was compiling files labeled "Miscellaneous Negroes." Hofheinz created a three-member panel of federal judges to determine the significance of the files and if they were obtained improperly. Questions about them continued to linger into 2011 since the judges technically kept them secret. The people with access to them have said over the years that they amounted to scarcely more than newspaper clippings and similar public records.[14]

His suspicions heightened, Lynn bugged his own office when Singleton came in to talk to him. Lynn wanted Singleton fired; instead, he retired and Hofheinz immediately appointed him chief clerk of the Municipal Courts. Singleton always denied any wrongdoing even though the wiretap issue didn't go away. Officers found out about Lynn's covert taping effort, angering practically everyone in the department but those working closely with him. The chief, in essence, was trying to wiretap and record in order to entrap one of his fellow officers.[15]

In addition to dealing with the secret files, Lynn fired two officers in February for alleged sexual abuse of a prostitute. A month later he pledged to end wiretapping in the department after federal indictments against current and former officers in "one of the largest scandals ever" in HPD. Ultimately, six officers were convicted of conspiracy to violate prisoners' rights and were assessed prison terms ranging from three to eight years.[16]

Later that year, Lynn took the heat that came from allegations he used a private investigator, J. L. Patterson, to wire the chief's office so that Lynn could tape record officers he was questioning about illegal wiretaps. Patterson used special equipment to find bugs on Lynn's home and office phones. He later went to federal prison in connection with defrauding Southwestern Bell Telephone Company and cooperated with authorities seeking evi-

Mayor Fred Hofheinz pins
the sergeant's badge on J. C.
Hartman, the first African
American HPD police sergeant
in 1974. (J. C. Hartman)

dence against Lynn. Later, Lynn refused to discuss his ultimate conviction
and prison term. He admitted in hindsight that "it was a terrible error on my
part." He said HPD had no Internal Affairs at the time and he couldn't trust
anybody else to investigate wiretapping allegations.[17]

By November, the Houston Police Officers Association, representing all
3,500 officers in HPD, accused Lynn of secretly taping conversations with
police officers in his office. Five members of City Council said if this were
true, Lynn needed to resign. Two months later the HPOA decried the department's low morale.

Lynn admitted he taped "a good number of officers to cover my backside"
and establish a record for what transpired behind the closed doors of his office. Lynn testified before both a Texas Senate subcommittee and a U.S. House
Judiciary panel in Washington that illegal wiretaps in Houston "probably
numbered in the thousands." He was unable to tell the district attorney, Carol
Vance, any specifics, saying it would be impossible to compile such a list.[18]

To make Lynn's growing list of controversies and serious police-oriented
questions even more complicated, on June 1, 1975, the *Houston Chronicle* reported he handled the dismissal of about fifty parking tickets in 1971 through
1973, most involving employees of companies doing business with private se-

curity firms in which he was involved while off-duty. No criminal charges ever resulted. The chief also faced accusations based on information coming from police sources that he and two other officers shook down gamblers and bookies for $2,000 a month for police to lay off Houston's gambling operations.[19]

Many of Lynn's detractors believed that his problems resulted from his absence from the HPD good-ol'-boy network. He just didn't have many friends in the department. The pay raise Hofheinz sponsored lingered in the background behind the host of problems dogging Lynn. The problems overshadowed the successful effort to recruit more minorities and women for the department. HPD Cadet Class No. 67 contained the largest number of females in history. The total class of sixty-eight included twenty-four women and five blacks, the result of Hofheinz getting the help of black and Hispanic leaders to help HPD find qualified candidates. They also encouraged more minority officers to take the sergeant and detective tests.

Minority recruitment was the lynchpin of Lynn's policing program. The chief also transcended the tradition of appointing policewomen to serve only in the Juvenile and Jail divisions. He put them in Accident and Traffic Enforcement.[20]

At Hofheinz' request, Lynn resigned as chief on June 28, 1975, after serving eighteen months and still short of the twenty years needed to retire. He dropped down to the rank of inspector while Hofheinz appointed another police captain he had known and trusted, Byron G. "Pappy" Bond, as chief of police.[21]

Pappy Bond wanted changes in his command staff that Fred Hofheinz was ready and willing to make. Bond was a captain who got the same icy reaction as Lynn when he took office on January 21, 1976, after Inspector R. J. Clark played HPD's caretaker role as acting chief for about six months. Hofheinz regarded Clark as "a well respected cop in the department" not known for causing controversy and on the verge of retirement.[22]

The jovial, rotund man everyone called "Pappy" felt the title of "inspector" was out-dated and inappropriate. An inspector handled meat or put his label inside new clothing as a stamp of approval. Chief Bond thought "deputy chief" sounded more authoritative. And when the iciness of his deputy chiefs didn't settle well, he persuaded Hofheinz and City Council to re-establish the new command staff-level rank of *assistant chief*. George Seber held the title, which was retired with him. HPD needed three such administrative managers.

First HPD Asian-Americans

Carrol Lynn's service as chief did see another "first" in the history of the Houston Police Department. On June 10, 1974, the chief swore in Steven Lee as the department's first Asian-American police officer. The second Asian-American joined the force almost a year to the day later, June 9, 1975. He was Herman Mar. Lee and Mar were followed by the first Asian-American policewoman, Lily Yep, on May 23, 1977.

On May 22, 1998, Police Chief Clarence O. "Brad" Bradford and Mayor Lee P. Brown approved the promotion of N. D. Wong to assistant chief, the first Asian-American to achieve that high rank. Wong had joined HPD on December 19, 1977. The growth of Asian-American officers in the department reached almost 198 officers by 2009, including 181 males and 17 females, with membership of the Houston Law Enforcement Association of Asian Pacifics reaching more than 100 members.

Then fate took over. Promotions to assistant chief came from a promotional list that included most of the former inspectors-turned-deputy chiefs. Number one on the list was Deputy Chief Wallace L. Williams, who couldn't accept the job because he was about to be convicted in federal court of income tax evasion. This left the second-, third- and fourth-ranked men on the list eligible to promote. Number four was Carrol Lynn. The other assistants were Tommy Mitchell and B. K. Johnson. Bond first promoted Mitchell and Johnson and a short time later made Lynn an assistant chief when Williams officially retired.

Number five on the list was Harry Caldwell, who persuaded Bond that HPD needed *four* assistant chiefs to handle the growing amount of administrative duties. By the time Assistant Chief Caldwell was sworn in, the three other assistants had staked out office turf. Caldwell ended up downtown in office space leased by the Recruiting Division, the only assistant not at 61 Riesner.[23]

Lynn took over as head of Support Command, which included communications, dispatching, garage, jail, supply, crime lab, Houston Crime Information Center, identification and polygraph. According to court records, while quietly serving in this capacity in November 1977, Lynn contacted John Vincent Holden, the sales manager of Tri-State Oil and Gas Company about a federal investigation. By January 1978, a federal grand jury indicted Holden for mail fraud in violation of security regulations in connection with making false representations in oil lease sales.[24]

Lynn told Holden that for $45,000 he could have former Houston City Controller Leonel Castillo persuade U. S. Attorney Tony Canales to drop the charges. Gerald Birnberg, Holden's attorney, contacted Castillo, the director of the U.S. Immigration and Naturalization Service under President Jimmy Carter. Castillo barely knew Lynn and certainly hadn't heard of this plan. Soon, Canales launched an investigation.[25]

On April 11, 1978, FBI agents arrested the forty-five-year-old Lynn on charges of obstruction of justice in an extortion plot. He posted a $50,000 bond and was released, while facing five years imprisonment and a $5,000 fine. Interestingly, eight days earlier, attorney Birnberg was shot in the hand by two men in front of his home. There was never any evidence linking Lynn to the shooting. Coincidentally, Birnberg later became a Hofheinz law partner.

The assistant chief refused two opportunities to resign, the first on April 18, offered by Police Chief Harry Caldwell, and the second two days later by Assistant City Attorney Al Levin. On April 21, 1978, Lynn was fired, the highest-ranking Houston police officer ever to be dismissed. Caldwell made his decision to fire Lynn based on the facts in the FBI affidavit about the case. Since Lynn served twenty-two years with the department, he was entitled to his pension even if convicted. On May 18, he dropped his appeal of the firing.[26]

Lynn was indicted in June 1978 on two counts of perjury, two counts of obstruction of justice and one count of extortion. On January 29, 1979, a federal judge sentenced him to twelve years in federal prison and a $10,000 fine after a jury found him guilty as charged on Christmas Eve 1978. The judge added a ten-year sentence probated for five years to begin after he served the twelve-year sentence. Lynn went to prison on February 25, 1979, and served almost five years before earning parole. As a retiree of HPD, he received a monthly pension of $1,319.07.[27] Twenty years later, Lynn was aging into his 70s and keeping a low profile in retirement.

Upon learning of the charges, Chief Caldwell was so angered that he immediately ordered Lynn's picture removed from the wall at headquarters where portraits of HPD chiefs reverently hung. He also abolished the same fourth assistant chief position that he had served in prior to his appointment to be chief. The pictures in the hall were shifted accordingly so that there was no blank space.[28]

20

ALL 7'S

The first African-American officers in the Houston Police Department served in 1870 during Reconstruction. Those first blacks were believed to be state police officers whose job was to counteract Reconstruction Era violence against black citizens in Houston and around the state of Texas. These were known as "special officers"—a term used for decades to refer to African-Americans without the full authority of their white counterparts.

HPD African-American police historian May Walker wrote *The History of the Black Police Officers in the Houston Police Department 1878–1988*, which revealed that three of HPD's twenty-two officers in 1892 were the first black officers with full police authority. Hardly any records exist to show the names of these men, none of whom served more than five years. There is confusion over the years of service for the first fully identified black officer in HPD history. His name was Nathan Davis. His first year of service is reported as 1878; however, a picture of the twenty-six-member force in 1916 is the first and only departmental picture depicting Davis, a man approximately six-feet tall with a fully gray handlebar mustache. Officer Davis patrolled predominately black areas and had full authority with one exception—he could not arrest a white suspect without the assistance of a white officer, nor could he get a promotion.[1]

Davis didn't own an HPD badge. The first black officers to receive badges were Issac Hayden, Badge No. 119, and Moses Moss, Badge No. 9. The year was listed as 1889, although subsequent research shows it was perhaps 1913. Oscar P. Robinson was the first black officer promoted to the rank of special detective. The number of blacks in HPD fluctuated from one to seven through 1913. This part of the early century saw two special officers with only partial authority give all they had for HPD. They were killed in the line of duty, Special Officer Isaac "Ike" Parsons on May 24, 1914 and Special Detective Ed Jones on September 13, 1929.[2]

Despite ever-ready dedication like that exhibited by Parsons and Jones, the number of black officers didn't grow significantly throughout the decades leading to the 1950s.

One African American officer joined the Houston Police Department in Class No. 1 in 1948. Edward A. Thomas went on to serve longer than any other HPD officer in history. Thomas served sixty-three years until his retirement in 2011 at the age of ninety-two. Over those years he earned such respect among his peers that everyone from the police chiefs to the newest cadets addressed him as "Mr. Thomas." The veteran officer was particularly discreet—meaning he avoided news media interviews and refused all requests for pictures. The only published picture of Mr. Thomas, outside the photos of Class No. 1, appeared in a book about African Americans in HPD. He even refused the release of his police identification photo.

Mr. Thomas began his tenure during segregation and enforcement of the Jim Crow laws in Houston. He seldom shared his thoughts about his early days in the department with anyone and never thought he would ever work under a black police chief. That changed when Lee P. Brown became the city's first black chief in 1982. By the time Thomas retired, there had been four African-Americans in the position. Mr. Thomas was known to share his thoughts of the early days with the fourth person in that distinguished line, Police Chief Charles "Chuck" McClelland, appointed by Mayor Annise Parker in 2010.

According to Chief McClelland, who took to calling this most senior officer "Mr. T," Thomas was born in Louisiana. His father died when he was nine or ten years old, making him "the man of the house" that included his mother, a school teacher, and several sisters. The family lived in Nacogdoches in East Texas, where Mr. Thomas earned a high school diploma and attended Southern University in Baton Rouge, Louisiana. He also served as an infantryman during World War II, spending only nine weeks stateside before serving several years in the European campaign, including the Normandy invasion.

The slow process of police departments across the southern United States accepting African American officers began after the war. The process wasn't easy for Mr. Thomas and others who joined HPD. After fighting for his country, the young officer could not attend roll call with white officers and was not allowed to drive a police car or catch breakfast or lunch in the department's cafeteria. "He had to drink out of the 'colored' water fountain and could not arrest a white person without a white officer's authorization," McClelland said.

The retirement of Officer Edward A. Thomas was a major juncture in HPD history. The man referred to as "Mr. Thomas" served sixty-three years until his retirement in 2011 at the age of ninety-two. Thomas is pictured with Houston Police Officers Union President J. J. Berry on the left and Sgt. Dennis Carter on the right. Sgt. Carter was serving on the staff of Police Chief Charles McClelland at the time of Mr. Thomas' retirement. Berry was the first African American president of the Union. (J. J. Berry)

Since Mr. Thomas was not assigned a patrol car, he had to walk a miles-long beat that literally extended from Houston's Third Ward to the Fifth Ward. McClelland's recollection would exhaust anyone familiar with Bayou City geography: He had to walk from 2900 Dowling in Third Ward to near the corner of Hill and Lyons in Fifth Ward, a distance of three and a half miles. "He did it twice a day," Chief McClelland said, "and he worked the Evening Shift from something like 6 p.m. until 2 a.m." Although Mr. Thomas spent more than his share of time on patrol, his workload eased in his later years. When he retired in 2011, he could be seen frequently at the guard desk at Police Headquarters at 1200 Travis in downtown Houston. He shuttled mail and delivered messages. He told the many officers who asked that HPD was the only family he had left. "The two most difficult things I've had to do as police chief," McClelland said, "was to lay off 154 employees because of budget cuts and, secondly, to talk to Mr. Thomas when he made the decision to retire. It brought both of us to tears."[3]

HPD Officer A. V. Young was accepted in the same class as Mr. Thomas but didn't use the opportunity because he was unsure about becoming a police officer. Then he made up his mind to enter the second class in February 1949. In 2005, at age eighty-four, Young was the only surviving member of Class No. 2. While assigned to the Patrol Division, his duties were confined only to predominately black areas. Like Mr. Thomas, Young walked his beats. Only when Police Headquarters moved from 401 Caroline to 61 Riesner in 1953, did the department supply cars to black officers—the oldest models in the poorest running condition.[4] The slow growth taking place on police forces in Texas saw enough black officers that the Texas Negro Police Officers Association was formed. Young and other Houston officers joined it, dropping the "Negro" in 1955. Young founded the African-American Police Officers League in 1975.[5]

Young was the TPOA's fourth president and saw gradual progress toward the typical black officer goal "to be treated like everybody else." Young himself became an expert marksman who received numerous awards for excellence in competitions around the state and nation. He joined the National Rifle Association and entered a state competition in 1959, eligible to shoot only as a civilian since there couldn't be any competition between blacks and whites. He won the national pistol championships in 1969, 1970 and 1971. While most blacks of the era resented Herman Short, Young greatly admired him for making him the first black firearms instructor in the department.

HPD's practices toward black officers in the 1950s were much like those in any big city across the southern divide of the United States. There were separate roll calls, limited authority when arresting white persons, disrespectful reactions to black officers trying to do good jobs, patrol assignments only in predominately black sections of the city, practically non-existent promotional opportunities and no clear-cut effort to recruit more officers of color.

Despite such treatment, certain African-Americans in the Houston Police Department weren't deterred. Their names merit a special roll call:

Stockey Gray, Scoby Williams, E. J. "String" Stringfellow, Margie Duty, Leslie Magee, Claude White, Walter Irving, Billy Williams, L. T. Thomas, O. E. Brown, G. Crawford, Robert L. Crane, Leon Griggs, Albert Blair, Fred Black, Charles Howard, David Pierson and his brother Proncell. Many of these officers were deceased by the year 2011.

Griggs was the first-ever "fully authorized" black officer to die in the line of duty. A pistol-wielding supermarket robber on the southeast side murdered him from behind on January 31, 1970, while Griggs worked an extra job as security.[6]

Even Police Academy credits, which could be applied toward a college degree, were applied by way of segregated means. While white officers received academy credits from the University of Houston, under the G.I Bill, black officers were often required to get theirs from the predominately black Texas Southern University.[7]

The academy often drew the line with its training procedures. Officer Albert Blair, a forty-seven-year officer, said black officers at that time were not taught how to direct traffic and were not assigned to downtown street corners in a position highly visible to the entire community. When traffic train-

Officer E. J. Stringfellow became the first African American city marshal in 1980. "String" later became the chief in the city marshal's office. The Houston Police Department named its Southeast Command Center after Marshal Stringfellow in 1996. (May Walker)

ing was implemented, black cadets were told to take time off. Blair, a farmer's son from Malakoff, near Athens, came to Houston in 1948 to attend Texas State University for Negroes (later TSU). He spent two years majoring in electronics repair before going into the U. S. Army in time to become a veteran of the Korean War.[8]

The soft-spoken and articulate Blair described what he came home to:

> One thing that kind of really upset us after we finished our jobs over there protecting our country was we came back and couldn't really be first class citizens. We had to be seated in certain places. We had money, but couldn't enter hotels. We had money, but we couldn't enjoy a hamburger at a lunch counter.
>
> I think the thing that bothered us so much was that the other guys in uniform could sit down and enjoy these privileges, and we couldn't. It was very, very distasteful.
>
> I had given two and a half years to my country and my country decided I was not a first class citizen when I got back. I was a second class citizen, not because I was disrespectful in my conduct, but because I had a darker complexion and I didn't fit in.[9]

Blair used the G. I. Bill to finish his degree at TSU in 1955 and get a job first as a butcher and later as the only black licensed electrician in Houston, enabling him to buy a home for his growing family. As with many African-Americans with careers in HPD, Blair's adult life took a major turn for the better through the help and understanding of white businessmen who paid no attention to skin color. Blair's employers and mentors were white businessmen Harry Keep and Frank Stabler. Their inspiration prompted Blair to join HPD in 1957. When he retired forty-seven years later, Stabler's wife and children attended his retirement ceremony.[10]

Upon graduation in June 1957, Blair earned a monthly salary of $330 and got a $20 raise after completing probation. It was money that enabled him to pay a house note, electricity bills and $61 a month for a new Ford. Fred Black was the other African-American in Blair's cadet class. The two joined the other thirty blacks on a force of 1,000.[11]

The sergeant in charge of the academy eyed Blair and Black with suspicion on their first day. He made it clear that he was the authority. He told them they would probably bust out and reminded them that they could not eat in the cafeteria. Black pioneers in the HPD of the early 1950s were told to go in through the back entrance of the cafeteria. Many opted to bring sack lunches.[12]

When the sergeant told Blair and Black that they would not be a part of traffic directing exercises, they had to obey. One day, after separate roll calls, Blair and Black's cadet class entered a courtroom in orderly fashion and sat on the front rows. They all stood up as the judge entered and promptly asked the sergeant to "straighten the class out." The sergeant then ordered the two black cadets to move to the back row, away from their fellow class members. Use of the N-word was common every day in academy classes but never used to refer to the black cadets.[13]

After graduation, new black officers were usually assigned to the Patrol Division, always working exclusively in African-American neighborhoods. As the saying went, they were "all sevens." All black patrol units were identified by numbers that ended in seven. If you patrolled Third Ward and Sunnyside, you rode Unit 137. There was a large black population in the downtown and Fourth Ward area with its beer joints up and down West Gray and West Dallas. The black officers there were assigned Unit 127.[14]

On the other side of downtown in Fifth Ward, Unit 157 was on patrol. On back to Nance and Griggs, those areas were very difficult areas to police, as were Quitman and Collingsworth. Unit 147 went there and was known as "a roving car."

Blair, Black and other "seven" patrol officers went all over town, depending on the hot spot of the night shift. There were never enough black officers to maintain all areas. Black officers often had trouble getting respect from law-abiding black citizens. Like their Hispanic counterparts, these citizens desperately wanted more officers who looked like them and understood unique community problems. They also wanted African-American and Hispanic officers with authority equal to white officers. One notable occasion which illustrated this lack of authority happened when Blair and Charles Howard, long-time partners in several divisions together over the years, arrested a white man for driving while intoxicated. They booked him in the jail and returned to their beat.

It was common then for a white suspect to ignore orders from a black officer. Even more troublesome were white supervisors inclined to release white suspects without conferring with the black officers who made the arrests. When Blair and Howard got back on patrol, they received a call from Otto Vahldiek, the captain on duty. Vahldiek asked the officers if they had brought a drunken white man to the jail. "Why didn't you book him for DWI? He was drunk," Vahldiek said. When the captain heard what happened, he admonished the sergeant in question and told the black officers they could arrest white suspects.[15]

In the sixties, supervisors at the lieutenant and captain level carefully chose opportunities to stand up for the black officers. One of these supervisors was an instructor at the academy, Larry Fultz, for whom the library at the L. D. Morrison Sr. Police Academy was named. Fultz had a law degree and was known for his refinement, graciousness and well-spoken demeanor. He bonded with Blair and later asked him and Charles Howard to be two of twenty-one officers to participate in a public relations conference at Texas A&M University. Fultz was in charge of the whole program.[16]

When school officials learned Blair and Howard were black, they notified Fultz that these two would have to stay off-campus. Fultz told them that he wouldn't lead the program unless the officers stayed on campus with everyone else. He got his way.[17]

Even into the late 1960s, middle class black citizens had trouble getting served in restaurants and hotels. In the Weingarten's stores blacks could shop for groceries all day but weren't allowed to get a sandwich at the lunch counter. They could buy all the gasoline they needed to fill up the gas tanks of their vehicles but couldn't set foot in service station restrooms. Hotels had the same strict policies. When U.S. Supreme Court Justice Thurgood Marshall came to Houston for a speech, he couldn't stay in a hotel, but roomed instead in the home of prominent black political leader Judson Robinson Sr.

The lunchroom in the Harris County Courthouse was off limits to blacks, even black police officers. Black officers also were not considered the right color to be assigned to investigative divisions such as Homicide, Robbery and Burglary and Theft. These divisions "borrowed" blacks when they needed them but never assigned them permanently to primary investigative divisions—until about 1966, when Civil Rights demonstrations began to take place regularly at lunch counters and other no-blacks-allowed venues. Houston school integration was drawing the same highly emotional reaction as it did throughout the nation.

The department needed black officers to work undercover to get valuable intelligence about possible race-related disturbances before they happened. Initially, Albert Blair and Charles "Sideburn" Howard were lent to

Assistant Police Chief Dorothy Edwards became the highest-ranking African American female in the Houston Police Department. Edwards worked her way through the ranks, also becoming the "first" African American female lieutenant and captain. (Dorothy Edwards)

what became known as the Criminal Intelligence Division, undertaking a very touchy assignment in view of the fact that Houstonians of color were becoming aware of statistical information such as the one or two percent of police officers who were African-Americans.[18]

Blair and Howard, the first two permanent black CID officers, primarily served to protect visiting dignitaries, such Justice Marshall, Prince Charles and Presidents Johnson, Nixon, Ford, Carter and Reagan, along with Egyptian President Anwar Sadat. Most HPD officers didn't catch on to the real purpose of CID, thinking that it was a spy for the command staff of that day and time. CID's early-day goal was operation of the intelligence-gathering needed to monitor the mood, plans and level of possible violence used by the leaders of Civil Rights demonstrators.[19]

By 1967, Blair and Howard regularly worked lunch counters at Foley's, Weingarten's, Walgreen's, Kress' and Woolworth's in plain clothes. The two worked together fifteen years, reporting intelligence such as the need to provide a leader to answer the growing demand for equal treatment at eateries all over Houston. Outside of several notable demonstrations and the TSU situation in 1967, intelligence gathered by black officers served to curb the violence that marked race-oriented riots in America's big cities in other sections of the nation. Howard retired in the early 1980s, while Blair went on to serve twenty years in CID, leaving in 1986 to work in the Legal Services Division for Deputy Chief Sam Nuchia, later chief of police.[20]

E. J. Stringfellow was a street-savvy black officer whose work as an undercover officer in Narcotics with long-time partner H. M. "Stockey" Gray got positive results. Gray and Stringfellow were the first two blacks who worked the exciting world of Narcotics. Stronger enforcement of drug laws was new all over the nation. The two officers found a new frontier of opportunity since no Houston area drug dealers knew of the existence of black officers used for undercover work. They worked together for ten years obtaining evidence and eyewitness testimony that sent dealers to prison for the then-unheard-of terms of ten years or more.

Over two decades "String" arrested more than 500 suspects, a record so prolific that the Texas Department of Public Safety, which had no black officers over most of this period, "borrowed" him to work drug cases all over the state.[21] Stringfellow was the first and maybe *only* Houston police officer who had a song written about him. No one remembered the song's writer but they know words that include that "low-down, cold-blooded, badge-carryin', gun-totin' law machine" with a refrain that went "String's gonna get you! String's gonna get you!"[22]

Mayor Jim McConn (1978–1982) named Stringfellow one of three assistant chief clerks for the city's municipal courts upon his retirement from the department in 1980. A year later McConn named him the first chief city marshal in Houston, a position he held until he retired in February 1995. The following year the city renamed HPD's Southeast Command Station at 8300 Mykawa Road the Edward J. Stringfellow South Police Station. As retired HPD Sergeant J. C. Mosier told the *Chronicle* at the time, "They don't name a station after you if you're not a legend."[23]

String gained that legendary status beginning in 1954 when twelve of just more than 1,000 HPD officers were black. By the date of the Stringfellow building dedication, February 6, 1996, HPD had a total of 5,150 officers; 697 were blacks and 740 were Hispanics. String died on March 22, 2001. He was seventy-one years old.[24]

The female jail facility at police headquarters at 61 Riesner began to require a growing number of female officers by the early 1970s. This was one of two assignment posts (Juvenile Division was the other) that saw an increased number of African American female officers on a regular basis. These archival photos from September 20, 1977 depict the operations in the female section. (HPD Archives)

Frederick D. Black was like Albert Blair in many ways: he was church-going, college-educated and a Korean War veteran when he joined HPD. Black earned a biology degree with a math minor at Huston-Tillotson College in Austin, entered the University of Texas Dental School and studied there until money got tight. He started with HPD "to keep the wolf from the back door." He thought he might return to dental school; instead, he took serious an HPD recruiting poster he saw on a bus, became a cop and stayed a cop. He was in Class 16 with Albert Blair. Black joined the department when there were less than forty African-Americans on the force, hoping to make a difference. He got the feeling, however, that there would never be more than forty black officers.[25]

Black also spent a long time on the force—thirty years. He lived in the Hillwood section of Sunnyside on Houston's southeast side with other black middle class families with strong work ethics and steady ties to established churches. Gradually, the neighbors recognized Black as a hard-working officer, breadwinner and effective role model for the growing number of young men in the neighborhood. As a result, he provided the law enforcement/public service role model to inspire many of these youngsters to join the department. Black's actions and results demonstrated the slow but steady growth of the sphere of influence early black officers had. His neighborhood and church produced once and future HPD Officers Leon Booker, Selwyn Ellis, Henry Davis and Mattie Simms, the wife of an HFD firefighter. Black also advised Army buddies of his son Benjamin about becoming officers. Two of them, Sabrina Noble and Shawn Freeman, joined HPD.[26]

Fred Black cited his "easy-going nature" as his way of getting through tough times in HPD, especially the two years he spent in the Internal Affairs Division, where he went in with the second wave of officers investigating officers for alleged violations of departmental policies—an often unpopular assignment.

Black was the second black officer promoted to the rank of detective after Earl "Scoby" Williams, another academy-trained pioneer black officer. Williams graduated from the Police Academy on April 16, 1948, serving just one week in Patrol before joining what was called the Morals Division, a combination of the Narcotics Division and the Vice Squad. He stayed in Morals for one year before joining the Crime Prevention Division, now called Juvenile, the second black officer assigned there. His job description: investigate all cases involving black people, including murder, rape and any other crime in which the victim or perpetrator was a black juvenile. He was joined in the division by Margie Duty in 1954. Blacks in Juvenile didn't encounter as much prejudice as those in divisions such as Patrol and Morals.[27]

Williams was serving in Juvenile when he became HPD's first black detective on December 16, 1957 and remained there for most of a career that ended with his retirement in 1975. Williams found Juvenile was a challenge for some black officers because they could see that they were doing some good, helping some youngsters go straight. Following Williams and Black to the detective ranks were Mcloy Medlock in August 1971, Lloyd Rivers in October 1971 and Oliver E. Brown in March 1974.[28]

Sergeant Jerry R. Jones became Houston's first African-American lieutenant on April 3, 1982, and the first captain on February 15, 1986. Three more blacks were promoted to the rank of lieutenant in the 1980s. They were Claude Whitaker and David L. Walker on September 28, 1985, and Marcus Davis on December 19, 1986.

///

Margie Duty was the Houston Police Department's first black female officer. She was considered a "matron" with no police academy training. Police Chief L. D. Morrison Sr. swore in Duty in July 1953 and immediately assigned her to the Juvenile Division. There were two other black officers, both males. Duty had never considered that police work would be her career, but once she got her earliest on-the-job training she began to believe that she was truly doing the Lord's work. She spent twenty-three years in Juvenile as a plain-clothes officer and eleven more in the Jail Division before retiring in 1986 after thirty-four years of service.[29]

Six years passed before Duty had any company. On September 14, 1959, Barbara Ellison and Johnnie V. Greene became HPD's first two academy-trained black female officers. Ellison and Greene experienced the same differences in training schedules and back-door requirement at lunchtime. They were given an extra five minutes during restroom breaks because they had to take a circuitous route across a parking lot to the ladies room. Physical training consisting of judo lessons taught by a private instructor in the gym required an additional two hours after regular daily classes. They received no training in Dispatch or the Jail Division and no formal training in how to write tickets or direct traffic.[30]

Ellison and Greene learned the same lesson as their white female predecessors—that if they wanted uniforms, they would have to make their own. They each bought khaki military-style outfits and a matching military-style hat they could wear at the academy. Between 1962 and 1970, no black females went through the academy. When Ruby Allum and Robbie Fields-Phelps entered in 1969, they were the first two in seven years. Marilyn Batts-Henry became a cadet later that year. Then the three-year period between 1969 and 1972 resulted in an increase of black female officers by just one—Joyce Pomares.[31]

The Juvenile Division instituted its own version of segregation through the seniority list. There was a white seniority list and a black seniority list. Only two or three black officers got enough seniority to get weekends off. The black women in Juvenile were instructed not to answer the phone or handle white prisoners. They were to be seen, not heard. They found themselves relegated to the back office with little to do, often while white officers were swamped with phone calls and prisoners. No female officers were assigned to direct traffic or go on patrol during these tough transition years when any black officer was perceived as a troublemaker if he or she started asking questions about unwritten policies.

Election years affected the fate of female cadets. When Houston elected Fred Hofheinz mayor in 1973, he named Carrol Lynn police chief when there were less than seventy-five black officers in the department. Lynn made sure the department hired a large number of female cadets. Academy Class No. 67 contained more females than ever before—a total of twenty-six of the seventy-three cadets, including four black females, three of whom graduated—Marcella Guidry, Rachael Julian and May Walker.

The twenty-five female graduates of Class No. 67 received unprecedented opportunities. For the first time, these women graduates were sent to the Special Operations, Accident and Enforcement divisions, most of them on desk duty. A few were sent to Special Operations to direct downtown traffic and patrol assigned street corners on foot, giving women in blue more public recognition than ever before, a fact that greatly concerned male officers not accustomed to the competition.

Under Lynn during the first six months of 1975, the history of black HPD officers reached another milestone. Females had entered Radio Patrol and Officer Shirley D. Linwood Williams became the first black female officer assigned to a unit there.

21

BUFFALO HUNTERS
AND A NEW UNION

Pappy Bond had a plan in late 1974. The new captain in Narcotics had taken over a division troubled by unsafe arrest practices and accusations of brutality, wiretapping and other questionable activities that often turned the tide in the criminals' favor. Bond attacked the growing drug problem in the Bayou City through a special inter-departmental recruitment technique. He perused the lists of arrests from Patrol and wrote down the names of the arresting officers most often appearing.

On his yellow notepad, he scribbled the names of the top three from Central Patrol, Northeast, Shepherd and Park Place. He interviewed each of them, flattered their egos by citing their aggressiveness, and appealed to their purposeful demeanor as being just what HPD needed to take on drug dealers.

He sought and signed up the people who later nicknamed themselves the "Buffalo Hunters" on the day shift. The night shift became known as "Ripley's Raiders" after Narcotics Lieutenant Billy Ripley. These hunters and raiders were younger officers unafraid to plunge head-on into the more challenging and dangerous police situations and live to write detailed reports. One of them was Bob Thomas, who endured his share of meanness and violence as a patrolman in Third Ward and with the Park Place Rangers, known in the 1970s as HPD's toughest patrol division. In his three years on the force, Thomas had heard more shots fired and saw more blood than hundreds of officers with far more years on any beat.[1]

The Buffalo Hunters met for the first time in early 1975, each finding himself in a roomful of strangers, a condition that quickly changed. Thomas threw in with Officer Doyle Green of Central Patrol. The modus operandi meant working in groups on shifts. Thomas' group worked days and also included Rick Ashwood, Kenny Williamson and Joe Otis. The narcs worked undercover, using tips from street people and informants to make buys of heroin

Bob Thomas was the leader of the founders of the Houston Police Patrolmen's Union (HPPU) on October 22, 1979. Thomas was one of four officers who suffered serious injuries when they attempted to serve a drug arrest warrant one December night in 1975. Their subsequent on-duty treatment was a decisive factor in the formation of the Houston Police Patrolmen's Union. HPPU advocated better legal representation and insurance benefits than the rival Houston Police Officers Association. (Bob Thomas)

and large amounts of marijuana. They grew long hair and beards and dressed the part. They put in long hours together and frequently socialized off-duty.

Thomas grew up in Oak Forest on Houston's Northside, an ideal backdrop for conscientious young men and women of the early sixties. Many graduates of Waltrip High School, Thomas' alma mater, became Houston police officers. An especially poignant fact in history is that three Waltrip graduates were police officers killed in the line of duty: John Bamsch, shot to death by a robbery suspect in 1975; Timothy L. Hearn, killed by a pistol-wielding drug suspect in 1978; and John Anthony Salvaggio, killed by a hit-and-run driver in 1990.

The twenty-one-year-old Thomas realized that Waltrip's HPD tradition, his three years as a UH business major and sixteen weeks in the police academy prepared him for the Houston streets—but only to a degree. He got the same on-the-job experience as thousands of his predecessors. He graduated high enough in his academy class to pick his poison. Choosing nights in Central Patrol, he quickly became intimate with the Third Ward culture despite the fact he had never been able to vote or buy weapons or ammunition, had never gotten drunk and always locked his patrol car doors.

Many officers learned before decade's end that Thomas knew the meaning of perseverance. He persevered through the bloodshed and the tough initiation dished out by the department. He even was *recruited* by the Park Place Rangers, the only way a young officer could join the rugged, no-nonsense patrol known for taking no prisoners. Instead of worrying about the lack of legal representation for officers involved in shootings or fretting over insurance co-pays that added up too quickly on pay day, Thomas built a solid reputation for the savvy needed to make cases that stood up with supervisors and later in courts.

Thomas was a quick study in drug culture. He dressed the part, talked the part and became an integral part of it just like colleagues Doyle Green, Rick Ashwood, Kenny Williamson, Jim Kilty, Tim Hearn and others. He learned the dangerous trade from more seasoned narcs such as Frank Miller, Mike Woods and Joe T. Dugger.[2]

Narcs cultivated their snitches, discreetly dropping charges against suspects in return for certain introductions. Bartering for a dismissal, the defendant was required to introduce the narcs to three people who sold drugs. The informant might participate in the first dirty buy. Then the narcs would make two more on their own, building up trust and carefully working their way through the drug-dealing chain. Captain Bond was looking good, too. By the middle of 1975, the Buffalo Hunters and Ripley's Raiders developed and cultivated a vast network of drug dealers. In their first year, the Narcotics Division saw a 300 percent increase in drug arrests, a stark contrast to the squad of predecessors disbanded because of its own way of doing things.

The narcs set records for blowing the division's monthly drug budget the first three days of a new month because they were making bigger busts, requiring much larger sums. On the night shift, Lieutenant Billy Ripley, Jim Kilty and his aggressors in the war on drugs were doing the same thing. Each of the narcs learned to always be part of a task force that involved Harris County officers, the U. S. Drug Enforcement Agency and the Texas Department of Public Safety. One task force member or another always had the money the underfunded HPD officers needed for their next bust.

The workload added up, especially the time spent in court. The narcs worked sixteen-hour days and sometimes on their days off. Thomas kept his marriage to his high school sweetheart together by spending every day off with her and his daughters. Others weren't so lucky. The HPD divorce rate grew higher, particularly among narcs. The narcs' workload grew heavier and, as they learned on a December night in 1975, it also became more dangerous.

In the 1970s, Jim Kilty was a patrol officer in the drug culture/hippie community known as Montrose. He promoted a Pigs-versus-Hippies softball game that proved to be a successful bonding experience between these natural adversaries. Kilty became a Narcotics officer and was shot and killed during the arrest of a drug suspect on April 18, 1976. The badge he wore that day is depicted on the cover of *Houston Blue*. (Nelson Zoch)

Critics of the Narcotics Division of the late seventies believed narcs were overly aggressive and careless. Too often they initiated arrest operations without fully assessing the dangers. Justices of the peace, particularly Judge Lawrence H. Wayne, eagerly demonstrated their anti-drug stance by signing search warrants without posing detailed questions about the perilous predicament in which arresting officers would soon immerse themselves.[3]

Early the evening of December 8, 1975, Officers Mike Woods and June Cain were en route to a darkened and rundown multiple-unit dwelling on Golfcrest on the southeast side. The twenty-year-old Cain was still wet behind the ears. She grew up in Pasadena and always wanted to be a cop. Cain graduated from the academy at age nineteen and spent a half-year in Recruiting because she was one of only a few females who could pass HPD's tricky agility test. She became HPD's second female narc, with braces on her teeth and a Sunday school image.[4]

She had been a narc for only three months when the Golfcrest warrant situation arose. Woods needed help to gain entry to the apartment and secure the occupants inside. He radioed Thomas as he worked late from the day shift. Doyle Green bumped him and they also got Nathan Brumley to volunteer to participate. The sergeant going to the scene was Gene Cox.

The sergeant and three other officers arrived and shared information about the case. The guy in the apartment was sixty-year-old Thomas Garza

Malone, the poster boy for the early release program in the Texas prisons of the seventies. He served ten years of a ninety-nine-year sentence for murder. Once paroled, he killed another man in a bar fight and did another twelve years of hard time on a life sentence for murder.

Malone had nineteen-year-old stripper Bonnie Sue Hollis with him. Hollis had recently sold heroin to a narc. The Buffalo Hunters would have sweet, innocent-sounding Cain knock on the door and say, "It's me," which usually prompted the drug-dealer to open up, triggering officers to hit the door with their shoulders and order the occupants up against the wall. The ruse worked—until this night.

Hollis didn't open up. Malone jammed a two-by-four against the door knob, burying the other end into the carpet. The officers heard the toilet flush down evidence as they kicked down the door. Flushing continued steadily as several minutes passed before the narcs gained entry to the darkened one-bedroom apartment.

Green took the lead with his shotgun. He grabbed Hollis by the arm, eased past a small Christmas tree and stepped down a hallway. Green aimed his shotgun as he rounded the corner toward the bedroom. Malone was in a shooter's stance with a five-shot, snub-nosed .38.

POW! POW ...

Malone's first shot struck Green's left hand on the stock side of the shotgun. The bullet hit the third knuckle of his left index finger and traveled up into his wrist where it tried to exit the palm side. Deflected by the face of Green's watch, it then continued up his arm and came to rest near his elbow.

Malone aimed his .38 carefully. The memories of what happened in the next few seconds consist of the fiery yellow orange muzzle of the .38, ungodly intense pain, death and the strong desire to catch the bad guy whodunit.[5]

POW! POW!! POW!!!

Woods and Thomas returned the fire in uncertain directions, unable to zero in on Malone as he aimed the gun barrel precisely in their direction. All of this happened in split seconds.[6]

Malone's second bullet struck Woods' gun, deflecting the slug down through the officer's groin. Woods' gun jammed helplessly after he got off two rounds, and he took cover behind Brumley after a third slug traveled dead center through Brumley's chest cavity. Brumley was shocked back to life three times that night, living in physical and mental pain for the rest of his life.[7]

"I saw the muzzle and his face," Thomas recalled the instant a slug—believed to be from Malone's fourth shot—tore through his stomach and stuck between two vertebrae, barely missing his spinal column. The officer returned a total of fourteen rounds.[8]

Green was down near the dinette table. He had his regular duty weapon in his "jack ass" shoulder holster, but he was left-handed with the wound putting his left hand out of commission. So he just lay there—shot, bloody and scared—wondering if he should try to get his gun out of his holster and shoot right-handed. He later said he was afraid he would be too slow or miss, and Malone would take it away from him and shoot him with it. Playing possum was his best decision.[9]

Woods retreated out the front door, where Thomas had difficulty standing and walking. Woods and Thomas thought Green and Brumley were dead.[10]

Malone went into the bedroom to put on a t-shirt, came back out and picked up Green's shotgun, wanting to shoot the possum. Malone started pulling what he thought was the trigger while pointing the shotgun at Green's head. In his confusion Malone actually caused the slide to release and eject one live round and pump another one into the chamber. He kept pumping until the gun was empty and Green was still alive.[11]

Thomas and Cain were shoulder-to-shoulder, side-by-side in the doorway when the shots rang out. The shot that hit Thomas in the gut caused blood to spill out over his left hand, which was holding his stomach. "I've been shot!" Thomas said to Cain. "Get me some help!" He continued shooting, thinking he had hit Malone. The bullet in Thomas' vertebrae pressed against the nerve that put his right leg to sleep. Woods picked up Brumley from a pool of fresh red blood and pulled him out, while Green hugged the floor, ever the possum.[12]

Malone was shot one time, through the sagging skin that hung below his bicep area. It was never determined whose bullet hit him.

Thomas' leg was numb and he couldn't stand up. He heard the racking of Green's shotgun and thought Malone was trying to kill him. The gun wasn't working. It never fired. Malone never released the safety. He pointed the shotgun at Thomas twice, tried to pull the trigger and ejected at least two rounds. Thomas had seven rounds left and wanted to sit there and keep him in this apartment. But he couldn't see what he was doing behind the counter of the living room, only hearing the racking of the shotgun.[13]

In less than another split second, twenty-year-old June Cain had to make a decision of what to do. Cain saw the muzzle blasting of a gun like it was in slow motion. She cocked her gun and pointed it at Bonnie Sue Hollis, whose hands were spread out on the carpet. Cain had to get help for her partners. This meant sprinting down the stairway to a police radio. Officers had Walkie Talkies in 1975 that were useless in "dead zones" like this run-down apartment. Not taking a chance on a dead zone, Cain got to the stair steps and yelled to Sergeant Cox to throw her the keys to the police car so she could get to a reliable radio.[14]

Then Malone got help from an unexpected source, the apartment manager who mistook Thomas for the drug dealer. The manager was about three-hundred pounds and clad in a sleeveless t-shirt and boxer shorts. He barked at the wounded Thomas: "Drop your gun! I've called the police!" Then he fired a shot that barely missed the officer's head. Thomas painfully tossed his badge in the man's direction. "Anybody can get a badge," he responded, and fired more shots.[15]

Thomas limped down the steps, dodging more bullets. The pistol-packing manager soon surrendered to somebody who set him straight.

Cain radioed, "Officers down," asking for help and ambulances. Before she could put down the radio mike, she heard sirens and saw Thomas out in the street waving for help. Cain told him to sit down, hearing him state, "June, I've got to get these patrol cars and ambulances in here. I think Doyle's dead."[16]

Meanwhile, Malone tiptoed over the wounded Green, left his apartment and crept down the narrow second-story walkway to the apartment unit of an older woman two doors down.

Almost as chaotic as the actual shooting scene was the narrow Golfcrest Street with cars parked on both sides, virtually blocking the ambulances and responding officers. Cain and four others actually picked up the back end of a car parked on the side of the road and moved it toward the drainage ditch so ambulances could get through.

Despite his four hits with five pistol shots and seeming to have luck on his side, Malone couldn't find an adequate escape route. Sergeant Cox arrested him at the apartment unit down the walkway as Houston Fire Department paramedics carefully placed four wounded officers into three ambulances. A few miracles kept all four alive or else the Houston Police Department would have experienced its second bloodiest night in history next to the Camp Logan Riot.

The four officers survived serious line-of-duty wounds and returned to duty six months later. Instead of heroes, they become "morale problems." Their overall treatment led Bob Thomas and others to seriously question departmental philosophies and benefits enough to initiate a new, more aggressive police union within three and a half years.[17]

Thomas felt he was alive because Malone mishandled the shotgun and that the trigger-happy apartment manager missed shooting a man he didn't know was a police officer. Malone was able to launch his escape attempt when Thomas left Green and sought shelter from the manager's shooting attack behind a parked vehicle downstairs.

About twenty-five to thirty apartment dwellers gathered downstairs after hearing the shots. They spotted Malone and pointed toward his temporary haven as Sergeant Cox rushed in to arrest the man whose shootings came within inches of killing four officers.

Fire Department paramedics placed Green and Woods in one ambulance and Thomas and Brumley in another. Nathan Brumley "died" at the scene. Paramedics quickly resuscitated him and laid him and Thomas side-by-side in their ambulance. Halfway to Ben Taub General Hospital, they lost Brumley again. They pulled over to the side of the road, again shocked him back to life, and rushed him to Ben Taub while leaving the still-breathing Thomas with a paramedic. Within seconds another ambulance arrived to pick them up.

Brumley "died" yet a third time and underwent an out-of-body experience as one of the best emergency doctors in the business, Dr. Ken Maddox, brought him back to life in the Ben Taub Emergency Room. Later, Brumley told his fellow officers that he remembered looking down from above his body and seeing Maddox. "He was ripping me apart like a watermelon and I could feel his fingers in my chest. I kept trying to talk. There was no pain, but I could feel the sensation. I was up above and could see a light. I was looking down at my body."[18]

Green underwent surgery and his arm was placed in a cast. He needed two more surgeries. Woods felt lucky the bullet deflected off his watch or else he would have suffered a more serious chest wound. Both rested at home in bed for several months.

Doctors cut a hole for a tube in Thomas' abdomen to drain an abscess. They also installed a colostomy bag he used for four months before undergoing surgery to repair the damage. For the next four months he endured a low-grade fever caused by two different infections. His weight dropped sixty pounds to 135.

Pappy Bond was police chief by this time and visited each of his wounded narcs on Sunday afternoons at their residences or personally called each one at his home. The four men longed to get back to normal working routines and closely bonded during their recovery process. Two months passed before the quartet was instructed to return on a limited-duty basis, Thomas still running a fever with his colostomy bag and drainage tube in tow.

Narcotics underwent another series of supervisory changes, largely the result of the Golfcrest shooting, a separate shootout that wounded several narcs and the April 8, 1976 line-of-duty death of Jim Kilty. Most of the supervisors didn't know Woods, Brumley, Green and Thomas, and didn't like the fact they were physically incapable of working the streets. Brumley was in the poorest shape. While off-duty in recovery, he couldn't hold a gun, and once back on duty he started shaking at the sound of loud noises. The cruel jokers popped sacks behind his back, causing obvious responses of fright.

The four wounded officers orchestrated their return on the same day. Woods returned to regular duty, but the other three were assigned to answer phones. Within two weeks, their supervisors called them into the office for a conference. They told them that they were a lingering reminder of the danger of Narcotics, a negative morale factor. They each were to be transferred.

All hell broke loose. The new brass wanted all four in lighter duty, maybe even back in uniform. The officers hobbled down to find the former captain who teamed up the Buffalo Hunters. There in the chief's office sat Pappy Bond, who screamed, cussed and dressed down the new Narcotics captain. Green and Brumley transferred to the Helicopter Division, while Woods and Thomas stayed in Narcotics. Thomas went back on injury leave for his colostomy closure surgery and returned to work in June 1976. Woods was named the 100 Club's 1976 Officer of the Year.

Conditions worsened for narcs on the streets. Three more were shot in February 1976, and Jim Kilty was killed in the line of duty during an arrest on April 8. Captains and lieutenants were replaced and most of the sergeants transferred. Thomas got paperwork from two doctors saying he was fit for full-time duty. He spent time on surveillance without making any arrests through the summer. By September, he was again buying drugs and making cases. Eventually he and his two closest friends in Narcotics, Ashwood and Williamson, were transferred out against their wishes.

Three of the four officers stuck it out until retirement. Three of them pursued other careers, Green in U.S. Customs, Woods in land investment and

Thomas as a lawyer. Brumley didn't make it. Cancer struck him down and affected "every organ the bullet struck." He died in 1981.

The quickly-seasoned June Cain stayed in Narcotics, later married an assistant police chief, Tommy Shane, and became the first female police helicopter pilot in HPD history. She retired in 2006 with thirty-one years on the job.

Thomas Garza Malone was sentenced to life imprisonment for his deadly assaults on the officers. After serving five years, Malone died behind bars in Huntsville.

It was only a matter of time before this case and its aftermath would change the course of HPD history.

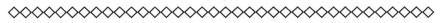

Officer James F. Kilty

Officer Jim Kilty went down as one of the most aggressive Narcotics officers in HPD history. Popular among his colleagues and judges at the courthouse, Kilty, a graduate of Police Cadet Class No. 28, was a member of Ripley's Raiders who often led or participated in an average of two search warrants and/or six subpoenas served each shift. Narcs in the 1970s earned "$50 within what a captain made" with overtime and court time figured in. The One Hundred Club of Houston named Kilty its 1973 Officer of the Year in the Radio Patrol-Investigative Field.

In addition, Kilty, single and available for tons of overtime, regularly bought drugs from hitchhikers and soon developed a broad network of snitches who led him and other Raiders to the big dealers. Many of them hailed from the Montrose-Westheimer hippie subcultures. Kilty was a softball player who one day observed with partner John R. Hake some hippies playing softball in Montrose. The friendly, outgoing officer proceeded to organize a softball game billed as "the Pigs versus the Hippies." This first of its kind event drew national news media attention.

The early morning of April 8, 1976, Kilty and other Ripley's Raiders were in the process of executing a search warrant involving a cook at a Southwest Freeway hostelry when the suspect shot Kilty. HPD officers were still years away from the regular use of bullet-proof vests. Kilty was dead on arrival at

Ben Taub General Hospital after his fellow narcs transported him there. Several of his fellow Raiders shot and killed the suspect, Willie Howard.

Many throughout HPD felt Jim Kilty embodied the spirit and drive of the ideal police officer. For many years after his death the annual Jim Kilty Law Enforcement Softball Tournament was held in his honor. In 1978, Kilty's brother Mark became an HPD officer out of Class No. 80, and one of Mark Kilty's sons is a namesake for Jim Kilty. Mark Kilty later also spent time with Ripley's Raiders. But one of the greatest tributes came within a year of Kilty's tragic line of duty death when the Houston Police Officers Association (now HPOU) distributed a bumper sticker which read, THE BADGE MEANS YOU CARE. The badge depicted was Kilty's No. 1856.[19]

Patrol brass put Bob Thomas in "the armpit of the police force"—riding on the evening shift of the Northeast substation. Then the two men in Thomas' corner, Pappy Bond and Lieutenant Eli Rivera—the only brass that understood the plight of the wounded narcs—retired to security jobs at Tenneco.

Thomas and the other three seriously injured narcs were the first in history whose injuries were subjected to worker's compensation laws amended in September 1975 to cover municipal employees. Heretofore, officers injured in the line of duty could not take off for sprained backs, broken bones or injuries affecting soft tissue. The department ordered Thomas to work light duty with a colostomy bag and a low-grade infection.

Initially, the shabby treatment disappointed and angered four men considered to be good officers. Thomas took the sergeant's examination and scored high except for a captain's low evaluation given him for failing to write at least two moving tickets per day when most of Thomas' citations involved expired plates or license stickers. When the Houston Police Officers Association wouldn't furnish an attorney to fight the low evaluation, Thomas hired his own lawyer to argue against the captain's unfair evaluation.[20]

Other promotion lists were similarly affected. The chances of one lieutenant, Tom Koby, died when Koby was No. 1 on the captain's promotional list three years in a row. Thomas' case resulted in enough alterations in the evaluations to place him fifteen slots higher on the sergeant's list, thus attracting the attention of Harry Caldwell, acting chief until Mayor Jim McConn made the appointment permanent in McConn's first term in 1978.

Thomas learned he was enjoined from entering the Northeast Substation, subject to arrest if he did. He was then ordered to report immediately to the Property Room, long established as a duty station for injured officers during physical recovery periods. The reassignment had all the earmarks of punishment since HPD had no opening at the Property Room. There were five officers assigned there—three with heart problems, another who had suffered a nervous breakdown and a fifth with a glass eye. Thomas had Wednesdays and Thursdays off on the evening shift.[21]

The officer had the reputation for voicing disagreement over the way narcotics cases were handled at the courthouse. Thomas' record, combined with high recommendations from past supervisors, assistant district attorneys and a high test score, made him a prime candidate for the FBI. He passed the background check, yet when word leaked that he was headed to the Feds, suddenly he became known as a malcontent who questioned authority and didn't follow orders.[22]

Had Thomas left for the FBI, the HPPU never would have taken shape. His case for change was mounting, beginning with wounded officers' treatment in the aftermath of the December 1975 shootout; second was the torpedo from above that ruined his chances of getting into the FBI; and, third, an experience that clearly showed that civil service laws didn't provide an officer with due process after a suspension.[23]

The latter experience in January 1975 emerged during the third week Thomas was assigned to Narcotics and involved the sexual proclivity and demands of a night shift Narcotics sergeant. The sergeant took sexual advantages of female narcotics suspects in return for dropping charges against them. The department fired the sergeant, who otherwise had an exemplary record, a wife and six children, and nineteen years and nine months service with HPD—three months away from vesting. The logical plan might have been to allow him to retire in three months. Instead, the department quietly fired him, causing him to lose a retirement that amounted to thirty percent of his salary, medical benefits and forfeiture of more than $25,000 he had contributed to his pension fund.[24]

Thomas thought that the errant sergeant should have gotten back the money he had earned and contributed to a pension fund. The young officer also was struck by the fact the sergeant had no recourse through an independent appeals process and restricted due process. The process at the time entailed a hearing before a three-member Civil Service Commission appointed by the mayor with the later option of appealing to a state district court. This procedure was a far cry from the modern day practice of independent arbitration.[25]

The treatment of the sergeant set the stage for the formation of a new union and an eventual reform movement that finally saw the necessary changes in procedures that would have allowed him to keep his accrued benefits.

Within six months of Thomas' assignment to the Property Room in 1978, the department conducted a surprise audit, unannounced and the first in five years. Previous Property Room audits were openly scheduled at least three months prior to the auditors' appearance. Thomas was ready for them, taking care to log in money and pornographic films and videotapes. The audit turned up nothing negative, but it sent signals to many other officers in the department that if the higher-ups were after you, they would stop at nothing to nail you.

As 1979 began, Thomas had enough ammunition to strike a mighty blow for largely overlooked Patrol officers, present and future. Like the Houston police officers who met secretly to write state laws granting them civil service protection in the 1940s, Thomas and a widening inner circle started thinking about a new union separate and apart from the HPOA.

Formed in 1945, the HPOA was there for every rank. Many of those forming the group had graduated to sergeants, lieutenants and above. In 1979, the association was perceived as being too soft on representation and in bed with the police administration and City Hall. The oil-rich Houston economy of the seventies enabled the city to pay for two generous back-to-back pay raises under Mayor Jim McConn. Despite these lifts in morale, Bob Thomas and other leaders found shortcomings in legal representation, health insurance and job security.[26]

The economy elsewhere in the United States wasn't as prosperous. Detroit and other cities laid off officers. So down to Houston these officers came from New York and the Midwest to enroll in HPD cadet classes. These new officers signalled a major change in HPD demographics. Instead of a force consisting of Texas country boys and former members of one military service branch or another, a growing number had some college behind them, talked differently, were more demanding and knew the power of unions.

Thomas garnered a multitude of issues after serving on the HPOA board for two years. He knew if he and his friends couldn't dramatically change HPOA, they would initiate an ambitious plan to get aggressive legal representation, more inclusive insurance coverage and due process. By the end of the 1979 session of the Texas Legislature, Thomas and his fellow Waltrip High School alumnus, state Representative John Whitmire, had a notch on their political gun. Whitmire sponsored a measure to require refundability of police pension contributions if an officer left the department before twenty years of vested service—like the Narcotics sergeant earlier in the 1970s.

Withholding these contributions was highly hypocritical since the city refunded them for firefighters and municipal employees. City lobbyists killed bills in two previous sessions that would have achieved this goal. Thomas and some other HPOA board members believed that many of HPD's sharpest and brightest young officers were leaving to work in other law enforcement agencies, not wanting to contribute pension monies that they knew they would never get back unless they were around for twenty years.

An HPOA meeting with the pension board members was especially rancorous. One or two of them yelled at Thomas and the others. Coincidentally, Chief Caldwell was the long-term Pension Board chairman during this period. Thomas pushed the issue at the next HPOA board meeting by requesting an unprecedented roll call vote for the Whitmire legislation. It passed unanimously and the proposed measure became the association's sole goal in the upcoming Legislature. The bill exclusively required refundability of pension contributions and became law despite the Pension Board's backroom effort to fight it.[27]

Conflicts like these solidified the growing belief that HPOA was not representing the average officer on the street. The association board members came mostly from areas like Burglary and Theft and Community Services. The new officers from the north and northeast, some of whom were referred to as "the Detroit Tigers," were familiar enough with police union affiliations to provide sources of information for Thomas, Raymond McFarland and Rick Ashwood. Although Thomas was the founding president of the Houston Police Patrolmen's Union (HPPU), Ashwood was the primary instigator.[28]

Like the HPD Civil Service advocates of the 1940s, the first HPPU members met in secret. At 11 p.m. on October 29, 1979 at the Holiday Inn on Memorial and Sawyer, just west of 61 Riesner, they started flocking into a meeting room. Each person brought a $10 initiation fee. A total of fifty-three people joined on the spot. The union would alter the future benefit package for all Houston officers by embarking on a crusade for improved insurance, legal representation that included due process and even higher salaries.

These steps resulted in a growing number of young police officers believing that the Houston Police Officers Association was too close with the city administration. The HPOA spent $40,000 annually on athletic events that included sponsorship of Little League teams and the establishment and financing of softball leagues for its members. Younger, more aggressive officers from states in the Northeast and Midwest expected more than a time-honored brotherhood and were bothered that HPOA budgeted a mere $15,000 for legal services.[29]

Low dues reflected low expectations. HPOA's major thrust was the yearly study of city finances and the recommendation of salary increases. Parity was in effect, meaning that a sergeant shared the same pay scale as a fire captain, etc., on up the line. Council members felt they had to give firefighters and municipal employees the same percentage raise they gave officers.

Active terms like "collective bargaining," "grievance procedure" and even "due process" weren't commonly used. Feelings intensified among officers that they had fewer rights of due process than common crooks. When an officer was transferred to the jail, Dispatch or the property room as punishment, he didn't speak out for fear his work life would worsen or he would be labeled a malcontent for the rest of his career. "Firings" weren't labeled as such. The affected officer literally cleaned out his locker and was "allowed to resign for personal reasons." HPD kept no record of the number of times this happened.

More aggressive members of the HPOA board started to keep score and voiced concern that younger officers got no legal representation. They preferred that money be designated for legal assistance rather than nighttime softball leagues. The scorekeepers found that the retention rate of officers had reached a new low point. New recruits in town expected a totally different philosophy than the mild-mannered HPOA. Some association members had growing families and felt unions like those in the Northeast endorsed work stoppages and strikes. HPOA President Bill Elkin and the association wanted nothing to do with an organized union. Elkin's leadership resulted in the appointment of the organization's first African-American board member, J. J. Berry.

A growing number of new HPD officers hailed from Chicago, New York, Philadelphia and Boston. Many of these officers had walked picket lines with their dads, while Texas-born officers had lived in a right-to-work state. About the same time Bob Thomas of Central Patrol became a more active HPOA member, so did Tommy Britt of North Shepherd, Rick Ashwood of Central, Raymond McFarland of North Shepherd, Doug Carr of Central/North Shepherd and Chris Gillespie of Northeast. Gillespie was from the Midwest and had a college degree. "It was almost like the perfect storm of people coming together," Britt said. Each had his own strengths. Gillespie, for example, introduced the idea of collective bargaining, grievance procedures and career development.[30]

Vast differences existed with the older, more influential HPOA members. The younger faction had some college hours. These six activists each worked in uniform on weekends and nights or evenings, while the majority of HPOA board members had 8-to-5 desk jobs, take-home cars and didn't have to wear uniforms. Each of the younger challengers had a grievance of one kind or another and sought the strength in numbers to resolve their problems. They felt the need to take a more strident involvement in the organization to deal with their perception that some of the people running the department had a moral compass that wasn't running true north.

As early as 1978, Britt, Bob Thomas and four others ran as "a reform slate" for the HPOA board. Thomas and Ashwood were already board members but unsuccessfully sought board leadership offices, causing them to believe they needed a new union.

Thomas soon got the reputation as a troublemaker. Older members weren't reluctant to express their desire to give him a good old-fashioned "whupping." The bitterness from his 1975 near-death line-of-duty experience remained a chip on his shoulder, and he sometimes came across as a smart aleck. Yet his leadership was effective enough for Britt and many others to later conclude that most of the good things that happened to officers took place because of Thomas' leadership.[31]

These new activists were soon known by a new universal identifier, "Baby Boomers," the first generation to grow up in the sixties, affected by protests for civil rights and women's liberation or against the Vietnam War. The officers figured they could conduct their own form of protest and maybe get somewhere. Yet the priority for HPOA President A. J. Burke, a popular solo motorcycle officer, was a new location for the association's headquarters. Real estate sources offered two intriguing possibilities. One was the Brazos

Hotel in downtown, the other the Atascocita Country Club property on the northeast side.

Both had high asking prices, discouraging most HPOA members. The association could have used the golf course for its golf-playing members and sold off most of the remaining acreage to a developer. Instead, the board decided to lease a building on Jackson Street in downtown that once housed the Salvation Army and was later torn down to make way for the George R. Brown Convention Center.

HPOA then purchased property at 1600 State Street, two blocks from 61 Riesner, where it constructed an 8,975-square-foot building that opened in 1983. It cost $553,000 and was later dedicated to the late Lieutenant Breck Porter, a hero in the establishment of state civil service protection for officers. (The structure was remodelled in 2009 at a cost of $463,000). To help pay for what became the Breck Porter Building, HPOA sponsored a country and western concert with Roy Clark as one of the headliners in the old Coliseum. Outside supporters bought steers at the Houston Livestock Show & Rodeo and donated the proceeds to HPOA; the beef was used at benefit barbecues.

Not until grand juries stepped up investigations of police brutality cases did HPOA hire a lawyer to represent members who were targets in these investigative procedures. The first lawyer hired was a former HPD officer, John Lohmann, through his firm Lohmann, Glazer and Irwin. Another legal counselor, D. Reid Walker, also was hired through Lohmann's firm and became an authority in state civil service law.

Thomas and a growing list of ardent followers of uniformed patrol officers on duty after dark readily asserted that pay raises were one thing but legal representation and insurance benefits were quite another. At the birth of the Houston Police Patrolmen's Union on October 29, 1979, founding President Thomas stressed points like these and backed up his words at frequent news conferences. The new union concerned Mayor McConn, Police Chief Caldwell and long-time political movers and shakers more than a Category Five hurricane. Thomas thought he would be fired and postponed the first secret organizational meeting for the union until his wife Pam gave birth to their youngest daughter in September. He didn't want to lose maternity benefits.[32]

Summoned to Caldwell's office on the day he announced formation of the new union, Thomas became physically ill, thinking he would be dismissed along with other union founders. From outside Caldwell's office, he heard the chief rant and rave about the union and the disloyal officers who formed it. As the minutes ticked into hours, Thomas remained apprehensive, but his confidence slowly grew. He later learned that influential Houston area AFL-CIO labor leader Don Horn wised up McConn. The mayor was about to win his second term with Horn's political influence and listened on the phone as Horn posed important questions: What had Thomas done other than what any other officer was entitled to do under the Constitution? What law had he broken? Was the city ready to combat the lawsuit that would result from a firing?

According to McConn, he told Chief Caldwell to use every resource to discredit Thomas, thinking it was just a matter of time before they broke up HPPU. But HPPU membership grew by leaps and bounds because Thomas and union leaders were hitting HPOA in its weakest spots—its inability to publicly articulate the issues impacting working officers.

Having staff attorneys to provide legal advice to members was in high demand by officers anxious about situations like the infamous Joyvies and Webster incidents. The union felt that having a lawyer at either of these cases might have completely changed the dynamics of the resulting investigations. As it was, people were fired and lives destroyed at the feet of the HPOA, whose dues were $3.50 a month, a sum which HPPU contended was not enough to hire lawyers.

Thomas argued that a lawyer at the scene in which officers said suspect Randy Webster was armed with a pistol would have made a dramatic difference. Had a union lawyer been there to sort out the facts, the investigation would have shown the case to be what many HPD officers believed it really was—an accidental shooting at the hands of one officer. The findings could well have been that his gun safety was horrendous, but it wasn't an indictable offense. The union leaders suggested that when you have a lawyer come up and say, "What happened?" ninety-nine percent of the time officers are going to do the right thing.

HPPU pioneers also believed the most controversial case in HPD history—the in-custody death of Joe Campos Torres—may not have happened had there been a strong police union in place pressing issues such as the faulty, under-budgeted jail conditions at the time of the events of May 5–7, 1977. HPD had a clinic in the basement of the jail since the building opened in the 1950s but never manned it. Officers with an injured suspect routinely went to Ben Taub General Hospital.[33]

22

THE DARKEST DAY

Mayor Fred Hofheinz wasn't about to make another mistake at HPD after Carrol Lynn. Hofheinz couldn't persuade council members to consider an outsider and waited until after his 1975 re-election to select another insider.[1]

Hofheinz had known Byron Glenn "Pappy" Bond throughout his twenty-two-year HPD career. The rotund captain grew up in the elder Mayor Hofheinz' administration in 1953 when Fred was in his teens, making him a "comfort factor" for the young mayor. In a serious interview with Bond about the chief's job, the mayor was concerned about the man's fluctuating weight and asked, "Pappy, you're overweight, aren't you?"

"Who told you?" Bond deadpanned.

"Pappy" was much more likeable than his predecessor. Practically everyone used the same terms to describe him: rotund, jovial, friendly, honest, likeable, qualified, fair. Altogether, the newest chief would serve eighteen months on the job, the same tenure almost to the number of days as Carrol Lynn. Bond started with the same quick wit for which he was well known. As the job took a strong toll, his weight grew to more than three hundred pounds, while the patented Pappy smile faded to a frequent frown as reports of brutality and throw-down guns emerged.[2]

Bond faced an unprecedented number of highly publicized police brutality cases. Despite his sincere efforts to court Houston's Hispanic community to get its members more involved in recruiting, he incurred its collective wrath. Instead of positive bonding with Pappy, many Hispanic leaders emphasized the department's negatives.

There were more smiles than frowns when Hofheinz made the official announcement and the chief-designate made it clear from the beginning that there would be happier days at 61 Riesner. "Be happy with Pappy" was his campaign slogan when he ran for University of Houston student body president. Once at the HPD helm, Bond told *Houston Post* police reporter Ann

POLICE CHIEF B. G. "PAPPY" BOND, JANUARY 21, 1976–JUNE 10, 1977 (HPD ARCHIVES)

James, "It'll be that way around here."[3] *Post* editorial writers picked up on the projected leadership of a large, jovial chief by concluding, "Captain Bond has had a fine career as a police officer. He will undoubtedly continue to govern by the weight of his convictions."[4]

City Council confirmed him on January 21, 1976. As expected, Bond did what practically every other newly christened chief does—he shook up the command staff. Former Chief Lynn was moved to night command; Fred Bankston took over special services from Harry Caldwell; and T. D. "Tommy" Mitchell was assigned to head a special investigation bureau consisting of Narcotics, Vice and Juvenile. The latter division was added to Special Investigations because Bond felt narcotics crimes had begun to include too many minor offenders.[5]

Former Acting Chief R. J. Clark headed the new inspections bureau that included Criminal Intelligence, Organized Crime and Planning and Research. Clark was just getting back in the fold after having suffered a heart attack just weeks before Bond's appointment. Five deputy chiefs were retained in their previous assignments: R. G. McKeehan in Patrol, W. R. Waycott in Traffic, B. K. Johnson in Criminal Investigations, W. L. Williams in Technical Services and Leroy Mouser in Administration. Deputy Chief Caldwell was assigned to

Staff Services, which included training and recruiting. Caldwell was studying for his doctorate in criminal justice at Sam Houston State University.

Bond succeeded in getting the mayor and council to create three *assistant chief* positions, creating another level of command. At the suggestion of his academy classmate, Caldwell, Bond quickly returned to council to get a fourth assistant chief for the command staff hierarchy. The person next on the peg for the position was Caldwell.

Bond was the first and only chief to hold court in the basement cafeteria at 61 Riesner. He bantered about with the troops, answering their questions about any ongoing policy changes or rumors. The sessions established a direct line of communication for the rank and file. Sometimes four or five tables were arranged to accommodate all the officers who wanted to hear what the chief had to say on any subject.[6]

The chief was much more of a PR man than either of his predecessors. Instead of short and private promotion sessions like Herman Short conducted, Bond made it a full-blown ceremony that included officers' families, something Lynn actually started with the huge promotion ceremony involving twenty-five new sergeants. Bond always insisted that the promoted officers bring their younger family members. He kept a pile of quarters on his desk and provided them to the kids to "get yourself an ice cream."[7]

Early on, Bond wanted every uniformed officer to have a portable radio in order to stay in constant contact with the dispatcher.[8] He held back his opinions about the six narcotics officers facing federal charges in connection with alleged illegal wiretaps and theft of money from narcotics suspects. But in February 1976, Bond stood up for them when he was called as a witness. He said he would return them to work should they be acquitted. However, once they were convicted, he took steps to fire them.[9]

These six weren't the only HPD personnel who saw the inside of a federal courtroom from the defense table that year. A federal jury hearing evidence of illegal wiretapping acquitted M. L. "Joe" Singleton and nine Houston officers on March 31. Singleton, a retired lieutenant, was then reinstated to his Hofheinz appointment as chief clerk of the Municipal Court System. The not guilty verdict greatly pleased the mayor, the chief, City Council and HPD. The Houston Police Officers Association generated a $25,000 legal defense fund for the group.[10]

Bond followed up the verdict by announcing his support of a proposed wiretap bill in the Legislature that required a law enforcement agency to get permission to wiretap from a district attorney or the state attorney general.

He later dropped the effort and endorsed a more cooperative effort with the Drug Enforcement Agency that would work better to "attack the big heroin peddlers in Texas."[11] Federal agencies had been authorized to use court-supervised wiretaps since the Omnibus Crime Act of 1968.

Bond also instituted better enforcement of rules affecting two tender spots with officers—take-home cars and the dress code. Ever since HPD's fleet of cars began to grow as the city annexed more square miles, Patrol and the investigative divisions needed more maneuverability. Take-home cars became highly desired perks, based on rank and seniority. Yet the department had no rules governing their use. A growing number of officers in the mid-1970s were moving to the suburbs, not having to worry about the added gasoline cost of getting to work because they had take-home cars. The increases in the gasoline budget called attention to this problem. In his initial response Bond decided that officers through the rank of sergeant and detective would be deprived of cars used to go to and from work.

By July 1976, the chief estimated that a $300,000 annual savings in the department's fuel budget was derived after 150 desk officers surrendered their cars. Not only was the department saving money, it also was about to provide better automobiles for the officers really needing them. Bond issued an order on August 6, 1976 that forbade officers from using city cars to drive more than thirty-five miles to their homes and mandated that officers in fixed-post assignments would not be given cars except for use on official police business.[12]

Younger officers desiring longer hair got a boost in April when Bond spent four and a half hours with the HPOA. He emerged from the meeting to announce that longer hair would be permitted. Younger officers wanted to wear mustaches and longer hair and go without their hats. The chief quipped, "We have a large number of young officers. When they finish their stressful assignments, I feel that they ought to relax. I feel like I'm saying that because I don't have hair."[13]

He later announced a new hair code that for the first time since the Gay Nineties allowed police officers to grow mustaches and modest sideburns—but no beards. Immediate supervisors used rulers to make sure hair length was no more than a half inch over the top of the collar in back while standing upright. An officer could have his hair not more than a half inch over the ear and no longer than mid-forehead in front. Hair should not be flared or bunched or make headgear fit poorly. Mustaches may not stretch more than a half inch beyond each corner of the mouth nor more than a half inch below the top of the upper lip.

The chief conceded that going "hatless" was permitted because hats got in the way while riding in patrol cars.

Chief Bond established the Cabs on Patrol (COP) program that allowed the city's 600 Yellow Cabs to help police track down wanted persons and vehicles and to report crimes by way of direct telephone linkups with the dispatcher.[14]

He also tried to enable the department to better communicate with the city's growing Hispanic population, even setting up Spanish classes for officers. HPD had only 147 Mexican-American officers on a force of 2,739. But other officers were fluent in the language and were called on to interpret in crisis situations. About fifty officers enrolled in Spanish language classes that required them to spend three nights a week in a classroom.

On May 4, 1976, Bond set up an internal police review committee consisting of three deputy chiefs whose job was to investigate undesirables on the force. The committee met from time to time and recommended action, which could result in "reassignment, retraining, psychiatric counseling or resignation from the force." Members of the committee were deputy chiefs Caldwell, McKeehan and Mitchell. Bond also set up a Commendation Board to form a system of recognizing officers who display exceptional heroism in dangerous situations. There were four types of awards—a medal of valor, which could be awarded posthumously; meritorious service; lifesaving and the chief of police commendation. Officer James F. Kilty, killed in the line of duty on April 8, 1976, received the first medal of valor on July 15, 1976.[15]

President John F. Kennedy's 1961 executive order to honor the nation's law enforcement officers established National Police Week in the month of May. Bond initiated an annual ceremony on the steps of police headquarters during the week of the observance. The mayor and City Council showed up when the first awards for excellence were presented to officers with their families present. The May ceremony has continued at the site of the Houston Police Officers Memorial on Memorial Drive just west of 61 Riesner. Presentations of valor, meritorious service, lifesaving awards and the police chief's commendations continue to be held throughout the year at the Academy.

The department purchased five new four-seat Hughes turbine helicopters, bringing the police fleet up to sixteen and making HPD the operator of the largest fleet of police helicopters in the world. Bond needed more back-page good news like this to counteract the Page One news his deputy chiefs B. K. Johnson and Wallace Williams were making by mid-year. Johnson endorsed a candidate for sheriff in neighboring Montgomery County on letterhead containing a deputy chief's badge and notation of Johnson's rank and assignment. The Houston city attorney later decided that Johnson did not violate any law in using his name and office in this sheriff's campaign. Johnson apologized, saying, "I find that I have made an error in judgment." The legal opinion found that the deputy chief was not in violation of the Firemen's and Policemen's Civil Service Act. The only problem was the misleading letterhead.[16]

Williams' problem was much more serious. On September 29, 1976, a federal grand jury indicted him on charges that he made false statements on his income tax returns for 1970, 1971 and 1972. The unreported income involved amounts Williams received for providing off-duty police officers for use as security guards for Southwestern Bell Telephone Co.[17]

On April 11, 1977, a federal jury found Williams guilty of filing false statements on his income taxes. The amount of unreported income was $349,000 in gross receipts from outside security services he ran from 1970 to 1972. The court sentenced Williams to six years in prison and ordered him to pay a $5,000 fine at the rate of $100 monthly. Bond suspended the twenty-one-year HPD veteran, who took his retirement.[18]

A federal grant enabled the department to embark on a recruiting campaign Bond said was needed to increase the number of blacks and Hispanics on the force. The slogan *The Badge Means You Care* was introduced alongside the depiction of a badge containing the number of the shield worn by Officer Jim Kilty. Bond followed Carrol Lynn's minority recruitment program by using a set of in-house advisors consisting of three minority officers who voiced concerns about the jobs and opportunities of minority officers and suggested ways to improve recruitment. He also regularly met with minority leaders to enlist their help. The minority recruitment effort—the first of its kind in the department's history—took place at precisely the same time a growing number of suspects, most of them blacks or Hispanics, were identifying themselves as alleged victims of police brutality.[19]

There also was a Bond initiative to set up an internal affairs unit to deal with allegations of police misconduct. Houston was the only major city police department in the nation without an internal affairs unit.[20] If established, this permanent unit would replace the current mechanism in place to handle alleged brutality. Supervisors and sometimes police administrative personnel committees would investigate officers' conduct when an issue, usually well publicized, cropped up. Bond figured that an internal affairs unit answered the demand from a growing number of minority leaders to establish a citizens' review committee. Then again, as *The Houston Post* pointed out, a grand jury had the ultimate say-so as to whether a police officer over-stepped his bounds.

The cadet class trained in May 1977 included nine Hispanic men, twelve African-American men and two women and one Asian-American female—the first in HPD history. These numbers showed a minority cadet class enrollment of 36.4 percent. One problem was that HPD had only a few minority officers of rank. Of 145 blacks, only two were sergeants and five were detectives, while among the 157 Hispanics, there were just two lieutenants. The 2,700-member department had twenty-four black and thirteen Hispanic females.

Further complicating the challenging situation was a federal lawsuit alleging sex discrimination in the height requirement for applicants to the academy. Carol F. Aldridge, a former police officer in Washington, D.C., was denied application to HPD because she was two inches shorter than the minimum five-foot-six-inch requirement for females. Aldridge's suit also contended that the department's arbitrary standards had no relation to job performance. Portions of the agility test required that candidates must run 880 feet in seventy-five seconds, drag 150 pounds for sixty feet in fifteen seconds and jump six feet from a standing position. The lawsuit was the first of a number of allegations that HPD's academy standards were designed to discriminate against females.

As for recruiting minorities, Bond stated his belief that the effort could have been better had minority leaders been more persuasive. "I thought we did a good job," Bond told *The Post*. "However, I thought I would gather a lot more cooperation from the minority community." Minority leaders cited the growing list of brutality cases as a major deterrent.[21]

None of the newspaper accounts of the February 20, 1977 death of Tommy Hanning, a thirty-nine-year-old resident of the Star of Hope Mission, said that he was a member of any minority race. But the account of a rookie officer shooting Hanning thirteen times—by reloading his gun at least once—when he caught the man breaking into a west Houston tire store, raised a red flag. Hanning was found to be armed only with a pair of scissors. The officer was put in a desk job and the case got ink in the newspapers for several weeks before a grand jury no-billed the officer.[22]

On Friday, March 11, 1977, another incident hit the news, again because of the action of a rookie officer. This time the alleged victim was a twenty-year-old black construction worker. Demas Benoit Jr. ran his car through a red light and refused when police officers ordered him to pull over. A high-speed chase ensued involving about twenty police cars and a helicopter. Benoit stopped his car in front of his house on the northeast side and some officers at the scene later reported that he then struck an officer with a beer bottle after getting out of his automobile. Officers handcuffed him.[23]

Benoit later claimed the officers beat him up while he was handcuffed, a story supported by rookie Officer Alan Nichols as well as a Catholic priest who came to the scene from his nearby church after hearing the sirens. Father Jack McGinnis said police smashed Benoit's head against the sidewalk. Benoit filed suit against the department in federal court, buoyed by testimony from McGinnis and Nichols, who said he failed to get his fellow officers to stop.

No less than fifteen officers disputed Nichols' account. Many of them said Benoit continued to bite the finger of an officer even after he was handcuffed. Mayor Hofheinz supported the officer's right to offer his side of the story; so did Chief Bond. The incident grew more complicated when Father McGinnis went on a two-week fast to protest the actions of HPD. Another of McGinnis' parishioners, Milton Glover, was killed one year earlier when officers shot him when he whipped a Bible from his back pocket, mistaking it for a weapon. A grand jury no-billed the officers and the incident became a lesson used in academy training.[24]

Two other newsworthy cases contributed to the negative trend. One involved the police shooting death of Houston lawyer and known drug user Sanford Radinsky in January 1977 when at least sixteen officers knocked on the door of his Rice Hotel residence where he was sleeping in the nude with two women. Police believed Radinsky was producing pornographic films and selling drugs at the location. Officers opened fire when Radinsky pointed a gun at one of them; their shots killed Radinsky. The women in bed with him disputed the officers' account but a grand jury decided not to indict the officer who fired most of the shots.[25]

The second case was put to the small screen in a CBS made-for-television movie entitled *The Killing of Randy Webster*. The events leading to the production happened in February 1977, when Houston police chased Webster, a white seventeen-year-old high school dropout in the process of stealing a custom van from a Dodge dealership. At the end of the chase, officers said Webster was shot when he attempted to fire a pistol at them. An autopsy showed Webster died of a bullet that entered the back of his head in a downward path. "There was also a half-inch elliptical gunshot wound in the palm of his right hand, which is consistent, since only one shot was fired, with Webster raising his hand to his head in self-defense," *Texas Monthly* reported. "This was the hand he supposedly pointed the gun at the police with. The gun found at the scene was unloaded. The only other thing known about it was that it had been shipped to Globe Discount Stores in Houston in 1964."[26]

A cab driver/witness at the scene of the confrontation said he saw police shoot Webster at close range at the end of the chase. He said the bullet was obviously fatal. Then he quickly drove away, fearing the men in blue, one of whom he saw with a smoking gun in his hand. The cab driver, Billy Junior Dolan, later told his story of "cold-blooded murder" to a homicide detective. "The police told me I lied about everything." Dolan said, "but I know what I saw."[27]

The evidence cited by *Texas Monthly*, indicating the gun wasn't loaded, contributed to the coining of a phrase in the lingo used by HPD detractors everywhere; it was a "throw-down gun."

One of the few indicators that Bond had some semblance of control came on April 25, when he announced a new pursuit policy that limited participation in a high-speed police chase involving a traffic violation to "no more than a lead car, a follow car and a helicopter."[28] The policy was Bond's response to the furor following the March 11 arrest of Demas Benoit Jr. The chief said it was very difficult for some officers to abandon a pursuit but often it was the most intelligent decision to make. The policy drew mixed reactions from the rank and file. The high-speed chase policy became a regular source of controversy for the next three decades at HPD.

Bond also was fighting a personal battle—his weight. The chief got a scare on October 13, 1976 when he was rushed to a hospital with chest pains, only to find out it was severe indigestion. Two weeks later, he asked his ranking officers to consult their doctors about a proposed weight loss program. Standing at five-foot-seven and weighing 250 pounds, Bond often referred to himself as the most visible fat man in Houston. He vowed to have a mandatory weight loss program ready in February or March 1977. The program never took hold.

A nationwide study by the Law Enforcement Assistance Administration (LEAA) said unhealthy officers will not perform as well as expected on the job.[29] HPD had no continuing program to keep officers fit. People who worked regularly with Bond, including office personnel, later said his moods were often reflective of his diet. Pappy wasn't happy. The jolly side turned dark in Pappy's last days as chief. The table-jamming sessions in the basement cafeteria gave way to private meals in the solitude of his office.

///

Bond held regular meetings with the board of the Houston Police Officers Association. "What's on your mind?" the chief asked. It was like opening up a flood gate. Bond calmly listened and took notes on his ever-present yellow legal pad.[30]

"There's people trapped in the jail and can't get out," one board member pointed out, citing a sore subject with the troops. It was an unwritten policy that if an officer abused a prisoner or failed to contribute to the annual United Fund drives, he was sent to the jail or Dispatch. The board told Pappy that he knew of an officer who was sent to the jail division years ago as punishment "and now he can't get out."[31]

Bond responded by starting a policy where officers rotated into the jail. The least senior officer off probation would be brought to the jail to replace an officer eligible to come out. "The jail rotation policy" worked well until the department had to cut down on cadet classes. Then police administrators went back to other cadet classes with members who had not yet taken a turn in the jail or dispatch, starting with officers whose names began with the later letters of the alphabet. Officers marched across the stage at graduation in alphabetical order; therefore, the order of seniority went from Z to A, from the last person to get his or her diploma to the first.

The list came to a solo officer who said, "I can't do this." The process required to replace him for six months was drawn out and complicated. The department agreed not to rotate Winston J. Rawlins to the jail for six months in 1982, unknowingly setting up one of the saddest ironies in HPD history. On March 29, 1982, Rawlins was one of two motorcycle officers killed in the line of duty in separate fiery freeway accidents with other vehicles.[32]

United Fund contributions were a constant source of irritation for officers throughout the 1950s, 1960s and 1970s. Mayors put pressure on chiefs, especially Herman Short, to make sure that HPD had a 100 percent contribution rate—or as close to it as possible. The high-pressure effort subjected officers needing to squeeze their every penny. Should they fail to make a contribution, many of them were sent to the jail, Dispatch or to a night shift with Tuesdays and Wednesdays off. It also could mean an officer got a lower efficiency rating or was passed over for promotion.

Bond started the "Extra Employment Section" by providing the Personnel Division an additional sergeant and four police officers to investigate every extra job location. There often were problems with officers working extra jobs in bars. Bond, tiring of dealing with the news media, appointed the department's first public information officer, Rick Hartley, a reporter for KTRK—Channel 13—and later KPRC—Channel 2.

Bond continued the practice of issuing special notices from the chief's office that defined changes in departmental rules and policies. The notices would be posted on bulletin boards and often only stayed in effect until somebody thumb-tacked another notice over them. Bond got especially angry at some of his deputy chiefs, angry enough at one juncture to have a sergeant prepare a seven-page paper on whether or not he had the authority under civil service law to demote them.

The police chief realized that Hofheinz was not planning to seek a third two-year term in November 1977. Although the mayor was not ready to make the decision public, Bond was ready to take action. Bond announced his decision to retire on Friday, May 6, 1977, effective June 10. He said he had accomplished "everything I wanted to accomplish." He expressed disappointment in minority recruiting efforts.[33]

A few weeks after Hofheinz announced his decision, Bond threw his hat in the mayoral election ring. The "campaign" didn't last long, and he soon withdrew to become head of security for Tenneco in downtown Houston. Many factors entered into his decision to leave. The Randall Webster "throw-down gun" case greatly disappointed him, especially when the gun was traced back to the department's property room. Details of the case didn't become official until 1979, when an U.S. Department of Justice investigation showed that two high-ranking officers had signed papers saying the gun had been melted down with many other pistols to be used in metal to make manhole covers. The same pattern held true in another case involving a dead suspect in probably the darkest day in HPD history.

On the morning of May 6, 1977, Officer Louis Elliott Sr., who hailed from a family rich in HPD tradition, detected a noticeable change in the attitude of his younger son, Carless, an enthusiastic rookie fresh out of the academy. As the two ate breakfast at the Avenue Grill near Police Headquarters, Carless didn't eat and had very little to say. His father knew something was wrong. Not long after the two departed, Carless called his father and asked to meet him again.

The rookie then told his dad the same story he recounted in forty-eight hours of court testimony in what will be forever known as "the Joe Campos

Torres case." Shocked and stunned, Louis Elliott well knew the Blue Line's "code of silence" and instantly feared his son would be drummed out for reporting what had happened. The elder Elliott quickly called a fellow Mason he highly respected—Assistant Chief B. K. Johnson.

Carless Elliott detailed for Johnson the story of a rowdy, unruly Hispanic man picked up at a disturbance in an east side bar and later taken to an old dock on Buffalo Bayou near the Harris County Courthouse complex. Johnson told Chief Pappy Bond, who launched an immediate investigation. The body of Joe Campos Torres later washed up on the banks of the bayou two days after Elliott told his story. The date was Sunday, May 8, 1977—Mother's Day.

The Torres story made national news, detailing conduct that angered many and established a reputation that HPD found difficult to live down. The *Texas Monthly* version of the story also included the series of brutal police-related episodes that had plagued Pappy Bond in 1976 and 1977. The headline: "NEW GANG IN TOWN What Happens When Cops Run Wild?"[34]

Torres was a twenty-three-year-old Army veteran and a laborer for a glass contractor. Bond established the Internal Affairs Division as a result of this episode. The IAD investigated and presented the following facts, quoted in *Texas Monthly* and other major news media.[35]

HPD Officer M. G. Oropeza was summoned to deal with a fight in a club in the 4900 block of Canal in the city's predominately Hispanic east side. Oropeza asked the Dispatcher for another patrol unit to be sent to the bar before heading there himself. It was just after 11:35 p.m. Thursday, May 5 when he walked into the darkened cantina to find the manager trying to eject Torres for quarrelling with two other customers. Torres had a drinking problem serious enough to be discharged from the Army. At the time of the confrontation he was at the end of a twelve-hour drinking bout. Oropeza and two other patrol officers, Stephen Orlando and Carless Elliott, arrived and wrestled with Torres, handcuffed him and put him in the backseat of their patrol car.

When two other patrol cars then arrived, Orlando informed the four additional officers that the prisoner had put up a fight. Officer Joseph Janish suggested that the officers try to quiet him. As Oropeza returned to duty, a total of six officers in three patrol cars carried Torres to a rundown warehouse area just across Buffalo Bayou from the courthouse complex. They drove down an embankment to the south bank of the bayou, below street level and out of sight.

There, each one of the officers except Elliott took turns striking Torres while he was handcuffed. One of the officers, Terry Denson, remarked that he had always wanted to watch a prisoner swim the bayou. The group then took Torres to the city jail where the duty sergeant told them to take their prisoner to Ben Taub General Hospital for treatment prior to his official booking.

Orlando thought about letting Torres go rather than spending several hours at the hospital and then only being able to charge the prisoner with being drunk and disorderly. Once back in the police car, Torres cursed the officers, prompting Orlando to call Janish and Denson to suggest another meeting on the bayou. Officers Lewis Kinney and Glenn Brinkmeyer, participants in the earlier beating, heard Orlando's call and returned to the scene. Perched on a location about twenty feet from the oft-polluted waters of Buffalo Bayou, the six officers stood with Torres while Elliott removed the handcuffs and immediately left to answer a dispatcher's call. "Let's see if the wetback can swim," Denson said. Torres supposedly assured the officer that he could swim. Then Denson shoved him over the edge. Elliott returned to the other five officers and handed Torres' wallet to Denson, who tossed it in the water as one or two of the others shined their lights on Torres and later said they saw him swimming across the bayou on his back. The body was found three days later. The medical examiner ruled that the cause of death was drowning.

Chief Bond spent all day the next day in meetings and emerged early Tuesday to tell the news media that murder charges had been filed against Officer Terry Denson, age twenty-seven, in the drowning death of Joe Campos Torres. The chief said Denson was one of six officers thought to be involved.

Bond took the case to a grand jury on Tuesday and secured an indictment against Denson. The chief relieved the other five officers of duty, pending the outcome of further investigation by grand jurors. Bond named Captain Les Wunsche to be the first head of Internal Affairs. Wunsche prepared by attending a ten-day internal affairs school at the University of Louisville in Kentucky. Some of the first members of the Internal Affairs team were Joe Gamino, Don McWilliams, Ed Whitehead, Larry Ott, Eli Uresti, Pokey Sammons and Lloyd Rivers. Wunsche set up shop in the north end of the building at 61 Riesner. They immediately were flooded with cases. The captain tried to be fair by hearing "both sides" of every case. He didn't tackle the Torres case, which was already in Homicide's bailiwick.[36]

A total of six officers were on the hot seat. Two of them, Carless Elliott and Stephen Orlando, were sons of Houston police officers. The other three,

Brinkmeyer, Janish and Kinney, each had less than four years with HPD. None of the six had any previous disciplinary actions.

On May 13—less than a week after Torres' body was found—Chief Bond fired five of the six officers. He allowed Elliott to stay on the force, relieved of duty with pay. Houston's Hispanic community was incensed and called for justice, which leaders said meant more than just being fired. Fifty people, including Torres' mother Margaret, demonstrated outside City Hall. Joe Campos Torres Sr., the dead man's father, went to the FBI and asked for a Department of Justice investigation. The Houston chapter of the League of United Latin American Citizens (LULAC) joined the effort as did an aggressive state representative from the east side, Ben T. Reyes, later the first Hispanic member of the Houston City Council. The Torres family blamed a prejudiced system for requiring a bond of only $10,000 for Denson, who posted it and went free.[37]

The community's anger spilled over into minor incidents involving Hispanics and officers. Statistics from the months following the incident showed a significant increase in the crime rate, coupled with a much lower clearance rate. Officers interviewed by the news media lamented the fact that the entire department was being judged based on the actions of five or six police officers. Bond met on a regular basis with Hispanic community leaders and their groups, including the local Political Association of Spanish-speaking Organizations (PASO).

More than thirty years later, Hispanic activists still cited what happened to Torres; incidents that resulted in the shooting deaths of two Hispanic teenagers caused one leader to voice the sarcastic insinuation that HPD officers "used to throw us in the bayou and we had a chance to swim; now they just shoot us."[38]

Mayor Fred Hofheinz was out of the country on city business when Torres died. The incident struck the very nerve center of a major Hofheinz constituency. He had pledged to blacks and Hispanics to reform the department by putting a stop to brutal acts against minority suspects and making it more open to minority applicants. The mayor literally spit fire when he met with reporters on his first day back at City Hall. "I think there is something loose in this city that is an illness," he said, defining illness as the "attitude of some people—including a lot of community leaders, people in charge of mass communications—believing that whatever a Houston police officer does is okay." Hofheinz apologized to his constituencies for his previously expressed views that instances of police misconduct were "isolated events."[39]

HPOA President R. C. Rich told *The Post* that bad news about the department always received more public attention than the good news. Yet this was the straw that broke the camel's back, and he predicted that the community would "try every officer in the department" over the actions of a few. Eventually the grand jury also indicted Officer Steve Orlando for murder in Torres' death.[40]

Hofheinz persuaded Bond to stay on for another month before he retired to become the director of corporate security for Tenneco. Bond relished the well-paid private security job in contrast to the public pressure applied daily. He hired away Lieutenant Eli Rivera from a job he loved after twenty-one years in HPD. Bond's health started going downhill in the summer of 1986 when he seemed depressed with cancer. His weight even dipped from 275 pounds to 220. On election night in November 1986, Rivera bade Bond good evening. Hours later, there was a shooting at Pappy's home. The retired chief used a pistol to take his own life.[41]

23

THE DRILL INSTRUCTOR

Harry Caldwell met the Joe Campos Torres and throw-down gun nightmares head-on and stood stridently in his approach to easing the pains they caused. He delegated little authority and generally rubbed both the street officers and the brass the wrong way. He frequently engaged in his own public relations campaigns without involving anyone else.

Caldwell found himself heading a department with extremely low morale dealing with a high crime rate amidst stern criticism from intolerant Hispanic and African-American community leaders. For the first time in his career, Caldwell saw grown men in blue with tears in their eyes because of the lack of public trust caused by the Torres incident. Pappy Bond admitted to Caldwell shortly before announcing his retirement that his nerves couldn't take being police chief any longer.[1]

Caldwell inherited a number of controversies. On April 26, 1978, he fired the three officers involved in a notable throw-down case that resulted in the death of Billy Keith Joyvies. They were Sergeant Walter Earl Plaster and Officers John Stephen White and Clarence M. Burkett. Plaster and White were indicted in federal court on charges they conspired to violate Joyvies' civil rights. Burkett was an unindicted conspirator. In a trial before U.S. District Judge John V. Singleton Jr., Burkett, under a grant of immunity, testified that he fired a .25-caliber automatic pistol provided by his partner, White, who minutes later handed the gun to Plaster. Burkett, later a private investigator, testified that the actions of the officers were necessary to make things flow smoother after Joyvies "obviously dumped" a gun he was firing at the officers during a high-speed chase on July 11, 1975.

Singleton issued a directed verdict of acquittal on July 25, 1979, after concluding that the prosecution had produced insufficient evidence. A strong believer in removing police officers who violated rules and regulations, Chief Caldwell was not encouraging about reinstatement of any of the three officers.

**POLICE CHIEF HARRY
CALDWELL, JUNE 11,
1977–FEBRUARY 29, 1980
(HPD ARCHIVES)**

Caldwell dealt with three notable cases (Torres, Webster and Joyvies) that attracted national attention. The news coverage, plus concerned and angry minority citizens, resulted in an action that Caldwell claimed that only he knew about.

The chief was unsure of the initiation date of his next big challenge or the particular person who delivered the message to him. Over the years he has claimed in public statements that a high-ranking U.S. Department of Justice official told him in a 1978 phone call that the DOJ was giving serious consideration to placing the Houston Police Department in federal receivership. Caldwell quoted the individual as saying he was on the verge of going to federal court over the matter. It would require the appointment of a master to oversee HPD.[2]

Caldwell has maintained that he urgently requested that the official give him a month to make improvements in the department. He also asked that the possible move not be made public so the chief could preserve what little morale remained. Efforts to substantiate Caldwell's account were unsuccessful. The chief has asserted that he was granted a thirty-day reprieve. He immediately put into effect a new policy that said officers could only use deadly force if they felt a life was in imminent danger. The chief also ordered officers to remove their beads, shine their shoes and get away from cowboy outfits. Right in the middle of Houston's rodeo season, he told them they couldn't wear cowboy boots. In retirement Caldwell admitted getting rid of "this cowboy image" was not his best decision.

The chief required sergeants to make raids with officers and issued a mandate requiring every firearm carried by officers to be registered with the department. The chief generally reacted in a hurry.

Before he became a Houston police officer, Caldwell was in fact a drill instructor for the United States Marine Corps. From the start of his policing career, the man with the booming voice knew he would not be satisfied until he had a high rank. He rose to lieutenant in no time, his eyes immediately on the next rung on the administrative ladder and his sharp mind constantly aware of the need to have more high-ranking officers in a fast-growing city.

People who worked under him knew his terse attitude and commanding personality, accentuated by a deep baritone voice that became authoritative on radio and television. Even his words in the black and white of a newspaper echoed down the page with unmistakable jabs at adversaries. He once playfully suggested that, "The ACLU favors firing squads in a circular fashion where everyone gets shot in the end."[3]

Later, commenting on Houston's 1979 rise in violent crime, particularly homicides, the chief said, "Almost everybody has a pistol and carries it with them at all times.... Homicides and assaults are personal sorts of offenses which cannot be prevented unless a policeman were stationed in everybody's front room."[4]

It was almost as if Caldwell wanted to demonstrate that he had a master's degree in sound bites more than in his true academic disciplines of sociology and abnormal psychology.

Underscoring his effort to learn African-American and Hispanic perceptions of police, the chief said, "I'm not only meeting with the grass roots people, I'm meeting with the 'tap roots' people." If Pappy Bond played the news media game with good humor, the erudite, brow-beating Caldwell used an incessant blend of highly opinionated, emotional expressions of compassion and authority to communicate his messages in public. He didn't always rub people the right way, nor did he ever have any intention of doing so.

By late 1979, he had been Houston's chief for two and a half years and was under attack by African-American Justice of the Peace Alexander Green in connection with the controversial September 26, 1979 police shooting and killing of a black man, Reggie Lee Jackson. The officers involved claimed

Jackson pulled a gun on them while trying to flee from them. Green, elected to the U. S. Congress in 2004, representing Texas' 9th District, strongly criticized the investigation of the case, especially critical of the fact that Mamie Garcia, the chief's liaison to Houston's Hispanic community, served on the grand jury investigating the case. The media played up the Caldwell stance until the grand jury cleared both officers involved on January 9, 1980.

The drill instructor barked an order for all uniformed officers to wear their police caps on duty, a rule the easier-going Pappy Bond had withdrawn or ignored. No one dared question Caldwell's authority. He was *the* authority on policing whether in a speech at Rotary Club, a cadet class, the elevator at headquarters or the men's room.

HPD Chaplains

Under Police Chief Harry Caldwell in 1980, the department named a family assistance officer, Jim Hudson. Before then, Officer Harold L. "Bubba" Hannah Jr., an ordained minister, served as HPD's volunteer chaplain. When Hannah retired in 1984, there was no chaplain, and Hudson assisted the grieving families of officers appropriately.

From 1984 until 1993, no officer served in a chaplain capacity. In 1993, the department named Senior Police Officer Ed Davis as the first official police chaplain. Davis served thirteen years until 2006, when he was succeeded by Senior Police Officer Monty B. Montgomery. Hudson was succeeded as family assistance officer by Senior Police Officer Matt Perales. In 1997, Senior Police Officer Mike Newsome was added to the Family Assistance staff when it became a two-person operation.

Caldwell despised disorganization and lax attitudes. Caldwell's general orders were neatly placed in a four-inch, loose-leaf notebook. The orders were specific—overly detailed, in fact—typed out and placed in a nice, convenient manual, a first in modern HPD history. Caldwell remained proud of this achievement even after his tenure as chief was over. He believed that this product of his Planning and Research Division helped to implant discipline, improve appearance and restore accountability.

Mayor Fred Hofheinz appointed Caldwell police chief on June 11, 1977 after telling him that he would be on his own after the mayor left office and his successor took over. There was no guarantee the new mayor would keep the city's third police chief in four years once he made his key personnel decisions. Hofheinz regretted not appointing Caldwell as his first police chief. His selection committee thought the drill instructor too controversial and intimidating.[5]

Jim McConn, Hofheinz' successor, kept Caldwell, removing the "acting" from the chief's title after he was in office at least six months. Changes were in the wind, not the least of which was an increase in the make-up of City Council from a nine-member body consisting of the mayor and eight members elected at-large to a fifteen-member group comprised of the mayor, nine members elected by geographic district and five at-large. The smaller council had always consisted of all males. Only one black man had ever been elected to it, Judson Robinson Jr. The larger governing group included more blacks, females and one Hispanic elected in the 1979 city elections. They took office in January 1980.

HPD GROWTH

Mayor Jim McConn's Tenure

Year	Officers	Cadets
1978	2,903	178
1979	2,971	207
1980	3,079	253
1981	3,117	424

McConn and Caldwell got along like fraternity brothers. They even made a few crime scenes one night after having a few drinks together, telling anyone who made a fuss that the actual imbibing took place "after hours" even though they were on duty 24-seven. McConn occasionally visited officers at 61 Riesner, one time even learning that Homicide was short of typewriters and ordering eighteen of them to be sent over the next day.

First Female Sergeant

Chief Caldwell made the history Herman Short rejected a few years earlier when he signed the paperwork necessary to promote HPD's first-ever female sergeant in 1978. Appropriately, she later became a part of a renowned policing family, the Masseys.

Sergeant Cynthia Jones "Cindy" Landry (Massey) later became Lt. Chester Massey's daughter-in-law. Chester's sons Richard and David also were HPD officers of rank. Cindy became David's wife. The limbs of the Massey family tree extended further. Richard's son Richard Junior and David's son Chris also made HPD a career.

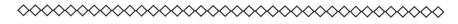

Houston Police Officers Association President Jim Albright, a captain by rank, was a controversial figure in the 1970s, always on the wrong side of Harry Caldwell. Like Caldwell, Albright was a Marine Corps veteran who joined HPD after his discharge. A graduate of Police Cadet Class No. 14 in 1956, Albright was a classmate of Carrol Lynn, with whom he worked and studied when opportunities arose to take promotional examinations. Albright worked his way through the ranks, but was left No. 1 on the captain's promotional list five times. Once he finally became captain, he was in line to be a deputy chief. When he was captain in vice, he had a sign on his desk that said, "It's a thousand times better to have common sense without knowledge than to have knowledge without common sense." Harry Caldwell inspired the sign.

The same position of "fourth assistant police chief" that Chief Bond established so that Caldwell would be promoted to deputy chief was effectively abolished when Albright was No. 1 on the promotional list for the same position in 1977. This action meant that the services of a fourth assistant chief were only required for the eighteen months Caldwell held the job. Albright filed suit over his lack of promotion and won in the trial court; however, he ultimately lost on appeal due to an attorney's filing error.[6]

Caldwell's strict rules lowered the dismal morale and set the stage for Albright to raise hell through renewed activism in the Houston Police Officers

Association. He and Bob Thomas, an active, outspoken Narcotics officer, vied for the HPOA presidency in 1979, becoming the sharpest, most outspoken Caldwell detractors.[7]

Bond had established the practice of meeting regularly with the HPOA board. Caldwell, an HPOA member, tried to communicate in similar fashion. Thomas was elected to the board in 1977 and was present during a stormy session with Caldwell in the summer of 1978 in which the chief yelled, cursed and screamed about the HPOA report about the department's low morale after the indictment of Carrol Lynn. The board never invited Caldwell to another meeting. Thomas soon died on the sergeant's promotional list and learned that Caldwell had blackballed him from the FBI.[8]

Had Caldwell not opined to the FBI that Thomas was a trouble-making malcontent who couldn't obey orders, Thomas may well have left HPD for the federal job. Then he never would have become the primary motivator behind a new police union. After the volatile meeting Thomas was instrumental in the association's vote of no-confidence against Caldwell.

About forty percent of association members voted and fifty-four percent went against the incumbent chief in the no-confidence vote taken just before Albright became HPOA president in an emotion-pitched campaign against Thomas and six other candidates. Caldwell responded with one of his most remembered one-liners, a sound bite that was widely broadcast. "I'll be here as long as there is one vote in my favor," he said, "the vote of the mayor of this city."[9]

On April 4, 1979, Officers Danny H. Mays, thirty-two years old, and Norval Wayne Holloway Jr., thirty, were convicted of conspiring to plant "a throw-down gun" beside the dying Randall Alan Webster on February 8, 1977, to justify his shooting death and afterward lying about it to a federal grand jury. Paul D. Dillon, a sergeant at the time of the incident, was acquitted of all charges—accessory, conspiracy and perjury. Five weeks later, the judge in the case, U.S. District Judge Finis Cowan sentenced Mays and Holloway to five years' probation.[10]

Cowan criticized the handling of the case by U.S. District Attorney J. A. "Tony" Canales, but he also praised Canales and his staff for exposing the practice of some members of the Houston Police Department of using throw-down guns to cover up facts involving police shootings in which the suspect died. A state grand jury actually no-billed Mays in the Webster

In 1978, Police Chief Harry Caldwell promoted Cynthia Jones "Cindy" Landry Massey (top center in white hat) to sergeant, making her the first ever female to hold the rank. Clockwise from there are Maggie Marques, black female officer Regina Young, Phyliss Serna Wunsche, Lavonda Hobbs. Wunsche later became the first Hispanic assistant chief. (Cindy Massey)

shooting case, but a subsequent federal grand jury investigation unveiled the fact that the .22-caliber pistol found beside Webster had been reported destroyed with other police property room evidence in 1968. The court record showed that prosecutors got testimony from former Officers John Thomas Olin and William E. Byrd in exchange for immunity.

Judge Cowan openly stated that he was persuaded that "the practice of using 'throwdown' guns is not and has never been widespread in HPD."[11] Even though no prison time was assessed to any officer, the judge said he thought the case had discouraged other officers from engaging in similar "reckless conduct."

Caldwell made one statement to the media that he thought the department had done what it thought was "proper and appropriate" regarding the initial cover-up.[12] As a footnote to Cowan's decision and subsequent written remarks, a state district judge ordered the October 1983 reinstatement of Lieutenant Paul D. Dillon with back pay "as though he never left."[13] Dillon served until early 1985 before retiring.

The Moody Park Riot happened at a Cinco de Mayo celebration on Sunday, May 8, 1978, violently manipulated by a few members of a radical group to keep alive an awareness of the death of Joe Campos Torres. Many members of the Hispanic community were incensed with the verdict returned by a Huntsville state court jury on October 6, 1977. The trial was moved to the town best known for housing many state prison units, including Death Row, on a change of venue. The jurors found former officers Terry Wayne Denson and Stephen Orlando guilty of negligent homicide, a misdemeanor. The two received probated sentences and were ordered to pay fines of $1 each.

This trial was not the end of court sessions in the Torres case. One year later, on October 30, 1979, a federal judge in Houston resentenced Denson, Orlando and former Officer Joseph James Janish in connection with their 1978 conviction for violating Torres' civil rights. U.S. District Judge Ross N. Sterling assessed felony prison sentences of one year and one day concurrent with one-year federal misdemeanor terms they already faced. The three former officers immediately dropped appeals of their convictions since the judge's action rendered them eligible for parole after a third of their terms. They began serving their sentences within a month of Sterling's decision.

Another former officer present when Torres went into the bayou, Glenn Lee Brinkmeyer, pleaded guilty to a misdemeanor in an agreement to testify

◇◇

Psych Services Established

Harry Caldwell appointed the first HPD psychologist to help officers deal with "continuous and tremendous stress" in 1979. Dr. Greg Riede's job description also included developing methods for selecting recruits and teaching at the police academy. Houston was about the fifth department in the nation to see the need for a psychologist.[14]

After retiring in 2004, Dr. Riede recounted that he was recommended by Assistant Chief John Bales, a mainstay on the Command Staff through at least three chiefs. Psych Services was Bales's idea. Suicide was "a real problem" among HPD officers at the time Riede was named the department's first psychologist on January 4, 1979. Three officers took their own lives in 1977 and three more in 1978, more than one officer per 1,000 and a record that was ten times the national suicide rate. Riede rode with many officers and soon had a full schedule of free counseling sessions every day, often working after dark and sometimes in emergency situations. Caldwell gave him autonomy and always approved Riede's requests.

Eventually the unit consisted of Riede, six other psychologists and four clerical employees to run a full schedule of counseling sessions. Budget problems and retirements saw the number cut to four psychologists and one secretary by 2005. To help officers feel more at ease, counseling took place away from headquarters and the substations. Over the years, the counseling center was located in the Heights, on West 34th Street near Highway 290, on Imperial Valley north of Beltway 8, and on the North Freeway at Greens Road.

In 2000, due to budget constraints, the counseling center was actually at the new station at 1200 Travis but located in a part of the building that enabled officers to discreetly attend sessions. Psych Services grew to be one of the most widely recognized services of its kind in the nation and was instrumental in the formation of HPD's Crisis Intervention Team, specially trained officers who deal with police situations involving mentally ill citizens. CIT grew into the largest program of its kind in the country.

◇◇

for the government along with Officer Carless Elliott, the state's star witness. Also indicted for civil rights violations was former Officer Louis Glenn Kinney, but he was severed from the other three defendants and got probation at the government's recommendation. Only Elliott stayed with HPD.

By the time Cinco de Mayo rolled around in 1978, one year after the Torres debacle, Hispanic leaders had expressed their outrage at the light sentences given the former officers. They were even more outraged by the time Judge Sterling lightened the federal punishment. Caldwell fostered friendships and built up higher levels of trust during this period; still, young Hispanic revolutionaries like Travis Morales kept the Torres flame burning brightly. Morales was affiliated with People United to Fight Police Brutality and the Revolutionary Communist Party. Older, more seasoned Hispanic leaders disassociated themselves from Morales and his small group of followers, but the vociferous leader became media savvy and spoke loudly at every opportunity to decry the death of Torres and cast derisive blame on Caldwell and the department.

Morales referred to Houston officers as "pigs" and spread the message that revolution was the only way to end the persecution of long-suffering Hispanics.[15] He attracted hundreds of followers, most of them in their teens or early twenties, attempting to rain on the growing parade of community believers paying more attention to Caldwell.

The riot itself began as a Cinco de Mayo celebration on a Sunday afternoon, complete with beer and food. The park in which the riot took place is located at the corner of Fulton and Collingsworth, just a few blocks east of Interstate 45 (the Gulf Freeway). A portion of the crowd in the park grew unruly early Sunday evening and began throwing bricks, rocks and bottles at any officer they spotted.

"I don't think I'll ever forget the sound a brick makes when it ricochets off a car hood," long-time KPRC—Channel 2 news reporter Phil Archer said, recalling the incident in *The Fault Does Not Lie With Your Set,* a book recounting the first forty years of Houston television, spotlighting the city's first network station, Channel 2 and NBC. Archer was a cameraman at the time, assigned to cover the night police beat. On this day, Archer worked with the best sourced and best loved police reporter in Houston television history—Jack Cato.[16]

The rioters in the crowd set fire to several businesses in a nearby strip shopping center. Cato and Archer, the only reporters on the scene with a TV camera, saw a burning overturned car through the trees. They had already seen two police officers, one with blood on his face from being hit by a bottle, leading a prisoner out of the park. They heard a woman's voice alternately speaking English and Spanish through a bull horn. Officers told them that a man had been stabbed inside the park and a confrontation resulted when a fire department ambulance attempted to treat the victim. The HFD paramedic and the injured man had to battle their way out. An ambulance supervisor abandoned his car and rode out with them. The mob turned over his car and set it on fire.

The relentless reporters headed toward the burning car, obviously a most desired video opportunity, despite warnings that the crowd was incited toward violence and might not spare men with cameras. The speaker in the background continued to espouse hatred toward HPD officers and say "that the people needed to show their hate for the treatment they had been given," according Cato. Archer shot video while Cato asked around to find out details. Someone picked up a bicycle and threw it at Archer, striking the camera he had on his shoulders. Then someone threw a rock that struck Cato in the face as three young men jumped Archer, causing him to drop his camera. The stunned Cato was stabbed in the back. The street-smart Cato knew "you die when you're stabbed in the back" and thought he might bleed to death before paramedics got him to a hospital.[17]

One attacker grabbed Archer's camera and jumped up and down on it along with a companion. A brick flew out of the crowd, striking the cameraman between the eyes and knocking him out. Several friendly kids dragged the unstable victim toward police lines where officers who knew Archer also helped. One of the attackers had stabbed Archer on the lower left buttock, his light blue pants quickly turning red with blood. He realized the same possibility as Cato—when a person is stabbed in the buttocks he can easily bleed to death. Archer lapsed into shock. Police officers responded, thinking the unruly group had castrated the cameraman.[18]

Cato's new station news car was flipped over and burned "like a torch." Officers took Archer to Northwest Memorial Hospital when the crowd made it too difficult for an ambulance to get through. Archer owed his life to the two boys who dragged him to safety. Channel 2 management later rewarded them without publicity. Hispanics in these times were reluctant to accept positive attention from police because of HPD's negative image in their community. Archer's left thigh was left permanently numb but he still had the normal use of his legs. Police never made a case on the suspect in the Archer incident. Cato identified his attacker, who eventually was sentenced to five years' probation and later died of a drug overdose.

Caldwell was out of town during the riot. HPD was used to leaders with decisive action plans. At Moody Park, only one officer almost lost his life. Tommy Britt was intentionally run over, hit by a rioter in a car and sustained a broken leg.

The riot saw police cars overturned—some set afire—nearby businesses burned and other establishments looted. Among an estimated 1,500 people in the park that day, police wound up arresting forty people, while a total of fifteen others, including Cato, Archer and three police officers, were treated at hospitals. Two businesses were burned to the ground, seven firms looted and others heavily damaged to the tune of $500,000. Three members of the Revolutionary Communist Party and People United to Fight Police Brutality were arrested and charged with rioting. They were Travis Morales, Mara Youngdahl and Thomas Hirschi. By May 1985, the three were given credit for time served in jail. They paid their fines and were released.

Morales stayed true to his Communist philosophy and participated in whatever radical, publicity-grabbing demonstrations that availed themselves. In a 1988 interview with *Houston Chronicle* minority affairs specialist Lori Rodriquez, Morales verified that he has remained "a die-hard, unrepentant, Maoist, revolutionary Communist." He still had very few followers.[19]

Harry Caldwell worked from daylight past dark trying to improve HPD's relationship with the Hispanic community. He often spent the night in his office and dictated memos and letters to his secretary from inside his private restroom during the day. Underneath his Marine-tough exterior, Caldwell was kind and understanding at times, but tried not to show it in a general sense. At Christmas he took the jail shift to allow young officers to be with their families. The chief regularly alternated hour upon hour, being holed up in his office with walking a "beat" that included each of the investigative offices in 61 Riesner.[20]

Caldwell was the first chief to realize a societal irony, learn lessons from it and make necessary changes in the relationship HPD officers had with the minority communities. The irony: Police officers were generally great citizens who chose a career in law enforcement. Yet once they donned the uniform with a badge and gun, they appeared to be in conflict with the community.

As chief, Caldwell tried to implement change too rapidly, tearing through his reform agenda with "a failure to delegate." He felt he and he alone was accountable to the federal government and the local Hispanic community. He therefore failed to extend authority to higher-ranking staff members because he didn't want them facing the heat for him.[21]

Caldwell burned the midnight oil preparing for appearances before the U.S. Commission on Civil Rights both in Washington, D.C., and Houston. Although shutting the doors of his office to the staff, he opened them to Hispanic leaders for their help. Any improvement plan had to be not just *his* plan or *their* plan but *our plan.* Before Hispanic leaders met with Caldwell, there had never been a meal, holding hands or shaking hands with the chief of police.[22]

Historically, the League of United Latin American Citizens was instrumental in gaining entry into HPD for certain qualified Hispanic men tall enough to meet entrance requirements. Mamie Garcia, a social worker, was an elected LULAC District 8 director during the time of the Joe Campos Torres incident and the Moody Park Riot. She teamed with other LULAC leaders to draw up a three-page proposal to present to Caldwell and HPD. Unlike Travis Morales, the group was constructive. It consisted of Garcia and her husband Julian, John and Jeanie Aleman, Rita Arevalo, and two Hispanic activist attorneys, Ellis Barrera and Frumencio Reyes. The group hit upon the idea of Mamie Garcia serving as HPD's volunteer liaison to the Hispanic community. Garcia served twenty-five years in this capacity.[23]

Before Torres there had never been any opportunity to open genuine communication with police officials to earnestly tackle the cultural barriers that prevented the department from representing all of the city's diversified communities. Caldwell was the first to knock down these barriers. Before Caldwell there weren't meetings between the neighborhoods and the police officers who patrolled them. Hispanics deemed his actions to speak louder than news media rhetoric. The Garcia group presented the three pages of requests and goals that included the naming of Mamie Garcia to be the liaison, first temporarily then permanently. Garcia reported directly to the chief and helped him prepare for Department of Justice meetings in both Washington and Houston, documenting every request and every meeting involving HPD and the community for the federal government's consumption.[24]

The liaison also handled a multitude of requests from Hispanic citizens regarding policing matters—everything from paying parking tickets to bailing citizens out of jail. She discovered that HPD would arrest illegal immigrants and leave them in jail for months before sending them back to Mexico. In response, she helped to establish a better working relationship with the Consulate of Mexico, which undertook the task of paying transportation costs to return immigrants to their homeland.

Garcia developed a heretofore unseen trust in a police chief and spread her feelings to others in the community, endorsing the drill sergeant's attitude of accountability as he responded to thoughtful requests. Caldwell worked up to a September appearance before the U.S. Commission on Civil Rights in Houston by espousing the need for more Hispanic officers through recruiting in places like LULAC conventions and conducting more Hispanic-oriented seminars for officers. At a June 14, 1979 LULAC convention in Houston, Caldwell presented a special plaque to outspoken police critic Ruben Bonilla "for his innovative, pioneering and courageous efforts in establishing better relationships and understanding between Hispanic citizens and law enforcement officers of the state of Texas."[25]

Bonilla conceded that there had been progress in the lines of communication with police within the past year—a previously unheard-of stance. By September's hearing, the Civil Rights Commission was saying positive things about HPD and Houston Hispanics, a far cry from Philadelphia where the commission filed suit against the police department. The commission singled out the chief for being more open and cooperative than Philadelphia police officials.

Only three weeks before the hearing, newly named U.S. Attorney General Benjamin Civiletti stated that the Justice Department had no plans to lodge charges of police brutality against HPD. The statement came as no surprise to Caldwell, who told *The Houston Post* "that's what Mr. Civiletti told me more than a month ago." Civiletti never confirmed that he was the government official who suggested to Caldwell that HPD could wind up in federal receivership. But Caldwell said it was about this time that a high-ranking official from the Justice Department called him and said the department would not be placed in federal receivership.[26]

The following month, *The Post* published a series entitled "Crime in the City" that decried the Houston Police Department's lack of technology and long-range planning, two areas Caldwell had said needed to be addressed if he ever got to be police chief. They remained high priorities in his heart, but not on a realistic HPD agenda whose highest goal was Hispanic relations. "Houston police officials admit they can barely keep track of crime, much less check its wild growth," the story said. Crime was up considerably in 1979, while felony arrests were down and final case dispositions down to 15.4 percent. A new speedy-trial rule that moved cases through the courts more quickly resulted in increases in convictions, from 9,405 to 11,382 since 1975.[27]

As usual, Patrol officers bore the brunt of problems created by an under-staffed, overloaded workday in which prioritized calls often resulted in citizens having to wait more than an hour to see an officer. In essence, "crime is controlling the police department more than the police department is controlling crime." One of the problems was the decade in which Police Chief Herman Short followed Mayor Louie Welch's policy of accepting no federal funding, putting HPD far behind in police-related technological advancements.

Caldwell pointed out that officers had less time for fighting street crime when they had to answer so many calls for service, due in part to recent court decisions precluding the police from being pro-active and making them be more "reactive". The same held true for practically every department in the nation during this period. The chief decried low salaries and an understaffed department in which only 350 uniformed officers were on patrol during the prime hours for criminal activity—from 3 p.m. until 11 p.m. Houston's sprawling city limits, consisting of 558 square miles, translated to having one officer for every 1.6 square miles and 5,000 citizens—the lowest ratio in the nation.

The problem was not just budgetary since lack of funds was the primary reason the department was underpaid, understaffed and under-equipped throughout its history. These problems discouraged recruiting efforts. It was difficult to find qualified officers willing to be shot at, abused and second-guessed for a starting salary of $16,000 a year. Not only did Caldwell envision a police force 5,000 strong but also annual salaries starting at $24,000.[28]

Without federal funds, HPD continued to use an age-old manual reporting system. Vital reports of rapes, robberies and burglaries sometimes took several days to pass from the street to investigators, leaving cold trails to suspects. Civilian employees also were sorely underpaid. The department employed 634 of them in June 1979, paying an average of $141 a week. Later, the department developed an on-line offense reporting system that was regarded as the best in the country. Federal funds were used to pay for it.

The issue of a money-saving plan to turn over the jail to Harris County for full-time staffing in order to eliminate the need to book a prisoner twice, once in the city jail and later in the county jail, cropped up. It wasn't the first time, nor would it be the last. In 1979, the department estimated that 142 officers and supervisors would be freed up for street duty if such a plan were initiated.

Caldwell created the Field Training Division in his constant effort to improve training and education. While overbearing at times and often too authoritative, the chief continued to step out on a limb, but he seldom patted the troops on the back. He believed in better education and standards high enough so nobody could become an officer if he were not of high moral character. He was the first chief to recognize that HPD had to generate good public relations.[29]

Caldwell's hardened attitude really wore thin by the time his boss, Mayor Jim McConn, was re-elected to a second term in a 1979 November runoff election. Caldwell solidified his job security despite the baggage he carried with his troops and even his three assistant chiefs.

The Chicano Squad

The number of Hispanic officers increased throughout the 1980s and into the new century until one out of every five HPD officers were Hispanics. Under Chief Harry Caldwell in 1979, Homicide recorded eighteen murders in one weekend with most of the victims and suspects unable to speak English. Caldwell formed the Chicano Squad in the Homicide Division.

Captain Bobby Adams recruited squad members from other divisions. He went to Robbery and told Sergeant Jim Montero he needed him "on loan" for six months; he stayed there ten years. The identity of the group took on a catchy air that unsettled many in the Hispanic community. The term "Chicano Squad" was actually coined by two newspaper reporters, J. J. Garcia of *La Voz* and Rob Meckel of *The Houston Post*. Initially the name was viewed as being negative but grew to be positive because of improved case resolution.

Under Lieutenant Chuck Lofland and Detective (later Sergeant) Jim Montero, the first members of the squad were Officers Joe Selvera, Cecil Mosqueda, Bobby Gatewood, Joe DeLeon and U. P. Hernandez. Later, Officer Irma Sauceda became the first female member. After celebrating the squad's 25th anniversary in 2004, only Selvera and Mosqueda, a sergeant, were still on the same duty they began in 1979.[30]

The assistant chiefs, B. K. Johnson, Tommy Mitchell and R. G. McKeehan, each said in their own way that Caldwell was spending too much time on PR and not enough on providing basic police services. Their statements reflected the fact that the steadfast chief wasn't wearing well with the department's rank and file. The chief also had irked them with his expressed hope of changing civil service law to make assistant and deputy chief positions appointive and not totally dependent on tests. There was another problem from a quote Caldwell made in Fort Worth, in which he referred to the average age of his officers. "I don't have sergeants anymore," he said, "I have room mothers."[31]

Johnson conceded that Caldwell had had to deal with numerous touchy issues but caused "a hell of a lot of dissention." McKeehan and Mitchell voiced criticism for Caldwell's lack of an effective civilianization plan and his avowed dedication to "social policing," manifested in the large number of officers deployed when the police chief of Mexico City visited Houston. Still, purely and simply, the story called attention to the fact that the chief was unpopular because of his strict adherence to rules and regulations.

In the minds of many mid- and high-level managers, Caldwell had no common courtesy or horse sense. He was overly impulsive, a trait seen the day he issued a policy that detectives should no longer wear cowboy boots, another step away from the department's "cowboy" image. The order was typed and signed quicker than a heart beat, and all hell broke loose. Then it was quickly withdrawn. The chief got attention but not input, even in the form of polite suggestions.

Mamie Garcia handled the no-so-polite suggestions concerning even the smallest police-related matters in the Hispanic community, but by and large fielded the same question from numerous fathers and mothers in her community: What does it take for my children to become Houston police officers? The networking was paying off, and the trust was building. Still, all policing was not nearly perfect with minority communities.[32] On February 8, 1980, in what initially appeared to be another full year of Caldwell leadership, the federally funded Public Interest Advocacy Center issued a statement saying the Internal Affairs Division was "unresponsive" to complaints of police brutality. The findings were turned over to the newly formed Police Advisory Committee for Continued Improvement, a twenty-one-member committee set up by Mayor McConn.

Scarcely six weeks into the New Year of 1980, Harry Caldwell shocked Houston from Mayor Jim McConn to political leaders in the minority communities and the officers on the police force by announcing his plan to accept a job with Houston business entrepreneur and friend Wayne Goettsche. Caldwell would become director of security and community affairs at an undisclosed amount believed to be higher than his $57,000 salary.

The chief admitted to working sixty- to seventy-hour weeks meeting with people in his office, inspecting the troops and participating in innumerable nighttime community meetings and forums. He admitted to *Houston Post* police reporter Fred King that had he known the intensity of the stress involved in resolving crises involving the Torres case aftermath, the throwdown gun cases and the related community relations problems, he might not have taken the job.

Caldwell's retirement at age forty-eight was effective February 29. He told the news media he regretted not being able to communicate significantly with the entire spectrum of the community but that he was proud to deal with problems openly and on top of the table. He identified his major accomplishment as "having established an irrevocable commitment to moral integrity and accountability."[33]

Caldwell's most lasting impact came with the thawing of the Houston police department's icy relationship with the Hispanic community. A *Houston Chronicle* article by Lori Rodriguez on the ten-year anniversary date of the Moody Park Riot, quoted Captain E. F. "Frank" Leija as testifying to the changes that had taken place. Leija said HPD's Hispanic ranks had grown from 164 in 1978 to 472 more than ten years later. He said, "Where there were ten Hispanic detectives, eleven sergeants and five lieutenants ten years ago, there are now fifty-four sergeants, seven lieutenants and two captains."[34]

24

HISPANICS STAND TALL

In the year 1950, the Houston Police Department leadership perceived a problem with the Hispanic community. A Hispanic suspect killed an Anglo, prompting police to believe they needed a "Latin American Squad" to deal with cases involving similar circumstances. A called meeting at the Civil Courts Building attracted 200 people, including a number of prospective police cadets. The League of United Latin American Citizens wanted Hispanic officers selected "according to the same standards as real policemen."

The police representative present asked that each Hispanic male interested in joining the force to please stand up. Then he outlined basic requirements of a prospective cadet one at a time: You must be between the ages of 21 and 35, have a high school diploma and no criminal record. Some portion of the prospects sat down when they failed to meet these qualifications.[1]

"And you must stand 5-feet-10 1/2 inches tall," the recruiter said. Most of the remaining young men sat down. HPD immediately fell short of the number needed for a Latin American Squad. Only five remained and just one, Raul Martinez, a share cropper's son, really wanted the job. He was twenty-seven years old and saw nothing but problems with his job as an orderly that paid fifty cents an hour. Martinez soon got a call from highly respected Mexican restaurant owner, Felix Tijerina, who said to him, "We need you. Why don't you go down there and apply?"[2]

Thirty-nine years later, Martinez said he felt he could make a difference and went down to City Hall, officially applied and found it hard to believe his acceptance until he saw it in writing. Meanwhile, he trained to become a barber and earned seventy-five cents a cut every Saturday at the Gallegos Barber Shop on Preston. The barbering and his orderly job put Martinez in a high income bracket. The police job actually meant a pay cut and required him to work six days a week for a $60 salary.

The entire community encouraged him to become an officer since Houston had no uniformed Hispanic police officer at the time. Martinez faced tough recruiting questions from Ray Floyd, the Civil Service director at City Hall. Floyd cited Martinez' heavy accent and asked him how he would handle insulting comments from Anglos he might have to arrest. Martinez responded by saying he would be trained and paid to be called names he was called already.[3]

Martinez passed the written examination and the physical before undergoing more interrogation. The questioners gave him spirit when they never brought up the fact he was Hispanic. He entered the academy in March 1950, becoming the first academy-trained Hispanic police officer in HPD history. He went on to earn a college degree from the University of Houston under the GI Bill and served twenty-three years on the force before Harris County Judge Bill Elliott appointed him constable of Precinct 6. He served five terms there. He died on August 23, 1990. On September 17, 2003, Precinct 2 County Commissioner Sylvia Garcia led a dedication ceremony of the Raul C. Martinez East End Courthouse Annex.

Victor Trevino grew up on Houston's eastside in the 1950s, becoming adept with a broomstick from the time the broom stood taller than he was. Over the years as one of nine children parented by a Mexico-born day-laborer for Southern Pacific Railroad and his stay-at-home wife, Trevino worked in several mom-and-pop grocery stores, graduating from sweeper to stock boy, then sacker, and on to stocker, meat cutter and cashier.

As he became a teenager, Trevino loved helping people, a satisfaction that inspired a desire to become a police officer after he graduated from Austin High School. By 1970 the department lowered the police academy eligibility age to nineteen. Trevino was nineteen, biting at the bit to join up, but he faced a requirement he couldn't measure up to.[4]

The HPD height requirement was five-foot-ten; Trevino stood five-foot-seven. The height requirement ruled out all but the tallest Hispanics. So Trevino became a butcher at an east side Weingarten's during the Herman Short era in HPD when only Anglo officers patrolled Hispanic neighborhoods. There was only one Hispanic cop for the area and investigations were tough since Hispanics wouldn't talk to police.

Trevino thought that intelligence and policing ability had nothing to do with height. He wanted to enter HPD as early as 1975 but soon learned he faced yet another obstacle—he was not legally an American citizen. He had entered the country legally at age seven, and he assumed he was a citizen.

But he wasn't. He took courses at San Jacinto College, enabling him to earn citizenship in January 1976, just as HPD lowered its height requirement to five-foot-seven.

Over the years business leaders such as Houston restaurant entrepreneur Felix Tijerina instructed Hispanic applicants to apply first thing in the morning when they were taller. Next time, Trevino applied in the morning and qualified for HPD Cadet Class No. 74 in 1976 at age twenty-four. He was one of seven Hispanics to qualify, a new record at that point in history. One class member, Jesse Garza, became a sergeant, while another, Joe Zamarron, died in the line of duty on April 18, 1981, when he was struck by a car while directing traffic on Market Street.

The height policy changed again. In March 1977, with Harry Caldwell at the helm, a management consulting company conducted a study that changed the department's hiring practices. The firm was Lifson, Wilson, Ferguson and Winick Inc. LWFW surveyed all officers and their job descriptions and developed criteria to measure effectiveness. Among its findings was that since August 14, 1968, HPD had used a height and weight chart developed by the U.S. Air Force. In hindsight, many in the department believed the chart requirements had a disparate impact on females, blacks and Hispanics. Coincidentally, LWFW had earlier validated the agility test that critics felt effectively eliminated many female applicants. HPD changed the height policy in 1977 to be height in proportionate to weight—a major turning point in the recruitment of women and Hispanics.

Trevino succeeded another former Houston police officer, Raul Martinez, as constable in the predominately Hispanic Precinct 6 on the east side. He was a founding member of the Organization of Spanish Speaking Officers in 1981 and served as OSSO's second president. He looked back on the day in July 1976 that he was sworn in to wear a badge and gun with the Houston blue with good humor. He and the largest-ever graduating class waited for that memorable moment when Police Chief Pappy Bond pinned on their badges. Taking his turn, Victor Trevino stepped up and stood tall—all five-feet-seven-inches of him.

As Bond did the honors, Houston's newest police officer was looking down at a chief obviously shorter than he was.

The visibility of the improving numbers of Hispanics in HPD blue captured the attention of a teen-aged girl who thought she could become a police officer and make a difference. The department recruited more actively with minorities to develop a more positive image through outreach programs at weekend events and at high schools during the week. Martha Morena sensed there were still problematic issues—but none she couldn't handle.

Morena was born in Ecuador and came to Houston with her family at age five to live in the East End, just outside of downtown near the original Ninfa's Restaurant on Navigation. Hearing the recruiting pitch, Morena thought the pay and benefits HPD offered were extremely high for a young Hispanic female with a high school diploma from Incarnate Word Academy. Encouraged by the recruiting booths at East Side community events, she was impressed that the department actually viewed Hispanics as people different from the bad guys on the beats or in the lead story on the evening news. Hispanic recruiters were there, as were African-American and Anglo officers.[5]

Morena joined HPD in 1979, stepping into Police Cadet Class No. 90 and graduating in May 1980. In earlier years, HPD regularly assigned new female officers to either the Juvenile Division or the jail. Morena was assigned to Central Patrol, as were the other two African-Americans and two Anglos in her cadet class. Her first sergeant, Robert Hill, fit the old-school image—paternal, decisive and always eager to give advice applicable to both professional and private lives.[6]

Morena married and became Martha Montalvo. That was not the only change. She earned bachelors and masters degrees in Criminal Justice Management from the University of Houston—Downtown and Sam Houston State University, respectively. Montalvo found that the vast majority of officers accepted a Hispanic female officer as long as she was productive on the job and remained strong and determined to achieve her professional goals.

She felt a major turning point in public perception of the department happened when Mayor Kathy Whitmire appointed Lee P. Brown to become the first African-American police chief in 1982. Brown was eager to answer the hardest possible questions from all minority communities and to convince leaders he needed their support through both dialogue and positive actions. It wasn't easy coming from people who felt they were overly policed and targets of suspicious arrests and traffic tickets. Chief Brown required officers to dialog with community leaders and convince them that police were there to serve everyone.

Like many of her police contemporaries, Montalvo was seldom pleased with Whitmire's attitude toward police officers. She participated in demonstrations against the mayor by members of the Houston Police Patrolman's Union that

Martha Montalvo became the first Hispanic female to serve as executive assistant chief. In 2012, Montalvo headed Investigative Operations. (HPD Archives)

were common early in Whitmire's ten-year tenure. At one heavily attended HPPU meeting with Whitmire, members sat silently as the mayor entered the room, the clicking heels of her shoes echoing in the large meeting room. Montalvo sat on the end of a row and felt sorry for the trembling woman. She saw that the mayor feared police, definitely a bad omen for the city.[7]

Montalvo worked in Central Patrol after spending time at the academy as an instructor. She didn't let a stubborn mayor deter her from stepping up the management ladder. After being shifted back to Central, she became a sergeant in 1985 and promptly got assigned to the jail, where she worked with Lieutenant Robert Montalvo, the man she married. Montalvo went on to serve as one of four executive assistant police chiefs under Police Chief Harold Hurtt, the highest ranking Hispanic female in history.

Wilfred Navarro got out of the service in February 1948 and went from one job to another until 1950 when LULAC began its big push to get the police department to hire Hispanics. Navarro took notice of the articles in local newspapers and attended the same meeting in which Raul Martinez learned he was tall enough to qualify. B. W. Payne was police chief and an inspector, L. D. Morrison Sr., was Payne's spokesman at the meeting. Morrison said the reason that the department wasn't hiring Mexican Americans was that the majority weren't as tall as Martinez.[8]

Navarro met the requirement and told Morrison he would apply. Yet when he went to the ninth floor of City Hall, Civil Service Director Roy Floyd said he was five-eighths of an inch too short. Floyd suggested that Navarro become a firefighter and wound up getting the applicant a job as a junior police clerk because he could type. Navarro worked as a clerk under three lieutenants, R. J. Clark, Foy D. Melton and Sid Rowe. One day Rowe gave him the same advice as Tijerina: apply early in the day when you're taller.

When Navarro showed up, the man there to do the measurement was George Hogan, a clerk who later became the business manager for police chiefs from Jack Heard to Lee P. Brown. Hogan found him to be a half inch *above* the requirement.

Originally, Navarro was scheduled to start Police Cadet Class No. 4 in March 1950, the same as Martinez, but he was rescheduled for Class No. 5 in September because of a problem with his work as a police clerk. Police Chief L. D. Morrison Sr., the recruiter, pinned on Navarro's badge on December 28, 1950, and the new officer started his first duty on New Year's Eve.

Other Hispanics in Class 5 were Jesse Ontiveros, Roy Beltran and Pete Fuentes (all deceased). The four Hispanic cadets made a conscious decision not to hang around with each other in their effort to get to know all of their classmates and not seem standoffish. They all went to Patrol with the feeling they were disliked because of their race but believing only a small percentage of officers were actually prejudiced against them. They were encouraged that some higher-ranking officers such as A. C. Martindale, a leader in the Houston Police Officers Association, discouraged discrimination at every opportunity and accepted them as equals.

Navarro went on to work Dispatch, Evening Patrol and Day Patrol at the North Shepherd Substation until one day when Lieutenant Chester Massey called him to become his administrative officer to work the desk for Downtown Patrol. He worked there until 1970, when he went to Community Services to supervise school crossing guards and give safety talks at schools.[9]

When the incumbent chief of police at Houston's airports resigned, thirty-year veteran Navarro's name appeared at the top of Mayor Jim McConn's list of possible successors in 1979. Encouraged by Councilman Ben Reyes, Houston's first Hispanic City Council member, Navarro actively pursued the

Ephirne Leija became the first Hispanic captain in HPD history in 1980, a time when Chief Harry Caldwell was working diligently to improve HPD's relationship with Houston Hispanics in the wake of the death-in-custody of Jose Campos Torres. (HPD Archives)

job. On January 3, 1980, he retired from HPD to become chief of the Airport Police three days later. He was responsible for both Hobby and Intercontinental Airports, commanding 259 people.

Navarro worked under mayors McConn, Kathy Whitmire, Bob Lanier and Lee Brown. When the airport police merged with HPD in November 1992, he became an assistant chief, a civilian position made official by ordinance under Mayor Lanier. He improved working conditions and morale and raised the training standards at the airports, believing that his officers had undergone more training than HPD officers at the time of the merger. By the time he retired in 1999, Wilfred Navarro had spent just a few months short of fifty years in law enforcement.

Officially, Mercedes Halvorsen Singleton was the first-ever academy-trained female Hispanic Houston police officer, and Emily Rimmer Vasquez was the second. They actually graduated from the same academy class. Since cadets got their badges in alphabetical order, Vasquez ranked second in history's count. Velia "Belle" Ortega, a Houston native and 1951 graduate of Sam Houston High School, was an HPD Records clerk in the early 1950s when Singleton, Vasquez, Jean Smith and Jo Bankston were the first policewomen to be academy-trained.

Everyone called Ortega "Belle," a nickname that meant "young beautiful woman," and often sought her to translate Spanish. Sergeants begin to suggest to her, "If you are going to translate for the reports, why don't you try out for the academy?" She wound up in Class 15 and was sworn in on New Year's Day 1957, the third Hispanic female officer in HPD history. As was typical, Ortega replaced a matron who retired and alternated between Juvenile and the jail before spending eleven years in Crime Analysis. She was in her thirties and let "the younger women go and be brave" when policewomen were allowed to patrol the streets.[10]

Ortega's first taste of resentment of Hispanics came when she was a cadet and a high-ranking Command Staff member was conducting a class discussion and asked the class, "Anyone here speak Mexican?" She and other Hispanics took remarks like this one in stride and tried to do the job.

Having so few female officers caused frustrating scheduling problems. If another division needed a woman for special duty, Ortega was "loaned out" from Juvenile or the jail. Shift scheduling was inflexible. A female officer's schedule stayed the same until someone quit, retired or died. Ortega worked the night shift eighteen years before she was able to work days.

After her retirement, Belle Ortega served eleven years as a police service officer (PSO), a de facto desk officer who took police reports from citizens, performing virtually every duty but riding the streets. Ortega died August 11, 2008 from gunshot wounds she suffered in a July 21 drive-by shooting at her daughter's apartment. Her death was ruled a homicide. She was seventy-eight years old.

When the admittedly bright-eyed and bushy-tailed Art Contreras, age twenty-two, drove in from Baytown and walked into the Houston police recruiting office in the basement of City Hall, two Anglo recruiters stood between him and the police academy. The height requirement in 1961 was five-foot-nine. The first recruiter, an older man, tersely informed Contreras that he was too short and walked out of the room. Contreras stood in the middle of the room, too angry to move.[11]

The second Anglo recruiter—an Officer Hill—came in, measured Contreras and all of a sudden the recruit had grown an inch. Contreras always credited Hill with giving him a life-changing break that resulted in a career that lasted more than four decades. In November 1961, the son of a Humble Oil and Refining Company (later Exxon) safety inspector and LULAC activist entered the Houston Police Academy at Police Headquarters at 61 Riesner by commuting from Baytown.[12]

A tough-minded sergeant, Julius Knigge, required meticulous notes and gave hard tests. Each cadet turned in his notebook every day for grading. Knigge put strong stock in a cadet's ability to pick up details in even the most basic investigation. Knigge once asked cadets how many steps were there in front of this training building. Contreras always remembered that there were thirteen.

Contreras' father was a "color blind" Baytown reserve officer who urged his son to change the policing system "from within," an outlook that inspired the new officer to conclude that only certain *individuals* had racist problems. When Contreras started in 1961, there were less than 100 Hispanic officers. Overall, in his Class No. 25, there were six—Contreras, George Rodriguez, Humberto Moreno, Abel Casas, Robert Luna and Johnny Gonzalez.

Contreras' first job in 1962 was riding a three-wheeler, working downtown to make sure traffic didn't get backed up. He made sergeant in 1968, the third Hispanic sergeant behind Raul Martinez and Richard Castillo and the first one assigned as a supervisor in Patrol. All previous Hispanic sergeants were assigned to Dispatch or the jail. Weldon Waycott, his supervisor, emphasized the fact that he ran Patrol and made Contreras the Northside sergeant on the night shift. Contreras had a few attitudinal problems with subordinates but gradually worked through them.

He became a lieutenant in 1973, serving in Juvenile and Recruiting. In the latter division he worked hard at enhancing the message to Hispanics and African-American would-be cadets that there was upward mobility available to them. He was promoted to captain in 1982 and spent time in Night Command at Northeast and took the lead in the elimination of some sexually-oriented questions on the pre-employment polygraph test. The new set of questions and guidelines required that all inquiries be job-specific and not designed to satisfy voyeuristic tendencies, including questions involving homosexuality or sodomy.[13]

Contreras drafted a bilingual pay bill during the 1987 session of the Texas Legislature, trying to use better pay as a recruiting tool to encourage bilingual men and women. The bill's passage meant officers who could speak Spanish, Vietnamese, Mandarin, Cantonese and Korean began receiving bilingual pay. Another bill provided the city with the ability to offer shift differential pay.

Contreras became HPD's first Hispanic deputy police chief in 1990 and served in that capacity until his retirement after thirty-six years in HPD. He spent only two days "unemployed" when President Bill Clinton named him U.S. Marshal for the Southern District of Texas on March 10, 1998—the first Hispanic in history to serve in this capacity. He was there four and a half years. In his HPD career, Contreras was considered as a candidate for Houston's police chief by two mayors, Bob Lanier in 1996 and Bill White in 2003.

Phyllis Serna Wunsche recounted her HPD career as a true calling or blessing. Her recollections flow as if out of a storybook with a happy ending despite the inevitable conflicts along the path. Wunsche's most significant "first" was *pregnant* with controversy and changed a bad tradition and policy for a department which took aim to recruit more women in the changing times of the 1970s.[14]

Wunsche was "the first Hispanic female math degree holder" to become a Houston police officer. A March 1972 graduate of the academy, her rise was meteoric—she became a robbery detective in three years and later stair-stepped up to become the first Hispanic female assistant chief. She also was the female half of the first married couple on the Command Staff. Her husband, Les Wunsche, was the first head of the Internal Affairs Division. He retired in 1986.

The University of Houston graduate began her career in November 1971, when she was looking for a government job that would take advantage of her way with numbers. HPD had four openings for women in its next cadet class, only hiring women to replace those retiring or resigning. She never had any inclination to be a police officer but ultimately "never went through any burned-out period in twenty-three years." Always motivated by changes in assignments and promotion, her longest assignment was five and a half years as a robbery detective.[15]

Wunsche scarcely passed her six-month probation when she violated an unwritten HPD rule—she got pregnant. She already had a three-year-old child at a time when motherhood was discouraged for policewomen. There were no health benefits that enabled her to take a paid leave of absence to give birth. If a policewoman wanted to have a baby, she had to take a non-paid leave of absence. Police Chief Carrol Lynn rejected Wunsche's request to use sick leave time.

It was a *city* policy that affected any pregnant employee, whether in the police department or any other city department. The young officer learned from research that some other cities granted sick leave for pregnancies. She thought it was worth fighting the city of Houston for such an entitlement and sought help from Wilfred Navarro of the Houston Police Officers Association Board of Directors.

Wunsche went down the line with the association officers and none gave her any hope. Navarro, chairman of the Insurance Committee, presented the issue to the full board and said pregnancy should be recognized as a health issue. He took Wunsche to an HPOA meeting when she was "very pregnant" and had her stand up as he made the case.

The board then got Mayor Fred Hofheinz and City Council to grant sick leave for pregnant city employees as part of the city's health insurance plan. The measured passed a few weeks before Wunsche's delivery. She was later transferred to the midnight shift at the jail for rocking the boat.

Policewomen found it hard to raise any stink about another issue that touched them almost every day of their job assignment, their blue uniforms. In the Hofheinz/Lynn years the department saw a major influx of women. But there were no uniforms designed to fit them. Women had to wear men's pants and jackets usually three or four sizes too large. Many women were reduced to tears by the way they looked in a department that could fit 300-pound men but not 110-pound women. Many women altered their own blue, and in the 1990s Wunsche ordered a Navy cap, which became part of the female assistant chief's uniform.

Wunsche became the first female detective in Texas assigned to investigate armed robberies. In 1980, she was promoted to lieutenant with another aspiring policewoman, Elizabeth "Betsy" Watson. Every week Wunsche worked as a lieutenant on all three shifts—days, evenings and nights—in what was a special "swing shift." She didn't complain.

She was a lieutenant when Watson succeeded Lee Brown as chief in 1990. Watson eliminated the deputy chief position and increased the number of assistant chiefs reporting directly to her to eleven. Newly appointed assistant chiefs hereinafter were subject to City Council confirmation. Later, under Police Chief Sam Nuchia, the Command Staff consisted of five executive assistant chiefs and eight assistant chiefs.

Watson could fill vacancies by appointment and chose Wunsche as the first female assistant chief. The appointment finally came but not without controversy, complicated by Watson's lack of political experience with City Council. Watson first sought Wunsche's appointment along with two white males in 1990 but endured political heat before a more diverse list of five appointees got through the mayor and council on July 2, 1991. Wunsche was not the Hispanic community's choice and stayed in limbo while Watson held her ground.[16]

As Watson's budget administrator, Wunsche finally got to use her talent with numbers. Bob Lanier took office as mayor in 1992 and demoted Watson in favor of Nuchia. But Wunsche remained in her "numbers job" and mastered the details of the move of police headquarters to 1200 Travis in downtown. The department didn't want to lose her knowledge and talent until the project was almost completed. She was the only chief of any rank that Mayor Lanier and Chief Nuchia asked to stay. She went on to serve on the Presidential Commission on Organized Crime as the group's only Hispanic female police officer.

Adrian Garcia's desire to become a police officer started to unfurl when he was hanging out at his dad's gas station on the Northside at age ten. Garcia was in awe of the take-charge men in police uniforms that performed their daily duties while riding Harleys. These "solos" hung out at a Texaco across the street from his dad's station. One day he saw them pull over a man who was driving through the neighborhood. Since this driver only spoke Spanish, the solo officers had trouble communicating with him.

One of them approached Garcia and respectfully asked, "Can you translate?" The little boy was happy to do so and his work resulted in a better understanding between the officers and a citizen who had a malfunctioning tail light. The officers cautioned him and let him go. One of them said to Garcia, "You'll make a good police officer."[17]

In 1980, when the outreach toward Hispanics was greater than ever and the height requirement all but gone, Garcia got into the Houston Police Academy Class No. 93 at age nineteen. Many of Garcia's contemporaries called him a sell-out, while memories of Joe Campos Torres and the Moody Park Riot lingered in the community.

Like Martha Montalvo, Garcia credited Whitmire's choice of Lee Brown as the first-ever black police chief as a major turning point in the attitude of Hispanics. Minority recruiting went through the roof as the department instituted academic standards. Brown also included the Hispanic community more and more in his interworking and strategies. Garcia believed the initial changes came through Harry Caldwell and were truly embraced by Chief Brown.[18]

Garcia became the first-ever Houston police officer elected to the Houston City Council in 2003. In his HPD career he worked in Patrol in downtown and the Northside, in HPD's Criminal Intelligence Division's Organized Crime Squad, and served as a special investigator for the District Attorney's Office in the Special Crimes Division. He also served in HPD's Community Services Division before his appointment to be HPD's liaison to the Mayor's Anti-Gang Office in 1994, becoming director in 1999.

Before retiring after twenty-four years as a Houston police officer, Garcia saw Hispanics come to form a much larger percentage of the force. The number of high-ranking Hispanics in HPD became too long to list completely. In 2008, Adrian Garcia, a Democrat, became the first Hispanic elected Harris County sheriff.

Creation of OSSO

Hispanic officers in the Houston Police Department set up the Organization of Spanish Speaking Officers in 1981. Victor Trevino believed the term "Mexican" was deliberately not in the title of the new group because there were other Hispanics who were not Mexican. The primary goal of OSSO was to assist minorities in special issues that they face in their day-to-day work life. Jesse Garza was the first president, Trevino the second.

OSSO celebrated its twenty-fifth anniversary in 2008. Its stated objective "is strength through united effort, guided by intelligence. Such unity is essential for the mutual protection and advancement of interests and general welfare of law enforcement officers. We believe this is the hallmark of any organization." The organization represents officers in work-related issues "for safety, equality, dignity and respect."

Richard Rodriguez, OSSO president in 2008, said in a message to membership, "In the beginning Hispanic officers issues were seen as Hispanic only. But time has changed and so has our membership. Our diversity has given this organization a new outlook and strength." Members do not have to speak Spanish to join. In its silver anniversary year, OSSO had 320 active members and eighty retirees.[19]

25

THE OUTSIDER

The man who succeeded Harry Caldwell was as low key as Caldwell was confrontational and aggressive. B. K. Johnson smiled more often, listened silently but thoughtfully and doled out orders without bite and sting. When Caldwell announced his retirement in February 1980, Mayor Jim McConn quickly informed the City Hall press corps that he didn't feel the need to go outside. He soon decided on Johnson after pouring some Scotch for the current Command Staff members in order to solicit their candid opinions about the individual who would follow Caldwell.

In his brief tenure Johnson followed most of the policies Caldwell established without the same eloquent expressions of opinion before microphones and cameras. The HPD assistant and deputy chiefs and captains who despised Caldwell welcomed a decidedly low key leader who had had a wide range of experience since graduating from the same cadet class as both Caldwell and Pappy Bond. Johnson was talked up as "the high school dropout who became police chief." The man always identified as "B. K." was never thought to be slow and dumb. He took civil service promotion tests with the gray matter dexterity of a valedictorian, making some of the highest scores in history. "He was a good man, one of the sharpest individuals ever," said Chester Massey, an HPD legend. He had beaten Carrol Lynn on the exam in the mid-1970s, prompting Mayor Fred Hofheinz to ask him to step aside so Lynn could be the chief of police, promising to make him deputy chief the next day. It was hard to take but Johnson endured.[1]

Unlike some men in HPD blue who rose to the top, Johnson earned deep respect from the troops with his decisiveness and wit. Faced with a touchy hostage situation in his earliest days as police chief, Carrol Lynn quickly turned to Johnson to "take command" as he stood in the background and supported the command decisions. When Johnson officially took office, Pappy Bond, peacefully retired to a private industry security job, told the media his friend B. K. was just what Houston needed to lead the fight against criminals. The new chief was very different from the man he succeeded. In Johnson's previous assignments, especially as head of the Robbery Division, he preferred one-on-one interviews, often off the record or where he would be quoted anonymously.

Bond's description accurately identified Johnson as a member of the "old school of policing" from which Bond, Caldwell and Johnson graduated. This status meant Johnson would find it difficult to contend with minority community leaders in the process of building a higher profile with greater demands for improved police representation and service. The chief quickly got off on the wrong foot by reciting portions of the poem "Little Black Sambo" during a mike test before a press conference. It was what he later described as "an error in judgment" that misled the public about his feelings toward African-Americans. A quarter century after his twenty-three month tenure as chief, Johnson was still referred to as "the Little Black Sambo police chief."[2]

The moniker withstood time largely because Johnson's service was generally quiet with only a few miscues. Hispanic leaders praised him for the continuation of Caldwell's progressive inroads into their community. He met with them often enough to leave a favorable impression that the department was still trying to improve relations. But he never reached the high level of respect Caldwell attained. The "old school" hadn't taught him the proper political nuances well enough to keep away from missteps. Johnson still used frank appraisals, describing the large number of prisoners arrested in massive sweeps by downtown patrol officers as "vagrants and winos." He also failed to score points when he responded to the Hispanic community's urgent request to solve a large number of homicides in their neighborhoods by promising to send out fleets of patrol cars. City Council's nine-to-five vote to confirm Johnson was down racial lines. It signalled that many of Houston's minority citizens preferred an individual not so tied to policing methods of the past.

Like Herman Short, Johnson promoted through the detective route. His laid back management style was easier going on his assistants. Clerks from his years as chief said he never yelled at them or anybody else. Nor did he allow them to work overtime. There was no backlog. A chain smoker like Caldwell, Johnson was even more private than the chief who preceded him. He was not quoted as often in the news media, local or national. The March 23, 1981, issue of *Time Magazine* quoted him as saying that many Houstonians lived behind burglar bars with loaded shotguns by their beds. Such good ol' boy conservative talk was wearing thin on minority leaders and gay rights advocates longing to support a more progressive-thinking mayor who would be more inclusive of the city's more diverse population.[3]

Johnson hailed from a department loathe to accept federal funding until Bond became chief and slow to implement new ideas. He did initiate one key innovation, the idea of decentralization. Houston always maintained an aggressive annexation program. The square miles within the Bayou City's boundaries had grown to more than 500, quite a sprawl to handle when patrol cars were the highest possible profile in neighborhoods. Under Johnson, the department determined that construction of several substations in key locations would enable HPD to better use its strong suit, neighborhood patrols. Investigative divisions remained at 61 Riesner while these smaller outlying facilities each accommodated a small number of patrol vehicles and related patrol services. Under Johnson, Lieutenant Jerry DeFoor, head of HPD's long-range planning unit, determined that this policing concept was outmoded. DeFoor proposed "a multipurpose command center to serve the burgeoning western section of the city."[4] He recommended a decentralization of all policing functions, including detective work. Officers in investigative divisions saw the idea as an opportunity to go to a workplace much closer to homes located in the Westside suburbs.

DeFoor's 1979 study concluded that HPD needed a plan to integrate a facility that provided all policing functions into the nearby neighborhoods it served. At this historic juncture, west Houston had more population per

**Police Chief Bradley
K. Johnson, February
16, 1980–January 1,
1982 (HPD Archives)**

square mile and a higher crime rate than any other quadrant. The lieutenant promoted close contact with citizens, which later proved to be a primary characteristic of Police Chief Lee Brown's Neighborhood-Oriented Policing that came several years later. As outlined in Mark H. Moore's book, *Creating Public Value*, the concept was to create an intimacy where whatever function an officer or citizen might need on a daily basis "would be represented at the station, including detention facilities, courtrooms, motor pool, radio repair, administrative offices, male and female patrol facilities, detective offices and facilities for community activities."[5]

DeFoor's unit worked steadily through 1981 after Chief Johnson convened a Decentralization Study Group composed of "thirteen functional task forces representing each departmental interest likely to be affected by decentralization." The group had a plan ready for full presentation by July 1981, but Johnson put it on the back burner until after that year's city election. To open a command station on the west side, the mayor and council needed a more detailed plan to ensure minority members that the areas they represented would soon see similar facilities built to serve minority neighborhoods to the east and southeast.

Lee Brown, Johnson's successor, took the plan and ran with it since it fit perfectly into Neighborhood-Oriented Policing. Because of the ambitiousness of Brown's complex plan to reach out to Houston's diverse communities, he often got full credit for decentralization and the implementation of the command station concept. But he personally always made sure that B. K. Johnson was accurately identified as the first chief behind the plan.

As chief, Johnson implemented a bookkeeping measure that seriously cut down the period of time between the day the department hired an individual for a civilian job and the day he or she actually came to work. The change came in the form of a letter from Johnson to the Civil Service director requesting that all contacts between the department and Civil Service regarding hiring and promotions be sent directly to the HPD Personnel Division. Previously, if the department hired a clerk, the process entailed a slow chain of events that began with a background investigation, followed by a checkpoint process among the chain of command. The process often required two months and resulted in the would-be hire finding another job. By cutting the bureaucracy, Johnson enabled HPD to get a civilian on board within three working days.

As Johnson's second year as chief approached, Jim McConn finished third in the 1981 November General Election. City Controller Kathy Whitmire won, having had the undying support of gays, minorities and progressive-minded white urban professionals. Johnson resigned as chief on January 1, 1982, the day Whitmire took office. In doing so, he became the third chief in history to step back down to a lower rank. The previous two were Buddy McGill, fired by Welch in 1964 and moved down to an inspector and later deputy chief, and Carrol Lynn, who stepped down in 1975 to the deputy chief level. Johnson had enough years to retire but felt he still had a contribution to make. The well-respected John P. Bales took the reins as acting chief for four months before Whitmire appointed Lee Brown.

Mark H. Moore detailed the conditions of the department. Johnson left behind a high overall crime rate that included a doubled homicide rate and tripled number of rapes and a seventy percent increase in robberies. The department's 3,200-member force was still underfunded at $142 million and far undermanned with 1.9 sworn officers per 1,000 citizens—just more than half the national average of 3.5. Los Angeles had fifteen officers per square mile, Houston only six. The number of officers leaving the department had doubled from three to six percent. Exit interviews revealed that the two main reasons were lack of leadership and poor quality of vehicles and equipment.[6]

The most important appointment in Houston Police Department history was ironically initiated by the mayor most resented by police officers. Mayor Kathy Whitmire appointed Lee P. Brown as HPD's first African-American police chief in April 1982. Officers clearly despised the Bayou City's first female mayor for her aggressive attacks against their hard-earned benefits and the civil service law that protected them. Veteran officers at the time of Brown's appointment resented a chief from the outside, the first since the selection of Ray Ashworth of San Antonio just before World War II. Whitmire said she never disliked police but felt the department was in dire need of reform and restoration of credibility. She ardently believed Lee Brown could do the job.[7]

Still, the perception lingered throughout her ten years in office that the mayor was incapable of anything but the harshest treatment of the men and women in Houston blue. Well into the new century, veteran officers still remembered Whitmire taking away a pay raise, an action that actually reduced the take-home pay they had before she took office.

Brown, the outsider, instituted what became known as "Neighborhood-Oriented Policing," a practice that created working relationships with minority communities throughout the nation's fourth largest city for the first time

Mayor Kathy Whitmire took the bold step of appointing Houston's
first African American police chief, Lee P. Brown, who later served
six years as mayor of the Bayou City. (Kathy Whitmire)

in history. Brown's tireless efforts to attend luncheon and evening meetings
with community leaders of all factions and constituencies gradually changed
the players in the age-old "us-versus-them" scenario. More and more gays
and minorities joined the police side. The chief, who held a doctoral degree,

built an image one-hundred and eighty degrees from that of Herman Short, the hard-liner of the sixties and seventies thought to be too old-school and even "racist" to lead the policing of an increasingly diverse population without any open dialogue outside predominately white environs.

Chief Brown opened the HPD door even to the gay community in Montrose. Instead of setting up periodic raids of gay bars, Brown established a line of communications with leaders he found to be sincerely law-abiding. Coincident with this newly established openness, the chief made sure the department recruited more African-Americans and Hispanics and opened the promotion process to enable a steady increase of minority officers in the higher ranks. The mere fact that a black man was a chief who frequently appeared in Houston's numerous black neighborhoods encouraged more young black men and women to apply to HPD. Many sergeants, lieutenants and captains who joined HPD on the Whitmire/Brown watch later said when they saw a black man as chief of police, they felt they also could one day become chief.

Brown's community policing campaign—which hardly let up during his seven and a half years at the helm—continued in one form or another after he left in 1990 to become police commissioner of New York City. A former police association leader himself, Brown returned to Houston to serve six years as mayor of Houston and saw the approval of Houston's first-ever police "Meet and Confer agreement" in history, making officers the best paid in the state and Southwest.

While chief under a female mayor who seemed to be popular everywhere but 61 Riesner, Brown endured the management hardships that went with being a chief from outside who happened to be an African American. Whitmire was a politically active Democrat, certified public accountant and two-term city controller with the time and pencil-pushing inclination to keep close tabs on city finances. Many Houston officers supported Jack Heard, the incumbent Harris County sheriff and former HPD chief, and felt they didn't have a friend in the newly elected liberal female.

The fledgling Houston Police Patrolman's Union had endorsement discussions with Whitmire—literally checking their guns at the door of her Montrose residence. Yet they chose not to support either Whitmire or Heard, a direct slam at Heard as the result of their belief that he had not shot straight with them. When the city elected a real police reform candidate, HPPU and the less outspoken Houston Police Officers Association feared the worst.[8]

The HPOA endorsed Heard because, as Association President Bill Elkin saw it, "the blue blood factor kicked in." Whitmire sought the endorsement of HPOA but was denied because she was too close to the gay community. When she became mayor, she never forgot the snub. "She was unforgiving even though she was always cordial and presented the best protocol decorum," Elkin said. Whitmire had no reason to trust HPOA leaders after they failed to support McConn, who led two lucrative back-to-back salary increases.[9]

Police officers had a rancorous relationship with the five-foot blonde given to two-piece suits, businesslike management and conservative fiscal practices. A June 15, 1983 confrontation involving three hundred uniformed officers in the City Council Chambers frightened the mayor. The officers yelled obscenities at her and booed over increased health insurance costs and the absence of a pay raise in the new city budget. Whitmire feared that the officers were on the verge of a riot and prepared herself to call in Houston police to escort their fellow officers outside "an emotionally charged atmosphere." The officers called her "a coward" and "chicken." They asserted that the department would be better off with a male mayor.[10] It was a first-term example of the mayor and employee groups staying at one another's throats while "citizens who want better public safety are caught in the middle of this sour relationship."[11]

The adversaries underwent constant benefit battles in the Texas Legislature and sparred in a never-ending point-counterpoint over civil service protection and management authority. "I had a job to do," Whitmire later said. "The national news said that the Houston Police Department was using too much excessive force. I came into office knowing that that had to be changed. There was a concern about excessive force and the bad reputation of the department. Point number two was my concern that the people in the minority communities were not going to receive fair treatment from the police department." She felt that civil service benefits minimized the department's management authority and that those benefits had to be changed "and people resist change."[12]

In early 1982, trusted members of Whitmire's young, ambitious staff undertook the highly secretive selection processes for police chief and other city department heads. Whitmire designated Jack Drake, director of scheduling and office policy, as the leader of these important undertakings. Like a real detective, Drake checked every detail of every resume that came forth. Whitmire also listened to many sources, private company CEOs and board chairmen among them. Three primary resources, particularly in her search for a police chief, were Harry Wallingford of Texas Eastern, Jim Kettleson of Tenneco and John Cater of Compass Bank.[13]

Whitmire interviewed each member of the HPD Command Staff serving under Acting Chief John Bales. She became acquainted with all Command Staff members except B. K. Johnson through a series of private meetings. She found three individuals who stood out: Bales, Dennis Storemski and Frank Yorek, Bales for his reform-oriented presence. Yet she felt a reform-minded mayor couldn't promote from within. Wallingford, Kettleson and Cater each advised Whitmire that when a private business got into financial difficulty, it invariably chose an outsider as its new chief executive officer to bring in a refreshing approach that entailed an accountability noticeably missing from the department.[14]

Drake was led to Spencer Stuart, an international search firm with expertise in finding big city police chiefs. Whitmire told Spencer Stuart representatives that she wanted someone with a college degree and serious police leadership experience, probably as an assistant chief of a large city. Two men stood out—an assistant chief in Los Angeles and the police, fire and emergency medical services commissioner of Atlanta, Georgia. It was the first time Whitmire had heard of Lee Patrick Brown, a leader in solving the Atlanta murder cases identified with the perpetrator, Wayne Williams. She and her staff relished the fact Brown was an African-American.

The mayor held a secret meeting with Brown at a hotel conference room near DFW Airport. She impressed the candidate with her thoughts on redeveloping the department out of control enough to spawn a large amount of negative national publicity. Whitmire felt Brown, as an African-American, would make a symbolic statement that her administration was out to solve the policing image problems even though he would have to take the HPD management team as it existed.

Brown was New York police commissioner and President Bill Clinton's drug czar before returning to Houston to serve six years as mayor. He said his job as Houston's chief was to establish a department of people from all communities, while conforming to Whitmire's value system and leadership philosophy. He felt a white mayor had strong reasons for being the first big-city mayor to hire a minority police chief. "She wasn't a police chief and didn't want to be one," Brown said upon reflection. "Kathy had a value system for policing and for government. The government and the police should serve the people and be part of the community. They should be professional and treat people right. Those are the issues where I saw that our values were common in reference to policing." In Brown's eyes, "The Houston police had been too tough with everybody. I'd seen a lot of the national publicity and the headlines saying it was out of control. They were an entity unto themselves. They did not even consider themselves part of city government, let alone the community.... Kathy's concern was that she wanted a police department that respected people and treated people right."[15]

Whitmire and Brown believed they could make the city safer by getting more people of all ethnicities, colors and lifestyles on their team, putting an end to the us-versus-them conditions between minorities and the police. Brown proved he had the ability to individually connect with members of *all* communities within the city. The biggest hurdle was the color of the new chief's skin.

Command Staff members never perceived that their stock was rising to the level needed for her to pick any of them to be chief. John Bales soon decided he didn't want the job under any circumstances and removed his name from a short list it was never really on. Whitmire's staff kept the Lee Brown secret until the mayor finally made the official announcement in April 1982.

Bales felt Mayor Whitmire didn't like or trust Houston cops. He told the woman who always considered him a true professional that he would help her new appointee in every way possible—even if that person were an outsider. Bales earned the special respect of Whitmire and Brown for his willingness to help the new chief.[16]

Whitmire didn't need to go out and make any moves with the communities by using the police department to establish liaisons as in past mayoral administrations. Whitmire had black and Hispanic support for police reform. The support was further solidified by Brown. After that, any doubt was over.[17]

All but two of the fourteen City Council members voted for Brown's appointment, the "nays" contending they preferred promoting from inside HPD. An hour before she publicly announced the appointment, the mayor invited leaders of the HPOA and the HPPU to her office to meet the new chief. But she didn't mention his ethnicity beforehand to Bill Elkin and Dave Collier of the HPOA nor Bob Thomas and Tommy Britt of HPPU. When Brown walked into the spacious mayor's office on cue, the four police group leaders reacted with cool, trying to make sure their jaws didn't hit the floor. Underneath their cordial façade, Elkin and Collier vowed to conduct a thorough investigation of the new chief's resume and reputation.[18]

Lee Brown felt no warmth, nor would he be warmly greeted in his first Command Staff gathering that came after his confirmation. "I was an outsider coming in," he said. The unions sent representatives on a fact-finding mission to Atlanta. Somebody pointed out to the news media that the new chief would be required to take the tests to become an officially licensed Texas peace officer. Within several short months, Brown crammed and passed the basic entry-level test with ease. Efforts to find a skeleton in his Atlanta closet went in vain.[19]

Soon, both the HPOA and HPPU expressed doubt that Brown could change the complexion of the department without lowering standards. Officers wasted no time making race-oriented jokes and viewed Brown as Whitmire's yes man with no loyalty to the 1269m Civil Service statute that preserved their jobs and benefits.

The first major upheaval in management practices happened immediately after Brown's confirmation. He initiated something no previous HPD Command Staff members ever had on their calendars—regularly scheduled staff meetings with agendas. The first meeting lasted less than five minutes. The prevailing attitude was: *We're not going to help this guy!* Only John Bales responded as a professional, which was something Brown never forgot. He later hired Bales in his mayoral administration.

Brown used his academic background as none of his predecessors ever did. He had a civilian assistant do a complete analysis of the department. While not popular at first, the proposed solutions eventually appealed to true professionals desirous of new directions needed to earn respect from more of the people they were sworn to protect. One of his findings and recommendations concerned uniform apparel. He wanted officers in uniform to wear ties. Many openly disputed the order and suggested that a crook fighting with an officer might grab the tie and use it to choke him. Brown leafed through the annals of police history and never found an officer choked to death by his necktie. He suggested that officers could wear clip-on ties if they liked.

Whitmire left change to the chief. Any discussions about specific concerns took place in their weekly meeting in her office. Brown used research from sergeants and lieutenants who looked into problems and studied solutions and took copies of the ensuing reports to the Command Staff on the first staff retreat in history. The chief rented a conference room for a day, provided each staff member a copy of the issues and asked how each of them would correct them. One major comment overheard in the session was, "How did he find that out so quickly?" They then developed a road map for the future.[20]

One road led to Centerville, about 130 miles north of the Bayou City on Interstate 45. Brown thought the department was too insulated with no conferences, training programs or interaction with other departments in the state. HPD's Command Staff didn't know its Dallas counterpart until they met halfway—in Centerville.

The chief found three rising stars he grew to count on to help implement change—Tom Koby, Larry Kendrick and Elizabeth Watson, by far the most noteworthy female rising in the ranks. He mentored the three and depended on them to implement important management decisions and policies. Brown frequently attended out-of-town seminars at venues such as Harvard University, earning him the nickname "Out-of-Town" Brown; he always said, however, that he went on his own time.

Officers found Brown was even-tempered and never yelled at subordinates. He treated everyone with respect and didn't dress them down for perceived slights. "Brown himself was the nicest person you ever wanted to deal with," Homicide Captain Bobby Adams said of the Brown years. "He was especially interested in officer shootings and he'd call me. I always had the habit of finding the detective that made the scene and sending him directly to his office. He respected the fact that he was getting information first hand and not getting my interpretation."[21] When supervisors took stands different from Brown, he didn't hold it against them or transfer them to another division.

High on Brown's priority list for change were Civil Service laws and the widely held perception that officers were to be feared, even by law-abiding citizens. When Brown came to Houston, there were only eight black sergeants. After careful study, the chief felt that Civil Service protection and the promotion process served to severely hinder the promotions of blacks from sergeant to captain. For example, in the past, should an African-American officer rank No. 12 on the sergeant's list, management would see to it that only eleven officers made sergeant.

Brown took extra steps against discrimination in promotions. If the person on the list was black or Hispanic, he/she got the job. A qualified person on the list could not be passed over unless for good reason. The change gave African-Americans new hope for promotion instead of feeling like they didn't stand a chance no matter how hard they studied. Brown spent many hours discussing the pros and cons of 1269m. He knew he could not easily make the changes in the HPD culture if he relied on the old guard. He placed the assistants he inherited wherever he wanted them to be. He put Bales in charge of Field Operations and made B. K. Johnson chief of detectives.

Still, the biggest surprise the chief found came during a get-acquainted session with a group of doctors and their wives. The wives firmly stated that they were scared of the police, an oft-repeated opinion that groups like this one shared with the outsider more candidly than they had with previous chiefs. The women told Brown that if they were stopped by an officer for a traffic violation, they would pull their cars over to a location with plenty of witnesses. The chief realized the department had a long way to go.[22]

The new chief changed the culture of the department by going to meetings every day and every night of the week. He knew he couldn't expect his impressionable mid-level professionals to interface with communities unless they saw leadership from the top. It took several years but he saw a growing number of officers at civic association meetings sharing the same values he expressed.

Brown demanded accountability. He knew that individuals seeking the highest level of professionalism expected to be held accountable. As a result, he fired a lot of officers in 1982 and 1983. Even HPOA and HPPU got the message: If an officer is proven to have abused a suspect or violated their rights, they could be expected to be fired and sent to the district attorney for prosecution. There was no wavering. Brown even made it clear to every police academy class.

The employee groups, especially the more aggressive Houston Police Patrolman's Union, wanted binding arbitration, enabling an outside arbitrator to hear officer suspension cases instead of the three-member Civil Service Commission appointed by the mayor. An officer who lost his/her job via commission ruling could appeal the case to state district court. Whitmire and Brown opposed the proposal. The issue was one of the many offshoots of Whitmire's undying effort to change the perception of HPD through reform. Brown's public relations effort gradually eased the fear of police and became a recruiting tool.

Lee Brown believed the best recruiters were police officers. The department would do specified minority recruiting with help from minority leaders such as Councilman Judson Robinson Jr., the first black elected to City Council and the mayor pro tem, influential physician Dr. John B. Coleman, Councilman Anthony Hall and the Reverend Bill Lawson, pastor of the Wheeler Avenue Baptist Church. Brown turned around many negatives by helping to found Houston Ministers Against Crime, following it up with similarly named groups for Hispanics and Asians.

Whitmire's record showed a hefty increase in the size of the department despite going two lean years in the mid-eighties without adding one new officer to the force. It grew from 3,270 in 1982 to 4,054 in 1991. The number actually reached 4,516 in 1987 but levelled down with high attrition. Minorities made up an increased portion of new cadet classes and unquestionably changed pervasive us-versus-them conditions. The "us" included the ministerial groups and another program, the Positive Interaction Program, which came to fruition on the Brown watch. It actually had roots when John Bales was at the helm and chose the term Positive Interaction Program—PIP—where the department gave responsibility to captains in the stations to identify the community leaders throughout their area and invite them in as an advisory group to them and their officers.[23]

HPD GROWTH

The Whitmire/Brown Years[24]

Year	Officers	Cadets
1982	3,270	493
1983	3,634	443
1984	3,909	469
1985	4,188	389
1986	4,481	199
1987	4,516	0
1988	4,323	0
1989	4,165	131
1990	4,104	130
1991	4,054	230

From day one, there were lots of community activists who felt free to talk to Brown. At every possible opportunity he left the impression with officers that "it's a new day" and he expected them to be professionals. Brown was non-confrontational, while demonstrating his professionalism. He got a professional response from B. K. Johnson when he requested a stricter take-home car policy during a time the city was going through a tough funding period.[25]

By 1983, Brown's second full year at the helm, the HPPU steadily raised a beef about cadets with as many as twelve traffic violations on their record.

Why didn't the department do printouts of applicants' driving histories? A ruling on a lawsuit said HPD could no longer interfere with an officer's credit history. The very nature of the Union's business was to zero in on weaknesses. The average reading comprehension of graduates of Houston high schools was at the tenth grade level, while some cadets were found to read well below that.

The test failure rate increase prompted the chief to initiate remedial classes. If a cadet failed a test, he/she was required to take a two-hour remedial tutoring class. Traditionally, if a cadet failed two tests, he/she was thrown out. Often, cadets were allowed to take the same test three times. HPPU found that cadets of all colors were failing tests because they didn't have the educational background. But the union's protests went to no avail. One person familiar with the recruiting practices quipped in hindsight, "The standards started falling. They'd just wash you off with a water hose and let you in the academy."[26]

HPPU believed recruiting was overly subjective. More minorities were accepted at the expense of white applicants being rejected for flimsy reasons. The Union asserted there were people turned down that met every requirement needed to become an officer. But for some "personal reason" known only to Brown's recruiters, they were rejected. The HPOA was more subdued in its claims, its leaders continuing to work closely with City Council and the Texas Legislature. The association knew it might need to use its trump cards as Whitmire stepped up her attacks on civil service protection and the Police Pension System.

The HPPU openly touted its achievements. Its attorneys went to bat for a black officer who lost his job and got him reinstated. The HPOA was far less vocal and endured the picture that Bob Thomas and other HPPU leaders painted of the association's members always being too close to the city administration, a characteristic cited in the Union's continued assault on the older organization's membership. The chief remained impartial and met with both groups, as well as with the African-American Police Officers League and the Organization of Spanish-Speaking Officers. The HPPU hit him hardest and gradually Brown earned their respect because he responded to their concerns and often took action.[27]

HPPU told Brown about a problem with a captain in one of the HPD commands, causing many officers to consider mutiny. When Union leaders listed the problems for Brown, the chief dispatched two veteran "old school" officers to the division in question to investigate. They came back recommending a change as soon as possible. The chief acted immediately and called HPPU officials to tell them their concerns were well documented enough to remove a captain. The unprecedented action caused HPPU to develop a renewed respect of the chief. The union presented Brown with a twenty-page report, the product of two or three special HPPU board meetings. He acted on at least two of the expressed concerns—placing "buddy bumpers" on a number of patrol cars and increasing the size and number of identifying decals on each patrol car. The devices enabled patrol officers to push stalled vehicles out of major roadways, preventing traffic tie-ups. Previously, there were not large enough decals to enable citizens to know, beyond any doubt, that they were being chased by a police officer. Another major change took place when the department ended the use of flap holsters, giving way to open holsters for all uniformed officers, a practice which went unchanged into the 21st Century.

Brown made another noteworthy change in 1983 when he converted the department's 366 detectives to sergeants, effectively abolishing the rank of detective. Under the old system, detectives could only do investigative work, while sergeants only served as supervisors. The change gave the chief flexibility. Under the new system, a sergeant could be both investigator and supervisor. City Council passed the necessary personnel ordinance on August 23, 1983, effective a month later. Detectives got new badges matching those of the 322 HPD sergeants. Although Brown never stated it publicly, the personnel move also gave him power to re-assign ineffective or lazy detectives-turned-sergeants.[28]

Gays in HPD

No one in HPD officially keeps track, but people inside the department estimated in 2011 that the department had at least 400 gay officers, some in higher ranks. As HPD has grown closer to being as diverse as the community it patrols and protects, officers have grown more tolerant of gay colleagues.

The first time Ruston "Rusty" Alsbrooks encountered Houston officers, they stopped him in Montrose and harassed him. The year was 1978, a time when HPD had a reputation for bashing gays and raiding gay bars. If they roughed up bar patrons, they seldom faced punishment. Police attitudes like these prevailed for many years in Montrose, a long-time bastion of gay activism and social life. In the early 1970s, gays were generally afraid of officers.

In the early 1990s, Alsbrooks figured he could become a police officer, aside from one big problem. Although he graduated No. 1 in his Houston Community College police cadet class in 1993, he was refused entry into an HPD academy when he told a recruiter he was gay. He soon established that not all officers were prejudiced against gays when he went on a ride-along with a gay officer who touted the real, down-to-earth job of policing.

He discussed the problem with gay activists Annise Parker and Ray Hill, who urged him to persevere. HPD accepted him for Class No. 163 and he graduated seventeenth in a class of sixty-nine in April 1995. He was assigned to a Patrol beat in Montrose. He also worked other patrol beats, Traffic Enforcement, the Tactical Unit and Solo Motorcycles.

Alsbrooks was the first openly gay officer in HPD. "It wasn't going to be kept secret," he said. "I knew that when I came out. All of my partners on the Police Department are some of my best friends to this day. They have all been straight."

The department has a General Order governing sexual harassment and hostile work environments. Employees can receive discipline for violating any portion of it. Officers also must not use derogatory epithets when referring to any minority group without facing disciplinary measures.[29]

26

NEIGHBORHOOD-ORIENTED POLICING

There was some belief that HPD was on the verge of a war with the community with tension reaching palpable proportions to street officers until Mayor Kathy Whitmire picked Lee P. Brown as Houston's police chief. The prevalent attitude among gays, African-Americans and Hispanics was that the department felt no obligation to reach out for support. The battle line remained us-versus-them and "them" was the Houston Police Department.

That attitude changed with Brown and Neighborhood-Oriented Policing. Instead of the enemy, a growing number of officers began to be regarded as allies. Brown achieved this dramatic change by gradually meeting with every representative community group and demonstrating that the HPD would be more responsive to their unique police-related problems. He soon learned that African-Americans, Hispanics and gays felt police didn't care about the unique perplexities of communities such as Fifth Ward, Denver Harbor or Montrose. The department itself didn't reflect the entire community. Under Brown's leadership, it developed steadier recruitment of minority cadets.

As the chief developed plans for increased citizen involvement, he wrestled with the appropriate buzzword or phrase. Soon he found it: Neighborhood-Oriented Policing.[1] Brown's police administration developed the command station concept right alongside "NOP". But the first step was another catchy acronym, DART, the acronym for Directed Area Response Team, which was on the department's drawing board before Brown. The new chief placed DART into operation. It became familiar before NOP, a national concept embraced by many departments and directed toward fighting teenage drug use. The department learned from the DART experiment, prompting the chief and upcoming mid-level managers such as Lieutenant Tim Oettmeier to start thinking about the service delivery needs for the near future.[2]

Citizens Review Committee

Lee P. Brown rejected the desire of minority groups to establish and become a part of a citizens review commission with subpoena power and policy-shaping capabilities by instituting the Citizens Review Committee. The action came after the black community demonstrated against the police-involved Ida Lee Delaney shooting on Houston's Southwest Freeway the early morning of October 31, 1991.

As constituted, the committee had no subpoena power but had access to all records used in police officer disciplinary actions. CRC members reviewed the entire disciplinary process, even an officer's employment and performance records—anything that the Internal Affairs Division saw. CRC's job was to look at investigations of officer conduct and make sure they were made properly and that the right questions were asked.

Brown safeguarded the process that keeps the ultimate disciplinary actions in the hands of the chief of police. He also helped to put into place a committee of solid citizens with a strong devotion to an objective decision-making process instead of trying to fulfill a political agenda. Brown felt the system gave an added level of review to a group of people from the community who can review the cases after the investigation is completed.

Annise Parker was once a CRC member before her successful run for the District C council seat, city controller and mayor of Houston. The CRC consisted of three seven-member panels, a total of twenty-one appointees made by the mayor usually at the suggestion of council members or community leaders. The committee was considered to be one of the most effective by-products of Neighborhood-Oriented Policing.

When Parker became mayor of Houston, she set up an appointed independent police oversight board to replace the Citizens Review Committee. Parker felt the change was an appropriate response to a heightened concern about police misconduct and brutality.

In his earliest Command Staff meetings in 1982 the chief often voiced the concept of "putting ourselves in the neighborhoods and thinking about policing them differently." The actual term Neighborhood-Oriented Policing was a derivative of his speeches in these meetings. Not everybody relished the philosophy but among those who did were the more idealistic Command Staff members whose sphere of influence grew early in Brown's tenure. Both the later HPOU and HPPU characterized NOP as "Never on Patrol." Old-line officers refused to see it as a different reiteration of the old policing concept of walking a beat. Yet the primary characteristic called for an alliance between police and the communities, which resulted in a greater involvement and participation in the crime-fighting process.[3]

NOP took the five historical stables of police work—calls, tickets, reports, investigations and patrolling—and appropriately intermingled them with sit-down visits with citizens to discuss the causes and possible prevention of crimes that occurred closest to where they lived. The typical HPD patrol officers felt it took too much time away from answering calls. They didn't want the change and used it as part of their repertoire of criticism. Brown and his protégés were up for the challenge. They developed a color-coded Houston map that divided the city into twenty-three districts that clearly defined beats and neighborhoods. The goal was to realize that every neighborhood was different and had its own unique problems and leaders and to recognize hotspots and work with movers and shakers to get the best policing handle on solving the problems. "Go in there and customize your service delivery for them," became the order of the day.

NOP offered citizens a time and place to be part of the crime-fighting solution. HPD's old guard contended it provided fewer opportunities for officers to respond and ventured to say that the department would self destruct if it pursued this course. There wouldn't be enough officers to respond to calls for help. More crooks would get away from crime scenes. They would laugh at the police. Whitmire's more liberal constituencies would keep voting for her since she put the police in their place. Marijuana smokers and drug dealers would thrive. Yet crime victims embraced the idea and said that they never thought they would see anything like this proactive concept. Bill Elkin, the HPOA president at the time, later in reflection said that gradually officers came to accept the concept after realizing that HPD was still doing its job by fighting crime.[4]

Brown used the opportunity to offer autonomy to members of his Command Staff. When asked how to implement the concept, the chief told his

Houston Police Officers' Memorial

Artist Jesus Bautista Moroles designed and constructed the Houston Police Officers' Memorial on Memorial Drive in the shadows of the downtown skyline in 1990. The granite sculpture, shaped like a Greek cross and consisting of five stepped pyramids, is dedicated to HPD officers who gave their lives in the line of duty. The $630,000 work was given by the citizens of Houston with significant contributions from Houston Endowment, the Wortham Foundation, the Linbeck Foundation, the Knox Foundation, the Cullen Foundation, Fayez Sarofim and Co., the Rockwell Fund, the Brown Foundation, the M. D. Anderson Foundation, the Scurlock Foundation, Neva West and Albert and Margret Alkek. The wreath-laying ceremony at the site during Police Week each year in May pays special tribute to fallen officers.

leaders to figure it out for themselves and get busy. One deputy chief, Elizabeth Watson, began leading community meetings about problem-solving and tactical teams. She and others visited other cities and tried to learn from their mistakes. They learned that involvement of lieutenants and captains was a key to success because they were the backbone of mid-management. Oettmeier and Assistant Chief John Bales became the real architects of NOP. Future Assistant Chief Tom Koby also was instrumental in taking steps such as organizing workshops for Patrol officers.

Brown believed NOP was the antithesis of the Herman Short management school and would become the very best method for involving all segments and races in policing. Every officer was committed to getting to know the beat and the people on it. They were to deemphasize numbers of tickets in favor of positive interaction by engaging the community when they weren't on call. Often the younger officers thought of the concept as social work, while old-timers felt it was what they did back in the old days.[5]

The program continuously stressed that the department must allow citizens to ask questions and get feedback on how policing tactics related to citizens' lives. Some officers took to the redefined assignment like fish to water. Others developed disdain for the "out-of-services" that left the real

The annual Police Week Memorial ceremony at the Houston Police Officers
Memorial always draws a very large crowd to honor the fallen heroes of the Bayou
City. This photo was taken at the 2012 memorial ceremony. (Gary Hicks Sr.)

street officers to answer all the calls. Often, officers were left to sort out the
workload, a new task that didn't sit well with older veterans.

Twenty years later citizens generally had positive appraisals of Neighborhood-Oriented Policing, not necessarily for NOP in particular but for some
of the programs that were its outgrowth. Storefronts were a prime example. Early in the HPD effort to orient officers to the policing needs of every
neighborhood, the storefront concept began to take hold. A research paper
inspired by Chief Brown and Hubert Williams, president of the Police Foundation and former police director of Newark, New Jersey, provided a detailed analysis of similar community-oriented policing (COP) programs in
Houston, a new and prospering city, and Newark, an older, problematic city.

The study identified police storefronts as "another strategy designed to
reduce the physical and psychological distance between Houston police and
residents of one neighborhood."[6] Initially, a small office conducive to walk-in
traffic from the neighborhood was set up in a small, one-story commercial

office complex, modestly but comfortably furnished to be non-threatening. It was staffed by two patrol officers on both day and evening shifts, along with a civilian coordinator and three police aides. The programs initiated by the results of the study included monthly neighborhood meetings, a truancy reduction plan, a fingerprinting procedure designed to easily identify lost children, a park vandalism reduction plan, a walk-in blood pressure screening procedure, a ride-along program and the distribution of a monthly police newsletter spotlighting local crime information and prevention tips.

Brown used the findings outlined in the study as proof that he and his administration experienced success when the chief from the outside took the lead down the reform path aimed at greater citizen support in the crime-fighting process. His effort was later identified nationally as the "most notable" effort of its kind in the United States. Officers were becoming friends and not members of an oppressive occupational force. Brown was the first chief to expand "civilianization", a process using non-commissioned personnel to perform specified duties, to almost every part of the department where Brown found many officers lacked the necessary training and experience. His answer was civilianization. Among these civilian specialists he hired were:

- Bob Wasserman, Executive Assistant to the Chief
- Donald Hollingsworth, Director of Communications
- Cindy Sulton, Director of Planning
- Gene Darling, Director of Fleet Maintenance
- Cheryl Dotson, Budget Director
- Waynette Chan, Chief of Staff

Brown's frequent interaction with distinctive communities all over Houston confirmed his belief that citizens felt abandonment from officers. By the mid-1980s, the department initiated five test programs, each with varying degrees of success. These efforts provided time for officers to discuss crime with people in neighborhoods on a regular basis and develop programs that responded to their concerns. Initially, response was more positive in predominately white neighborhoods but gradually changed as HPD intensified its recruitment of blacks and Hispanics. Neither newsletters nor the victim re-contact strategy program produced positive measurable effects. The neighborhood "storefronts" increased interaction with citizens, created more neighborhood organizations and succeeded in decentralizing the department.

Houston City Council members learned that Chief Brown was willing to work directly with them on plans to attack neighborhood crime in a positive manner without input from Mayor Whitmire, who experienced on-and-off-again working relationships with council members.

One crime-fighting success story involved District C Councilman Vince Ryan, who was seldom one of the mayor's allies. With the help of the beat officers in the southern portion of his very politically active district, Ryan endorsed a wide-sweeping cleanup effort in Link Valley, a large group of run-down apartment complexes on the south side near the 610 Loop. The area became known as "Death Valley" because of nightly drug deals and gunshots that could be heard from neighborhoods across the freeway. Police coordinated some of the apartment owners and neighborhood activists in a weekend clean-up, the first major step that led to improvements to many of the complexes and to the arrest or removal of many drug dealers.

The Case against Brown's Civilianization

A lawsuit initiated in the Lee Brown years by a lieutenant and directed at civilianization bounced around the Texas appellate court system for the better part of a decade. The lieutenant and another fifteen colleagues who later joined him as plaintiffs ultimately won a Texas Supreme Court decision issued on March 6, 1991.[7]

The ruling was clear: Civilian supervisors in HPD were operating outside of state civil service law and in no way met the legal qualifications to act in supervisory capacities. The high court's decision earned promotions for each plaintiff and back pay to the date they would have been promoted to the next highest rank under the provisions of the state's civil service laws.

For Richard W. Lee, the lead plaintiff, it meant a higher pension since Lee filed the first lawsuit in the early 1980s after Chief Brown put a civilian in a supervisory job normally held by a captain. The title was director of Planning and Research. Soon Brown also appointed a civilian director of Fleet Maintenance.

The suit contended that Lee was denied promotion to captain because of Brown's civilian appointments to positions previously held by police brass. This meant civilians had to supervise and command police officers, a violation of state civil

service law. Brown appointed sixteen civilians to positions
previously held by captains and deputy chiefs. When four civilians got supervisory positions in HPD, it meant that four
captains on the peg for deputy chief were denied promotion.
In turn, four lieutenants would not be made captain, four sergeants wouldn't become lieutenants and four officers wouldn't
be promoted to sergeant.

A state district judge heard the case filed against the City
and ruled in favor of Lee and his colleagues, but the City appealed and won in the 1st Court of Appeals in Houston, providing Mayor Whitmire and Chief Brown the victory. However, Lee, the other plaintiffs and the Houston Police Officers
Association appealed to the Texas Supreme Court, the state's
highest civil appeals court. The argument boiled down to the
definitions of "civilian" and "classified police officer." Apparently the court didn't believe that a fleet maintenance or planning and research supervisor had to rise in the classified officer ranks to gain the knowledge necessary to do their jobs.

Richard W. Lee retired on March 24, 1990, about one year
before the ruling came down. He had the pleasure of seeing
his pension increased from an amount based on a lieutenant's
to a higher amount based on a captain's salary. The back pay
came in a lump sum. The court also ploughed unprecedented
ground by requiring the City to pay the plaintiffs' legal fees of
$200,000. The ruling meant that three captains were promoted
to deputy chief and awarded back pay. They were Ellis Milam,
Milton Simmons and Art Contreras. Lee was promoted to captain, as were Lieutenants Jerry DeFoor, Delvin Hendrick, Merv
Yates and Sam Merrill, effective on the March 1986 date.[8]

The chief consistently contended that NOP did not add costs to HPD's operations, a very important pitch in the 1980s when a bad economy required
cuts in the city budget and two years without new cadet classes. This, coupled with a higher than normal attrition rate, created a manpower shortage.
By its very nature, NOP required officers to use uncommitted time to meet
with community leaders and develop strategies to address specified neighborhood crimes. This wasn't easy when a dwindling force was addressing an

increasing number of calls from all over the city. The economic downturn cost HPD 500 to 600 officers.

Houston policing strategies became more effective, albeit not flawless, through long-term communications with individual communities through storefronts such as the one sponsored by the Near Town Association in Montrose, the first one set up on Brown's watch. An earlier version formed in Third Ward before Brown's tenure with no identification with NOP or COP.

The department formed the Positive Interaction Program, set up to hold monthly meetings featuring speakers from different divisions who would explain how their divisions operated in ways that enabled citizens to know what to expect if they ever needed the police. Community police also resulted in the creation of the Citizens Police Academy to educate citizens on the jobs of police officers. By 2009, Houston had fifty-five PIP programs in all sections.

Brown authorized the development of the Houston Police Activities League, a group of police officers serving as caring, supportive, responsible, adult role models to thousands of school-aged children. The target population was at-risk youth ranging in age from eight to eighteen, mostly from low-income, single-parent households. Like most of Brown's programs, it was a first for Houston.

Brown also formed the Police Advisory Council, the Law Enforcement Explorer Scout Program, the Youth Police Advisory Council and the Ministers Against Crime, a group of black ministers who worked closely with the department on community-related issues. Later, the Hispanic Ministers Against Crime and Asian Ministers Against Crime were formed. Brown hired the first Vietnamese police officer in America. He also used his Atlanta experiences to foster a better police relationship with the Houston gay community.

Brown, in theory, opened the first police storefronts, a practice that became a department tradition and served to keep police/community relationships on a high plain. Yet Sergeant Victor Trevino, who later became the Harris County Precinct 6 constable, staffed "the first storefront in history" at Ripley House at the direction of Police Chief Harry Caldwell in 1977 along with fellow Hispanic officer, Wilfred Navarro. The later storefronts were technically the first under the NOP program that Brown set up.

Brown opened the first storefront that was officially a part of NOP at the Wesley Community Center. Trevino and an African-American officer, J. J. Berry, became the "black-Hispanic team" that worked at out of a library at Wesley for half a day. They then traveled to South Park, which was later named Martin Luther King Jr., and Van Fleet to a former church the city purchased. It became known as HELP Center and housed other offices such as Juvenile Probation.

Gay leaders began to feel that the chief listened to their problems and worked with them to co-exist without raids on gay bars. Police administrators learned that many Montrose gays were law-abiding and wanted better communication with police under the right circumstances. The very first storefront opened in Brown's tenure was the one sponsored by the Near Town Association at 802 Westheimer in the middle of Montrose. This was known as the chief's first storefront but the Neighborhood-Oriented Policing umbrella had not yet been instituted.

Aside from "firsts," the department revived the HPD Mounted Patrol in 1984. Funds for its establishment were provided through a grant from the Downtown Central Business District, and it later became a part of the Special Operations Division under the Tactical Support Command. The detail was located at a stable at 300 North Post Oak on the southwest side. It primarily worked the downtown area as well as Memorial and Hermann Parks. The increased height enabled officers to be as effective as a human who stands ten to twelve feet tall. Councilwoman Eleanor Tinsley led the crusade to re-establish the outfit in 1984. The detail stood out as a great crowd control and public relations asset during the 2004 Major League All-Star Game, the 2005 Super Bowl and 2005 World Series.

The media quoted Brown as saying that sixty percent of all police departments nationwide adopted NOP in one form or another. As chief from 1982 until 1989, Lee Brown got credit for getting more police officers into the communities of Houston, vastly improving citizen/officer communications and the public's perception of officers in general.

27

BETSY AND THE POSTER BOY

Lee P. Brown served as chief from April 19, 1982 until January 19, 1990—seven years and nine months, compared to Herman Short's nine years and two months. He left Houston to become New York City's police commissioner and served there two years before becoming drug czar in President Bill Clinton's administration. Then he served three terms as mayor of Houston from 1998 until 2004.

When Brown left, Mayor Kathy Whitmire was in her final two-year term, still with no friends in the higher ranks of the Houston Police Department. Whitmire had inspired the troops in blue like a despised head football coach who openly taunts a rival team. Her attitude moved police lobbyists to study the legislative process more fervently than ever before and use ambitious political gambits designed to keep beneficial laws from changing in the five legislative sessions in which the mayor fought against them.

With this as a backdrop, two individuals stood out as Brown's possible successor, Assistant Chief Tom Koby and Deputy Chief Elizabeth "Betsy" Watson, the highest-ranking and most ambitious female in the department. Koby was progressive, even viewed as liberal, as well as being an ardent supporter of Neighborhood-Oriented Policing. But Whitmire and Koby never hit it off, both too independent to be compatible.

Brown recommended Watson based on his feeling that she understood NOP better than anyone. The chief felt that Watson was a good manager who had gotten valuable experience in a variety of key positions, especially as the "first inspector" to audit the records in each unit or division. She spent time in every unit to examine its efficiency, often using unannounced auditing sections.[1]

Whitmire denied that she appointed Watson solely because of the gender factor. She relied heavily on Brown's recommendation of her. As she did be-

Police Chief Elizabeth
"Betsy" Watson, January
19, 1990–March 3, 1992
(HPD Archives)

fore Brown's appointment, the mayor interviewed all Command Staff members, including Dennis Storemski, who later recalled the mayor asking him in a three-hour interview, "What do you think the department would think about a woman chief?" The writing was on the City Hall wall: Houston's first African-American chief would be succeeded by its first female chief, her appointment official on January 19, 1990.[2]

The forty-year-old Watson was the daughter of a NASA space engineer and a mother with strong ties to law enforcement. Watson's maternal grandfather was a Philadelphia officer, as were her mother's brothers and two cousins. Her father's work at NASA during the Apollo era led to her ambition to seek federal government employment after graduating from Houston's Jesse Jones High School. She was doing stenography work at City Hall until the day she learned HPD needed female cadets in its next class. She applied on a lunch break and two weeks later started Police Cadet Class No. 57 in 1972 as "something to do until something more interesting came along."[3]

She finished No. 2 in her class and chose to go to the Juvenile Division, hoping to make a positive difference in the lives of many young people. She went from Juvenile to the jail and then to CID—the Criminal Intelligence Division, Recruiting and Planning section—the later assignment at a time when the department was starting its first crime analysis on note cards with no computer. Watson followed the stiff-upper-lip formula passed along by policewomen pioneers like Jo Bankston in Juvenile. Bankston was the go-to "mom" for younger female officers. Her advice to them: You just work hard, do the best you can do and don't sweat the small stuff.

A captain at the police academy named Bill Higgins, a mentor to many officers over the years, urged Watson to take the sergeant's examination; instead, she went the detective route, went from Planning to SWAT, became a detective and served in Burglary and Theft and Homicide. She was promoted to lieutenant from Homicide. By 1984, she worked in Records under Higgins and was No. 1 on the captain peg when she went to Northeast Patrol, having no experience on the streets. So Lieutenant Watson volunteered to ride with different "partners" at night just to get patrol experience at shootings, knifings and car thefts. Officers thought she was pulling the duty to check up on their work ethic. But Watson did it solely for the experience she knew she needed to succeed as a supervisor.[4]

Higgins was the first to set any parameters for Watson's conduct as a ranking officer in the department. She learned to argue in private, support in public. Watson worked in six major divisions after her promotion to detective in 1976. She became the first female captain, first female deputy chief and head of the city's first command station, Westside, in 1987. Adding to her police lineage that traced back to Philadelphia was the fact that she was married to Robert L. Watson, a sergeant in the Accident Division. Watson also went down as the first police chief of a major American city to become pregnant.

By the time Whitmire appointed her police chief, Watson had more than seventeen years of experience and realized that officers were overworked and underpaid. She knew most officers thought morale hit rock bottom when Whitmire was mayor and they went five years without pay raises. Nationally, most polls taken showed that police morale in big cities was generally low and that, in Watson's words, "We whined a lot to each other. We were misunderstood and always grumbling about inequities."[5]

Watson remembered sitting in a room with Chief Pappy Bond one day and after she became a detective and joking with Bond that she would have his job in ten years. Everybody present laughed. It actually took fourteen.

Watson played up the fact that she had paid her dues and that she was no Lee Brown. She was "acting chief" for nineteen days before City Council approved her as permanent. Reaction was positive from all around. Feminists hailed the appointment, minority leaders said they would judge Watson by her performance rather than her gender and police groups cited her lengthy experience in the department. Most council members were initially pleased.

The new chief vowed to continue the precepts of "partnership with the community," stressing open lines of communications. However, she was not the same smooth communicator as her mentor and was unable to interact effectively with Houston's diverse communities or City Council. Watson faced significant hills to ascend during her brief honeymoon. Not only had four officers been fired the week before her appointment, but support in the black community was noticeably weakening. The biggest problem was the growing rift between Whitmire and HPD's rank and file. Nevertheless, the appointment of "one of our own" drew praise from leaders like Mike Howard, president of the Houston Police Patrolmen's Union, who did not believe Watson's gender would have a negative impact on her ability to lead.

It also didn't hurt that both Chief Brown and Assistant Chief Koby, Watson's former supervisor who joked about "Betsy's payback time," appeared at the news conference announcing the appointment. The move became official on February 7, and the honeymoon was over less than six weeks later when Watson didn't appoint the community's choice for the city's first-ever Hispanic assistant police chief. Watson tried to end the department's militaristic structure. Instead of a Command Staff, she set up an "executive board," saying, "I think we have to structure the department in such a way that collaboration and communication are facilitated. And I think that the paramilitary organization works counter to that."[6]

She wasn't the face of the department's public image like Brown had been, but instead relied on executive board members to oversee the department and represent her in various public appearances. After a staff retreat, she unveiled a plan to abolish the positions of deputy chiefs, who attained the rank through Civil Service testing, and replace them with assistant chiefs appointed by her and subject to City Council approval. Watson stressed that, "I will be taking less of the credit and more of the blame. *All* of the blame."[7]

The new chief made it clear that her executive board would reflect Houston's diversity, and she promoted an African-American sergeant, Jimmy Dotson, to assistant chief. Hispanic groups expressed outrage that there was no Hispanic assistant chief and by August, City Council rejected Watson's assistant chief appointees because they lacked racial balance. The appointees were two white men and a Hispanic woman.

As part of a reorganization plan approved by the council earlier in the summer, Watson had six new assistant chief positions to fill, which increased the HPD total number to eleven. Her first three nominees were Lieutenant Phyllis Serna Wunsche, Captain Joe L. Breshears and Captain William A. Young. Getting council rejection of the three, Watson heard complaints that Wunsche, a Hispanic, did not represent their community. Hispanic leaders wanted Captain Hiram A. "Artie" Contreras.[8]

African-American leaders quoted Watson from 1981 when she had said that blacks did not fare well on Civil Service examinations because they didn't study hard enough. A coalition of black and Hispanic community leaders outlined demands that the "executive board" have two blacks, two Hispanics and two females, contentions that drew council support.

Watson remained steadfast, saying she would consider only the best qualified persons for the assistant chief positions, a stance Whitmire supported. However, she criticizing the Legislature for its failure to approve an affirmative action program allowing police departments to promote more minorities to positions where they could gain the experience necessary to gain assistant chief qualifications. Mike Howard's successor, Officer Greg Bisso, said, "I really take my hat off to Watson because she didn't bow down to their pressure. She appointed the people she thought were best for the job."[9]

The year 1991 began with Watson's first year at the HPD helm getting mixed reviews, with endless comparisons to Lee Brown. Officers told the media that they appreciated the chief's efforts to improve morale, partially by the establishment of a senior police officer rank that enabled officers to earn higher pay by remaining "on the streets" below the rank of sergeant. The minority community's adverse reaction to Watson's first assistant chief nominations stood as what the *Houston Chronicle* called "the watershed event of her first year."[10] Had she had the same political awareness and bent toward community interaction as Brown, the appointment controversy might have easily faded into the background. Her community profile was decidedly lower, a condition complicated by Watson being on six-week maternity leave at the time of her first anniversary.

Although Watson promised a new list of more diverse assistant chief nominees as soon as possible, about five months passed without it, angering the African-American and Hispanic critics. The chief said improving minority representation within HPD was one of her first priorities in the New Year. To that end, she prepared a step-by-step plan to increase the number of minorities in HPD's top ranks, revealing no details. She called the assistant chief appointment episode the most difficult and enlightening of her tenure, "a classic case of miscommunication"—just the thing she said she hoped to avoid. But she accepted "the full blame."[11]

Watson didn't realize that her critics were expecting her to help quickly rectify many years of racial discrimination and believed that the officers of color that she wanted to appoint "were not ready." There were no deputy or assistant chiefs of color and only one black captain. She said she needed an assistant chief good with numbers, and Wunsche had a math degree.

Whitmire did not share with Watson the knowledge she had of minority communities and their decades of frustration stemming from the lack of minority officers. The chief also lacked the independence and authority of her male predecessor at a time when the two women at the top lacked a close personal relationship. They were true professionals in their high-profile jobs but remained businesslike in their communications with each other. Watson never felt Whitmire understood the police and resented the fact that HPD got the lion's share of the city budget while also continuing to pick up community sentiment.[12]

Whitmire's inability to know and understand Houston police officers had problematic results at practically every turn. Coupled with Watson's political naïveté, Whitmire's inability or refusal to help her chief navigate the troublesome political waters amplified the problems and never raised the already low departmental morale. The chief sensed a lack of support from the mayor's top managers, who also failed to adequately enlighten her with cultural relationships that would have been helpful. She went through her last year in office with the feeling she had too many bosses and too little support. It had been different with an outsider. Having a chief "from within" under these circumstances didn't serve the city well at a time when HPD was 500 officers short on the street. Officers were still sore over the aborted pay raise episode, which resulted in the nation's fourth largest city dropping to the lower twenty percent in pay.[13]

The two women leaders never bonded. When Brown held the job, he and Whitmire had a standing weekly meeting for an update on policing issues. Later in Brown's tenure, the meetings often weren't necessary. Conversely, Watson had to go through high-ranking aides to communicate and wasn't made to feel as welcome. This lack of a close relationship resulted in a classic case of miscommunication. Every department head but Watson got a pay raise. She learned much later what went wrong. Al Haines, a high-ranking Whitmire assistant, prevailed upon Watson to perform a task she considered "political." She ignored Haines and forgot about his request, thinking that she answered only to the mayor, finally learning in the last week Whitmire was in office that she answered to Haines on the organization chart, a practice acknowledged by Whitmire aides in later years.

Watson's tenure featured the usual trivial pursuits that affect police chiefs. She discovered Lee Brown had five chauffeurs. She kept only one and reassigned the other four. Watson revamped the dispatch call system, resulting in a dramatic reduction in response time from eleven minutes to less than five. She tried to improve the disciplinary process, making it fairer to officers, while regularly meeting with all employee groups.

Officers praised the chief for helping them win a six percent pay raise in 1990. They also liked the fact that she made minor policy changes that made officers' lives easier. Instead of setting a specific day in concrete as the day officers must change from short-sleeved to long-sleeved uniform shirts, Watson let them decide for themselves, a policy that remained in effect long after she retired.

Because of the terrible economic times, City Council was unable to fund any police cadet classes in 1987 and 1988. HPD trained 131 cadets in 1989. Then in Watson's term, it put through 130 cadets in 1990 and 230 in 1991, bringing the force to 4,054.

HPD saw a growing number of women in higher ranks in the 1990s—but not without a price. Promotion-eligible males felt Watson stood in their way. Those who were promoted or already held high rank felt she was unapproachable.[14]

Insiders believed that Watson's early conflict with City Council adversely affected her two years and six weeks as chief. The nine months between Watson's controversial appointments of Joe Breshears, Phyllis Wunsche and Bill Young as her assistants and the council finally accepting a larger, more diverse set of appointees, severely hindered implementation of Watson's vision. She never got off track.[15] Watson talked the three appointees out of filing, contending that they weren't getting promoted because they were white. Nine months later she promoted them along with Art Contreras and Clarence Bradford, an African-American sergeant, to assistant chief positions.

Watson made speeches without notes, using what some critics termed "a forked tongue; her message always depended on who she was talking to." She spent long periods discussing how to spin messages to the media. Many in Houston's policing community believed Watson was rushed into the position and should have had more experience. Her management style received greater attention because she was a woman. She turned on the feminine charm or yelled and screamed. Responding to criticism she said, "Either I'm a weak leader and I won't make a decision or I'm arrogant and stubborn."[16]

Bob Lanier defeated incumbent Mayor Kathy Whitmire and his runoff opponent, state Representative Sylvester Turner, in the 1991 city election largely through his adept study of numbers and relating "the math" to the voters. Lanier studied contemporary policing methods and learned that Neighborhood-Oriented Policing took numerous officers off patrol and increased response times. He also developed an awareness of the safety concern created by having too many patrol cars with only one officer. He discovered that for the first time in modern history, African-Americans, Hispanics and gays freely expressed themselves about the ways and means needed to fight crime in their communities. Ironically, the improved communication was a by-product of Neighborhood-Oriented Policing.

During his campaign Lanier hit incumbent Whitmire where it hurt the most—the numbers showing that the city's crime rate was growing. Lanier contended that NOP was taking its toll on HPD's day-to-day crime-fighting capabilities. A lifeless economy caused Whitmire to close down the police academy for two years at a time when HPD saw unprecedented retirement numbers. Numbers were Lanier's forte. In all his years as a developer, chairman of both the Texas Highway Commission and the Metropolitan Transit Authority and during his six years as mayor, Lanier seldom lost a political battle when numbers were the primary focus.

This mayor could spit them and instantaneously enunciate elaborate correlations to current conditions, whether they involved library books, weeded ditches or the crime rate. Once the challenger had his numbers ready to be communicated so that voters easily understood them, he launched the simple attack that put him in office. As soon as he was sworn in, Lanier saw to it that the Metropolitan Transit Authority devoted twenty-five percent of its funding to street maintenance work throughout its service area, thereby enhancing the street repair programs for every member city. Street widening and traffic control engineering updates were an essential part of Metro's mission statement. No one knew that better than the former Metro board chairman and recognized expert in state highway funding mechanisms. The extra street funding allowed Houston to free up millions of additional dollars for HPD's manpower expansion and provide tools needed to capture more criminals and prevent more crimes.

In his campaign, Lanier trotted out a number that beat another noted numbers cruncher at her own game. The number was "655". It represented the number of additional officers placed on the streets through the use of a creative overtime program. Lanier said he would implement the plan in the first ninety days of his new administration. It didn't mean he instantly hired that many new officers; it meant his police chief scheduled enough overtime with current officers to put the equivalent on duty. The Lanier numerical campaign strategy worked so well that before the election Chief Watson asked her division commanders to find a way to put three hundred more officers on the streets. It was too little too late. Watson was not politically clever, and Whitmire lacked the police savvy to put a program in place quickly enough to impress voters.[17]

The mayor achieved "655", or "the Metro plan", by appointing the majority of the Metro board. Besides, his authority and close attention to the math earned him high respect from board members representing member cities outside his appointed jurisdiction. These member cities could improve the streets *and* the quality of policing for the people electing them.

Sexual Harassment Issues

The Houston Police Department formed the Women's Advisory Council on January 10, 1995, to review the concerns of the department's growing number of female officers (eleven percent, or 500 officers). The fourteen-member group, composed of civilians and officers of all ranks, discussed women-related issues such as day care, sexual harassment in the workplace and promotions and training. The council relayed primary concerns to the police chief.

Female officers had seen their numbers grow slowly but steadily since Fred Hofheinz became Houston's mayor in 1974 and made HPD more accepting of minorities and women. One of the leaders who emerged was Sergeant Jeannine Maughmer, the niece of legendary Houston Police Officers Association co-founder Earl Maughmer. Sergeant Maughmer believed that pioneering female officers in Patrol had to act like a man, walk like a man and be "tough" like a man.

Leaders like Maughmer and another sergeant, Vicki King, later an assistant chief, urged their 1990s contemporaries to remain feminine, not compromise their ability to do the job, maintain a sense of humor and make the most of wearing uniforms basically designed for men. While male and female partners were unique in the 1980s, the practice became more prominent in the 1990s, when more women were reaching the higher ranks. In 1997, Police Chief Clarence O. "Brad" Bradford promoted Lieutenant Tammie Y. Pace to become the first African-American female captain. The following year, HPD named Officer Beth Ann Kreuzer the first female solo motorcycle officer.

Despite all the positive signs and indicators, HPD still suffered from the same gremlin as many other large departments—sexual harassment, perceived and some of it real enough for court. Three federal lawsuits resulted. In 1996, a jury awarded Officer Linda Williamson $128,000 after finding a male officer had sexually harassed her over a number of years and a supervisor had retaliated against her for complaining.

In 1997, a jury awarded Officer Patrice Sharp $110,000, finding she was the victim of a code of silence for complaining about sexual harassment. The court also assessed two supervisors $15,000 each in civil penalties. The third suit involved Officer Kreuzer. On April 27, 2005, a jury awarded her $600,000, finding that her supervisor had sexually harassed her and that his supervisors failed to take action.[18]

To lead the department under this program, Lanier didn't want a more academic, less militaristic police chief; he picked a no-nonsense, highly experienced leader to use this new manpower to get crooks off the streets. The thoughtful new mayor's precedent-setting policy proved to be so popular that no challenger got on the outer edges of voter radar screens in the next two city elections. Lanier set records in the voter-approval category with regular decreases in the crime rate. As soon as Whitmire was voted out of office, it was clearly understood that Watson's days as chief were numbered.

The men that Lanier named to select his first police chief stood out in Houston's political subculture for their use of quiet discretion in their backroom decision-making processes. From the inside, Lanier chose Dave Walden,

POLICE CHIEF SAM NUCHIA,
MARCH 4, 1992 – DEC. 30,
1996 (HPD ARCHIVES)

his co-chief of staff, along with Public Works Director Jimmie Schindewolf. From the community, the mayor picked Metro Board Chairman Billy Burge and civic leader Oscar Holcombe Crosswell II—real estate investor, a director of CenterPoint Energy Inc. and the grandson of the Old Gray Fox himself. Burge was a forthright leader with deep political roots. To round out the group, Lanier chose former Police Chief Harry Caldwell. The new mayor felt Watson's leadership suffered because Whitmire "never gave me a chance" and, as such, didn't think she could lead HPD.[19]

The pickers narrowed the field down to assistant chiefs Dennis Storemski and Tommy Shane, and HPD retiree Sam Nuchia, an assistant U. S. attorney in Houston. They were unanimous in picking Nuchia. Caldwell later said, "He's the HPD poster boy."[20]

Nuchia grew up in the Herman Short get-tough-on-crime years. He spent four years as a patrolman, served stints as a detective sergeant in the Robbery Division, and acted as lieutenant over the northwest Patrol and Recruiting divisions. He then graduated to captain heading the night command, internal affairs and criminal intelligence division and to deputy chief over the West Patrol Bureau. Before leaving to become a federal prosecutor in 1987, he succeeded Tim James as the department's general counsel. Few leaders from inside had comparable work experiences. He attended night classes at

South Texas College of Law while directing the internal affairs and criminal intelligence divisions, graduating with honors in 1983. As an assistant U.S. attorney, he prosecuted narcotics cases.

Nuchia shared almost heroic status with other investigators and prosecutors in the celebrated case of state District Judge Garth Bates, while assigned to the District Attorney's Special Crimes Division under the direction of Johnny Holmes when Carol Vance was district attorney. A state jury convicted Bates in 1976 for accepting a $59,000 bribe from a robbery defendant ready to stand trial in his court. The judge served four months of an eight-year sentence before another judge invoked "shock probation."

Nuchia was forty-six years old—four years older than his predecessor—and would earn $96,000 a year. Just before Lanier introduced Nuchia at a news conference, he was behind closed doors informing Watson that she would be demoted to assistant chief at $70,000.[21] He liked her, admired her for working her way up the HPD ladder but felt police hostility toward Whitmire made her an ineffective leader.

Lanier enabled Nuchia to implement the solutions needed to raise morale problems and solve ongoing crime problems. Lanier liked to study police and provide the resources that enabled officers to carry out their duties. He wanted Nuchia to give Neighborhood-Oriented Policing a lower priority than patrol with two officers in a car and a quicker response time.[22]

Nuchia started his tenure with the "655 program" as his highest priority. From his first day on the job, March 4, 1992, until the day he left the office to become an appellate judge on December 30, 1996, he had Lanier's full commitment, "like a pro football team owner saying to the general manager, 'I got the money. Get the players you need and go out there and win some games.'"[23]

Everything at HPD went in the opposite direction. There was a raise, improved morale and more officers on the streets. Nuchia vowed to return to the back-to-the-basics style of policing. One of his first directives was to reverse a Lee Brown policy of writing tickets to persons caught in Class C Misdemeanor thefts. "They're thieves no matter how you look at it," the new chief said, "take them to jail."[24]

Both Nuchia and Lanier believed the Whitmire/Brown era used too many consultants and theories and not enough crime-fighting innovations.[25] Nuchia literally flushed down the toilets at 61 Riesner all of the papers and directives related to Neighborhood-Oriented Policing. In truth, Nuchia and Brown seldom saw eye to eye, a condition prompting Nuchia to retire at the twenty-year mark.

◇◇◇◇◇◇◇◇◇◇◇◇◇◇◇◇◇◇◇◇◇◇◇◇◇◇◇◇◇◇◇◇◇◇◇◇◇◇◇

Assist the Officer Foundation

Assist the Officer Foundation was formed in 1991 to provide financial help for officers seriously injured in the line of duty. Throughout HPD history, the men and women in blue have always turned out like true brothers and sisters when one of their own dies or is critically injured.

The death of one of Houston's finest on June 27, 1990 prompted an exceptional departmental fundraising effort by the Houston Police Officers Association (later HPOU) to support the family of the solo motorcycle officer involved, Jim Irby. It became evident that officers needed a formal structure to make their generous contributions. Another tragic event contributed one key step toward such a formality. Solo Motorcycle Officer Michael Mitchell was involved in a catastrophic accident on February 28, 1991. His injuries required numerous operations over a long period of hospitalization and rehabilitation.

Many of the same officers involved in the Irby fundraising effort came together to assist Mitchell and his family. Once Mitchell was back on his feet, he took a disability retirement. He was genuinely moved by the support from the blue, joined with the leaders of the special fundraising effort and set into motion a more formalized method to help officers seriously injured in the line of duty. The core group of founders also included M. A. D. Martin, Hans Marticiuc, Gary Blankinship and Wayne Mosley.

Articles of incorporation established ATO as a non-profit organization that would provide benefits to officers seriously or catastrophically injured in the line of duty. Mitchell became the executive director and the group set up its own Board of Directors. When an officer was seriously injured, ATO provided $1,000 cash and assisted in other fundraising activities. By the mid-1990s, the organization successfully sought to change state legislation so that permanently disabled officers and their families receive the same state-sponsored benefits as those killed in the line of duty. Besides financial help for their medical needs, affected officers also are entitled to college tuition at a state college or university for each of their children.

◇◇◇◇◇◇◇◇◇◇◇◇◇◇◇◇◇◇◇◇◇◇◇◇◇◇◇◇◇◇◇◇◇◇◇◇◇◇◇

Nuchia believed in fighting crime first and listening to theories about it later. This meant running calls using two-man patrols and making citizens and the officers themselves feel safer. It didn't mean excessive management, decisions by committee or studying and then restudying problems through the use of consultants and an extra layer of bureaucracy. "Simply put," the *Chronicle* stated, "Nuchia believes police should police."[26]

The new chief inherited a roster of officers who had an almost anarchist sentiment toward Whitmire. He immediately released a steady stream of crime rate reports over the next five years that always saw reductions in every major category. His and Lanier's message that "more officers mean less crime and more arrests" continued to ring true. Morale in the department grew higher when Lanier got unanimous City Council approval for an almost $100 gross monthly pay raise for officers, firefighters, marshals and airport police. Lanier said he wanted to maintain pay parity and catapult Houston police and firefighters ahead of their counterparts in the other big cities in Texas.

Doug Elder, president of the Houston Police Officers Association, cited a survey that indicated officers were paid 116.6 percent of the average salary of officers nationwide in 1982 but only 84 percent of the average by the end of 1991, an interesting comparison for Lanier, the numbers man. The association contended that the increased retirement rate had seriously hindered recruiting efforts and increased the crime rate. By April 28, 1994, early in his second two-year term, Lanier got City Council to approve a three-and-a-half-cent tax increase that would help pay for an additional fifty officers by 1996.

HPD on the Lanier/Nuchia Watch

Year	Officers	Classes	Growth
1992	4,167	5	327
1993	4,628	5	331
1994	4,839	5	335
1995	5,056	5	335
1996	5,298	3	167
1997	5,363	3	191

◇◇◇◇◇◇◇◇◇◇◇◇◇◇◇◇◇◇◇◇◇◇◇◇◇◇◇◇◇◇◇◇◇◇◇◇◇◇

Edwards v. City of Houston

Two plaintiff officers brought suits against the city in 1975 and 1976 when Fred Hofheinz was mayor, alleging that HPD's promotional examinations were racially discriminatory. The plaintiffs were Kelley and Comeaux and their suit lay dormant in the federal courthouse due to the City's unwillingness to produce a settlement and the plaintiffs' lack of funding needed to push the case forward.

African-American and Hispanic officers moved to intervene, getting more adamant and specific about alleged discrimination in promotional examinations. They were backed by the African-American Police Officers League and the Organization of Spanish-Speaking Officers. The interveners alleged that they had been "harmed by racially discriminatory promotional examinations for the ranks of sergeant and lieutenant in the HPD." A U. S. District Court ordered the plaintiffs to file a new lawsuit, which they did on August 19, 1992, when Bob Lanier was in his first term as mayor. The lead plaintiff was Dorothy Edwards, who later became an assistant police chief. The case became known as "the Edwards lawsuit".

Settlement of the case left a large blemish on the legacy of Lanier's police chief, Sam Nuchia, and built up resentment among many officers who did not believe that third-party officers should suffer because of the department's past practices that may or may not have been discriminatory. The final court order mandated the department promote a total of 106 minority officers to the ranks of sergeant and lieutenant. Many veteran officers in the still largely Anglo department believed that the order effectively caused many of them to suffer because the department was following long-established promotional guidelines. HPD's promotional process consisted of a written test score, with additional points given applicants for longevity and efficiency rating grades. According to a federal court summary, "This process resulted in a rank-ordered list based upon the sum of these different criteria. Officers were promoted off the list in the order they appeared on the rank-ordered list."

Many officers resented the fact that the remedial list resulting from the consent decree waived this process. They also
couldn't believe that Nuchia, a long-time officer known for his
dedication to doing things by the HPD book, would allow an
unfair settlement of a promotion issue best resolved by adherence to a long-held process.

The Edwards lawsuit claimed that the department's promotional exams had the effect of disproportionately excluding
African-Americans and Hispanics from promotion to sergeant and African-Americans from promotion to lieutenant
since the year 1982—the first year Lee Brown served as Houston's first police chief of color. Federal court records specified that there was no inclusion of Hispanic officers who took
the lieutenant's exam from 1982 through 1992 since the city's
records did not indicate the exam excluded Hispanic officers
from promotion to lieutenant.

The Edwards lawsuit bothered Mayor Bob Lanier. His predecessor, Kathy Whitmire, had relied heavily on minority
support in the city election. He wanted the same thing after
having defeated an African-American runoff challenger, state
Representative Sylvester Turner. He knew that in a city as diverse as Houston, race-related issues inevitably would crop
up. But he wanted his police department free of the burden of
a discrimination lawsuit. Lanier was looking for ways to settle the suit and to that end he consulted with two of his most
trusted department heads, Police Chief Nuchia and City Attorney Benjamin Hall.

Nuchia thought the city could not legally win the lawsuit.
He told Lanier the city should try to reach a settlement with
the plaintiffs. Hall, an African-American, joked that he would
have to leave the country if called to testify. But, in all seriousness, he ventured to say that he didn't think the plaintiffs had
the money for a prompt trial.

All three believed that no matter which side prevailed, the
testimony would damage the city's relations with the minority community. Lanier didn't want that to happen. Nuchia believed settlement was the right thing to do although he knew
it would have adverse effects on his policing legacy.

Finally, Lanier made the decision: the city, with Nuchia and Hall taking the lead, would work up a settlement and get this emotional issue behind everyone involved. Hall was teary-eyed and later said of Lanier: "What a great human being this man is. He's as big as he looks."[27]

The Fifth Circuit backed up the final decree and legally set it in concrete on October 22, 2002, setting the stage for the department to promote seventy-one persons, most of them African-Americans or Hispanics. It remains the occasion in which the largest number of minorities was promoted in a single ceremony.[28]

Lanier's studies found that the city needed $28 million to train more officers, necessitating a tax increase that would raise $25 million. The difference was made up through savings in other budget line items, as well as an actual reduction in the police overtime program, which saved money. Newspaper reports said that the additional officers would bring HPD's staffing level from 4,673 to 5,223. Records at the Morrison Police Academy show this 1994 assessment was close to being on the money. By the end of Lanier's final term in 1997, the department reached a record 5,363 officers.[29]

Low crime rate reports continued right up through Lanier's final days in office. The new officers were assigned to the neediest divisions—the Gang Task Force, the Domestic Violence Unit, which grew from one to fourteen officers, and the Juvenile Division, which was seeing an overwhelming increase in juvenile-related crimes. As the crime rate went down, so did response times. HPD improved from an average response time of 22.48 minutes for all types of police calls in 1991 to 14.89 minutes for the first five months of 1992, drops that came as soon as Nuchia started the "655 program". Officers also cleared cases faster: 19.9 percent in 1992, compared to 16.6 percent over the same period the year before.

While Nuchia abandoned NOP, he had enough new officers to better interact with the community and cover the beats than HPD had had in several decades. Lanier played up the improved condition to the benefit of his administration, particularly his innovative Neighborhoods to Standard program and his crusade for park improvements, a highly successful high-profile pet project of his wife, Elise.

Given this feel-good situation, little was left but the inevitable nit picking that faces any police chief in a large American city. Gay-rights leaders
complained to City Council about the way Houston police handled a large
group of AIDS activists outside the Republican National Convention held
in the Astrodome in August 1992. Videotapes of the confrontation with police showed no excessive force. Gay rights activists, however, complained of
being assaulted with Billy clubs and trampled by HPD horses, a response
Lanier thought appropriate since marchers threw plastic water bottles to
spook horses. They also set fire to barricades. Initially, minority and gay
rights leaders expressed concern that Nuchia used an old-school redneck
management style in confrontations like this one.

Ironically, by late 1992, the chief ordered HPD officials to stop asking recruits about their sexual orientation when gay leaders told him that they
knew of gays in HPD, the Houston Fire Department, the Harris County
Sheriff's Department and even the Texas Rangers. Nuchia made the policy
change official after conferring with the boss.[30]

Despite minor political squabbles—one questioning the chief's ethics over
the investigation of a council member for alleged fraud—Nuchia weathered
almost all the expected storms until December 1994. He implied to the news
media that he didn't believe accounts that as many as twenty HPD patrol
cars chased a drunken driving suspect to Huntsville, seventy miles north of
Houston. The chase forced several motorists off freeways and accentuated
the fact that ten people were killed during police chases in 1994, six of them
involving bystanders.

Nuchia argued that the freedom to chase was essential to maintaining respect for authority and deterring criminals. He had opposition from critics who contended that research showed the subjects of most police chases
were errant traffic violators, many of them young car thieves. To chase such
wrongdoers exposed the public to needless danger. The final count in 1994
showed that eleven people were killed and sixty-two injured from a total of
191 motorist pursuits. About forty-five percent were for traffic violations.
The *Houston Chronicle* studied ten years of fatalities from police chases and
reached almost the same conclusions as the published critics. Six of the accidents, including one that killed Officer Michael Roman on January 6, 1994,
involved stolen vehicles.[31]

Nuchia held fast to his 1993 high-speed chase policy and said that police
policymakers must weigh the tragic consequences against the greater good.
Before the tragedies, the HPD policy stated that any officer considering pur-

suit "should minimize the risk of injury to officers and citizens alike." However, it left the decision wholly in the hands of the officer and allowed him to pursue anyone suspected of violating the law. Nuchia released the department's new policy at the end of 1994.

Unchanged was the basic provision that allowed officers to chase fleeing suspects whenever authorities believed a violation occurred. Revisions included detailed procedures for engaging police helicopters in chases. Before the policy change, HPD helicopters were used in less than one third of pursuits. The revised policy limited the number of cars permitted in a chase to three, plus a helicopter. It allowed unmarked cars to initiate a pursuit until a marked vehicle arrived to take over.

On June 23, 1995, the department announced the punishments handed down to eight HPD officers involved in the Huntsville chase. Each involved violations of the old pursuit policy. The stiffest penalty was levied against a sergeant whose car was videotaped during the chase, which overall involved twenty-three HPD units, twenty from eight other agencies and several tow trucks. The sergeant was suspended one day without pay.[32]

The Nuchia years embraced a full complement of problems with the African-American and gay communities, saw newly emerging police communications issues with the ever-growing Asian communities, and the police chief's in-your-face dealings with HPOA and HPPU. Nuchia incurred many of the same problems of his recent predecessors, with his number of critics growing with the years he spent at the helm. They often expressed their belief that he was becoming more autocratic each day. Meanwhile, homicides were down and the homicide clearance rate grew higher.

Nuchia's watch saw a continuation of the HPD decentralization plan with an important new twist. Central police headquarters would no longer be the aging 61 Riesner facility. On October 12, 1994, the Houston City Council unanimously approved the purchase of 1200 Travis in downtown Houston for $6.8 million.[33] After more than forty years at the Riesner location, HPD would be relocated in a twenty-six-story high-rise. Some police functions, such as the jail, dispatch and communications, central patrol and fleet maintenance would remain at the old location. Department personnel and administration were housed not only at 61 Riesner, but in 142,000 square feet of leased space in other locations. Nuchia succeeded in convincing the council that the new headquarters was not a "Taj Mahal" and was considerably less costly than construction of a new building the same size.

What became known as "1200 Travis" was not the only new HPD facility to open. On July 1, 1995, HPD formally opened the Northeast Command Station at 803 Crosstimbers. The year before, on September 19, 1994, the chief broke ground for the Northwest Police Station in the 9300 block of West Montgomery Road. The opening in this location was indicative of the strengthening relationship the department had with the African-American community. The station replaced the North Shepherd Station and thrilled community leaders in Acres Homes.

Partnerships like this in traditionally high-crime areas were once thought to be impossible. The ground breakings and subsequent openings brought to fruition the 1980 plan for four command stations. In all, three mayors were involved. The four-facility decentralization plan was created under Mayor Jim McConn. After years of delay, his successor Kathy Whitmire opened the high-priority Westside Command Center at 3203 South Dairy Ashford in September 1988, while in an economic crunch that caused a police hiring freeze. In 1992, Bob Lanier's first year in office, the department opened the Southeast Command Center at 8300 Mykawa Road.

HPD learned from each experience. For instance, the plans for the Northwest Station were modified based on the Westside experience; therefore, it had no jail or court, both of which became meeting rooms so that the station could serve as a community outreach center. Lanier and Nuchia scheduled ground breaking for the Northeast Police Station for early 1993 in the 8100 block of Ley. It was the last of the four command centers envisioned even before Lee Brown was chief of police.

28

THE MAN IN THE UNIFORM

Clarence O. "Brad" Bradford grew up on a farm outside Newellton in Tensas Parish, Louisiana, near the Mississippi River, four hundred miles from Houston. He was one of twelve children born to the farm's owners—a well disciplined African-American and his wife, a college woman dedicated to teaching her kids all good manners, hard work and the benefit of an education. Bradford also had five step-brothers and sisters. When the first son graduated from Newellton High School in 1973, he had his choice of five academic scholarships. Instead, he became an auto mechanic, attended Grambling State University and scored high on the state trooper examination.

Assigned to a cadet class that started in six months, Bradford decided to see if the Houston Police Department was interested. He arrived in the Bayou City in May 1979 and started HPD Police Cadet Class No. 88 in July, a Criminal Justice degree already under his belt. Bradford graduated on January 11, 1980, with Police Chief Harry Caldwell pinning the badge to his brand new uniform.

Bradford alternated between Patrol and the jail before reaching the rank of sergeant in 1983. Bradford spent time as a field training officer in the Traffic and Accident divisions before his transfer to the Emergency Communications Division, where he was placed in a watch command position, "monitoring the computer screen to see what's going on and report[ing] to the captain." By 1986, he became an academy instructor. During this period, the department fully implemented computer terminals in all patrol cars in what became known as Computer-Aided Dispatch. In 1990, Police Chief Elizabeth Watson assigned Bradford to the Organizational Development Unit to evaluate programs and strategies related to Community-Oriented Policing.[1]

Brown accelerated the promotion of blacks to sergeants but couldn't enhance their promotion to the lieutenant and captain levels, much less assistant chief. Later, Chief Watson had one black captain, Jerry Jones, and three black lieutenants, Claude Whitaker, David Walker and Marcus Davis. Jones

POLICE CHIEF CLARENCE
BRADFORD, DECEMBER
31, 1996–SEPTEMBER 22,
2003 (HPD ARCHIVES)

filed suit against Lee Brown for his failure to promote him, and Davis was a relatively new lieutenant. There were not too many choices for promotion.

Sergeant Bradford earned a Bachelor of Arts in Public Administration at Texas Southern University, graduating magna cum laude through night duty and day classes. Later, he earned a master's at TSU and alternated his night work with his class days, determined to become a lawyer. Watson promoted the sergeant to assistant chief in June 1991, one year before he earned his University of Houston law degree. His policing duties encompassed technical support—communications, fleet operations, records, property and supply. When Bob Lanier replaced Watson with Sam Nuchia, Nuchia moved Bradford to the Professional Development Command—recruiting, personnel, the academy, disciplinary system and psych services.

Bradford served there until the end of 1995, when Nuchia made him head of West Control Command, by far the largest patrol command in the department, encompassing the Westside, Northwest, Southwest and North Shepherd stations. Nuchia became a judge on the First Court of Appeals on January 1, 1997. Bob Lanier had one more year in office and needed a new chief.

It didn't take the mayor long to call Harry Caldwell and get him to lead yet another police chief selection process. Caldwell met with each of sixteen initial candidates, including twelve from within the department, for one-on-one interviews. The former chief reduced the number to nine before turning over the next phase of the process to a small group of trusted Lanier insiders. African-American businessman Jodie Jiles was one of them. Bradford was the consensus of the group. Nuchia also approved of the choice.[2]

Besides Bradford, the other finalists were Assistant Dennis Storemski and Mike Thaler. Bradford had a habit that suited him well. He wore his uniform almost every day, and in doing so projected the same effect as Sam Nuchia; he preferred the field uniform to the dress uniform and thought nothing of wearing it to the interviews. About six months into Bradford's first year as chief, he sat in Lanier's office where the mayor routinely propped his feet upon his desk. Mayor Bob said, "I was pretty sure you'd do a good job. I knew you'd be a good chief. Besides, you were the only one who wore the uniform." Lanier thought he wore his uniform like it was a badge.[3]

When Bradford took office January 9, 1997, he decided to leave several assistant chiefs assigned to their current areas of command and make a few well-tailored shifts. For instance, he assigned two rather than four assistant chiefs to be over the patrol divisions. Assistant Chief J. R. Jones headed the South Patrol Command and Assistant Chief Mike Thaler commanded the North Patrol Division. Assistant Chief Joe Breshears, who headed the former Southeast Patrol Command, became operations coordinator, overseeing the five commands headed by Assistant Chiefs John Gallemore, Hiram "Arty" Contreras, Dennis Storemski, Jones and Thaler. Jimmie Dotson began service as administration coordinator over the commands of Milt Simmons, Geraldine Stewart and Frank Yorek, who took over the Professional Development Command that Dotson headed. Dotson later became police chief of Chattanooga, Tennessee.[4]

The new chief made one move he knew would improve morale; on March 8, 1997, he stopped moving investigative sergeants into patrol divisions. Further boosting morale was his decision to allow those investigative sergeants moved out of their divisions under Nuchia to return to their old jobs, with the same hours and days off they previously had.[5]

From the time Caldwell was chief, the department had—sometimes impressively—developed better communications with Hispanics. The time had come to exert the same approach with Asians, a growing number of whom were becoming victims of crime and were afraid to communicate with officers. Among the scores of new methods and specialized units developed under Bradford was the establishment of the HPD's Middle Eastern and South Asian Community Liaison with Officer Muzaffar Siddiqui serving as the first appointment. Siddiqui was successful in establishing a greater trust between this growing community and Houston officers. Also, Bradford appointed Officer Shawn Sokhan Kang as liaison to the city's Korean community.

Police union leaders felt Nuchia's four-years-and-nine-month tenure was too long and felt he needed to leave. Bradford wanted to open up the internal communications that Nuchia closed. Nuchia had quit communicating completely with HPOA and HPPU, who had fiercely competed for members until they began to realize that one strong union would make a Meet and Confer process work for all officers.

Besides regular monthly meetings with the news media, Bradford kept in close contact with HPOU leaders and established his own version of open-door Command Staff meetings. He set up weekly meetings. Those in the first and third weeks were closed; those on the second and fourth were open to any officer. Bradford didn't want to make high-level decisions without hearing from the troops.[6]

Bradford's style was "participatory management." He heard from as many officers as possible before making policy decisions. Sometimes his Command Staff members didn't care for the open meetings. But others, like Union leaders Hans Marticiuc and Mark Clark, were present every minute and welcomed by Bradford.

The chief opened the door of his office every Wednesday at 1:30 p.m. Anyone of any rank or assignment could come in, usually by appointment, to discuss anything on his/her mind. It became a way of resolving often touchy issues when supervisors were caught in the middle or officers on a patrol beat felt their concerns were being ignored. Officers discussed with the chief issues such as their lack of firepower when dealing with heavily armed suspects and one captain's practice of treating officers in a non-professional manner. Bradford later started the Patrol Carbine Program, allowing officers to use carbine rifles in patrol settings as a way to counteract danger from possible terrorist acts.

One particularly significant event in Bradford's administration was the opening of the new Houston Police Department Headquarters at 1200 Travis Street on Friday, December 12, 1997. Mayor-elect Lee P. Brown and outgoing Mayor Bob Lanier led the formal opening of the newly renovated twenty-six-story downtown office tower. The new facility experienced structural problems requiring massive renovation. It also lacked holding cells, necessitating trips back to the old station for prisoner interviews.

The department added four new substations, Northeast Police Station on Ley Road, Clear Lake station on Bay Area Boulevard, Kingwood station on Rustic Woods Drive and Fondren station on Fondren. New police storefronts opened in five locations: East Freeway, Fifth Ward, Leija, Sunnyside and Westwood Mall. HPD also enlarged or relocated four other storefront facilities including Heights, Hiram Clark, Neartown and Northline.

On August 11, 1999—almost two years and two months before a new state law required all Texas police officers to do so—Houston officers began collecting data on the age, race, sex and reason for the stop of every person with whom they initiated contact. They also recorded the date, time and location of the stop, their police division and patrol beat. More significantly, officers said on their report form whether the person was arrested, ticketed or released. Chief Bradford ordered the requirement to determine if officers were detaining, questioning or otherwise initiating contact with people because of their race.[7]

Both Mayor Brown and the chief expressed strong doubt that "racial profiling" was a common practice. Their press conference announcing the move included the presence of three of the department's employee groups, including the Houston Police Officers Union. The *Houston Chronicle* praised the move as being an enhancement to crime-fighting through a greater trust in law enforcement. Bradford amended his requirements so that officers could note the additional required information on their regular incident reports instead of using a separate form.[8]

A study of the first two months the policy was in effect showed a twenty percent decrease in tickets in August and thirty percent in September, compared with the same months a year earlier. The number of tickets written was nearly 40,000 under the number for the same two-month period in 1998, a number that caused City Controller Sylvia Garcia to forecast a $7.6 million city revenue shortfall. HPOU President Hans Marticiuc said, "I think some officers wonder why they should jeopardize their careers and personal finances if the rules or threshold for determining racial profiling have not been established."[9]

The 2001 Texas Legislature passed a law requiring all Texas law enforcement agencies to compile virtually the same information Bradford required. This made actions of Houston officers subject to state law instead of just interdepartmental sanctions. The new law specified that officers include the

The HPD Mounted Patrol became one of the nation's best-trained units of its kind at crowd control. The officers and their police horses also became some of the Department's best public relations representatives. (Houston Police Officers Union)

reason why they initiated each of their traffic stops. The definition of "traffic stop" also included pedestrians that officers stopped for questioning.

A study of the compiled figures one year after the state law was in effect showed that Houston officers were detaining more African-Americans and Hispanics than Anglos. An HPD report covering 2002 showed that officers stopped 191,066 blacks, 158,874 Hispanics and 172,533 Anglos. Those stops resulted in the arrest of 26,723 blacks, 15,897 Hispanics but only 7,393 Anglos. The department promptly requested criminal justice educators at Sam Houston State University in Huntsville to analyze the data to determine if racial profiling was taking place, amid contentions by minority groups and the American Civil Liberties Union that the figures supported their belief that race indeed played a factor.

On May 1, 2003, Sam Houston State released the study that found that socioeconomic status, not racism, accounted for Houston police stopping a greater percentage of minority suspects. The study found that officers were disproportionately deployed to high-demand beats populated by lower income minority residents. The analysts said it is "universally true" that economically challenged neighborhoods tend to have higher crime rates than more affluent areas. Accusations of HPD racial profiling continued to crop up, particularly in cases where an African-American or Hispanic was killed or seriously injured during a police confrontation.[10]

The department experienced many "firsts" under Bradford, who also was the top cop when various debacles unfurled. The chief faced another low point in history—the July 12, 1998 police shooting of Pedro Oregon Navarro during what an investigation found to be a botched drug raid at a southwest Houston apartment.

Oregon died and six officers were fired. As if that controversy weren't enough to re-ignite the fires of Joe Campos Torres in 1977, Bradford became entangled in three of the biggest HPD controversies in history. One involved the incredible inconsistencies of the department's crime lab, which caused City Council members to call for the chief's resignation and set up the likely reversal of hundreds of convictions. Another would be known by the scene of the event itself, "the Kmart incident"; this event took place on the west side and caused the department embarrassment, regret and anguish. And, finally, Bradford became the first sitting police chief to face a felony indictment.

Bradford went from the sergeant's rank to assistant chief in June 1991, where he served five and a half years before Mayor Lanier named him chief. Still, he never really shed the sergeant-to-chief reputation. He was known as a leader who raised his voice to subordinates, using what some would term foul language.[11]

Captain Mark Aguirre played a prominent role in the Bradford record book. Not only did he lead the ignominious August 18, 2002, Kmart raid, another action caused the chief even more headaches. In September 2002, Bradford was accused of lying under oath about whether he had called Assistant Chief Breshears an obscene name. The allegation sprang from a grievance hearing about Aguirre's use of profane and threatening language toward subordinates. The captain alleged that Bradford used obscene terms on a regular basis in a threatening manner toward subordinates that included Breshears.[12]

At Aguirre's disciplinary hearing in May 2002, Bradford denied the allegation under oath. Later, Breshears' testimony contradicted the chief, who allegedly called Breshears a derogatory term during a discussion about an incident that left Mayor Brown's wife without a security guard at a time the mayor had received death threats. Bradford contended that he used the term

but didn't call Breshears the name. A grand jury indicted Bradford for perjury after hearing evidence of the chief's sworn testimony. The action made
Bradford the first Houston chief of police in history to be indicted while still
serving in office. Carrol Lynn was fired in 1979 and later sentenced to twelve
years in prison for extortion, perjury and obstruction of justice. But he was
serving as deputy chief at the time he was arrested. Brown relieved Bradford
of duty with pay, pending the outcome of his trial and appointed Assistant
Chief Tim Oettmeier to serve as acting chief while Bradford faced up to ten
years in prison and a fine of up to $10,000.

At first a lawyer for Aguirre expressed hope that the Bradford indictment
would result in the reinstatement of the suspended captain. No such action
ever took place. A jury before State District Judge Brian Rains heard the
prosecution's case and found the evidence too weak to continue the trial and
dismissed it on January 23, 2003. Later, the case was expunged, leaving Bradford with no official criminal history. All twelve jurors later said they were
going to throw it out anyway.[13]

Prosecutors in Aguirre's trial on official oppression charges argued that
the Kmart raid on Westheimer became "a cattle-herding operation" under
Aguirre's direction. The raid resulted in hundreds of citizens, mostly teenagers, being handcuffed and their cars towed away. Many of them spent a
night in jail and within a short period of time at least sixty-five of them sued
the city. All 278 people arrested later saw the charges against them dropped.
Aguirre, captain of the South Central Patrol Division, said the operation's
original purpose was to thwart drag racing on Westheimer.

The department fired Aguirre, but a jury later acquitted him. The same
charge was then dismissed against a sergeant who resigned from the department. By June 2008, the city settled a lawsuit brought by fifty-nine plaintiffs
for a total of $474,117. Each plaintiff got $4,000 although one got $5,000.
Another suit resulted in forty-three plaintiffs each getting between $2,500
and $3,500. Eight other lawsuits stemming from the Kmart raid had been
settled and four others dismissed. HPD worked to expunge the arrest records
of those caught up in the sweep.[14]

By far the most complex problem Bradford encountered was the HPD
Crime Lab. The city and the department continued to experience embarrassment over the issue of tainted evidence that was mishandled over the
past few years leading up to 2011. While Bradford was on suspension pending his perjury trial, Acting Chief Oettmeier closed the DNA testing division
of the department's crime lab on December 13, 2002 after an audit disclosed

numerous problems that included poorly trained employees and improper evidence storage. By the following March, a man serving time for rape was released from prison after tests showed the Crime Lab had incorrectly analyzed the evidence prosecutors used to convict him.[15]

Bradford announced he would retire on July 19, 2003, his twenty-fourth anniversary date with HPD. The decision surprised no one, Bradford having spent the past year dealing with one crisis after another. He actually spent the day of his announcement testifying before a Harris County grand jury about the growing number of problems in the Crime Lab. The chief steadfastly avoided acceptance of any blame for the Crime Lab fiasco.

Also on the Bradford watch was a Meet and Confer agreement that totally restructured and improved the HPD salary structure and other employee relations. But this change didn't enable the chief to overcome the three hot spots that adversely affected morale. Yet Mayor Brown never once doubted his integrity and ability to lead despite nine of the fifteen Houston City Council members calling for his resignation. HPOU President Hans Marticiuc gave Bradford an overall job performance grade of an A-minus. Bradford ended up working with Brown in a consulting company after the mayor left office. In 2009, Bradford won election to council At-Large Position 4.

29

HANS MARTICIUC AND GREATER BENEFITS

For fifteen years, Houston's police employee groups stepped up the age-old fight to get better salaries and benefits at a feverish pace by lobbying sympathetic legislators for laws that provided officers with significant bargaining rights with the city. Their most ardent adversary was Kathy Whitmire, the mayor with a perceived disdain for police who fought them bitterly over every money issue.

More than a decade and a half after Whitmire left office, older officers remembered the salary cut she instituted. She got City Council to approve a three percent pay raise, only to rescind it a short time later because of faltering economic conditions. Street officers did the math. A three percent raise for someone who earned $30,000 meant an annual raise of $900 to a new $30,900 level. However, when rescinded, the three percent was subtracted from the *adjusted* salary and resulted in a net loss of $27. Twenty-seven bucks might not seem like much. But it was a net loss and slap in the face.

By the early 1990s, the Houston Police Officers Association and the Houston Police Patrolmen's Union strategized in their own different styles to fight the legislative battles designed to improve the woeful salary and benefit conditions. By and large, leaders in both organizations reached the same conclusion—police employee groups would continue to go nowhere unless they merged into one united group vocal about local bargaining rights for officers. While the HPOA committed to embark on the merger course, HPPU's Board of Directors always had problems with acceptance of HPOA in what amounted to a full partnership. HPPU never fully accepted Meet and Confer, a position attributed to the selfishness of new leaders and hired staff who felt a merger would effectively end their work with the union.

By the mid-1980s, the two groups ran neck-and-neck in membership. HPPU had an upper hand for several years and gained more members. But by the mid-1990s, effective leaders such as Bob Thomas and Tommy Britt no longer prevailed as the most influential force in the patrol-oriented organization. Thomas retired as a patrol sergeant. Both he and Britt realized that the Meet and Confer measure passed in the Legislature called for the city of Houston to meet with what was known as the "Majority Bargaining Agent". An MBA represented the most police officers and acted as the sole agent for *all* officers. If HPOA and HPPU kept fighting, their actions would preclude establishment of an MBA.

The first of two merger attempts took place in the early 1990s with both organizations selecting their representatives, Johnie Vollert for HPOA and Ed Lascano for HPPU. The two groups jointly hired noted the Houston law firm of Bracewell Patterson to oversee the process in order for all officers to legitimately believe that every move was open and fair.

In 1995, leaders from both groups discussed a merger to no avail. Some leaders and employees of HPPU were steadfastly against it. They felt if officers voted independently to choose a bargaining agent, they would likely be on the losing end. The association itself, with headquarters two blocks from Police Headquarters, had its own problems with in-fighting and lack of aggressiveness. It paid for a study, released on June 7, 1996, that showed officers with seventeen years of experience were being paid eight percent less than comparable officers in other major Texas cities. Overall, Houston ranked 210th in the salary comparisons of U.S. police departments in cities with at least 50,000 populations.[1]

Officer Mark Clark learned the ins and outs of the Legislature while serving six years (1985–1991) as HPOA president. His efforts in Austin in 1985 resulted in the passage of some major police labor milestones for HPD officers. Clark, in concern with Houston Professional Fire Fighters Association President Lester Tyra and HPPU President Tommy Britt, negotiated legislation that was passed into law. This new law created binding arbitration for officers and firefighters in administrative discipline cases that would be heard by independent examiners rather than mayoral appointees. These labor leaders also led the passage of the first ever grievance procedure for HPD officers and the state's first ever bill of rights for police officers. The ability of HPD officers to have administrative discipline appeals heard by an independent third-party hearing examiner became a game-changer that was on par with the adoption of civil service law for HPD officers in 1948.

Clark traveled in the far corners of the nation as part of HPD's recruiting team and used that experience to learn about police union success and failure in other big cities. During the early stages of his HPOA administration, he befriended Waynette Chan, Police Chief Lee P. Brown's chief of staff from 1983 until 1989. A former police officer, Chan had previously served in her local union in Portland, Oregon and visited with Clark about obstacles tackled by the Portland police union. Chan suggested to Clark that if he were ever in New York that he should meet Henry "Hank" Sheinkopf, a friend of hers who was a political consultant and police union advisor. Clark also learned that Sheinkopf himself was a former police officer who possessed a true talent for developing a strong and effective organizational message. Sheinkopf believed in building a solid political foundation that centered on the election of candidates who supported working police officers.

Association President Clark also developed a friendship with HPPU President Britt, HPPU's president from 1985 until 1989. Both of these leaders of rival groups knew that a unified voice would lead to the establishment of a formalized collective bargaining process that would benefit all HPD officers. Clark's vision of bargaining via the Meet and Confer process was the only way officers could get past the obstacles of low pay, shrinking benefits and general ineffectiveness. However, there was a big hurdle standing in the way: Britt's leadership successors in HPPU were on a different path of self survival. Their approach prevented HPD officers from making their own democratic decision regarding the selection of the unified organization that would serve to negotiate with the city at the bargaining table.

HPPU's position notwithstanding, the loudest answer to the question about where to go from here came in the form of a widely respected street cop with an unusual first and last name. Yet it wasn't long before the entire force knew Hans Marticiuc. The news media soon followed suit. More importantly, the mayor and council members knew who he was and where he and Houston police officers stood on important issues. Marticiuc came on the HPOA board in 1984 and stayed quiet for twelve years, learning enough about bargaining and unity to set the stage for action and not just talk when he took over as president in 1996.

Marticiuc proved himself to be—as Mark Clark later put it—"the perfect guy to captain the ship" to get Meet and Confer. It took him three years to accomplish the goal and change the course of history for officers at all levels. He described himself as "probably an introvert" who took his job and his position on the HPOA board very seriously. The talk around HPOA focused on the route to better salaries and benefits. But no one had found the right

Senior Police Officer Hans Marticiuc became the extra strident leader the Houston Police Officers Union needed to push for the unity and aggressiveness needed to set the stage for Meet and Confer and the city of Houston's first union contract with its police officers. (Houston Police Officers Union)

wheel to drive the train down the track. Marticiuc was the one to do it. He knew he had to move the organization away from its constant in-fighting.[2]

This officer was no flashy individual, kept his mouth shut and never had any intentions of becoming a union leader. He had a well-deserved reputation of being an excellent street officer and possessed solid credentials as a superb field training officer. He took office as HPOA president in January 1996, vowing to end the honeymoon with Mayor Lanier quickly and take the steps to merge HPOA and HPPU. Nearly overnight Marticiuc became a pit bulldog in defense of the working officers' plight in HPD. When he spoke out, it was with power and solidarity for the troops and the mayor and the chief quickly got the picture.

Mayor Lanier and Police Chief Sam Nuchia experienced so much success implementing Lanier's campaign promise to cut the crime rate to shreds that press releases with lower crime figures became old hat as Lanier's popularity rating soared into the upper ninetieth percentile. But neither of these powerful men provided pay raises because of a tight city budget. Even Lanier's glorious "655 program"—designed to put that police equivalent on Houston streets through overtime—got old. As the mayor increased the size of HPD, he curbed the need for so much overtime.

Nuchia expressed his desire for pay raises throughout his administration, a source of frustration into 1996, Lanier's last year as mayor. The first thing the new president did was throw down the gauntlet. "While many cities throughout the state and country have ensured that officers can live the middle class dream," Marticiuc wrote in the February 1996 *Badge & Gun*, "Houston shows little sympathy or concern for those who protect them from the evils of urbanization and society's extremists." Financial conditions were so bad that the association president contended, "we have officers who qualify for federal aid programs." Lanier made "pretty good concessions" in the police pension and disability insurance but in his final analysis didn't have the necessary funding to give police, fire and municipal employees the raises they deserved.[3]

This stance placed Lanier in the crosshairs of Marticiuc's political rifle. He was a "man of action" just like Lanier; they simply moved in opposite directions. Early in 1996, Marticiuc called for a police policy known as "a formal warning citation" so the hard-working citizens officers were so diligently protecting would not always have to pay high ticket costs. Just because officers suffered with their low salaries, ordinary civilians with limited means shouldn't have to help the city make its budget. The association president also dramatically underscored his point that the HPPU was a Lanier apologist. He set up a Page One cartoon in the *Badge & Gun* depicting the HPPU president bent over in a shower with Lanier, alongside "Don N. Out," a fictional personification of a typical down-and-out officer.

"Pick up my soap, officer!" the Lanier character ordered.

"Sure, Mr. Mayor ..." the HPPU president said.

Officer Don N. Out, in the background, said, "Thank goodness for soap on a rope!"

The cartoon established Marticiuc as a *ferocious* pit-bull. Many HPOA members, including Mark Clark, voiced objections to the dire tactic, but in the end the president prevailed. Lanier never saw the cartoon. He later said, "If you want to get into a fight with Hans, don't expect pleasantries."[4]

Nuchia called Marticiuc in on the carpet for his aggressiveness, one time throwing him out and causing the officer to fear losing his career. En route to getting Meet and Confer, he learned leadership tactics from his meetings with union leaders throughout the nation. His every gambit always considered how specific tactics had worked in situations elsewhere. His most important lesson learned: Unity is the engine that drives the train for all the officers. And unity made a night-and-day difference for all HPD officers.[5]

Senior Police Officer Mark Clark developed the sophisticated lobbying approach pioneered by the earliest members of the Houston Police Officers Association. Clark is credited with using strong leadership skills in political arenas such as the Houston City Council and the Texas Legislature to get police legislation passed. He closely followed the historic Meet and Confer measure every step to the desk of then-Gov. George W. Bush, where the man about to become the nation's 43rd president signed it into law. (Houston Police Officers Union)

By spring 1996, Marticiuc implemented a plan to convince HPPU members at roll calls that the best plan of action was one united organization, which would be known as a Majority Bargaining Agent. He wisely took along Jerry Clancy, one-time president of the San Antonio Police Association who spoke of unity and the benefits of a Political Action Committee, which quickly got the attention of elected politicians. Clancy's encouragement energized officers along with Marticiuc's willingness to lead the dissolution of HPOA through a visionary Board of Directors willing to resign their positions if a new organization was set up, as the fight went public.

Some key HPPU leaders torpedoed the unity effort. Their undermining effort was driven by board members who believed disunity worked and by HPPU employees who feared they would not retain their powerful, well-paid positions in a new organization. In fact, HPPU's efforts prevented HPD officers from gaining Meet and Confer rights in the 1993 and 1995 Legislatures.

During this period, Marticiuc and Clark became well acquainted with influential people in Austin who well knew about police labor-management relationships throughout the nation. One such expert was Ron DeLord, the long-time president of Combined Law Enforcement Association of Texas (CLEAT). DeLord knew the political ropes; he was a ten-year police officer himself and over the years had authored and published numerous books and articles on police unionism and political action.

Basically, DeLord helped to devise a meet and confer concept to avoid the expense and unpredictable nature of a public vote to establish a bargaining process for Houston police officers. His vision included the use of the collective bargaining provision of Section 174 of the Texas Local Government Code. Without using such trigger issues such as an impasse procedure and duty of good faith negotiations, which were weak features in Texas law, the key to the DeLord plan was to get union recognition as the sole and exclusive agent for police officers across Texas. The plan appeared sound in both the 1993 and 1995 legislative sessions. However, HPPU's stalling tactics kept the legislation from passing because they did not want HPD officers to have the ability to elect a sole and exclusive bargaining agent as part of the bargaining process.

Marticiuc was confident that the HPOA's more strident public stance would lure HPPU members to a newly constituted union. This was an early step—even without a meet and confer law for Houston officers—to establish a Majority Bargaining Agent (MBA). During this effort, a growing number of officers began to view HPPU's stance as that of total obstructionist. HPOA's membership began to grow like summer weeds on Buffalo Bayou. In July 1996, the HPOA voted to become the Houston Police Officers Union. Eighty-three percent of HPOA members approved the change, which called for a board consisting of a president, vice president, secretary and thirteen positions held by men and women with the rank of police officer. Positions 14 and 15 could be held by either an officer or a sergeant and Positions 16, 17 and 18 by sergeants only.

Members of HPOU's Interim Board

President—Hans Marticiuc

Vice President—M. A. D. Martin

Secretary—Ray Hunt

From HPOA—Jeannine Maughmer, R. D. Perry, Wayne Mosley, Gary Blankinship, Max Williams, Matt Perales, Al Pena, David Webber, J. J. Morris, Robert Mireles and Johnie Vollert.

From HPPU—David Jones, Patrick Murray, James Chapman, George Hogwood, John Walsh, Bob Brown and Tom Hayes.

Marticiuc served as interim president and appointed an interim board consisting of both HPOA and HPPU members. The first HPOU election was in October 1996 in which board members were elected to two-year terms. Soon, the word got out. The *Badge & Gun* quoted HPOU's Veronica McDonough, who said that Texas' "newest and largest" police union was enrolling an average of twenty HPPU members each day. From April 1 through mid-July, 523 officers dropped the HPPU and joined. "They're flocking over," McDonough said. "We now have 3,455 active members on our rolls."[6]

Marticiuc had strong loyalty from many people. Clark's 1998 switch from governmental relations director of the Combined Law Enforcement Association of Texas to executive director of HPOU established him as a strong alter ego whose expertise in politics, police lobbying, and bargaining was second to none. Many strong supporters came from the first HPOU Board. They included Gary Blankinship, who followed Marticiuc as HPOU president in 2008, and Wayne Mosley, the long-time HPOU 2nd vice president. Not too far down the chronological line was J. J. Berry, the first-ever African-American member of HPOA/HPOU who served as 1st vice president and became known for his yeoman's service to Union members over many decades.

The year 1997 saw Marticiuc lead two important mayor-related endeavors. First, he worked with Lanier on Meet and Confer legislation on the docket of the 1997 Legislature. Lanier's obvious lack of opposition gave HPOU a major boost. It relied heavily on the efforts of Houston Senators Mario Gallegos Jr. and John Whitmire, both Democrats, and State Representatives Robert Talton, a Republican, and Kevin Bailey, a Democrat, to overcome the opposition of HPPU, OSSO and AAPOL in the hallways of the State Capitol. In fact, Clark had understood that these three groups would never agree to a process that—for the first time ever—would give all officers the opportunity to elect their bargaining agent. Accordingly, Clark was prepared to amend the Meet and Confer language in a shell bill he had Representative Talton file in the final stages of the session. Clark's instincts were accurate. Due to his preparedness in having a legislative vehicle available to close the deal, HPD officers were finally in a position to obtain the right to bargain.

No controversial, hard-fought bill becomes law until the governor signs it. HPOU faced a fourth quarter crisis when high-ranking gubernatorial aide Karl Rove, later a controversial White House advisor, had serious concerns about the Legislature mandating a local government to change its police salary and benefit structure. Then-Governor George W. Bush shared this feeling and seriously considered a veto. Mark Clark energetically stalked the enabling legislation process and pleaded the case for bargaining rights and what they would do for HPD officers. He ultimately communicated to Bush and Rove that the mayor and council were ready for Meet and Confer and realized the financial commitment brought by the change.

The man who became the nation's 43rd president backed away from the veto, thus enabling the historic legislation to become law. Recalling the historic occasion, DeLord said:

> The idea that Republicans would sign off on meet and confer when they opposed collective bargaining worked and Governor Bush allowed it to become law. Getting meet and confer changed the association from collective begging to real rights to determine their destiny. There is no doubt that obtaining meet and confer rights for HPD officers in 1997 and HPD officers' obtaining State Civil Service protection and establishing the Houston Police Officers' Pension System in 1948 were the three greatest organization accomplishments in the Houston Police Department's 176-year history. HPOA changed its name to HPOU, opened its doors to all officers and morphed into a world class police union. I was happy to have had the vision and it worked because Hans and Mark took the ball and made it a success.[7]

The legislative victory left HPOU in position to follow procedures established by the American Arbitration Association to set up a February 1998 election establishing the Union as the Majority Bargaining Agent for officers.

Before the end of the year, there was another mayor-related situation. Lanier was in his last year and former Police Chief Lee P. Brown and businessman Rob Mosbacher emerged as the leading candidates to succeed him. Both urgently needed the HPOU endorsement. Mosbacher offered a five percent across-the-board pay raise, yet he said nothing about Meet and Confer.

Brown's campaign aides placed the HPOU endorsement high on their priority list at a time when many officers remembered Brown as chief under Mayor Kathy Whitmire and, therefore, didn't like him. (The two Whitmires were not related by blood; John's late brother Jim had been Kathy Whitmire's first husband.) Initially, state Senator Whitmire, a decades-long supporter of Houston police, wanted to stay out of the November city election completely and told Brown campaign manager Craig Varoga it would not serve the Union well to take sides so early. Varoga was persistent, asserting that it would be in the best interests of the union and the officers if they endorsed Brown, who would in turn make them his highest priority.[8]

Whitmire knew Brown needed to be "a cops' mayor", but the rank and file officers didn't think he was going to be after going down in history as Kathy Whitmire's chief. The senator facilitated a private meeting that included candidate Brown, Marticiuc, Clark and Varoga in which Brown agreed to support Meet and Confer in order to make Houston officers the best compensated in the state. The next step was to convince the HPOU Board to endorse Brown and then get the rank and file to switch its support from Mosbacher to Brown. Marticiuc and Clark designated Whitmire to speak before the Board's Political Action Committee. At first the reaction was skepticism. "You can't make this guy mayor," one PAC member said. "I'll eat this pistol before I vote to endorse Lee Brown."[9]

"Do you want mustard or mayonnaise with it?" John Whitmire said, "because you're going to be eating it." Later, long-time board leaders such as Gary Blankinship, a veteran solo motorcycle officer, were grateful that John Whitmire sold the membership on the endorsement of a former chief when they had thought they "would really take a whipping." Brown proved to be the great friend John Whitmire said he would be.[10]

The Houston Police Patrolmen's Union had provided its members with good legal services and insurance benefits, both benefits giving the impression that it was better than what the Houston Police Officers Association offered. The city didn't provide dental and disability. Its medical insurance required twenty percent co-pay with the city's insurance covering eighty percent in its medical reimbursement plan. HPOU instituted the practice of regularly modifying its benefit package to cover out-of-pocket co-pays required by modern-day Health Maintenance Organization plans as well as the twenty percent in the Point of Service plans.

Due to the tremendous number of HPPU members dropping their membership and joining HPOU, Hans Marticiuc hired former HPPU insurance agents Burns and Hazen to come on board to assist HPOU insurance staff members Mike Mitchell and Veronica McDonough with HPOU insurance benefit administration. As the HPPU membership plummeted, Hans Marticiuc succeeded in adding Chris Burns and Rusty Hazen to its in-house insurance operation. The two well-respected partners in the business took the opportunity to serve HPOU in the same capacity as they had HPPU since 1982, prompting another 600 HPPU members to follow. Burns and Hazen became a vital part of the Union's effort to provide advice and counsel to members about their insurance benefits and financial investments. On a daily basis, they battled insurance companies reluctant to provide the fine-print coverage for officers and their family members.

HPOA/HPOU hired attorney Bob Armbruster, a highly respected retired Robbery detective, as a key member of the legal team. Two other former-officers-turned-lawyers, Sandy Bielstein and Fred Keys, also served as early members of the legal team along with Jan Rich.

HPOA's improvements were factors that laid the groundwork for merger talks. Marticiuc formed the Pro-Merger Committee to keep the effort moving. The Union later hired HPPU founding president Bob Thomas, who by this time was a retired HPD Patrol sergeant and practicing lawyer, to serve as chief general counsel. Between 1999 and 2001, the legal team also included Brett Ligon, Aaron Suder, Chad Hoffman and Sally Ring. Ligon was elected district attorney in Montgomery County in 2008.

Marticiuc worked with Mayor Brown and the police chief that Brown inherited from Lanier, Clarence O. "Brad" Bradford. Chief Bradford reopened his office to HPOU and opened his ears to the Union about any concern its leaders had about one officer or the entire force. Throughout his tenure, which lasted through most of Brown's six years in office, Bradford worked closely with Union leadership. Shortly after Bradford took office, Marticiuc and Clark sought his support for the new "collective bargaining" concept. Bradford said he would support the concept and needed the HPOU's help to change the promotional process from an exclusive A-B-C-D test and points for seniority. He also wanted agreement to an educational incentive pay plan. To this point in time, an officer earned an additional $27 biweekly if he/she had an associate arts degree and $55 with a bachelor's degree. Bradford wanted tuition reimbursement and better pay for college degree holders.

Bradford worked with the Union to prepare for the Meet and Confer bargaining table. City Human Resources Director Lonnie Vara headed the city's team, which also consisted of Finance and Administration Director Richard Lewis, Executive Assistant Police Chief Mike Thaler, HPD Chief Legal Counsel Craig Ferrell Jr. and Assistant City Attorney Connie Acosta.

Marticiuc assembled the Union's own "A" team, led by Mark Clark, arguably the person at the table who knew the most about police bargaining rights and tactics. Another key team member was Senator John Whitmire. Besides Clark and Whitmire, there were veteran HPOA board member M. A. D. Martin; first African-American HPOA Board Member J. J. Berry; Lieutenant Art Carson, representing HPD brass; Asian-American Officer Connie Park; Hispanic Sergeant Bob Mireles; Officer Ronny Martin; and political advisor Craig Varoga.

Varoga's work getting the Union together with Brown's first mayoral campaign laid the groundwork for the 1998 Meet and Confer agreement. Varoga recognized the "head fakes" of the city's management team and helped the Union team get over the hurdles and make things happen. He found that both sides wanted an agreement that was fair to officers. Once it was reached, Varoga then helped to make sure Union members and City Council approved the proposal while the taxpayers had confidence in the fiscal responsibility.

The state's Meet and Confer legislation entitled any employee group with at least three percent of HPD on its membership roles at the time the measure passed to be at the bargaining table but not the *negotiating* table. They could voice their priorities and opinions. The qualified groups were HPPU, the Organization of Spanish-Speaking Officers, the African-American Police Officers League, the Asian Officers Association and HPD Managers Group. These groups dropped out of the process when they didn't pay their shares of the cost of a compensation study.

The city and the Union hired Justex, a group of Sam Houston State University Criminal Justice professors, to do a compensation study of comparable departments. The study was the first move needed before HPOU went to the table. Justex found that Houston comparisons with other big cities throughout the nation didn't work as well as comparisons to other Texas cities. By May 1998, both sides were ready for negotiations.

The Union's biggest obstacle was the always touchy issue of parity. For decades the city had a policy that police officers and firefighters in equivalent ranks were paid the exact same salary. Various mayors showed favoritism toward firefighters because the Fire Department seemed to generate more heroes than problems. Firefighters had enough time on their hands to construct desks and other furniture for both the mayor and City Council members. Before the council was expanded to fifteen members in 1979, many council offices contained desks built by firefighters.

The generosity especially extended into election campaigns when fire-fighters manufactured campaign signs and placed them on the appropriate esplanades, fences, light poles and even yards. In 1998, all the firefighters had to do was sit back and allow the Meet and Confer team to negotiate a three-step salary increase beginning in 1999 and taking the police contract to the next negotiation cycle in 2001. Houston officers were liberated from parity in 2001. Until that time, the firefighters received what HPOU negotiated.

The problem in the initial negotiation phase was that HFD had more individuals in each of the higher-paying ranks than HPD did. For example, HPD had thirty-eight captains in 1998, while HFD had one hundred district chiefs, the rank equivalent. At the negotiating table, factors like these increased the total cost of the contract with absolutely no benefit to police officers. By 2001, HPOU used several vacancies in pay grades between police officer and sergeant and captain and assistant chief. The fire department had all of its grades filled. The Union created the senior police officer position and raised sergeants to lieutenant's pay grade, lieutenant's to captain's to the vacant deputy chief's pay grade, enabling the city to give all affected individuals money with no impact on Fire.

While parity was the biggest stumbling block in the Meet and Confer sessions, both sides reached an agreement in December 1998, making history and setting the stage for a vote to approve or reject it. Marticiuc, Clark, John Whitmire and others on the HPOU team were confident that henceforth Houston would have an attractive compensation package that would enable HPD to recruit and retain the best officers possible. Houston officers gave a ninety-

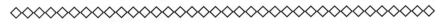

First Meet and Confer Benefits in 1998

- New Procedures for Promotions—Assessments
- A Contract Grievance Procedure
- Supervisory Intervention
- College Tuition Re-imbursement
- Educational Incentive Pay
- HPD Training Pay
- Equipment Pay
- Texas Police Trust—Contract Disability
- A Labor Relations Committee

three percent approval and City Council unanimously approved the contract that called for a three-step base pay increase over the next three years, putting officers on a pay scale equal to counterparts in other Texas cities.

Negotiations in the 2001 Meet and Confer session started in November 2000. Both sides agreed to a contract that was ratified by eighty-six percent of all officers in July 2001. Once again, City Council unanimously approved it. The package established a whole new set of benefits that included medical supplements from Texas Police Trust; an education component to promotions; a police-only Civil Service Commission; shift differential and weekend premium pay; the Senior Police Officer Grade III; and Paid Time Off, personal fitness training hours, the Phase Down program, a cost of living allowance and the Strategic Officer Staffing Program (SOSP).

The 2003 Meet and Confer amendments resulted in additional base pay increases for 2005 and 2006, compression of training pay, cost of living raises to a maximum of four percent of the Houston/Galveston CPI, an additional pay component of SOSP, increased medical supplements from Texas Police Trust and the positive discipline program. The amended contract specified that all officers would receive three percent pay raises in 2005, 2006 and 2007 and two percent increases in 2008, 2009 and 2010, by June of each year.

The 2004 Meet and Confer agreements resulted in a list of Phase Down options and a Paid Time Off schedule based on years of service. Officers with one to four years of experience, for instance, could receive 120 hours, or fifteen days, while those with fifteen years or more could receive at least thirty or no more than forty days.

Meet and Confer contracts negotiated in the Marticiuc years raised officer compensation to the highest in Texas, a marked contrast to the HPD rank prior to 1996 when the newly constituted Houston Police Officers Union under Marticiuc's leadership took the steps that changed history. By January 2008, the minimum salary calculation for first-year officer compensation, including base pay, longevity, training and equipment and shift differential was $43,075.

Future offices in the Houston Police Department can look back on the historic initial contract in December 1998 as the establishment of the most important benefit in the department's history. The first contract is the most important to get right because it is the solid foundation on which all future contracts are built. HPOU has been steadfast in its expressions of appreciation to two individuals who "made it happen"—Lee Brown and John

Whitmire. Both Brown and Whitmire have influenced HPD for more than a generation.

No longer does a new officer automatically face anxiety because of uncertain pay and benefits that could be challenged or changed based on the philosophy of a new mayor. The greatest legacy of the Hans Marticiuc era is that basic working conditions continue to improve for the greatest of reasons—that HPD officers *deserve* the salaries and benefits they receive. More importantly, the mechanism is in place to make even more improvements in future years.

30

THE CHIEF FROM PHOENIX

Bill White always did his homework. When he became mayor of Houston in 2003, he researched the Houston Police Department like a doctoral candidate, using the same fact-finding abilities and impressive menu of knowledge he employed to become a notable consensus builder in business and politics. White memorized the details of the department's three traditional "U's"—Underfunded, Undermanned and Under-equipped.

By talking to a large percentage of the department, sometimes more than a hundred officers at a time, the new mayor believed that the consensus was that the Command Staff had been in place too long and was out of touch. He included this finding in the major line of reasoning he used to pick an outsider as police chief for the third time in HPD history. White wanted a visionary with a high premium on professionalism and clear definition of policing roles at all levels. He wanted discipline without "management determined by internal affairs" after finding that half the HPD complaints were internal—not from the police interaction with citizens.

In his first year of 2004, the new mayor employed a police head hunter to find the best qualified outsiders and soon zeroed in on Phoenix Police Chief Harold Hurtt, a man he found to have self-confidence, experience and a belief in delegation, not micromanagement. Hurtt wanted one more major policing challenge before he retired. Why not Houston? White announced the city's sixty-fifth police chief on Friday, February 27, 2004.

Almost immediately, White and Hurtt undertook the touchy task of reassigning the two most senior members of the Command Staff, Executive Assistant Chiefs Joe Breshears and Dennis Storemski. Breshears served as acting chief upon the retirement of Clarence O. "Brad" Bradford on September 23, 2003. Storemski was seriously considered for the chief's appointment

POLICE CHIEF HAROLD
HURTT, FEBRUARY 27,
2004–DECEMBER 31,
2009 (HPD ARCHIVES)

by at least two previous mayors. Both men were very professional and highly respected men of rank with reputations for outspokenness.

Initially, Breshears didn't want the job on a permanent basis, but changed his mind and shared with White his views of various management issues. Breshears could come into a division, analyze a problem and fix it promptly, a talent he used in each of his major assignments. He held a biology degree from the University of Houston. Storemski, a UH Criminal Justice degree holder, became the only individual in history to serve in *every* rank from officer to executive assistant chief. Kathy Whitmire interviewed him twice for the chief's position, each time choosing others.

White wanted younger officers under a younger Command Staff. When he took office, he found HPD with an average age of forty-seven. He also inherited a force operating at almost 600 officers less than its peak roster of 5,435 in 1999. He and Hurtt instituted a plan designed to increase HPD to 5,450 officers by 2010—a plan that went unachieved. The new administration had hoped to accomplish this goal by effecting a management rotation with each assistant chief rotating assignments every two or three years. White considered rotation vital to having a senior leadership group that understood the entire organization.[1]

White handled Breshears and Storemski in his own way. He persuaded Breshears to accept a civilian position in his office to work on mobility issues and help establish the Safe Clear program, a new safety and mobility plan. David Saperstein, White's mobility guru, would work with Breshears, who would be director of Mobility. Twenty-four hours later, Breshears went into Phase Down and moved to City Hall. He was director of Mobility until he retired on October 14, 2006.

White offered Storemski the job of director of Homeland Security, another civilian position that also required HPD retirement. It was a good match. Storemski already had led impressive security efforts, including the 2004 Super Bowl at Reliant Stadium. He earned his security stripes when Houston hosted the 1992 Republican National Convention in the Astrodome. Storemski succeeded John Bales, another former executive assistant chief of police who had retired from his civilian position.

Harold Hurtt's background was similar in many ways to that of his predecessor, Clarence Bradford. He was the son of a hard-working farming couple in Virginia. His father worked two jobs, as a farmer during the day and a factory worker on the midnight shift. Hurtt went into policing after serving four years in the U.S. Air Force, winding up in Phoenix, where he joined the force in 1968 and began his career walking a beat. Hurtt learned the early concepts of Neighborhood-Oriented Policing on the streets. Only by getting acquainted with residents, businessmen and other street sources could he and his fellow officers effectively deal with the wide variety of police activities. Hurtt earned promotions every three or four years and volunteered for the department's committees. Along the way he earned a degree in sociology from Arizona State University and a master's in organizational management from the University of Phoenix. He left in 1991 after twenty-three years to become police chief in Oxnard, California, and returned to Phoenix to serve as chief from 1998 until 2004.

At first, Hurtt found difficulty in convincing his Houston troops that he was ready for a bigger policing league. He took over a department with an annual budget of $400 million and 5,500 officers and a support staff of about 1,250. In Phoenix he oversaw a $270 million budget with 3,700 classified and civilian personnel. The Houston City Council respected White's appointee enough to make him the highest paid city employee in Houston history at $170,000 a year, more than the mayor's $165,844, yet far below the Los Angeles chief's salary of $248,000.

Hurtt remedied Phoenix' deadly force problem by equipping his officers with Tasers, the so-called "stun guns" that had been around a number of years without being designated standard police equipment. He was the first major metropolitan police chief in the nation to arm each of his patrol officers with the device. Hurtt's first major order of business was to initiate this policy for HPD, which was experiencing the same bad deadly force rap as Phoenix. GT Distributors Inc., of Phoenix, got Houston's $4.7 million Taser contract. To cover the cost, the council borrowed money by issuing tax notes that would be repaid through the HPD budget over the next five years. In the first year of usage, HPD cut deadly force practice to its lowest rate in twenty-five years. The first eighteen months of usage showed more than $1 million in medical cost savings for injured officers now equipped with a non-deadly alternative to side arms.[2]

Houston officers' use of deadly force became controversial in 2003 when they shot and killed two unarmed Hispanic teenagers, fifteen-year-old Jose Vargas and fourteen-year-old Eli Escobar II. Although Tasers were credited with saving numerous serious injuries, they also drew notable controversy in the minority communities and the news media. A January 14, 2007, report in the Houston Chronicle analyzed more than 1,000 discharges from HPD Tasers between December 2004 and August 2006 and found that in ninety-five percent of those cases the Tasers were "not used to defuse situations in which suspects wielded weapons and deadly force clearly would have been justified." Taser incidents escalated from traffic stops, disturbance and nuisance complaints, and reports of suspicious people. Seventy-three percent of Taser targets were black suspects. The report found that no crime was committed in more than one third of the cases and usually resulted in misdemeanor charges, a point Hurtt countered by pointing out that the type of crime committed or whether charges resulted has little if any bearing on whether Taser use is justified.[3]

By far the most notable Taser case involved Fred Weary, an African-American six-foot-four, 308-pound Houston Texans lineman. Two HPD officers stopped Weary as he headed home after practice at Reliant Stadium when they saw that his vehicle didn't have a front license plate. The incident resulted in misdemeanor charges being dismissed and Weary filing a federal lawsuit against the city, although the department found that the officers acted according to procedure.[4] He dropped the suit in June 2009.

While the department assiduously contended that Taser use definitely offered an effective alternative to the use of deadly force, the Eli Escobar II case hung like a dark cloud over the department's reputation. Young Escobar's family pressed a lawsuit against HPD and on May 28, 2008, received a $1.5 million payout when City Council agreed to settle the case. The settlement required Mayor White to send the Escobar family a condolence letter and have the city locate a plaque honoring Escobar's life on city property. In addition to the new rule, the department expanded crisis intervention training for all officers.[5]

The Escobar case and the subsequent lawsuit portrayed HPD's firearms training as inadequate and claimed that the officer involved earned his badge and gun only because of the department's reliance on overall average performance scores at the police academy rather than success or failure in a particular area, such as use of force. Evidence showed the individual graded poorly in his mandatory Texas peace officers' test, including the "use-of-force law." The incident in question happened November 21, 2003, when the officer helped a fellow officer respond to a minor disturbance involving two boys in the Escobars' neighborhood. Young Eli was not involved in the incident but when he tried to leave the scene, the officer said his drawn pistol accidentally fired as he struggled with the young man, the bullet striking him in the head. The officer was allowed to resign from HPD.

In 2005, he was found guilty of criminally negligent homicide and sentenced to sixty days in jail and five years' probation. The city defended HPD's firearms training procedure and blamed the fatal incident on the officer's poor judgment and failure to follow that procedure. The court settlement established the Escobar Rule. The rule required officers to identify "articulable threat of deadly force, have sights of the weapon on the threat, protecting themselves or another person from imminent threat of death or serious bodily harm, must have made a conscious decision to fire before placing his/her finger on the restraining a person."[6]

Mayor White's Safe Clear program was being put into place before Hurtt arrived. The program used wreckers to timely clear stalled cars on freeways. After only a few months, Hurtt announced on April 29, 2004, a plan to install cameras at dangerous intersections and those near schools and hospitals. He said the move could make driving safer and free up more officers to investigate crime. Drivers faced $75 fines if the camera snapped a picture of the license plates on their vehicles as they motored through a camera-guarded red light. The process was used until voters in the 2010 election totally rejected the use of red-light cameras anywhere in Houston.[7]

When Chief Hurtt first took office, he discovered that the department's $440 million budget had a $30 million deficit in his boss' first two-year term as mayor. He had to do something quickly to make a good first impression within a context of a promised fourteen percent police pay raise and the unprecedented loss of personnel through retirements. Many officers had postponed their retirement until the raise took effect, therefore raising a pension based on their highest pay level.

The department, accustomed to a routine two percent attrition rate, set a new record for retirements. Shortly after the raise, fifty-nine officers with 1,823 years of experience submitted retirement papers. By the end of 2004, HPD's attrition totaled 481 officers, more than twice the largest attrition number of any previous year, at a time when budget limitations prevented the scheduling of any new cadet classes. Hurtt was taken aback because his predecessors had taken no steps for a succession process, including aggressive recruiting and a full academy schedule.

Hurtt combated the budget woes by cutting 345 civilians, including many jailers, from the HPD work force. Overall, the department was the biggest winner in White's first-ever city budget, seeing an increase of $47.6 million, most of which covered the $50 million needed for the raises. The jail staffing plan immediately drew criticism for taking commissioned officers off the streets in order to staff civilian positions. By cutting 240 civilian jailers, Hurtt saved $6.79 million. He also effectively increased the cost of running a jail since civilians earning an average annual salary of $24,745 were replaced by commissioned officers whose yearly base pay was $43,428.

Despite his vow to interact with community leaders and take seriously their ideas about fighting neighborhood crime, Hurtt cut two popular programs, the Drug Abuse Resistance Education program and the Police Activities League designed to keep young people from joining gangs. Hurtt retained the department's Explorer and high school intern programs for teenagers entertaining the idea of law enforcement careers.

On April 23, 2004, Hurtt said his younger, more diverse Command Staff would emphasize employee productivity and accountability. The reassignments of the longest-tenured and most influential executive assistant chiefs paved the way for Hurtt to make the biggest staff changes in history. White played a major role in the new assignments, but both he and Hurtt insisted that the changes were Hurtt's decisions, the chief insisting that White "was very, very hands-off in that." In making his choices, he developed "the top twenty and bottom twenty in the organization," got recommendations and made comparisons. Hurtt found a good consensus about the good leaders in the department.[8]

In the effort to increase the size of the department, HPD faced strong competition from other Texas cities, especially when HPD's salary structure fell behind San Antonio, Austin and Dallas. So by spring 2008, White led City Council to agree to $12,000 bonuses for newly recruited police cadets. But the bonus plan failed to fill the department's goal of seventy-member cadet classes. The Union termed the action a "Band-Aid solution" that ignored the need for across-the-board pay raises for all ranks. The Houston Police Officers Union found the bonuses "a bitter pill to swallow" since new officers just missed the opportunity and the bonuses created the perception that a veteran officer's value was not as much as that of a new applicant.[9]

In another historical trend, a U. S. Department of Justice study of America's big-city police departments in 2003 showed HPD to be the fifth largest in the nation but only twelfth in the percentage of female officers. Detroit led the nation with 26.09 percent of its police force consisting of policewomen. Practically all of the other big cities, including Dallas with 16.79 percent, led the Bayou City blue. Interestingly, the Phoenix Police Department, Hurtt's previous duty station, was the only major city behind Houston, with 12.70. Hurtt stressed that he was the first Houston chief to promote a woman (Martha Montalvo) to executive chief, the level just below his. Overall, HPD had three women serving at the level of assistant chief or above.

Hurtt weathered the storms caused by the record 2004 attrition rate one year later by citing a lower average response time to Priority 1 calls—from 4.75 minutes to 4.68 minutes. But Priority 2 call reports were not as fast. Response times increased to 8.85 minutes, up from 8.68 minutes over the 2004 figures. These time increases for responses to crimes such as robberies in progress backed up opinions the Union expressed about inconvenience for the greatest amount of citizens in need of police. Instead of getting a prompt response, victims were forced to wait longer while the perpetrators got away.

To help devote more attention to the growing investigative workload, the department made arrangements for twenty-four retired Houston officers to return to duty as part of a pilot program to increase staffing numbers in divisions like Homicide to handle extraordinary caseloads. The retirees would work no more than thirty hours per week and be confined to support functions as opposed to street work.

Hurtt felt heat over some officers working extra jobs in nightclubs and others working enough overtime hours to earn annual compensation adding up to more than the salaries of the mayor and police chief.

Five officers went on trial in August 2004 on charges they solicited bribes from local cantinas where they provided security in their extra jobs. The bribery cases focused attention on police extra jobs in Houston area nightclubs. These cases resulted in an October 4, 2004, opinion by Texas Attorney General Greg Abbott that off-duty police officers moonlighting at private security jobs were not violating a state law prohibiting them from accepting an honorarium for performing such services. Abbott's opinion settled the uncertainty about the long-standing practice of allowing peace officers to earn extra money as security guards. HPD fired the five officers. Prosecutors later reduced the charges to official oppression, a misdemeanor, in return for guilty pleas. The officers allegedly shook down as many as forty cantina owners in the northern and eastern parts of Houston.

Although HPD remained the nation's largest department that allowed its officers to moonlight in bars, Hurtt instituted closer supervision and monitoring. Effective November 1, 2004, all officers moonlighting at bars were required to attend a four-hour special training class designed by the Texas Alcoholic Beverage Commission in conjunction with HPD's Vice, Narcotics and Internal Affairs divisions. The training focused on enforcing rules and regulations in places that served alcohol. HPD supervisors also were trained to monitor moonlighting officers.

An in-depth April 2006 Chronicle story brought to light the subject of vast amounts of police overtime as related to HPD's traditional problem of understaffing. The story cited $100,000 in overtime pay earned by a senior police officer while working on the department's DWI Task Force. The officer's overall annual compensation of $172,000 earned him higher pay than White and rivaled Hurtt's $184,000 salary. The Chronicle investigation further showed that twenty-two officers earned more than $50,000 in overtime in 2005, "including seven who doubled their pay with the extra money." In all, these officers were among more than one hundred at the sergeant or officer level earning six-figure incomes.[10] Discussions at City Hall and 1200 Travis reminded the public that overtime was distinct from the income from extra jobs. Policy prohibited officers from working more than eighty hours a week for all jobs combined without a supervisor's approval. The whole system was laid out in the city's Meet and Confer agreement with its police officers negotiated in the mayoral administration of Mayor Lee Brown.[11]

HPD operated a state-of-the-art traffic control and security system in downtown Houston by the beginning of the new century. (Houston Police Officers Union)

Departmental spokesmen pointed out that overtime pay was absolutely necessary for the DWI Task Force because the nature of the work required officers to work at night when more drunken drivers were out on the roads. HPOU President Hans Marticiuc also took the opportunity to accentuate the staffing problem, insisting officers certainly deserved overtime if they were getting drunks off the streets, making arrests and going to trial. "If you're working it, then you have a right to it," the Union leader said.

Before the end of Hurtt's first calendar year, crime was down within the city limits. A year later, HPD kept the crime rate stable but Houstonians were uncertain about the steady influx of evacuees from Hurricane Katrina, which had displaced thousands of Louisiana residents. An unprecedented housing program offered by the newly formed Houston-Harris County Joint Hurricane Housing Task Force attracted increased numbers of evacuees, who could receive free housing and utility bills according to a Bill White-led process organized in conjunction with the Federal Emergency Management Agency. HPD responded with soaring overtime payments that put the equivalent of 150 officers on the street by the end of 2005. Within one year, the homicide rate began to rise to what became the deadliest year for the department in more than a decade, even with a $10.5 million overtime program dedicated to southwest Houston apartment complexes and the increased instances of gang violence from Katrina evacuees.[12]

Hurtt was disappointed that HPD was not able to identify homicide patterns "in a timely enough manner to be proactive."[13] For the first time in history, he appointed a captain to oversee the analysis of crime statistics and provide five-day updates on crime in each of the city's police divisions. The chief also restarted a program known as Blue Star, offering security training to apartment managers.

By 2007, violent crimes declined in Houston. Crime rates for murder, rape, robbery and aggravated assault decreased 5.4 percent during the first five months. Comparing that figure to the same period a year later, murders dropped from 162 to 148 and reported rapes from 369 to 268. Robberies and aggravated assaults also dropped. Nonviolent crime was a little different story; it increased by almost 2,000 over the same period a year earlier. Hurtt put the positive spin on the statistics by touting the Homicide Division's ongoing clearance rate of 91.1 percent and its average annual clearance rate of 81 percent, compared to the national average of 60 percent.

Hurtt established unique policies. Effective January 1, 2006, officers were not allowed to display visible tattoos or body art while on duty or wearing a uniform. The order required officers to cover their body art work only with their official police uniform, special assignment uniform or plain clothes. Forearm tattoos were required to be covered with long sleeves, even in sweltering summer months. Even bicycle officers with tattoos on their lower legs had to wear long pants. Laser removal was an option. The tattoo portion of the policy originally was to take effect on May 1, 2005, but HPOU persuaded the chief to delay the effective date so that officers could get through the long hot summer without having to wear long sleeves.

The grooming policy prohibited beards and goatees, a move that resulted in four African-Americans filing a federal lawsuit contending that the policy was discriminatory. The four plaintiffs suffered from a dermatological condition called *pseudofolliculitis barbae*, common in black men. They said that shaving required under the new order would cause them irritation, rashes and ingrown hairs.

Hurtt imposed the tattoo rule to ensure that officers presented a professional image when interacting with the public. He said the order would not apply to officers acting in an undercover capacity and contended that the prohibition of beards and goatees was necessary to protect officers who have to wear breathing masks when responding to chemical or biological emergencies. The plaintiffs in the lawsuit even made an appearance before City Council to inform the mayor and council members that they tested their gas masks and got good seals.

Hurtt had been in office two years when any perceived honeymoon with the officers' sole bargaining agent, the Houston Police Officers Union, reached a contentious end. The Union's forceful and influential leader, Hans Marticiuc, told the chief that a growing number of officers felt his leadership lacked a thorough understanding of the issues that most affected them. The Union's appropriate action came in the summer of 2006 in the form of a questionnaire sent to officers of every rank but chief of police. About 2,300 members responded and seventy-five percent expressed little confidence in the chief's leadership. The no-confidence percentages were similar throughout the HPD rank structure "from the first level supervisors—sergeants, lieutenants and captains—who were polled."[14] The Union unsuccessfully requested that Hurtt resign.

The Union also suggested that Hurtt choose his Command Staff based on ethnicity rather than policing abilities. The *Chronicle* editorialized on the issue, saying, "The union leaders' most substantive complaint was that the chief was not giving his officers backup. Unfortunately, Hurtt cannot give patrol officers the backup they need on the street unless the mayor and City Council give him a lot more money to replace the many veteran officers who are retiring." The editorial alluded to the two-year battle between the mayor and a group of anti-tax crusaders. Both sides did political battle in a 2004 election in which voters approved two tax-limiting measures in the city charter. The results complicated and confused the city's tax-collecting abilities and prompted a lawsuit and a follow-up 2006 charter change election. The measures passed in 2004 placed a cap on the public safety budgets, while the one on the 2006 ballot eased the limitation.[15]

On July 28, 2006, White called on Mike Nichols, senior vice president and general counsel at Sysco Corporation, to get both sides together and mediate. If Hurtt was to remain, he had to change his method of communications. Critics felt that Hurtt hadn't grasped the ways and means of a big city or its police union. This growing number of critics felt that the chief from Phoenix didn't realize that the Union had its hand firmly on the pulse of the department's rank and file.

Once again White's devotion to detail had a positive effect. Two other tacticians also entered the mediation picture. Famed Houston plaintiff's attorney John Eddie Williams Jr. went to bat for the Union, while Chuck Wexler, executive director of the Washington-based Police Executive Research Forum, spoke for Chief Hurtt. Wexler contended that Hurtt regularly found himself at odds with others because he frequently looked for new strategies to address controversial issues that typically went unaddressed. Weeks passed as the two groups met, allowed the furor to die down and eventually, both sides cooled off and tried to deal more cohesively with issues.

The department's often-revamped chase policy—the subject of one change or amendment after another over two decades—was the center of yet another conflict. In the mediation the chief backed off one part of his most recent chase policy change. He said officers in some situations involving minor violations would follow the vehicle only until they obtained a license plate number so they could arrest the suspect later.

Hurtt's credibility took a nosedive when he actually didn't back off at all on this part of the chase policy. His agreement to open the doors to the chief's office wider than before was a more important change that momentarily put the chase policy in the background. Hurtt claimed to have an open door for officers to air concerns. Marticiuc said officers wanted to see more results from the open discussions. The two sides agreed that Union representatives would be present during at least one meeting per month. In 2009, those monthly meetings usually included the Command Staff.

White's leadership was a key to success in the mediation scenario. The mayor won his first election with the strong backing of the Houston Police Officers Union. He kept his vow to listen to a group that had proven to be the voice of the typical police officer. He also vowed to his outside chief that he would not micromanage but keep close tabs. As a result, Hurtt got an important message and changed his management style to better communicate with the Union, paying more attention to the voice of the officers on the street. His adversaries believe he fixed "a leaderless ship" and turned around the early perceptions of his leadership style. He and the Union were still natural adversaries, continuing their fights over beards, tattoos and other policies the Union said had little to do with delivery of police services.

The Union believed Hurtt was completely unprepared to lead a police department the size of Houston's. His limitations made him slow to realize the political and working relationships that were already in place before he came to Houston. Union leaders had close interactions with the mayor, City Council members and City Hall staff members that the chief from Phoenix didn't understand. In the opinion of Union leaders, Hurtt never got the message. Furthermore, they believed he was a mediocre leader who had no true alliance to the organization or its officers.[16]

On September 21, 2006, an illegal Mexican immigrant and Houston landscaper named Juan Leonardo Quintero shot HPD Officer Rodney Johnson seven times, killing him instantly. Quintero had been arrested on traffic violations and Officer Johnson, working the Southeast side without a partner, didn't find Quintero's hidden pistol on the initial pat down. A jury later found Quintero guilty of capital murder and sentenced him to life without parole. Because the shooter was an illegal immigrant deported after being charged with a sex crime involving an under-aged girl, the demand for stronger enforcement of immigration laws began as soon as the news media deciphered Quintero's background. Exactly eleven days later, on October 2, 2006, HPD officially implemented two new changes in its immigration enforcement policy.

Even before Quintero murdered Johnson, the department was under fire for being too lenient toward illegal immigrants. Critics described the Bayou City as a "sanctuary" for this growing classification. Two out of every three robberies involved Spanish-speaking victims or perpetrators, many of whom were believed to be illegally in the United States. The policy changes did not allow officers to inquire about the immigration status of people they hadn't arrested, but put in place new procedures to allow more cooperation with federal agents trying to catch criminals living illegally in Houston.

Hurtt announced that HPD would hold people detained or arrested for traffic violations or other minor crimes—Class C misdemeanors—if warrant checks show they were wanted by federal agents for defying an order to leave the country or for returning after being deported in connection with a criminal case. Previous policy forbade officers generally from holding such people for federal authorities, even if they were aware of the federal warrants.

The department also would allow federal immigration officers access to the city's two jails, matching a similar policy allowed in the Harris County jail. Officers would start asking all arrestees whether they are citizens. The fingerprints of any suspect booked into city jails without proper identification would be checked against a national fingerprint database to determine if he or she was wanted for any serious immigration violation.

Even in the middle of his third term, Mayor White knew the Crime Lab problem could not be resolved overnight; what Houston really needed was a state-of-the-art facility that could produce DNA analysis faster than three weeks or a month. White found that HPD's biggest problem was getting back DNA analyses in prompt fashion, which he pointed out was a far cry from the United Kingdom's twenty-four-hour turnaround time. He wanted faster DNA analyses but never found the necessary funding policies to pay the salaries needed for highly qualified scientists.[17]

Houston officers were the highest paid among large cities in the state of Texas after the first Meet and Confer process in the last decade. But the pack had passed them, making the Houston blue further down the list in terms of overall compensation and benefits. As White served his last term, it was evident that the 2009 mayoral candidate who got Union support would be at City Hall at the time the new contract went into effect. Quite likely that individual would face the same problems that have stalked the Houston Police Department since its very beginnings: Underfunded. Understaffed. Under-equipped.

The Houston police officer of the early 21st Century was the most technologically advanced in history. HPD had come a long way since call boxes and radio broadcasts that shared time with an AM station. Every Patrol officer was equipped with his/her own handheld radio as well as a Mobile Data Terminal that enabled the track down of license plate information and criminal records instantaneously, never requiring a call to the dispatcher.

Patrol officers were able to communicate car-to-car or car-to-dispatcher via the MDT. The Global Position Satellite enabled them to know the exact locations of colleagues in the same Patrol district and the nature of the call responses in progress. It was not uncommon for officers to spend an entire shift without getting on the radio, while generally interacting via email, performing tasks such as picking up a call on the screen and proceeding to the location.

The high-tech gadgets were not without their own unique problems. By 2008, the Houston Police Officers Union advised officers that that same technology can just as easily come back and bite officers on the backside.

Standard patrol car equipment such as Automatic Vehicle Locators (AVLs), Crash Data Recorders and even cellular telephones could be problematic for their users. The primary purpose of AVLs was to enable the dispatch of units closest to a life-endangerment call for help. But the information also could be used to pinpoint an officer at an unreported location. The data might show that a large number of cars congregated in one location, an indicator that could be misleading, especially to the news media.

CDRs record speed data five seconds before the deployment of an airbag in case of a collision, thus establishing the rate of speed before impact. Caution advisories like these became more common in 2009 when officers became aware of ways the very tools they used to thwart wrongdoers could fall back into their own laps.

Greater technology was not the only dramatic change in the department. HPD's profile more closely mirrored the ethnic makeup of Houston better than ever before. In stark contrast to the prevalent standoffishness between black and white officers in the 1950s, 1960s and 1970s, the department in the earliest years of the 21st century saw racially mixed partners and a growing number of minority Command Staff members. These conditions became the rule, not the exception.

As a result, officer bonding took on a unique series of nicknames. Officer Joel "Sal" Salazar, a Hispanic, at one time partnered with Officer Ed Kwan, an Asian-American. Salazar was known as the "Beans" half of the "Beans and Rice" duo. The "Rice" was Kwan. The set was a variation of "salsa and soy sauce," the respective staples in the diet of Hispanics and Asian-Americans. In earlier times such references might have lacked the humor they now contained.[18]

Signs of policing change in Houston's recent history became evident in positive ways throughout the community. Thirty to fifty years ago the venting sessions in minority communities lasted into the late night. Stepped-up interaction with the city's widely diversified communities changed the entire concept of "us versus them." The "us" grew to be more diverse, just as Houston and its police department.

As a member of "the City Hall establishment," Anthony Hall noted the dramatic changes he had seen in the Houston Police Department over five decades. Hall served as Bill White's chief administrative officer in 2009 with responsibilities for implementing major priorities, including the budget process and oversight of all public safety issues. As a state representative and later a council member and Metro Board chairman, Hall attended his share of nighttime meetings in the wards and other predominately minority sections. Interested citizens devoted seventy percent of practically every neighborhood meeting to emotional discussions about HPD. The situation reached a community low point during the Herman Short years when the chief was perceived to be too tolerant of racist attitudes.

Hall said that the talk then didn't get around to libraries, streets or community condition; all of it was devoted to policing matters. In 2009, the long-time public servant still attended an abundance of public meetings in which "not ten percent" was spent on police issues. Hall never thought he would live to see that in Houston.[19]

The profile of the department also had changed dramatically. Instead of only a miniscule percentage of officers of color, two out of every five officers are African-American or Hispanic. While an overwhelming number had only high school diplomas or GEDs in Short's time, in 2011 more than fifty percent of HPD officers possessed college degrees, enabling them to earn higher salaries and greater benefits.

31

AN INSIDER AND
NEW TRUST

olice department histories are rife with irony and standard practice. The biggest irony in HPD history was the 1982 event in which the cops' most-resented mayor, Kathy Whitmire, appointed an outsider who markedly changed the quality of life of Houston officers and their policing techniques. The changes Police Chief Lee P. Brown brought to the department in the decade of the 1980s and followed up with administrative policies and the results of the Meet and Confer process when he served as mayor from 1998 until 2004 continue to influence the department in very positive ways. This outsider was truly a man for his time. It truly can be said that he took to the job and became a true "insider."

When she took office as mayor in 2010, Annise Parker chose her own insider to be chief, a decision based on years of experiences. Parker began compiling her study of the HPD as a 1970s Rice University student preparing a term paper on Houston homicides. Then she went on to become active in Houston's gay rights movement, learned the realities of police conflicts with the gay and lesbian community, and served as a civic association president before entering elective city politics in 1997. Unlike many other civic activists, Parker tried to understand both sides of every issue, giving particular attention to the job of street officers. HPD's relationship with Houston's diversified communities improved on Brown's watch as his Community-Oriented Policing policy spilled over into the new century. As Parker got to know more officers from the rank and file to the Command Staff, the budding politician grasped the overall benefit of officers working their way through the ranks to the top of their profession.

From 1998 until 2004, Parker served three terms as the City Council representative in District C, the most diversified council district and inarguably the one that has produced more mayors than any other section of the city.

The second-generation Houston native then was elected to three straight two-year terms as city controller before undertaking the challenge to become mayor in 2009 and thereby earning the distinction of being the only individual in history to hold all three offices. Parker herself was an *insider* in the truest sense.

Until her first run for mayor, Parker had received the solid support of the Houston Police Officers Union's Political Action Committee (PAC) after having proven her support of HPOU's goals for professional standards and salaries. She fully expected to receive its contributions in 2009. Yet the Union opted for African American civic leader Gene Locke. It was one of Parker's biggest disappointments in all of her years as a political activist and police supporter. She soundly defeated Locke and became the first mayor in recent history to be elected without HPOU support. Despite the perceived rift caused by the Union PAC decision, Parker didn't draw a line in the sand and dare the Union to get lost in the political sense. Instead, history shows that one night hardly went by before the mayor-elect was meeting with the Union leadership to throw the bygones out the window.

Since that meeting, the mayor, the Union and the HPD administration have stayed on one page with the understanding that what's best for Houstonians comes first with the emotional political issues that always come with police work following behind in an agreeable, prioritized order. The appointment of a chief was at the top of the priority list. Parker followed White's example by hiring an outside consultant to screen the candidates for chief. That was the only one of her predecessor's exemplars she used in the decision-making process. PERF, which stands for Police Executive Research Forum, conducted initial interviews and sent the top candidates to Parker. She wasn't surprised that four of them were from the current Command Staff. Executive Assistant Chief Charles A. McClelland Jr. stood out and quickly became her first choice for "his exemplary record and already-demonstrated leadership skills and his depth of understanding of various communities."[1]

When Harold Hurtt stepped down in the final days of Bill White's last term, coincidentally McClelland was on the peg to serve as acting chief, a position he held until his official City Council confirmation on April 13, 2010. During the interim period McClelland, the insider, knew what was expected by members of a Command Staff he had known since his rookie year in 1977. He presided at meetings but avoided any presumptions, such as sitting in the chief's chair at the Command Staff's conference table. The acting chief continued to stress the importance of working together in a way that demon-

**POLICE CHIEF CHARLES
A. "CHUCK" MCCLELLAND
JR., APRIL 13, 2010–
(HPD ARCHIVES)**

strated to the mayor that someone from inside of the organization was fully capable of being chief.[2]

Parker never seriously considered anyone from the outside. She knew that the chief from Phoenix brought outstanding credentials and an outside perspective that was useful in some management situations. Mayor Parker said:

> That perspective was helpful. But in my view there was talent in the department that could have been tapped. For whatever reason, Harold Hurtt never integrated himself into the life of Houston and never really gained an understanding of what it took to police in Houston. His technical abilities and approaches never really translated into the rank and file police officers because of that gap. He thought it was not important to engage communities in what communities expected after years of Neighborhood-Oriented Policing. They had expectations that their police chief would be accessible and available to the citizens of the communities.[3]

McClelland was trusted by community leaders. He knew the importance of being accessible at all times. Hurtt seldom ventured into Houston's diverse communities and officers soon realized that the chief from the outside didn't care if he rode the streets with them to get a genuine feel for walking in their shoes. "When it came my turn," Parker said, "I wanted to send that signal that they weren't a broken department and I didn't have to go looking outside for a chief. We had talent inside. I knew it would be a vote of confidence. The best chief was from inside. It was a signal to the community that there would be an openness with someone responsive to them."[4]

The year 2012 brought to the forefront a never-before-seen chemistry that many Houstonians didn't realize would well serve their city. There was no clearer demonstration of these active human chemicals than the January swearing-in ceremony of the Houston Police Officers Union Board of Directors. A smiling Mayor Parker led the formality and immediately asked the broadly-grinning Chief McClelland to join her, HPOU President Ray Hunt and the board members to pose for an historic picture. Everybody wore genuine smiles and not just for the split second benefit of a photographer.

Each of the chosen leaders present made it clear on that day and on many since that they are on the same policing page. In good times and bad, they each believed the doors of communication and understandings were wide open, something missing from most previous city administrations. Now, Houstonians had a mayor who had grown up knowing the Houston blue, a chief who almost lost his life on at least two occasions in his early days as a street cop, and a well-educated, street-smart Union leader who had demonstrated a knack for communication and fairness in even the toughest of times.

The political fates had put them at the forefront, each with a determination to work through tough economic times that promised to especially threaten a long-approved police pension system that some civic leaders were anxious to raid for the dollars involved.

Officer Charles A. McClelland Jr. was born in Center, Texas. He graduated in Class No. 78 in the Houston Police Academy in May 1977 and started his career on the streets, where he soon found himself in the most graphic and violent situations perhaps ever encountered by a young officer on a dangerous beat. In March 1980, McClelland answered an assist-the-officer call involving two suspects who had shot at an officer. Once at the scene, McClelland chased one of the suspects, who soon popped up with the barrels of two revolvers pointed at him. The suspect's bullet missed McClelland, whose return fire found its mark, instantly killing the armed individual.

Many HPD officers have heard Chief McClelland tell the story and describe the sick feeling he had when he realized that he had taken a human life, albeit to save his own. In the aftermath, the officer got strong support from his supervisor and his fellow officers. He didn't know it then, but in 2012, he reflected on the fact that the experience provided him with a deep understanding of what any Houston police officer could experience on any given day, especially while on patrol. On McClelland's watch as chief, HPD Psychological Services played a key role in counseling officers involved in shootouts or any event involving deadly or near-death experiences. McClelland went without this counseling more than thirty years, but his experiences on the *inside* have made him a prime counseling advocate today.[5]

This shooting wasn't the only life-threatening policing situation McClelland faced on the streets. A year or two earlier he and his partner got into a scuffle with some thugs at an accident scene on the southeast side. The bad actors were determined to seize the officers' guns, badges, flashlights and handcuffs. It was evident to McClelland that if they got a gun, one of them would shoot the officers. The calls for assistance got the attention of another young officer named Mark Clark. Clark and his partner soon entered the fracas, saving McClelland and the other officer from a life-threatening situation. More than three decades later Houston's chief of police remained clear in his assessment of the event: "Had not Mark Clark got there at the time he did, there was a good chance that one or two of us would have been killed."[6]

Clark went on to become president of the Houston Police Officers Association and in 2012 was serving as the executive director of the Houston Police Officers Union. He is also HPOU's chief lobbyist and a primary advocate of the effectiveness of a Political Action Committee. The latter stays active by helping to fund the campaigns of the mayor and City Council members as well as those of state representatives and senators. Clark is but one of the top three or four HPOU leaders, but when the Union discusses the issues at hand with the Command Staff, the police chief has no problem paying close attention to the fellow street officer who once answered a crucial call for help.

Many of McClelland's colleagues remember him as sporting a large Afro, goatee and mustache, allowing him to fit in with street people, as the best of the HPD undercover officers were adept at doing. "You had to play a role every day. It was exciting work but dangerous," he said in an interview with the *Badge & Gun*, HPOU's monthly newspaper, in January 2011. "You went to clubs, bars and massage parlors with no police ID or weapon. You really had to be a good actor but keep yourself safe. You looked like you could fit in with somebody on the street. That was the look you had to portray."[7]

McClelland evolved into a police chief who had once been the epitome of the HPD rank and file, a condition well appreciated by both the mayor and the Union. After more than two years as chief, McClelland said, "The major reason why I'm able to sit down with the Union is I came up in this organization and know people on a first-name basis, know their reputation and vice versa. It is a level of trust that has been built up over a number of years."[8] People in the community also know McClelland for implementing policies that affect the quality of police protection. He was, for instance, the executive assistant chief charged with maintaining a constant vigil over the department's Taser policy set up by Harold Hurtt. McClelland approached each day at work knowing community leaders trusted him to enforce laws with fairness and integrity.

This chief follows the dedicated approach of the community-minded Lee Brown, who spent hours into the night meeting in the far reaches of each and every Houston community to communicate about crime problems and specifically tailored ways to fight them. Brown's tenets from Neighborhood-Oriented Policing are quoted and used to this day. "Crime suppression and crime prevention go hand-in-hand," said Waynette Chan, a Lee Brown follower since their days together in the 1970s in Portland, Oregon, where Brown was the sheriff and Chan a police officer. The two knew they would work together one day and that day came in 1983 when Chan joined Brown's civilian staff in HPD. Union (then Association) leaders expressed skepticism about Chan's qualifications until they learned she was a former police union leader. Lines of communication opened up. Chan got to know Clark, became aware of the goals of Clark's organization and worked to iron out communications problems with the outsider chief. Chan later worked in the Department of Public Works and Engineering, giving her experience in two of the city's highest-funded departments, prompting Mayor Parker to name her chief of staff—establishing her as yet another major player on the city's police stage.[9]

Chan knew in great detail Chief Brown's 1980s plan to get HPD into the 20th Century through Neighborhood-Oriented Policing and, later as mayor, his plan to make Houston officers the highest-paid in the state and nation. On the night of the 2009 runoff election, she knew her friendship with Clark would have an immediate effect on the relationship between Mayor Parker and the Union. "True to his word," Chan said upon reflection, "Mark Clark called me the day after we won the mayor's race. We asked each other: Where do we agree? Can we sit down and iron all this out and let bygones be bygones."[10] In subsequent meetings both sides agreed to disagree when the need arose but did so in good faith without any surprises on the political front. No matter what the issue, they would always communicate fairly and honestly.

So the gamesmanship one usually finds in the complex relationship between a big-city mayor, her police chief and police union leaders was on the table and not behind any backs in 2012 and promised to continue. "The trust has returned," as Chan put it.

Houston police officers have maintained a union to improve their job security and salary structure since 1947. The early lobbying effort by the pioneers of what was initially known as the Houston Police Officers Association established the Houston blue as a major player in the Texas Legislature. What is now known as "the Police Union" closely watches every piece of legislation that affects Houston's finest.

While its record in the State Capitol in Austin has proven effective, the Union experienced some major credibility setbacks with its members in 2009 and 2010. First, one board member was charged with misappropriation of fiduciary funds and another with misapplication of Union funds. The following year a third board member was charged with misapplication of funds and theft of more than $600,000. All three pleaded guilty; two were required to make restitution and the third began serving a twenty-year sentence. HPOU President Gary Blankinship, a veteran solo motorcycle officer, vowed to take strong steps to re-establish the Union's credibility in the midst of harsh criticism from a growing number of members. Blankinship oversaw the most thorough audit in history. Every board member approved the strict measures and each one of them was thoroughly vetted in connection with any dollar he or she spent on the Union's behalf.

The HPOU president resigned in late 2011 as his second two-year term was coming to an end, thus paving the way for 1st Vice President J. J. Berry to become the Union's first-ever African American president. Berry had served on the organization's board for more than three decades, usually in the 1st vice president's position and almost always earning the elective position without opposition. Berry continued his service in 2012 in the capacity of immediate past president.

Berry's 2012 successor, Ray Hunt, believed the stepped-up audit and stronger accounting procedures put in place got the Union out of the woods with its membership. "We were living from check to check right after the thefts," Hunt said. "Now we're more than $1 million in the black. I couldn't have been handed a better situation than what Gary handed me." The Blankinship/Berry watch also ended with the Union's legal defense fund $1 million in the black. The monthly financial statements are now open to every member and the accounting of the Union's ever-growing PAC fund has become as transparent as Hunt and the board members can arrange it to be. Anybody in the public can see what goes in and what comes out right on the Internet. Hunt regularly points out that HPOU board members receive no stipend for their work and have set up "one of the lowest dues of any organization of this size in the nation."[11] The monthly dues average $46.71 or one percent of the paycheck of an eight-year officer.

Hunt also states confidently at every opportunity that the Union takes stands based on fairness and "not asking for the moon at every opportunity. We ask for what's fair. After all, if we bankrupt the city, we don't have jobs. That's why our Meet and Confer contracts have been approved one hundred percent by City Council."[12]

Blankinship and the board worked with leaders of the Houston Police Patrolmen's Union to disband HPPU with its members given the choice to join HPOU. The patrolmen's union, which had operated for just more than thirty years, voted to make this major change in 2010 on condition that HPOU affiliate with the National Fraternal Order of Police (FOP). The HPOU was already affiliated with the National Association of Police Organizations (NAPO) and eagerly looked forward to working with both organizations. "With the attack on police pensions," Hunt said, "we need all the help we can get in Washington."[13] In 2012, the sixty-two police officers who had not joined HPOU were considered long-time holdouts likely never comfortable with any police union but yet still eligible for the Union's negotiated benefits. Yet some of them trickled into HPOU as the year wore on.

In Union circles, the difference between Hurtt and McClelland greatly affected departmental morale. The belief was that Hurtt issued very unfair discipline and failed to understand the workings of a strong labor union. McClelland was viewed as being more reasonable, particularly with his understanding of disciplinary matters involving patrol officers. "If we make the case, he will listen to us," Hunt pointed out. "He may or may not lower the discipline if he agrees with us. Harold Hurtt didn't get it because our organization is strong. We're strong because we're fair." Indeed, the Union attorneys were highly successful in the reduction or total dismissal of the majority of Hurtt-issued punishments.[14]

Many HPD veterans described Hurtt as a nice guy who suffered because he was from the outside and never assimilated into his new duty station. "When Hurtt was chief, morale was very low among the rank and file. He came from the outside and never bought into the community," Hunt said. "I never saw him ride with officers. Chief McClelland rides with officers and tells his Command Staff that they have to do it, and they do."[15]

McClelland involves the Union in most Command Staff meetings, even those involving crime strategies. It makes a big difference when each party at a meeting has known the others' history for decades. Management and labor can distinguish the weightier financial matters from the day-to-day operations and policies that are so important to any police department. McClelland had three stated goals in mind when he took office: 1) Enhancing HPD's relationship with communities, especially minorities; 2) Improving internal communications in a department that includes 5,300 officers and 1,700 civilians; and 3) Responding to the economic challenges so prominent in the city governments and policing operations of today.

The chief had every reason to believe that his first year at the helm demonstrated that the communities were seeing positive changes. He saw 2011 produce only 1,077 citizen complaints, less than the average 1,200 per year for the past decade. Only 235 complaints were generated by the public, the lowest number in ten years, in a department that answers more than one million calls per year. The percentage is impressive: only 235 complaints in more than one million.

Over the past decade HPD, like the NYPD and most other major forces, has found itself in the position of having to do more with less. Many police forces have been hit with budget increases unrelated to hiring new officers, due to rising costs of salaries and skyrocketing increases in pension and health care benefits built into recent police contracts.[16] According to HPOU's contract with the city of Houston, the mayor cannot go to the Legislature to change any provision with conferring with the Union. Parker underscored this contractual tenet in an open Union meeting in February 2012, vowing to use the well-established communications path to tackle the details of any pension-related problem that cropped up. She also stressed her commitment

By 2012, the Houston Police Department was squeezing enough funds from a tight budget to run at least three cadet classes a year, still not enough new officers to keep up with the needs of the ever-growing city of Houston. (Houston Police Officers Union)

to all officers that she would see that the city honors everything in the latest Meet and Confer process. Given the economic conditions in Houston and elsewhere, she said there might be some devils in the details but they will be handled with all the political cards on the table. Significantly, both Hunt and the HPOU leadership, along with Chief McClelland, were on this same page.

Meanwhile, HPD has been forced to police America's fourth largest city with too few officers for each of its 579.4 square miles. Despite a budget that rose forty percent between 2004 and 2009, there was no increase in the number of officers on the streets.[17] HPD was caught in a no-win situation, along with other other cities who had to abolish mounted horse details, as well as the helicopter patrols, which have long acted as the eye in the sky for urban police. In interviews with the news media, McClelland said the "hardest thing I've had to do" was lay off 154 employees to maintain a balanced budget.[18]

There is a tendency from a hometown perspective to criticize local law enforcement any time crime goes up or there are missteps within the agency bureaucracy. In more controversial cases it becomes a media free-for-all where the truth is often obscured in the process. Several recent HPD cases highlight some of these contentious issues as the department continues to move into the 21st Century. No controversy has loomed larger over HPD in the past decade more than the storm of criticism over its crime lab. What goes unsaid is the fact that numerous crime labs, ranging from the FBI to the San Francisco and Oklahoma City police forces, have found themselves under the microscope for various failings.[19] This is no excuse, but is the result of several controllable factors, including funding and the quality of staff training. Others have suggested that as scientific labs become increasingly more complex that police departments should get out of the forensic business altogether. However, by most accounts significant progress has been made in reducing testing case backlogs in most divisions, leading one City Council member to comment, "I think we've made significant progress and we know where we are."[20] The resulting drawing board for solutions has included an as-yet-unfinished plan in 2012 to organize an independent forensic analysis organization.

Despite continued underfunding and lack of manpower for HPD, crime continues to fall. In the first six months of 2011, Houston recorded a substantial decline in most major crime categories. While a decrease in crime and a high crime resolution rate has often been used as a measure of a police department's effectiveness, there are too many factors to consider in explaining this thorny issue.[21]

Perhaps Chief McClelland put it best when he acknowledged to the media, "We don't control all of the factors when it comes to crime, but the factors that we do control, we do a very good job."[22] Following in the steps of New York City, which gave much of the credit for its crime drop to new high-tech-driven proactive police systems, McClelland believed Houston's crime drop could be attributed to the inauguration of the 24/7 Crime Center, which "has been instrumental in relaying crime trends and hot spots to patrol stations in order to deploy officers in a most strategic manner and efficient manner."[23]

HPD has come a long way from its horse-and-saddle days as a basically all-white police force. As recently as 1980, the force was eighty-five percent white. By 2010 it was only fifty-one percent and, as one reporter pointed out, the chances were "50-50" that the next officer hired would represent Houston's Hispanic, African American or Asian communities. Of these, the only group to match its population percentage was Asians at five percent. His-

On January 5, 2012, Mayor Annise Parker swore in the Houston Police Officers Union board members, led by HPOU President Ray Hunt (in center, next to the mayor). In a giant show of unity, the Union president and the mayor asked Police Chief Charles "Chuck" McClelland to be part of the historic photo. Pictured are, left to right, J. G. Garza, Tim Butler, Terry Wolfe, Terry Seagler, Police Chief McClelland, Robert Breiding, Jon Yencha, Dana Hitzman, Mayor Parker, Steve Turner, Bubba Caldwell (hidden), Tom Hayes, Paul Ogden, HPOU President Hunt, Will Reiser, 1st Vice President Doug Griffith, Jeff Wagner, Luis Menendez, Marsha Todd, George Shaw, Joslyn Johnson, Bill Booth, Lance Gibson, O. J. Latin, Secretary Joe Castaneda, Michael Navarro and Joseph Gamaldi. (Mary Pyland Photography)

panics made up forty-two percent of the population, but were twenty-three percent of the force; and African Americans, which were twenty-five percent of the community, were twenty-one percent of the force.[24]

Every officer wears the same Houston blue uniform, policing duds that were about to change their shades. In 2012, the department under McClelland had a consensus that many officers preferred a more rugged, military-style BDU—or Battle Dress Uniform—in a darker navy blue color. The proposed uniform would consist of modern synthetic fabrics, which would be a blend of polyester and wool—a cooler uniform for humid Houston, which often sees 70-degree weather even through the winter months. The new style and color would replace the custom-made military-style, light blue shirt with scalloped pocket flaps and epaulets. (Officers may choose either BDU-type pants or the more formal slacks with blue piping). The old uniforms were custom-made, cost more and often took longer to order, while the newly proposed style could be bought "off the shelf."

A badge policy change also was on the McClelland agenda. Since the earliest days of HPD, an officer received a different badge number when he was promoted to the rank of sergeant or above. Under a new proposal, officers would keep their same badge numbers no matter what their rank. One prototype under consideration but not yet finalized included a large badge that had a miniature of the existing HPD badge set inside an eagle. This prototype or any other could be upgraded with security features, including a locator microchip. These dramatic changes, along with yet another plan to return to the traditional black-and-white patrol cars, were designed to save money in the long run, but would require a budget increase on the near horizon—a condition that so often has been the story of the Houston Police Department since 1841.[25]

There also is still a number of gender and cultural barriers that need to be addressed by the department, such as the fact that only fourteen percent of the force is female, compared to forty-nine percent of the Houston population. Very few police forces in the United States have been able to match their percentage of staffing with the racial and ethnic profiles of the cities they police, but as one observer noted, it is essential to have a "police force that is culturally diverse" to better understand the culturally diverse community it protects and serves.[26]

In 2012, Houston was recognized as the most diverse city in America, and its police department was working to make itself more diverse while staying on the same page as city leaders to ensure that police policies were the fairest and safest for all Houstonians, no matter the shade of the Houston blue.

Appendix 1

Fallen Heroes of HPD

Mar. 10, 1860—C. Edward Foley—Shot

Mar. 17, 1883—Richard Snow—Shot

Feb. 8, 1886—Henry Williams—Shot

Mar. 15, 1891—James E. Fenn—Shot

July 30, 1901—William F. Weiss—Shot

Dec. 11, 1901—Herman Youngst—Shot

Dec. 11, 1901—John C. James—Shot

Apr. 1, 1910—William E. Murphy—Shot

Aug. 4, 1911—John M. Cain—Shot

Oct. 18, 1912—Joseph Robert Free—Shot

May 24, 1914—Isaac "Ike" Parsons—Shot

Aug. 23, 1917—Rufus H. Daniels—Shot/Mutilated

Aug. 23, 1917—E. G. Meinecke—Shot

Aug. 23, 1917—Horace Moody—Shot

Aug. 23, 1917—Ross Patton—Shot/Mutilated

Aug. 23, 1917—Ira D. Raney—Shot

Feb. 19, 1921—Johnnie Davidson—Shot

June 19, 1921—Jeter Young—Motorcycle Accident

June 27, 1921—Davie Murdock—Shot

Aug. 23, 1924—J. Clark Etheridge—Automobile Accident

Jan. 21, 1925—Pete Corrales—Shot

Sept. 17, 1925—E. C. Chavez—Shot

Jan. 30, 1927—Perry Page Jones—Shot

July 30, 1927—R. Q. Wells—Automobile Accident

Mar. 14, 1928—Carl Greene—Shot

Apr. 22, 1928—Paul W. Whitlock—Shot

June 17, 1928—Albert Worth Davis—Shot

June 22, 1929—Oscar Hope—Shot

Sept. 13, 1929—Ed Jones—Shot

Dec. 17, 1929—C. F. Thomas—Motorcycle Accident

Sept. 30, 1930—Edward D. Fitzgerald—Shot

Sept. 30, 1930—W. B. Pharres—Shot

Dec. 3, 1930—J. D. Landry—Motorcycle Accident

Oct. 16, 1933—Harry Mereness—Motorcycle Accident

Mar. 9, 1935—R. H. "Rimps" Sullivan—Shot

Dec. 1, 1936—James T. "Jim" Gambill—Heart Attack

Nov. 8, 1937—Adolph P. Martial—Automobile Accident

Mar. 24, 1938—Marion E. Palmer—Shot

June 30, 1939—George Edwards—Shot

Aug. 18, 1946—H. B. Hammond—Shot

Jan. 12, 1954—S. A. "Buster" Kent—Motorcycle Accident

Feb. 24, 1954—Fred Maddox Jr.—Shot

Apr. 30, 1955—Jack B. Beets—Shot

Apr. 30, 1955—Charles R. Gougenheim—Shot

Nov. 30, 1955—Frank L. Kellogg—Shot

Aug. 24, 1956—Robert Schultea—Shot

June 5, 1958—Noel R. Miller—Shot

Mar. 20, 1959—Claude E. Branon—Automobile Accident

Aug. 23, 1959—John W. Suttle—Auto/Pedestrian Accident

Feb. 28, 1960—Gonsalo Q. Gonzales—Automobile Accident

Mar. 8, 1963—James T. Walker—Automobile Accident

Aug. 4, 1963—Charles R. McDaniel—Automobile Accident

July 1, 1964—James F. Willis—Automobile Accident

Feb. 18, 1965—Herbert N. Planer—Shot

June 30, 1965—Floyd T. Deloach Jr.—Shot

Jan. 21, 1967—Louis L. Sander—Shot

May 17, 1967—Louis R. Kuba—Shot

June 26, 1968—Ben E. Gerhart—Shot

June 26, 1968—Bobby L. James—Automobile Accident

Nov. 26, 1969—Kenneth W. Moody—Shot

Jan. 31, 1970—Leon Griggs—Shot

Jan. 31, 1971—Robert W. Lee—Shot

Dec. 10, 1971—Claude R. Beck—Auto/Pedestrian Accident

June 17, 1972—David E. Noel—Stabbed to Death

Oct. 26, 1972—Jerry Leon Spruill—Shot

Jan. 9, 1973—Antonio Guzman Jr.—Shot

Sept. 19, 1973—David Huerta—Shot

June 18, 1974—Jerry L. Riley—Automobile Accident

Jan. 30, 1975—Johnny T. Bamsch—Shot

Aug. 2, 1975—F. E. Wright—Auto/Pedestrian Accident

Oct. 10, 1975—R. H. Calhoun—Shot

Jan. 28, 1976—George G. Rojas—Stabbed to Death

Apr. 8, 1976—James F. Kilty—Shot

June 8, 1978—Timothy L. Hearn—Shot

Aug. 16, 1979—Charles Baker—Shot

Oct. 2, 1980—Victor R. Wells III—Shot

Apr. 18, 1981—Jose A. Zamarron—Auto/Pedestrian Accident

Mar. 29, 1982—Winston J. Rawlins—Motorcycle Accident

Mar. 29, 1982—William E. DeLeon—Motorcycle Accident

Apr. 28, 1982—Daryl W. Shirley—Shot

July 13, 1982—James D. Harris—Shot

Aug. 18, 1982—Kathleen Schaefer—Shot

Feb. 23, 1983—Charles R. Coates—Auto/Pedestrian Accident

Sept. 12, 1983—William Moss—Automobile Accident

Apr. 10, 1987—Maria M. Groves—Auto/Pedestrian Accident

Feb. 18, 1988—Andrew Winzer—Automobile Accident/Drowning

July 19, 1988—Elston Howard—Shot

Nov. 10, 1989—Florentino M. Garcia Jr.—Automobile Accident

Dec. 9, 1989—James C. "Boz" Boswell—Shot

June 27, 1990—James B. Irby—Shot

Nov. 25, 1990—John A. Salvaggio—Auto/Pedestrian Accident

Apr. 12, 1991—Bruno D. Soboleski—Shot

Jan. 6, 1994—Michael P. Roman—Automobile Accident

Jan. 31, 1994—Guy P. Gaddis—Shot

Nov. 12, 1994—David M. Healy—Automobile Accident

Dec. 24, 1995—Dawn S. Erickson—Auto/Pedestrian Accident

Apr. 6, 1997—Cuong H. "Tony" Trinh—Shot

May 23, 1998—Kent D. Kincaid—Shot

May 19, 1999—Troy A. Blando—Shot

Sept. 20, 2000—Jerry K. Stowe—Beaten to Death

Jan. 10, 2001—Dennis E. Holmes—Heart Attack

May 22, 2001—Alberto Vasquez—Shot

Mar. 7, 2002—Keith A. Dees—Motorcycle Accident

Apr. 3, 2003—Charles R. Clark—Shot

Mar. 25, 2004—Frank M. Cantu Jr.—Automobile Accident

Oct. 26, 2005—Rueben B. Deleon—Shot

Sept. 21, 2006—Rodney Johnson—Shot

June 29, 2008—Gary Allen Gryder—Auto/Pedestrian Accident

Dec. 7, 2008—Timothy Abernethy—Shot

June 23, 2009—Henry Canales—Shot

May 19, 2010—Eydelmen Mani—Automobile Accident

May 29, 2011—Kevin Will—Auto/Pedestrian Accident

Source: *Fallen Heroes of the Bayou City* by Nelson J. Zoch (HPD Retired)

Appendix 2

Houston Mayors and Police Chiefs

Year-by-Year and Chief Selection Method

1837	James S. Holman	Elected	G. W. Holland	Constable
1838	Francis Moore Jr.	Elected	G. W. Holland	Constable
1839	George W. Lively	Elected	G. W. Holland	Constable
1840	Charles Bigelow	Elected	G. W. Holland	Constable
1841	John D. Andrews	Elected	Daniel Busby	Marshal
1842	John D. Andrews	Elected	Daniel Busby	Marshal
1843	Francis Moore Jr.	Elected	Joseph Waterman	Marshal
1844	Horace Baldwin	Elected	Joseph Waterman	Marshal
1845	W. W. Swain	Elected	James A. Young	Marshal
1846	James Bailey	Elected	William K. Smith	Marshal
1847	B. P. Buckner	Elected	Gatewood Hail	Marshal
1848	B. P. Buckner	Elected	M. Martin	Marshal
1849	Francis Moore Jr.	Elected	M. Martin	Marshal
1850	Francis Moore Jr.	Elected	M. Martin	Marshal
1851	Francis Moore Jr.	Elected	M. Martin	Marshal
1852	Francis Moore Jr.	Elected	M. Martin	Marshal
1853	Nathan Fuller	Elected	M. Martin	Marshal
1854	Nathan Fuller	Elected	J. P. Hogan	Marshal
1855	James H. Stevens	Elected	J. P. Hogan	Marshal
1856	James H. Stevens	Elected	J. P. Hogan	Marshal
1857	Cornelius Ennis	Elected	R. P. Boyce	Marshal

1858	Alexander McGowen	Elected	R. P. Boyce	Marshal
1859	William H. King	Elected	E. F. Williams	Marshal
1860	Thomas Whitmarsh	Elected	J. R. Proudfoot	Marshal
1861	William J. Hutchins	Elected	R. P. Boyce	Marshal
1862	Thomas W. House	Elected	H. F. Mathews	Marshal
1863	William Anders	Elected	Issac C. Lord	Marshal
1864	William Anders	Elected	Issac C. Lord	Marshal
1865	William Anders	Elected	Issac C. Lord	Marshal
1866	Horace D. Taylor	Elected	Issac C. Lord	Marshal
1867	Alexander McGowen	Elected	Issac C. Lord	Marshal
1868	Joseph R. Morris	Elected	Issac C. Lord	Marshal
1869	Joseph R. Morris	Appointed	A. K. Taylor	Marshal
1870	T. H. Scanlan	Appointed	M. E. Davis	Marshal
1871	T. H. Scanlan	Appointed	Joe Smallwood	Marshal
1872	T. H. Scanlan	Elected	R. Van Patten	Marshal
1873	T. H. Scanlan	Elected	R. Van Patten	Marshal
1874	James T. D. Wilson	Elected	Henry C. Thompson	Marshal
1875	Issac C. Lord	Elected	Alexander Erickson	Marshal
1876	Issac C. Lord	Elected	H. Lebuncom	Marshal
1877	James T. D. Wilson	Elected	F. U. Butt	Marshal
1878	James T. D. Wilson	Elected	F. U. Butt	Marshal
1879	Andrew J. Burke	Elected	John T. Morris	Marshal
1880	William R. Baker	Elected	Charles Wichman	Marshal
1881	William R. Baker	Elected	Charles Wichman	Marshal
1882	William R. Baker	Elected	Charles Wichman	Marshal
1883	William R. Baker	Elected	Charles Wichman	Marshal
1884	William R. Baker	Elected	Charles Wichman	Marshal
1885	William R. Baker	Elected	Charles Wichman	Marshal
1886	Daniel C. Smith	Elected	Charles Wichman	Marshal
1887	Daniel C. Smith	Elected	James Shaughnessy	Marshal
1888	Daniel C. Smith	Elected	John White	Marshal

1889	Daniel C. Smith	Elected	John White	Marshal
1890	Henry Scherffius	Elected	Charles Wichman	Marshal
1891	Henry Scherffius	Elected	Charles Wichman	Marshal
1892	John T. Browne	Elected	Alexander Erickson	Marshal
1893	John T. Browne	Elected	Alexander Erickson	Marshal
1894	John T. Browne	Elected	James H. Pruitt	Marshal
1895	John T. Browne	Elected	James H. Pruitt	Marshal
1896	John T. Browne	Elected	Charles August Heim	Marshal
1896	H. Baldwin Rice	Elected	Charles August Heim	Marshal
1897	H. Baldwin Rice	Elected	Charles August Heim	Marshal
1898	H. Baldwin Rice	Elected	Archer Anderson	Marshal
1899	Samuel H. Brashear	Elected	W. W. Bough	Marshal
1900	Samuel H. Brashear	Elected	John G. Blackburn	Marshal
1901	John D. Woolford	Appointed	George Ellis	Chief
1902	John D. Woolford	Appointed	George Ellis	Chief
1902	O. T. Holt	Appointed	George Ellis	Chief
1903	O. T. Holt	Appointed	George Ellis	Chief
1904	O. T. Holt	Appointed	George Ellis	Chief
1904	Andrew L. Jackson	Appointed	George Ellis	Chief
1905	Andrew L. Jackson	Appointed	George Ellis	Chief
1905	H. Baldwin Rice	Appointed	George Ellis	Chief
1906	H. Baldwin Rice	Appointed	George Ellis	Chief
1907	H. Baldwin Rice	Appointed	George Ellis	Chief
1908	H. Baldwin Rice	Appointed	George Ellis	Chief
1909	H. Baldwin Rice	Appointed	George Ellis	Chief
1910	H. Baldwin Rice	Appointed	James Maurice Ray	Chief
1911	H. Baldwin Rice	Appointed	John A. "Duff" Voss	Chief
1912	H. Baldwin Rice	Appointed	Henry Lee Ranson	Chief
1913	H. Baldwin Rice	Appointed	E. C. Noble	Chief
1913	Ben Campbell	Appointed	Ben S. Davison	Chief
1914	Ben Campbell	Appointed	Ben S. Davison	Chief

1915	Ben Campbell	Appointed	Ben S. Davison	Chief
1916	Ben Campbell	Appointed	Ben S. Davison	Chief
1917	Ben Campbell	Appoined	Clarence L. Brock	Chief
1917	J. J. Pastoriza	Appointed	Clarence L. Brock	Chief
1917	J. C. Hutcheson Jr.	Appointed	Clarence L. Brock	Chief
1918	J. C. Hutcheson Jr.	Appointed	Clarence L. Brock	Chief
1918	A. Earl Amerman	Appointed	Clarence L. Brock	Chief
1919	A. Earl Amerman	Appointed	Searcy Baker	Chief
1920	A. Earl Amerman	Appointed	Searcy Baker	Chief
1921	A. Earl Amerman	Appointed	Searcy Baker	Chief
1921	Oscar F. Holcombe	Appointed	Gordon L. Murphy	Chief
1922	Oscar F. Holcombe	Appointed	Gordon L. Murphy	Chief
1923	Oscar F. Holcombe	Appointed	Thomas Goodson	Chief
1924	Oscar F. Holcombe	Appointed	Thomas Goodson	Chief
1925	Oscar F. Holcombe	Appointed	Thomas Goodson	Chief
1926	Oscar F. Holcombe	Appointed	Thomas Goodson	Chief
1927	Oscar F. Holcombe	Appointed	Thomas Goodson	Chief
1928	Oscar F. Holcombe	Appointed	Thomas Goodson	Chief
1929	Oscar F. Holcombe	Appointed	Thomas Goodson	Chief
1929	Walter Monteith	Appointed	Charles W. McPhail	Chief
1930	Walter Monteith	Appointed	Percy F. Heard	Chief
1931	Walter Monteith	Appointed	Percy F. Heard	Chief
1932	Walter Monteith	Appointed	Percy F. Heard	Chief
1933	Walter Monteith	Appointed	Percy F. Heard	Chief
1933	Oscar F. Holcombe	Appointed	George Woods	Pub Safety Dir
1934	Oscar F. Holcombe	Appointed	B. W. Payne	Superintendent
1935	Oscar F. Holcombe	Appointed	Woods/Payne	Supt./Chief
1936	Oscar F. Holcombe	Appointed	Woods/Payne	Supt./Chief
1937	Oscar F. Holcombe	Appointed	Chester A. Williams	Superintendent
1937	R. H. Fonville	Appointed	Chester A. Williams	Superintendent
1938	R. H. Fonville	Appointed	Dave G. Turner	Acting Chief

1939	R. H. Fonville	Appointed	Lawrence C. Brown	Chief
1939	Oscar F. Holcombe	Appointed	Lawrence C. Brown	Chief
1940	Oscar F. Holcombe	Appointed	Lawrence C. Brown	Chief
1941	Oscar F. Holcombe	Appointed	Ray Ashworth	Chief
1941	Neal Cornelius Pickett	Appointed	Ray Ashworth	Chief
1942	Neal Cornelius Pickett	Appointed	Ray Ashworth	Chief
1943	Neal Cornelius Pickett	Appointed	Percy F. Heard	Chief
1943	Otis Massey	Appointed	Percy F. Heard	Chief
1944	Otis Massey	Appointed	Percy F. Heard	Chief
1945	Otis Massey	Appointed	Percy F. Heard	Chief
1946	Otis Massey	Appointed	Percy F. Heard	Chief
1947	Otis Massey	Appointed	Percy F. Heard	Chief
1947	Oscar F. Holcombe	Appointed	B. W. Payne	Chief
1948	Oscar F. Holcombe	Appointed	B. W. Payne	Chief
1949	Oscar F. Holcombe	Appointed	B. W. Payne	Chief
1950	Oscar F. Holcombe	Appointed	B. W. Payne	Chief
1951	Oscar F. Holcombe	Appointed	L. D. Morrison Sr.	Chief
1952	Oscar F. Holcombe	Appointed	L. D. Morrison Sr.	Chief
1953	Oscar F. Holcombe	Appointed	L. D. Morrison Sr.	Chief
1953	Roy M. Hofheinz	Appointed	L. D. Morrison Sr.	Chief
1954	Roy M. Hofheinz	Appointed	John F. "Jack" Heard	Chief
1955	Roy M. Hofheinz	Appointed	John F. "Jack" Heard	Chief
1956	Oscar F. Holcombe	Appointed	John F. "Jack" Heard	Chief
1957	Oscar F. Holcombe	Appointed	Carl L. Shuptrine	Chief
1958	Lewis W. Cutrer	Appointed	Carl L. Shuptrine	Chief
1959	Lewis W. Cutrer	Appointed	Carl L. Shuptrine	Chief
1960	Lewis W. Cutrer	Appointed	Carl L. Shuptrine	Chief
1961	Lewis W. Cutrer	Appointed	Carl L. Shuptrine	Chief
1962	Lewis W. Cutrer	Appointed	Carl L. Shuptrine	Chief
1963	Lewis W. Cutrer	Appointed	H. G. "Buddy" McGill	Chief
1964	Lewis W. Cutrer	Appointed	H. G. "Buddy" McGill	Chief

1964	Louie Welch	Appointed	Herman B. Short	Chief
1965	Louie Welch	Appointed	Herman B. Short	Chief
1966	Louie Welch	Appointed	Herman B. Short	Chief
1967	Louie Welch	Appointed	Herman B. Short	Chief
1968	Louie Welch	Appointed	Herman B. Short	Chief
1969	Louie Welch	Appointed	Herman B. Short	Chief
1970	Louie Welch	Appointed	Herman B. Short	Chief
1971	Louie Welch	Appointed	Herman B. Short	Chief
1972	Louie Welch	Appointed	Herman B. Short	Chief
1973	Louie Welch	Appointed	Herman B. Short	Chief
1974	Fred Hofheinz	Appointed	Carrol M. Lynn	Chief
1975	Fred Hofheinz	Appointed	R. J. "Joe" Clark	Acting Chief
1976	Fred Hofheinz	Appointed	B. G. "Pappy" Bond	Chief
1977	Fred Hofheinz	Appointed	Harry D. Caldwell	Chief
1978	Jim McConn	Appointed	Harry D. Caldwell	Chief
1979	Jim McConn	Appointed	Harry D. Caldwell	Chief
1980	Jim McConn	Appointed	B. K. Johnson	Chief
1981	Jim McConn	Appointed	B. K. Johnson	Chief
1982	Kathy Whitmire	Appointed	John P. Bales	Acting Chief
1983	Kathy Whitmire	Appointed	Lee P. Brown	Chief
1984	Kathy Whitmire	Appointed	Lee P. Brown	Chief
1985	Kathy Whitmire	Appointed	Lee P. Brown	Chief
1986	Kathy Whitmire	Appointed	Lee P. Brown	Chief
1987	Kathy Whitmire	Appointed	Lee P. Brown	Chief
1988	Kathy Whitmire	Appointed	Lee P. Brown	Chief
1989	Kathy Whitmire	Appointed	Lee P. Brown	Chief
1990	Kathy Whitmire	Appointed	Elizabeth M. Watson	Chief
1991	Kathy Whitmire	Appointed	Elizabeth M. Watson	Chief
1992	Bob Lanier	Appointed	Samuel A. Nuchia	Chief
1993	Bob Lanier	Appointed	Samuel A. Nuchia	Chief
1994	Bob Lanier	Appointed	Samuel A. Nuchia	Chief

1995	Bob Lanier	Appointed	Samuel A. Nuchia	Chief
1996	Bob Lanier	Appointed	Samuel A. Nuchia	Chief
1997	Bob Lanier	Appointed	C. O. "Brad" Bradford	Chief
1998	Lee Brown	Appointed	C. O. "Brad" Bradford	Chief
1999	Lee Brown	Appointed	C. O. "Brad" Bradford	Chief
2000	Lee Brown	Appointed	C. O. "Brad" Bradford	Chief
2001	Lee Brown	Appointed	C. O. "Brad" Bradford	Chief
2002	Lee Brown	Appointed	C. O. "Brad" Bradford	Chief
2003	Lee Brown	Appointed	C. O. "Brad" Bradford	Chief
2003	Lee Brown	Appointed	J. L. "Joe" Breshears	Acting Chief
2004	Bill White	Appointed	Harold Hurtt	Chief
2005	Bill White	Appointed	Harold Hurtt	Chief
2006	Bill White	Appointed	Harold Hurtt	Chief
2007	Bill White	Appointed	Harold Hurtt	Chief
2008	Bill White	Appointed	Harold Hurtt	Chief
2009	Bill White	Appointed	Harold Hurtt	Chief
2010	Annise Parker	Appointed	Charles McClelland	Chief
2011	Annise Parker	Appointed	Charles McClelland	Chief
2012	Annise Parker	Appointed	Charles McClelland	Chief

Source: Denny Hair, Houston Police Museum

Appendix 3

HPOA/HPOU Presidents

Year-by-Year 1945 to the Present

The Houston Police Officers Association was formed in 1945. It became the Houston Police Officers Union in 1996 with a change in its constitution. As an association, any commissioned Houston officer of any rank could serve as president. Effective with the new constitution and name, only a person serving in the police officer (or senior police officer) rank could serve as President and 1st or 2nd Vice President.

Houston Police Officers Association Presidents
1945–1946 Frank Murray
1946–1948 John Irwin
1948–1950 Breckenridge Porter
1950–1952 Earl Maughmer
1952–1953 A. C. Martindale
1953–1954 H. L. "Ham" Ellisor
1954–1955 Carl E. Buckner
1955–1956 Harry Cole
1956–1957 E. R. Goodnight
1957–1958 W. S. Whately
1958–1959 J. F. Willis
1959–1960 W. A. Evans
1960–1961 W. E. Crowder
1961–1962 W. A. Evans
1962–1965 Bernard Bueche
1965–1967 Earl Maughmer
1968–1970 B. J. Rodger
1970–1975 A. J. Burke

1975–1978 R. C. Rich
1978–1979 David Sheetz
1979–1980 James Albright
1980–1982 David Collier
1982–1985 William Elkin
1985–1991 Mark Clark
1991–1996 Doug Elder

Houston Police Officers Union Presidents
1996–2008 Hans Marticiuc
2008–2011 Gary Blankinship
2011–2012 J. J. Berry
2012– Ray Hunt

Notes

CHAPTER 1

1. Mrs. Dilue Harris (Rose), Reminiscences, 1833–38, SC134, Box 14, Folder 6, typescript, Houston Public Library Special Collections.
2. Richard Prassel, *The Western Peace Officer* (Norman: University of Oklahoma Press, 1981), 95.
3. *Texas in 1837: An Anonymous Contemporary Narrative*, ed. Andrew Forest Muir (Austin: University of Texas Press, 1958), 26.
4. David G. McComb, *Houston: The Bayou City* (1969; repr., Austin: University of Texas Press, 1981), 50–51.
5. Marguerite Johnston, *Houston: The Unknown City, 1836–1946* (College Station: Texas A&M University Press, 1991), 20.
6. *Texas in 1837*, 29.
7. Benajah H. Carroll, ed., *Standard History of Houston, Texas: From a Study of the Original Sources* (Knoxville, Tennessee: H. W. Crew and Company, 1912), 86.
8. McComb, 1981, 48.
9. Matilda Charlotte Houstoun, *Texas and the Gulf of Mexico: or, Yachting in the New World*, vol. 2 (London: John Murray, 1844), 102.
10. Francis Cynric Sheridan, *Galveston Island or, A Few Months off the Coast of Texas: the Journal of Francis C. Sheridan, 1839–1840*, ed. Willis Winslow Pratt (Austin: University of Texas Press, 1954), 112–113.
11. Mrs. Dilue Harris (Rose).
12. Branding as a form of exhibitory punishment can be traced back to the ancient Babylonians. Throughout most of history and before modern identification systems, it was common to brand malefactors with letters befitting their crimes, thus making the individual recognizable to the community. Vagabonds were branded with a *V*, robbers with an *R*, and so forth.
13. *Texas in 1837*, 160, 217n16.
14. *Texas in 1837*, 14.
15. Francis R. Lubbock, *Six Decades in Texas*, ed. C. W. Rains (Austin: Ben C. Jones, 1900), 46.
16. Ray Miller. *Ray Miller's Houston* (Austin: Capitol Printing, 1983), 80.
17. Linda J. Nanfria, "The Houston Police Department," in *1983 Houston Police Department Yearbook* (Delmar Company, 1983), 18. This 1983 history of the HPD was part of the 1983 *Houston Police Department Yearbook* and is the first published manuscript detailing the history of the force. However, it is not sourced and there are few attributions for references used.

18. Victoria Lynne Brooks, "Crime and Violence in Frontier Houston: A Study of the Criminal District Court in Harris County, 1872–1876," (master's thesis, Columbia University, May 1974), 7.

19. *Texas in 1837.*

20. Quoted in *Texas in 1837*, 193.

21. *Telegraph and Texas Register*, May 16, 1837.

22. Dora Fowler Arthur, ed., "Jottings from the Old Journal of Littleton Fowler," *Quarterly of the Texas State Historical Association* 2 (July 1898), 79–80; McComb, 1969, p. 62.

23. Sheridan to Garraway, 1840 in "British Correspondence Concerning Texas," ed. Ephraim Douglass Adams, *Quarterly of the Texas State Historical Society* 15 (July 1911–April 1912), 221.

24. Jonnie Lockhart Wallis and Laurance L. Hill, *Sixty Years on the Brazos: The Life and Letters of Dr. John Washington Lockhart, 1824-1900* (Waco: Texian Press, fascimile reprint, 1967), 80.

25. Denny Hair, "The Houston Police: A History and Legacy of the Houston Police Department, 1933–1992," unpublished manuscript, 14; *Morning Star*, Apr. 20, 1839.

26. Wallis and Hill, 80

27. Quoted in McComb, 63.

28. McComb, 64.

29. Writers' Program of the Works Project Administration in the State of Texas, *Houston, a History and Guide*, (Houston: Anson Jones Press, 1942), 49 (part of American Guide Series, hereafter referred to as AGS).

30. S. O. Young, *A Thumbnail History of the City of Houston Texas. From Its Founding in 1836 to the Year 1912* (Houston, 1912), 52.

31. Ed Blackburn, Jr., *Wanted: Historic County Jails of Texas* (College Station: Texas A&M Press, 2006), 153–154

32. Works Progress Administration (1942), 239.

33. S. O. Young, *A Thumbnail*, 53.

34. AGS, 1942, 53.

35. Blackburn and Richards, 1972.

36. Quoted in McComb, 19.

37. Quoted in McComb, 20.

38. Martin L. Friedland, *The Death of Old Man Rice: A True Story of Criminal Justice in America* (New York: New York University Press, 1994).

39. Quoted in McComb, 23.

40. The first surge of temperance activity was apparently unsuccessful according to Hair, who suggests the first temperance organization was on Jan. 9, 1841, p. 15.

41. Louis J. Marchiafava, *The Houston Police: 1878–1948* (Houston: Rice University Studies, 1977), 8.

42. William Ransom Hogan, *The Texas Republic: A Social and Economic History* (Austin: University of Texas Press, 1969), 260.

43. Quoted in Hogan, *The Texas Republic*, 260–61.

44. Hogan, *The Texas Republic*, 261.

45. Quoted in Hogan, *The Texas Republic*, 262.

CHAPTER 2

1. Ferdinand Roemer, *Texas, With Particular Reference to German Immigration and the Physical Appearance of the Country* (better known as *Roemer's Texas*), trans. Oswald Mueller (1935; repr., San Antonio: Standard Printing Company, 1983), 63.
2. Roemer, 63.
3. David R. Goldfield, *Cotton Fields and Skyscrapers: Southern City and Region, 1607–1980* (Baton Rouge: Louisiana State University Press, 1980), 40.
4. Roemer, 68.
5. Roemer, 67.
6. Roemer, 68
7. Marchiafava, 9; Dennis C. Rousey, *Policing the Southern City: New Orleans, 1805–1889* (Baton Rouge: Louisiana State University Press, 1996).
8. Marj Gurasich, *History of the Harris County Sheriff's Office, 1837–1983* (Harris County Sheriff's Deputies' Association, 1983), 10.
9. Gurasich, 11–13.
10. McComb, 1969, 52–53; Seventh Census of the U.S., Harris County, Texas, free schedule; Ninth Census, free schedule.
11. McComb, 1969, 68.
12. Quoted in Linda Nanfria, 20.
13. McComb, 1969.

CHAPTER 3

1. Killed in Action Memorial Book, HPD Archives (hereafter cited as KIA), p. 1.
2. Sally E. Hadden, *Slave Patrols: Law and Violence in Virginia and the Carolinas* (Cambridge: Harvard University Press, 2001), 21.
3. Passed Dec. 30, 1861; *Houston City Directory, 1867–1868*, 99.
4. Ibid.
5. Gurasich, 14.
6. Ibid.
7. Ibid.
8. Ibid.
9. Gurasich, 15.
10. H. W. Graber, *A Terry Texas Ranger, 1861–1865: The Life Record of H. W. Graber, 62 Years in Texas* (Dallas: Privately Printed, 1916), 30.
11. Johnston, 62.
12. Graber, 259.
13. Passed September 3, 1863
14. Compendium of Ordinances, Ordinances of the City of Houston, City Secretary's Office, Houston, Texas, 68–69.
15. Compendium of Ordinances, 68–69; Gurasich, 16.
16. *Houston City Directory, 1867–1868*, p. 99.
17. Quoted in AGS, 81.
18. Hair; Young, *A Thumbnail.*
19. Nanfria, 20
20. Ibid.
21. Ibid.

22. *Houston City Directory, 1866*, 64–65.
23. *Charter of Houston, 1866*, ch. 6, p. 77–80.
24. *Charter of Houston, 1866*, 6, sec. 17.
25. Gurasich, 17.
26. Gurasich, 18.
27. *Charter of Houston, 1866*, ch. 16, art. 310, p. 104.
28. Houston City Council Minutes, Jan. 25, 1866.
29. Rousey.
30. Rousey, 119.
31. Nanfria, 21.
32. McComb, 1969, 78.
33. Mitchel P. Roth, *Historical Dictionary of Law Enforcement* (Westport: Greenwood Press, 2001), 288; George E. Virgines, *Police Relics* (1982).
34. *Daily Houston Telegraph*, Vol. 34, No. 55, Whole No. 5376, May 30, 1868, typescript in HPD newspaper clippings file.
35. *Daily Houston Telegraph*, Vol. 1, No. 16, Sept. 29, 1868, typescript in HPD newspaper clippings file.
36. *Daily Houston Telegraph*, Vol. 1, No. 17, Sept. 30, 1868, typescript in HPD newspaper clippings file.
37. Quoted in William L. Richter, *The Army in Texas During Reconstruction, 1865–1870* (College Station: Texas A&M Press, 1987), 148.
38. *Houston City Directory 1895*, 8.
39. Marchiafava, 13.
40. Nov. 30, 1872, drafts of reports by Police Committee of the Board of Alderman, UH Special Collections.
41. Ibid.
42. Brooks, 103.
43. *Daily Houston Telegraph*, Feb. 8, 1873
44. Nanfria, 22; Marchiafava, 14.
45. Rousey, 163.
46. Marchiafava, 15
47. Ibid.
48. City County Resolution, 1879, UH Special Collections.
49. HPD historian Denny Hair cites 1873; Nanfria, 1875; and May Walker, 1870. May Walker, *The History of Black Police Officers in the Houston Police Department* (Houston: Houston Police Department, 1988).

CHAPTER 4

1. *Daily Houston Telegraph*, Feb. 8, 1873.
2. *Daily Houston Telegraph*, 1873.
3. Marchiafava, 9.
4. Ibid.
5. *Houston Telegraph*, June 24, 1875; AGS, 89.
6. Rousey.
7. Marchiafava, 25n26.
8. Walker, 9.
9. Ibid.

10. Ibid.

11. AGS, 89.

12. AGS, 91.

13. *Galveston Daily News*, Jan. 24, 1879.

14. *Daily Houston Telegraph*, Feb. 20, 1873.

15. Aug. 20, 1874; Brooks, 17.

16. Lawrence M. Friedman, *Crime and Punishment in American History* (New York: Basic Book, 1993), 127.

17. This draft was signed by Alderman W. H. Gavan of the First Ward, Fuermann Collection, UH Special Collections; Minutes of the Board of Alderman, May 2, 1879, May 2, 1879.

18. AGS, 106.

19. Carroll, 87; S. O. Young, *True Stories of Old Houston and Houstonians* (Galveston: Oscar Springer, 1913), 47–48.

20. Carroll, 87.

21. Carroll, 87; Young, *True Stories*, 48.

22. *Houston Post*, Nov. 3, 1885.

23. AGS, 97.

24. Carroll, 88.

25. KIA, 2.

26. KIA, 2–5; *Houston Post*, Nov. 3, 1885, 3.

27. Houston Post, Nov. 3, 1885, 3.

28. AGS, 99.

29. Trueman O'Quinn and Jenny Lind Porter, *Time to Write: How William Sidney Porter Became O. Henry* (Austin: Eakin Press, 1986), 8.

30. Gurasich, 23.

31. Gurasich, 25.

CHAPTER 5

1. *Houston Police Department Souvenir Yearbook*, 1901, Museum Accession Number 88.2.1, pp. 17, 25, 37, 39, Houston Police Archives (hereafter cited as *HPD Yearbook 1901*). According to former HPD Museum Director Denny Hair, this is the first yearbook produced by the HPD.

2. HPD Yearbook, *1901*, 35.

3. 1901 Roster, *Houston City Directory, 1902–03*, 484; *HPD Yearbook, 1901*, 19, 21, 23.

4. *HPD Yearbook, 1901*, 23, 25.

5. *HPD Yearbook, 1901*, 25.

6. *HPD Yearbook, 1901*, 31.

7. *HPD Yearbook, 1901*, 35, 37.

8. *Houston City Directory, 1908–1909*.

9. Perhaps one 19th century New York policeman put it best when after being promoted to captain and being rewarded with a transfer to the city's vice district where opportunities for graft were numerous, he famously exclaimed, "I've had nothing but chuck steak for a longtime and now I'm going to get a little tenderloin."

10. *City of Houston v. J. A. Estes*, Court of Civil Appeals of Texas, decided, Mar. 5, 1904.

11. Ibid.

12. *HPD Yearbook, 1901*, 45.

13. Mitchel P. Roth, *Crime and Punishment: A History of the Criminal Justice System* (Belmont, California: Cengage, 2010).

14. *HPD Yearbook, 1901*, 33.

15. Al H. Dunlap, "Police Department of Houston, Texas," *The Detective*, Municipal Section, vol. 32, no. 370, 1915, p. 7, HPD Archives [hereafter cited as *The Detective*, 1915].

16. *The Detective*, 7.

17. KIA, 6–9.

18. KIA, 8–10.

19. Ibid.

20. KIA, "Herman Youngst," Dec. 12, 1901."

21. 1901 Roster.

22. Annual Message of A. L. Jackson, Mayor of the City of Houston, *Annual Reports of City Officers for the year ending December 31, 1904*, 12.

23. Annual Message of A. L. Jackson, Mayor of the City of Houston, *Annual Reports of City Officers for the year ending December 31, 1904*, 108.

24. *Houston Daily Post*, Oct. 9, 1905.

25. *Houston Post*, Dec. 31, 1905; *Houston Post*, January 1, 1906; "When Carrie Nation Came to Houston," www.houstonarchitecture.com/haif/topic/402-when-carrie-nation-came-to -Houston/. This building, while significantly altered in appearance, is still standing at 1002 N. San Jacinto Street.

CHAPTER 6

1. "New Faces at Police Station," in "The Personal Scrapbook of James M. Ray, Chief of Police 1910," Accession Number 82.14.1, HPD, 3 (hereafter cited as Ray Scrapbook).

2. Gurasich, 22.

3. Gurasich, 22.

4. Annual Mayor's Message and Department Reports, City of Houston, 1910; Report of Chief of Police, Mar. 10, 1911, 167.

5. Annual Report of George Ellis, Chief of Police for the Year Ending Feb. 29, 1908 in *Annual Reports of City Officials for the Year Ending Feb. 29, 1908*, 38.

6. Ibid.

7. "New Faces at Police Station," Ray Scrapbook, 3.

8. Ibid.

9. Ray Scrapbook, 4.

10. "Show Results," *Houston Daily Post*, Sept. 4, 1910, Ray Scrapbook, p. 5.

11. The Progressive era lasted roughly between 1900 and 1920, a time of tumultuous change in America, as the nation's urban centers tried to accommodate waves of immigrants from eastern and southern Europe, as well as African Americans fleeing the Jim Crow South.

12. Thomas C. Mackey, "Thelma Denton and Associates: Houston's Red Light Reservation and a Question of Jim Crow," *The Houston Review*, 14.3 (1992), 139–152; See also Thomas C. Mackey, *Red Lights Out: A Legal History of Prostitution, Disorderly Houses, and Vice Districts, 1870–1917* (New York: Garand, 1987), 290–340.

13. "Morality of City Police," Ray Scrapbook, 9.

14. Annual Mayor's Message and Department Reports, Houston, 1913, Report of E. C. Noble, for the year ending Feb. 28, 1913, 201.

15. Ibid., 201–202.
16. International Association of Chiefs of Police, 1916 (hereafter referred to as IACP), 79.
17. IACP, 1916, 79.
18. IACP, 1916, 80.
19. *Charter of the City of Houston and General Ordinances Passes by the City Council from the 31st Day of October 1904, to and Including October 31st, 1910* (Houston: W. H. Coyle, 1910), 124–127.
20. The following account is based on several sources including a 24-page typescript/manuscript covering the shooting and subsequent trial from contemporary resources in the HPD Archives. Unfortunately there are no citations or attributions, but in any case this account appears to come from the local newspapers since it includes comments by Mayor Rice and testimony from the inquest. More informative was the master's thesis by Jim Dewey, "William E. Murphy, Deputy Chief of the Houston Police Department Killed While Seated in a Restaurant" (University of Houston-Downtown, 1984). Written by the great-grandson of the victim, this thesis also benefits from interviews with the victim's grandson and grand-daughter.
21. Ron Cartlidge, *Houdini's Texas Tours 1916 and 1923* (Austin: Ron Cartlidge Publications, 2002).
22. Charles Wolfe and Kip Lornell, *The Life and Legend of Leadbelly* (New York: Harper Collins, 1994), 82; see also Richard M. Garvin and Edmond G. Addeo, *The Midnight Special: The Legend of Leadbelly* (New York: Bernard Geis Associates, 1971).
23. Wolfe and Lornell, 88.
24. Wolfe and Lornell.
25. Ibid., 84.

CHAPTER 7

1. Robert V. Haynes, *A Night of Violence: The Houston Riot of 1917* (Baton Rouge: Louisiana State University Press, 1976), 18; *Houston City Directory, 1917*, 39. See also, C. Calvin Smith, "The Houston Riot of 1917, Revisited," *The Houston Review* 13.2 (1992), 85–102; Dixie Reid, "The Camp Logan Riot," *Houston Chronicle Magazine*, Aug. 30, 1981; Lynn Ashby, "Critical Spark," *Houston Post*, Aug. 23, 1978; Lynn Ashby, "Deadly Night," *Houston Post*, Aug. 24, 1978.
2. Haynes, 18.
3. Interview with John Bales.
4. Haynes, 6.

CHAPTER 8

1. Don. E. Carleton, *Red Scare!: Right-Wing Hysteria, Fifties Fanaticism, and Their Legacy in Texas* (Austin: Texas Monthly Press, 1985), 10.
2. The South Carolina Regulator formed in 1767, is generally considered America's first vigilante organization. It was formed by local gentry in response to the governor's pardoning of a number of criminals who had been convicted of horse theft and robbery following a terroristic campaign of rape, theft and murder. The vigilantes then extra-legally tried, convicted and punished the offenders.
3. Richard Maxwell Brown, *Strain of Violence: Historical Studies of American Violence and Vigilantism*, (New York: Oxford University Press, 1975), 3.

4. Danny Lee Alhfield, "Fraternalism Gone Awry: The Ku Klux Klan in Houston, 1920–1925" (master's thesis, University of Texas, 1984), 17.
5. Ahlfield, 7.
6. Kenneth T. Jackson, *The Ku Klux Klan in the City, 1915–1930* (New York: Oxford University Press, 1967), 83.
7. Jackson, *Ku Klux Klan*, 57.
8. Ahlfield, 19.
9. Ahlfield, 20.
10. Ahlfield, 20; Casey Greene, "Guardians Against Change: The Ku Klux Klan in Houston and Harris County, 1920–1925," *The Houston Review* 10.1 (1988), 10.
11. Ahlfield, 20.
12. Ibid.
13. Charles C. Alexander, *Crusade for Conformity: The Ku Klux Klan in Texas, 1920–1930* (Houston: Texas Gulf Coast Historical Association, 1984).
14. Ahlfield, 23.
15. Ahlfield, 106.

Chapter 9

1. 1925 Annual Police Report, Thomas C. Goodson, Superintendent of Police, Vice Investigating Squad, typescript, 1925, HPD archives.
2. Goodson joined the force on Oct. 2, 1911.
3. *Houston City Directory, 1923–1924*, 46.
4. "Houston Pioneered in Traffic Lights," *Houston Press*, June 18, 1930. According to this article the first traffic lights of any kind made their appearance in Cleveland in 1914.
5. "Mounted Traffic Force Abolished by Chief M'Phail," *Houston Chronicle*, May 11, 1929; "Taps Sounded for Mounties," *Houston Press*, May 11, 1929.
6. "'Cop Who Always Smiled' is Victim of Own Weapon," 1920, HPD archives clippings file.
7. "Hardened Police Amuse Thousands," 1920, HPD archives clippings file.
8. "Father Lee Jailed," Dec. 24, 1921; "His Palestine Record," Dec. 29, 1921, HPD archives clippings file.
9. KIA, "A. Worth Davis," HPD Archives.
10. Ibid.
11. 1925 Annual Police Report.
12. Approved by Congress in Dec. 1919 and ratified the following year by the states, the 18th Amendment made it illegal to manufacture, import, distribute or sell "intoxicating beverages"; these by definition were beverages with more than 0.5% alcohol.
13. *Houston Post-Dispatch*, June 30, 1929, p. 21.
14. "Police Force is Realigned by M'Phail," *Houston Press*, Jan. 31, 1930; "Police Shifts Put in Effect," *Houston Press*, Feb. 1, 1930.
15. "City's Finest Pass in Review," *Houston Press*, May 27, 1930.
16. "Arrests Made by Police Department for Violations of Prohibition Law," Chief L. C. Brown Collection, File 84.3.130, HPD Archives.
17. "Officer Phares Dies of Wounds Received in Fight with Bandit," *Houston Post*, Sept. 30, 1930; Nelson Zoch, "Killer of 2 HPD Officers Gets Swift Justice: 'The Chair' 69 Days Later," *Badge and Gun*, HPOU Online, KIA Files, HPD Archives.

18. Paul W. Barrett and Mary H. Barrett, *Young Brothers Massacre* (Columbia: University of Missouri Press, 1988).

19. Jan. 5, 1932; Barrett and Barrett, 88.

20. Quoted in Barrett and Barrett, 89.

21. Barrett and Barrett, 94.

22. Ibid.

23. Jan. 6, 1932; Barrett and Barrett, 95.

24. Barrett and Barrett, 1988.

25. Barrett and Barrett, 1988.

CHAPTER 10

1. "Shake-up in City Police Department Due Today," *Houston Post*, Apr. 29, 1933.

2. "Fire and Police Departments are Separated by Council Order," *Houston Post*, Aug. 15, 1935.

3. "Police Profiles," *Houston Post*, (undated) 1935, Jack Beets Scrapbook, Houston Police Museum Archival File, 1992; Last Roll Call, 1955.

4. "Police Radio Gets Baptism," *Houston Press*, Nov. 1, 1932.

5. "Houston Police Department is Directed by an Authority on Law Enforcement—Chief Payne," *Houston Press*, Feb. 11, 1935.

6. Marilyn M. Sibley, *Travelers in Texas, 17611860* (Austin: University of Texas Press, 1967), 176.

7. Don E. Carleton, *Red Scare!: Right Wing Hysteria, Fifties Fanaticism and Their Legacy in Texas* (Austin: Texas Monthly Press, 1985), 27.

8. H. Gordon Frost and John H. Jenkins, *I'm Frank Hamer: The Life of a Texas Peace Officer* (Austin: Pemberton, 1968), 263.

9. Frost and Jenkins.

10. "41 Husky 'Trouble Shooters' Mobilized for Duty in Event of City Dock Strike," *Houston Press*, Oct. 9, 1935.

11. "City Chooses 56 Police for Dock Patrol," *Houston Chronicle*, Oct. 5, 1935.

12. "Nazi Crew Mutinies," *New York Times*, Dec. 3, 1933, 4.

13. W. Marvin Dulaney, "The Texas Negro Peace Officers' Association: The Origins of Black Police Unionism," *The Houston Review* 12.2 (1990), 59.

14. Dulaney, *Texas Negro Peace Officers*, 60.

15. Ibid.

16. Dulaney, *Texas Negro Peace Officers*, 61.

17. Elliott M. Rudwick, *The Unequal Badge: Negro Policemen in the South* (Atlanta: Southern Regional Council, 1962).

18. Dulaney, *Texas Negro Peace Officers*, 64.

19. Ibid.

20. Joseph King, "Police Strikes of 1918 and 1919 in the United Kingdom and Boston and Their Effects," (doctoral dissertation, City University of New York, 1999).

21. Dulaney, *Texas Negro Peace Officers*.

22. Dulaney, *Texas Negro Peace Officers*, 63.

23. Ibid.

24. Cary D. Wintz, "Blacks," in *The Ethnic Groups of Houston*, ed. Fred R. Von der Mehden (Houston: Rice University, 1984), 940.

25. Ibid.

26. Ibid.

27. Griffenhagen and Associates, "City of Houston: The Police Department, Report No. 3," Dec. 28, 1939 (hereafter referred to as *Griffenhagen Report*), 13.

28. Ibid., 14.

29. Ibid., 27.

30. Ibid.

31. Ibid. This notion has been challenged by academics beginning in 1972 with a one year study conducted in Kansas City. The publication of the *Kansas City Preventive Patrol Experiment* report in 1974 concluded that police patrols, whether stepped up or diminished, had no significant impact on crime, police response time, public fears of crime or attitudes toward police.

32. Ibid.

33. Ibid., 28.

34. Ibid.

35. Ibid., 29.

36. F. Arturo Rosario, *"Pobre Raza!": Violence, Justice and Mobilization Among Mexico Lindo Immigrants, 19001936* (Austin: University of Texas Press, 1999), 76.

37. Rosario, 1999.

38. Maria-Christina Garcia, "Manuel Crespo," *Handbook of Texas Online*.

39. "Two Thompson submachine guns arrived—Sergeant R. B. Hooper to Train Men," *Houston Post Dispatch*, Dec. 3, 1930.

40. "Siamese Twins Baffle Officers," undated picture and caption in Personal Scrapbook of James Henry Tatum clippings file, Vol. 1, HPD Archives, Accession no. 82.26.1.

41. "Policemen Required to be Virtually Teetotalers Under New Manual Regulations," *Houston Chronicle*, July 8, 1936.

42. "'Forgotten Policemen' Now Forbidden to Contribute to Gifts for Their Superior Officers," undated article in Personal Scrapbook of James Henry Tatum clippings file, Vol. 1, HPD Archives, Accession no. 82.26.1.

CHAPTER 11

1. "Survey Shows Extensive Police Personnel Shakeup," *Houston Post*, Jan. 17, 1939.

2. Neal Pickett File Archive, Houston Public Library Texas Manuscript Collection (hereafter cited as Pickett Collection), C. T. Thomasen to Pickett, Jan. 1, 1941, W-1030, Neal Pickett Box #1.

3. Pickett Collection, H. S. Badger et al to Mayor Neal Pickett, Jan. 9, 1941, Neal Pickett Box #1, mss 3.

4. Pickett Collection, Alvis F. Day to Mayor Neal Pickett, Jan. 1, 1941; Alvis F. Day to Mayor Pickett, no date, Neal Pickett Box #1, mss 3.

5. Pickett Collection, C. W. (Ennis?) to Mayor Neal C. A. Pickett, Jan. 7, 1940, Neil Pickett Box #1, mss 3.

6. Pickett Collection, J. A. Collier to Mr. Neal Pickett, Jan. 24, 1941, Neil Pickett Box #1, mss 3.

7. Harry M. Johnston, "Ashworth Policy Firm, Direct," *Houston Chronicle*, Jan. 20, 1946.

8. Ibid.

9. "Ashworth's Blitzkrieg Bookie Raid Snares 70-Odd Hungry Gamblers," *Houston Post*, May 9, 1941; "80 Officers Raiding Houston 'Bookies'," *Houston Chronicle*, May 8, 1941; "Bookie Case Hearing reset for Friday," *Houston Post*, May 11, 1941.

10. "New Deal in Police Department," *Houston Press*, Apr. 30, 1942.

11. Ibid.

12. "Diamond Police Badges Banned by Chief Ashworth," *Houston Press*, Feb. 18, 1941.

13. "Chief Tells Police to 'Pipe Down' on Loud Sirens," *Houston Press*, Feb. 18, 1941.

14. Harry M. Johnston, "Police Rejoice Over New Chief," *Houston Post*, Apr. 30, 1942.

15. Ibid.

16. The Houstonian, "Our Congratulations to Chief Percy Heard, Who, is One of Us and Not a Fly-By-Night Official", *Houston Press*, May 22, 1942.

17. Ibid.

18. "Heard Returns Homicide Squad to Old Footing," *Houston Post*, May 14, 1942.

19. "Chief Heard Orders the Replacement of Sirens on Police Cars," *Houston Post*, July 22, 1942.

20. "Policemen and Firemen Will Get Pay Hike," *Houston Chronicle*, Sept. 22, 1942.

21. "Council Extends Maximum Age of Police Recruits," *Houston Post*, Aug. 12, 1942.

22. "First Dim-Out Here Short of Requirements," *Houston Chronicle*, Oct. 27, 1942.

23. "Special Police Squad to Handle Honky-Tonks," *Houston Chronicle*, Nov. 25, 1942.

24. "Jurors Begin Major Probe of Vice Here," *Houston Chronicle*, Nov. 18, 1942.

25. "Ordinances to Curb Vice Promised," *Houston Chronicle*, Dec. 1, 1942.

26. "Effort to Close Honky-Tonks at Midnight Flayed," *Houston Chronicle*, Dec. 3, 1942.

27. "Ordinance on Sale of Beer Passed Here," *Houston Chronicle*, Dec. 16, 1942.

28. "Gas Rationing Cuts Traffic 20 Per Cent; Crashes, 25 Per Cent," *Houston Chronicle*, Dec. 6. 1942.

29. "Health Head Pays Tribute to Vice Squad," *Houston Chronicle*, Jan. 13, 1943.

30. Orie Collins, "Police Radio Keeps Crooks in Constant Fear," *Houston Chronicle*, Jan. 9, 1943.

31. "City to Furnish Uniforms to 300 Auxiliary Police," n.d. *Houston Chronicle*; Heard Clippings File, 1943–44 volume; "Civilian Defense Unit Becomes Model for the Nation, n.d; John Murphy, "Houston's Auxiliary Police, *Houston Post*, n.d.

32. "Dentist Extracts Teeth, Police Extract Patient After Bookie Shop Raid," *Houston Chronicle*, Aug. 29, 1942; "Hides in Dental Chair—Suspect Loses 4 Teeth", *Houston Post*, Aug. 29, 1942.

33. "City Officer Dies of Heart Attack Here," *Houston Chronicle*, Aug. 21, 1942.

34. "Dangerous Escaped Enemy Alien Captured in Hotel Here by FBI," *Houston Post*, Dec. 2, 1942.

35. "25 Alien Japs Nabbed Here Face Hearing," *Houston Chronicle*, Oct. 26, 1942.

36. "Lad-de-Dah Burglar Nabbed in Chase Here, *Houston Post*, Sept. 15, 1942; see also "Jailed Youth Helps Police Clean up Many Burglaries," *Houston Chronicle*, Sept. 15, 1942.

37. *Houston Chronicle*, Mar. 9, 1943.

38. "Assistant Chief Eubanks Gets Demotion," *Houston Press*, Mar. 4, 1943; "Heard Will Run Police Force With Free Hand," *Houston Press*, Mar. 5, 1943.

39. "Policemen's Pocket Flaps Gone to War," *Houston Post*, Sept 25, 1943.

40. "Dance Hall Squad Being Created to Enforce New Law," *Houston Chronicle*, Apr. 8, 1943.

41. "Policewomen Here Launch Drive on 'Victory Girls," *Houston Chronicle*, June 23, 1943.

42. "Women Traffic Cops Suggested by Safety Official," *Houston Post*, Aug. 12, 1943, 1–2.

43. "Houston Criminals Strike Less Often, Get More Loot," *Houston Chronicle*, Apr. 15, 1943.

44. W. H. Kegans, 'Peaceful' Peace Officer for 45 Years, Dies Here," *Houston Post*, Oct. 20, 1943.
45. *Houston Chronicle*, June 18, 1943, 3.
46. "She Was Tired of Eating Beans," *Houston Post*, Jan. 2, 1944.
47. Community Chest was a chamber of commerce-type fundraising organization used in many American cities from 1919 until it became the United Way in 1963.
48. "Rank of Police Lieutenant Asked for Mrs. Inez Crawford," *Houston Post*, Jan. 5, 1944.
49. "John Blackburn, Former Police Chief, Dies at 83," *Houston Chronicle*, Jan. 31, 1944.
50. "Ruth Turrentine Flabbergasted by Windy Policeman," *Houston Chronicle*, Feb. 26, 1944.
51. "J. J. Kuykendall, 31 Years on Police Force Here, Dies," *Houston Post*, Feb. 20, 1944.
52. "Police Station So Crowded 16 Men Work in Offices Intended to Accommodate Only Two," *Houston Press*, May 2, 1944; see also, "City Jail Built for 88 Often Houses 200," *Houston Press*, May 1, 1944.
53. "Remodeling Police Station Pet Fancy of New Chiefs," *Houston Chronicle*, Aug. 8, 1943.
54. Ibid.
55. "City Jail Built for 88 Often Houses 200," *Houston Press*, May 1, 1944; "Police Station So Crowded 16 Men Work in Offices Intended to Accommodate Only Two," *Houston Press*, May 2, 1944; "Citizens Reporting Accidents to Police Often Must Wait Their Turns in Corridor," *Houston Press*, May 3, 1944; "More Room, Better Conditions Outstanding Need of Police Department, Chief Declares," *Houston Press*, May 4, 1944.
56. "Lost Painting of Former Detective Chief is Found," *Houston Chronicle*, Mar. 14, 1944.

CHAPTER 12

1. See for example, "More Mex-American Gang War," *Houston Post*, Sept. 16, 1944.
2. "Curfew for Delinquency," *Houston Post*, Feb. 11, 1944.
3. "More Negro Policemen, Stricter Enforcement of Liquor Laws Will Help to Curb Juvenile Delinquency," *Negro Labor News*, Mar. 25, 1944.
4. Ibid.
5. "'Magic' Employed to Find Body of Drowned Negro Boy," *Houston Chronicle*, Apr. 24, 1944; "Old Shirt and a Loaf of Bread 'Locate' Negro's Body in Bayou," *Houston Post*, Apr. 24, 1944.
6. "Police Employes (sic) Get 'Report Cards,'" *Houston Press*, May 31, 1944.
7. "Edy Tells 20 City Employes (sic) Rating System has Faults," *Houston Chronicle*, June 21, 1944.
8. "Police Chief Wants Crime Laboratory," *Houston Press*, Aug. 24, 1944.
9. "Woman Lieutenant Quits Police Force," *Houston Press*, Aug. 2, 1944.
10. "Larger Police Force Urged by Grand Jury," *Houston Chronicle*, Aug. 4, 1944.
11. "A. C. Thornton, Detective, To Quit March 15," *Houston Chronicle*, Feb. 26, 1945.
12. "Crime Record Declared Set in Houston," *Houston Chronicle*, Feb. 15, 1945.
13. "Houston Leads In Its Population Class in Crimes," *Houston Chronicle*, May 19, 1945.
14. Orie Collins, "Survey Shows Houston Inadequately Policed," *Houston Chronicle*, July 8, 1945.
15. "Lt. W. J. Heard, Son of Police Chief, Killed," *Houston Chronicle*, Apr. 19, 1945; "Lieut. Billy Heard of Marines Killed on Okinawa," *Houston Post*, Apr. 19, 1945.
16. Joseph Hopkins," Famed Houston Woman Sleuth Ends Half-Century as Detective," Nov. 8, 1945.

17. See announcement, "Police Association to Elect officers," in *Houston Chronicle*, Jan. 3, 1946.

18. "Houston Police May Form United Front Association," *Houston Chronicle*, Nov. 29, 1945.

19. "Burton Returns to Police Force," *Houston Post*, Jan. 3, 1946; "Burton is the Winner in Police Row on 'Who Ranks Whom,'" *Houston Chronicle*, Jan. 4, 1946.

20. Sam C. Johnson, "Ashworth Has Inside Track, Mayor Admits," *Houston Post*, Jan. 19, 1946.

21. Ben Kaplan, "Army Records Clear Ashworth for Chief's Job," *Houston Press*, 1-2.

22. Bud Myers, "Army Changed Ashworth Little; City Hall Call Proves Bombshell," *Houston Press*, Jan. 18, 1946, 11.

23. "Validity of Ordinances By Which Ashworth Got Leave Questioned," *Houston Chronicle*, Jan. 21, 1946.

24. "Houston Murders for Month Double June Total in '45," *Houston Post*, July 10, 1946.

25. "Mrs. Hartsfield Assumes Duties of Policewoman," *Houston Chronicle*, Aug. 24, 1946.

26. "Supervisor of Policewomen to Use Badge to Help Others," *Houston Press*, Aug. 28, 1946.

27. Bob Cone, "Officers are complaining of Spare-Time Police Job System," *Houston Post*, Sept. 12, 1946.

28. "Houston's 'Finest," *Houston Press*, Sept. 19, 1946.

29. "City Urged to Add 450 Policemen," *Houston Press*, Sept. 30, 1946.

30. "Take Police Chief Out of Politics, Says Safety Expert," *Houston Press*, Oct. 22, 1946; see also "Traffic Specialist Says More Police Needed in Houston," *Houston Press*, Oct. 1, 1946.

31. "Troubles of Police Under Holcombe Related by Eikel," *Houston Press*, Oct. 25, 1946.

CHAPTER 13

1. Diane J. Kleiner, "Holcombe, Oscar Fitzallen," *Handbook of Texas Online*; *Houston History: 1836–2008 Great Citizens.* "Oscar Fitzallen Holcombe".

2. "Survey Shows Extensive Police Personnel Shake-up," *Houston Post*, Jan. 17, 1939.

3. Marchiafava, 1977.

4. Earl Maughmer, Jr., Interview, Tape Recording, Houston Metropolitan Research Center, Houston Public Library (hereafter cited as Maughmer interview, 1974).

5. Maughmer interview, 1974.

6. Ibid.

7. Marchiafava, 82.

8. Maughmer interview, 1974.

9. Ibid.

CHAPTER 14

1. Interview with Breck Porter, Jr., Feb. 18, 2004.

2. Ibid.

3. Nelson Zoch, "Biography of Breck Porter," *Badge and Gun*, May 2003; Interview with Frances Porter, Feb. 25, 2004.

4. Ibid.

5. Frances Porter interview.

6. Zoch, 2003; Porter, Jr. interview.
7. Richard W. Lee, "The Legacy of Earl Maughmer Jr.," *Badge and Gun*, 1985.
8. Ibid.
9. Frances Porter interview, Feb. 25, 2004.
10. Maughmer interview, 1974.
11. Ibid.
12. Ibid.
13. Maughmer interview, 1974; Lee, *Badge and Gun*.
14. Marchiafava; Jack Heard interview, June 7, 2004.
15. HPOA circular.
16. Lee, *Badge and Gun*.
17. Marchiafava.
18. Ibid.
19. Maughmer interview, 1974.
20. Maughmer interview, 1974; Lee, *Badge and Gun*.
21. Marchiafava.
22. Ibid., 92.

CHAPTER 15

1. "Buddy McGill is Named New Police Chief," *Houston Post*, Mar. 29, 1963; Jack Heard interview.
2. For more on Larry Fultz see Harold Scarlett, "Juvenile 'Guardian' Still Has Jaunty Spirit of His Young Charges," *Houston Post*, May 8, 1966; "Larry Fultz Becomes Youngest Inspector," *Houston Post*, Dec. 6, 1958; and Mike Thorne, "Words of Lawyer Influenced Cop," *Houston Post*, Jan. 6, 1959; "UH Hires Fultz to be Chief of Campus Security," *Houston Post*, Aug 15, 1969; "Larry W. Fultz, ex-Law, Probation Official, Dies at 54," *Houston Post*, Jan. 24, 1974.
3. Ibid.
4. Ibid.
5. *Houston Press*, Oct. 20, 1954, in Denny Hair, History of HPD, unpublished manuscript, Houston Police Department Museum Archives.
6. Heard interview.
7. Ed Norton, "Meet Chief Heard's Family, He Keeps Law and Order Over 5 Kids," *Houston Press*, Sept. 2, 1954.
8. Heard interview.
9. 100 Club website; interviews with Jack Heard, Marvin Zindler, and Rick Hartley.
10. Heard scrapbooks.
11. Heard interview.
12. Jack Heard Interview.
13. Jo Bankston interview.
14. Bankston interview.
15. Heard interview.
16. Short interview with Denny Hair, 1982.
17. Marvin Zindler interview.
18. "Councilmen Do Well to Withstand Fight to Get at Police Chief Heard,"*Houston Chronicle*, Feb. 25, 1956.
19. Heard interview.

20. Ibid.
21. Ibid.

Chapter 16

1. "Carl L. Shuptrine Named Police Chief," *Houston Post*, Aug. 16, 1956.
2. Ibid.
3. Jack Heard interview.
4. George Fuermann, *Houston: Land of Big Rich* (New York: Doubleday, 1951).
5. "Kessler Assails 2 Unit Heads," *Houston Press*, July 11, 1957.
6. "Carl L. Shuptrine Named Police Chief," *Houston Post*, Aug. 16, 1956.
7. Saul Friedman, "Former Teacher is Chief of Police," *Houston Chronicle*, Nov. 2, 1956.
8. Jim Criswell, "Shuptrine Nears End of 5th Years as Chief," *Houston Post*, Aug. 13, 1961.
9. Saul Friedman, "Former Teacher is Chief of Police," *Houston Chronicle*, Nov. 2, 1956.
10. "$121 Monthly Not Bad in '32," *Houston Post*, Sept. 30, 1956.
11. Ellen Middlebrook, "Mayor Says Shuptrine Will Be Renamed Chief, *Houston Post*, Dec. 11, 1959.
12. Bobby Adams interview.
13. Jim Criswell, "Shuptrine Nears End of 5th Years as Chief," *Houston Post*, Aug. 13, 1961.
14. Ibid.
15. "Council Approves 3 New Inspectors for Police," *Houston Post*, Dec. 21, 1961.
16. Diane J. Kleiner, "Holcombe, Oscar Fitzallen," *Handbook of Texas Online*.
17. Bob Cargill, "Security McGill Aim in Switch to Police," *Houston Post*, Mar 31, 1963.
18. Ibid; Pat McGill interview.
19. Pat McGill interview.
20. Cargill, Mar. 31, 1963; Pat McGill interview.
21. Ibid.
22. Charles Schneider, "McGill Makes 2 Changes in Top Police Positions," *Houston Post*, Apr. 8, 1963.
23. "New Area of Police Inquiry Discovered," *Houston Post*, Apr. 24, 1964; Louis Welch interview.
24. Welch interview; Ellen Middlebrook, "Police Dept Shake-up is Foreseen," *Houston Post*, Apr. 25, 1964; John Moore, "Garrison Coming Here to Testify in Police Probe," *Houston Post*, Apr. 28, 1964.
25. Ibid.
26. Ibid.
27. Ronnie Bookman, "McGill, Grand Jury Hold 'Social' Meeting," *Houston Post*, May 15, 1964.
28. John Moore, "No Police Vice Link Evidence, Jury Says," *Houston Post*, Apr. 26, 1964.
29. Bob Saile, "'Heat' Always on Vice in Houston, McGill Replies," *Houston Post*, May 11, 1964.
30. "Police Chief Against Survey Plan," *Houston Post*, May 28, 1964.
31. Ellen Middlebrook, "Police Dept. Shake-up is foreseen," Houston Post, Apr. 25, 1964.
32. "Harmony Returns as Welch, McGill Talk Over Probe. Clear Job of Chief Now Safe," *Houston Post*, Apr. 29, 1964.
33. Ellen Middlebrook, "Councilman Frown on McGill's Ouster," *Houston Post*, Sept. 29, 1964.
34. Ibid.; McGill died in 1976 at 69, while Welch died on Jan. 27, 2008 at 89.

35. Welch interview.
36. Ibid.
37. Welch interview.
38. John Moore, "McGill is termed 'Tall in the Saddle,'" *Houston Post*, Oct. 26, 1964.

CHAPTER 17

1. Welch interview.
2. Ibid.
3. Ibid.
4. Houston Police Officers' Union, "Choosing a Chief," *Badge and Gun*, Jan. 2012.
5. Herman Short was interviewed as part of an oral history project conducted by the Houston Metropolitan Research Center at the Houston Public Library. Hereafter cited as Short interview.
6. Ibid.
7. Short interview; Welch interview.
8. Albert Black interview; Al Blair interview.
9. Short Interview.
10. Short Interview.
11. Welch interview; Bill Lawson interview.
12. Welch interview.
13. Mosier interview.
14. Tom Kennedy, "Profile: Police Chief Herman Short," *Badge and Gun*, Jan. 2012.
15. Bob Martin interview.
16. Judy Martin interview; Jack Cato interview.
17. Thomas Thompson, *Blood and Money* (Garden City: Doubleday, 1976); Hugh Gardenier and Martha Gardenier, *The Ice Box Murders* (Redbud Publishing, 2003); Jack Olsen, *The Man With the Candy: The Story of the Houston Mass Murders* (New York: Simon and Schuster, 1974).
18. Gardenier and Gardenier.
19. Massey interview.
20. Thompson, 1976.
21. Thompson, 1976; McKittrick interview.
22. Olsen.
23. Cato interview.
24. Welch interview; Short interview.
25. Short interview.
26. Short interview.
27. Bobby Adams interview.
28. Welch interview.
29. "Short shrugs off Wallace FBI job talk," *Houston Post*, Dec. 4, 1971.
30. Nelson Zoch interview; Mosier interview.
31. Daigle interview.
32. Ibid.
33. Welch interview; Mosier interview.
34. *Badge and Gun*, Interview with Officer David Freytag (father of the Honor Guard), Sept. 20, 2011.
35. Caldwell interview.

36. Bob and Judy Martin interview; Al Blair interview.
37. Caldwell interview.
38. Welch interview.
39. Judy Martin interview, Aug. 7, 2006.
40. Judy Martin interview.
41. Chief Short's Wife Killed by Pickup Truck," *Houston Post*, May 9, 1970.
42. Wright interview; Jack Heard interview.
43. Alan Bernstein, "Former Police Chief Short is Dead at 71," *Houston Chronicle*, Dec. 29, 1989.

Chapter 18

1. "Official Report by the Houston Police Department of the Riot at Texas Southern University," compiled and prepared by Planning and Research Division, n.d. Houston Police Museum Archives.
2. Ibid.; Interviews with Officers R. G. "Bobby" Blaylock and Al Blair.
3. "Texas: Hate in Houston," *Time Magazine*, May 26, 1967.
4. Blaylock interview.
5. Welch interview; Lawson interview.
6. Lawson interview.
7. Charley Schneider interview.
8. Lawson interview.
9. Storemski interview.
10. "Texas: Hate in Houston," *Time Magazine*, May 26, 1967.
11. Albert Blair interview; Blair Justice interview.
12. John Whitmire interview.
13. Carl Smith interview; Gould Beech interview.
14. Gene Locke interview.
15. Blair Justice, *Violence in the City* (Fort Worth: Texas Christian University Press, 1969); Blair Justice interview.
16. The 1993 Los Angeles Riots would demonstrate that mass riot control was still an Achilles heel for municipal police forces, which time and time again have proven how unprepared city police are for handling widespread civil unrest.
17. Storemski interview; Blaylock interview.
18. Cato interview; Justice interview; Justice, *Violence in the City*.
19. Storemski, Cato, Schneider, and Blaylock interviews.
20. Welch interview.
21. Welch and Lawson interviews.
22. Welch interview.
23. Blaylock interview; "Police keep watch in wake of clash," *Houston Post*, July 28, 1970.

Chapter 19

1. Mosier interview.
2. Interview with former Mayor Roy Hofheinz.
3. Interview with former HPD Chief Carrol Lynn.
4. Lynn interview.
5. Hofheinz interview.

6. Ibid.
7. Massey, Mosier, Lynn interviews.
8. Hofheinz, Caldwell, and Rankin interviews.
9. Lynn interview.
10. Sandy Wall interview; Noskrent interview.
11. Hofheinz, Lynn, Bob Martin, and J. C. Hartman interviews.
12. Lynn interview; "Past Police Spying Here Denied," *Houston Post*, Jan. 7, 1975;
13. "Past Police Spying Here Denied."
14. Dave Petro, "Police Files Sorting Set," *Houston Post*, Apr. 5, 1975.
15. Lynn interview.
16. Phyllis Spittler, "The Controversial Career of Carrol Lynn," *Houston Chronicle*, Apr. 11, 1978.
17. Lynn interview, Jan. 16, 2005.
18. Lynn interview, Jan. 16, 2005.
19. Martin Ralbovsky, "Chief Lynn Accused of Fixing Traffic Tickets," *Houston Chronicle*, June 1, 1975.
20. Hofheinz and Lynn interviews.
21. Hofheinz interview.
22. Hofheinz interview.
23. Bob Martin interview, Aug. 7, 2006.
24. Tom Kennedy, "Lynn Only Houston Chief to Serve Prison Term," *Badge and Gun*, Feb. 2012.
25. "FBI Looks for Possible Link in 2nd Shooting, Lynn Case, *Houston Chronicle*, Apr. 12, 1978.
26. Tom Moran, "Lynn given chance to resign by Chief Caldwell after arrest," *Houston Chronicle*, Apr. 12, 1978; Moselle Boland, "Birnberg convinced Lynn is key figure," *Houston Chronicle*, Apr. 12, 1978; Christy Drennan, "Lynn fired," *Houston Chronicle*, Apr. 21, 1978; Caldwell interviews.
27. Moselle Boland, "Lynn gets 12 years," *Houston Chronicle*, Jan. 29, 1979.
28. Hair interview with Caldwell; Bob Martin interview; Caldwell interview.

Chapter 20

1. Walker.
2. Walker; Nelson J. Zoch, *Fallen Heroes of the Bayou City* (Dallas: Taylor, 2007).
3. Chief McClelland interview, Feb. 21, 2012.
4. A. V. Young interview.
5. Young interview; W. Marvin Dulaney, *Black Police in America* (Bloomington: University of Indiana Press, 1996), 145.
6. Zoch, *Fallen Heroes*.
7. Walker.
8. Albert Blair interview
9. Ibid.
10. Ibid.
11. Blair interview; Fred Black interview.
12. Ibid.
13. Ibid.
14. Blair, Black and Denny Hair interviews.

15. Blair interview.
16. *Houston Post* and Larry Fultz; Blair interview.
17. Blair interview.
18. Blair interview; Howard interview.
19. Blair interview.
20. Blair and Nuchia interviews.
21. *Houston Post* feature on Stringfellow; Mosier interview.
22. Mosier interview.
23. Mosier in *Houston Chronicle.*
24. *Houston Chronicle*, Mar. 23, 2001.
25. Black interview.
26. Black interview; Selwyn Lewis interview.
27. Walker, 1988.
28. Ibid.
29. Ibid.
30. Ibid.
31. Ibid.

CHAPTER 21

1. Bob Thomas interview.
2. Thomas interview.
3. Judge Lawrence H. Wayne interview.
4. June Cain Shane interview.
5. Cain Shane interview.
6. Doyle Green interview.
7. Green, Thomas interviews.
8. Thomas interview.
9. Green interview.
10. Thomas interview.
11. Green interview.
12. Thomas, Cain interviews.
13. Thomas interview.
14. Cain Shane interview.
15. Thomas interview.
16. Cain Shane interview.
17. Thomas interview.
18. Green, Thomas and Cain Shane interviews.
19. Nelson Zoch J., *Fallen Heroes.*
20. Thomas interview.
21. Thomas interview.
22. Ibid.
23. Ibid.
24. Ibid.
25. Ibid.
26. Maughmer, Porter Jr. interviews.
27. Whitmire interview.
28. Rick Ashwood, Thomas interviews.

29. Thomas Britt interview.
30. Britt interview.
31. Ibid.
32. Thomas interview.
33. Thomas interview.

CHAPTER 22

1. Hofheinz interview.
2. Bob Martin interview; Mosier interview.
3. Ann James, "'Pappy' Bond Sees 'Happy' Department if He's Made Chief," *Houston Post*, Jan. 13, 1976.
4. "Oh, Lard," *Houston Post* editorial, Jan. 22, 1976.
5. Ann James, "Chief Bond Announces Deputy Chiefs Shake-Up," *Houston Post*, Jan. 28, 1976.
6. Martin interview; Storemski interview.
7. Storemski interview.
8. "Chief Bond Wants Portable Radios for Officers," *Houston Post*, Feb. 14, 1976.
9. Janice Allen and Jorjanna Price, "Bond Raps 6 Officers' Accusers," *Houston Post*, Feb. 27, 1976; Jorjanna Price, "Chief Bond Seeks Suspension for 6, Asks Legal Opinion," *Houston Post*, Mar. 5, 1976.
10. Ann James and Frank David, "Verdict Pleases Officials," *Houston Post*, Apr. 1, 1976.
11. "Wiretaps Needed to Nab Drug Suspects, Bond Says," *Houston Post*, Oct. 13, 1976; Ann James, "Bond Alters His Position on Wiretaps," *Houston Post*, Nov. 6, 1976.
12. "Bond to Cut Police Car Commuting," *Houston Post*, July 21, 1976.
13. "Bond to Change Police Dress Code," *Houston Post*, Apr. 8, 1976.
14. "Cab Patrols Get Approval from Chief Bond," *Houston Post*, May 27, 1976.
15. Ann James, "Chief Bond starts review panel," *Houston Post*, May 5, 1976.
16. Monica Reeves, "Police Official Campaigning," *Houston Post*, May 29, 1976.
17. "Grand Jury Indicts Deputy Police Chief Over Income Taxes," *Houston Post*, Sept. 30, 1976.
18. Jorjanna Price and Larry Troutt, "Deputy Chief Can Receive Retirement Pay in Prison," *Houston Post*, Apr. 12, 1977.
19. "Houston Police Reveal Minority Recruiting Drive," *Houston Post*, Oct. 12, 1976.
20. Larry Troutt, "Bond Considering Police Internal Affairs Unit," *Houston Post*, Apr. 20, 1977.
21. Marc T. Henderson, "Bond Pleased with Minority Recruiting," *Houston Post*, May 30, 1977.
22. Larry Troutt, "Physical Condition of Slain Suspect Checked by Police," *Houston Post*, Feb. 23, 1977; Larry Troutt, "Disciplinary Action Hinted for Officer Who Shot Suspect," *Houston Post*, Feb. 25, 1977; "Officer Who Killed Man Reassigned," *Houston Post*, Mar. 5, 1977.
23. Tom Curtis, "Support Your Local Police or Else," *Texas Monthly* (Sept. 1977), 82–89, 156, 158–159.
24. Phil Hevener, "Priest in 9th Day of Fast," *Houston Post*, Mar. 22, 1977; Larry Troutt, "Dismissal Allegedly Urged for Officer Claiming Brutality," *Houston Post*, Mar. 23, 1977; Larry Troutt and Fred King, "Bond to Discuss Brutality Charges," *Houston Post*, Mar. 25, 1977; Larry Troutt, "Police Rookie Resumes Duties," *Houston Post*, Mar. 26, 1977.

25. Donald Katz, *The Valley of Fallen and Other Places* (Random House, 2001); Curtis, "Support Your Local Police."
26. Curtis, "Support Your Local Police," 85.
27. Curtis, "Support Your Local Police," 84.
28. "New Pursuit Policy Readied," *Houston Post*, Apr. 26, 1977.
29. Larry Troutt, "Chief to 'Shape Up' Force," *Houston Post*, Nov. 21, 1976.
30. Robert "Bob" L. Martin interview, 2004; Robert L. Martin, *HPD: What Went Wrong and Why: Houston Police Department Problems in the 70s and 80s* (Outskirts Press, 2009).
31. Martin, *HPD*.
32. Zoch, 2007; Martin interview.
33. Larry Troutt, "Bond plans to resign before elections," *Houston Post*, May 7, 1977.
34. Curtis, "Support Your Local Police."
35. Curtis, "Support Your Local Police"; Larry Troutt, "Officer Charged with Murder," *Houston Post*, May 10, 1977; Larry Troutt, "Bond Talks with Death Probe Jury," *Houston Post*, May 11, 1977.
36. Les Wunsche interview; Larry Troutt, "Bond Going 'In Direction' of Firing 5 in Torres Case," *Houston Post*, May 12, 1977.
37. Larry Troutt, "5 of 6 Officers Fired in Torres Death Case," *Houston Post*, May 13, 1977.
38. Larry Troutt, "5 of 6 Officers Fired".
39. Hofheinz interview; Frank Davis and Larry Troutt, "Mayor Calls Police Image 'Illness,'" *Houston Post*, May 17, 1977.
40. Curtis, "Support Your Local Police," 85–88; Frank Davis and Larry Troutt, "Mayor Calls Police".
41. Eli Rivera interview; *Houston Post* Nov. 6, 1986.

CHAPTER 23

1. Caldwell interview.
2. Caldwell interview.
3. Ed Jahn, "Caldwell Claims Little Antagonisms with ACLU Critics," *Houston Post*, Feb. 14, 1979.
4. "Houston Crime Rate Increases 18.2 pct., Police Report Shows," *Houston Post*, Apr. 28, 1979.
5. Hofheinz interview.
6. Jim Albright interview.
7. Thomas interview; Albright interview.
8. Thomas interview.
9. Thomas, Albright, Caldwell interviews.
10. "Some Accept Webster Case Verdict," *Houston Post*, Apr. 5, 1979.
11. Pete Wittenberg, "2 Ex-Officers Receive Probate Sentences," *Houston Post*, May 15, 1979.
12. Ibid.
13. Nelson Zoch, "HPD Blue Heart: Paul Dillon Shot While Apprehending Burglar," *Badge and Gun*, Jan. 2009.
14. "New HPD Psychologist to Join Patrol Officers for Close Look at Stress," *Houston Post*, Jan. 5, 1979.

15. Travis Morales, "Echoes of the Moody Park Rebellion," *Revolutionary Worker* 960 (June 7, 1998), rwor.org.
16. Jack Harris, Jack McGrew, and Paul Huhndorff, *The Fault Does Not Lie With Your Set: The First Forty Years of Houston Television* (Austin: Eakin Press, 1989); Phil Archer interview; Cato interview.
17. Cato interview.
18. Phil Archer interview.
19. Lori Rodriguez, "Moody Riots Helped Tear Down the 'Barrier' to HPD," *Houston Chronicle*, May 8, 1988.
20. Judy Martin interview.
21. Caldwell interview.
22. Mamie Garcia interview.
23. Ibid.
24. Garcia, Caldwell, and Johnny Mata interviews.
25. Ed Jahn, "LULAC Convention," *Houston Post*, June 15, 1979; Mamie Garcia interview.
26. "Houston Not Target of Justice Suit, Civiletti Confirms," *Houston Post*, Aug. 20, 1979.
27. Fred King, "'Most Crimes' Clearance Ratios Dip During first Half of Year," *Houston Post*, Aug. 3, 1979.
28. Caldwell interview.
29. Mosier interview.
30. Rob Meckel interview.
31. Fred King, "3 Caldwell Assistants Mum on Boss Keeping Job," *Houston Post*, Nov. 18, 1979; "Caldwell Says Question 'Moot' on Changing of Police Chiefs," *Houston Post*, Nov. 21, 1979.
32. Garcia interview.
33. Fred King, "Caldwell Wanted to Create 'Athens' of Profession," *Houston Post*, Feb. 14, 1980.
34. Lori Rodriguez, "Moody Riots Helped Tear Down the 'Barrier' to HPD," *Houston Chronicle*, May 8, 1988.

CHAPTER 24

1. Raul Martinez, recorded interview; Thomas H. Kreneck, *Mexican-American Odyssey, Felix Tijerina, Entrepreneur and Civic leader, 1905–1965* (College Station: Texas A&M University Press, 2001) Wilfred Navarro interview.
2. Kreneck, *Mexican American Legacy*.
3. Martinez interview.
4. Victor Trevino interview.
5. Martha Moreno Montalvo interview.
6. Ibid.
7. Ibid.
8. Wilfred Navarro interview.
9. Ibid.
10. Velia Ortega interview.
11. Art Contreras interview.
12. Ibid.
13. Ibid.
14. Phyllis Serna Wunsche interview.

15. Ibid.
16. Watson, Wunsche, and Lanier interviews.
17. Adrian Garcia interview.
18. Ibid.
19. Richard Rodriguez interview.

CHAPTER 25

1. Massey interview.
2. Bob Martin interview, Aug. 7, 2006.
3. Ed Magnuson, "The Curse of Violent Crime," *Time Magazine*, Mar. 23, 1981.
4. Jerry DeFoor, *Study of Organizational and Facility Needs of the Houston Police Department Through the Year 2000* (Dec. 1980).
5. Mark H. Moore, *Creating Public Value* (Replica Books, 1997).
6. Ibid.
7. Interview with former Mayor Kathy Whitmire.
8. Britt and Thomas interviews.
9. K. Whitmire and Elkin interviews.
10. Tom Kennedy, "300 Officers Jam Council Meeting," *Houston Post*, June 16, 1983, 1A, 27A.
11. Ibid.
12. K. Whitmire interview.
13. John Cater and Jack Drake interviews.
14. K. Whitmire interview.
15. Interview with former Police Chief Lee Brown.
16. K. Whitmire, Brown and John Bales interviews.
17. David Jones interview.
18. Elkin interview.
19. Lee Brown interview.
20. Bales, Oetmeier and Storemski interviews.
21. Bobby Adams interview.
22. Brown interview.
23. Bales interview.
24. HPD Annual Reports, Houston Police Museum Archives.
25. Brown interview.
26. Joe Weikerth interview.
27. Thomas and Britt interviews.
28. J. C. Mosier, Bob Martin, Brown and Thomas interviews.
29. Ray Hill and Ruston "Rusty" Alsbrooks interviews.

CHAPTER 26

1. William Pack, "HPD initiates new beat policy," *Houston Post*, Oct. 16, 1984; Mary Ann Wycoff and Timothy N. Oettmeier, *Planning and Implementation Issues for Community Oriented Policing: The Houston Experience*, 1996, p. 5.
2. Tim Oettmeier interview, Aug. 5, 2004; Michael Haederle, "Brown describes experiments to cut crimes," *Houston Post*, Oct. 2, 1984.
3. Oettmeier interview.

4. Elkin interview, Aug. 4, 2004.

5. Watson interview, Nov. 12, 2004.

6. Anthony M. Pate, Mary Ann Wycoff, Wesley G. Skogan, and Lawrence W. Sherman, *Reducing Fear of Crime in Houston and Newark, a Summary Report* (Washington, DC: Police Foundation, 1986).

7. See *Richard W. Lee, et al., v. The CITY OF HOUSTON,* Supreme Court of Texas, Mar. 6 1997, No. C-8285, *807 South Western Reporter,* 2nd Series, 291.

8. *Richard W. Lee et al., v. The Honorable Dan DOWNEY,* Supreme Court of Texas, Oct. 7, 1992, No. D-1439, *842 South Western Reporter, 2nd Series,* 646–655 (rehearing Dec. 16, 1992).

CHAPTER 27

1. Brown and Watson interviews.

2. K. Whitmire interview.

3. Elizabeth Watson interview.

4. Watson interview.

5. Ibid.

6. Ibid.

7. James Robinson, "Honeymoon Over as Watson Begins to Restructure HPD," *Houston Chronicle,* Mar. 12, 1990.

8. Ibid.

9. Greg Bisso interview.

10. *Houston Chronicle,* Jan. 20, 1991.

11. Ibid.

12. Watson interview.

13. Ibid.

14. Joe Breshears, Storemski interviews.

15. Breshears interview.

16. James Robinson and Eric Hanson, "Watson's Legacy/Woman Police Chief Fought City Hall as Well as Crime," *Houston Chronicle,* Mar. 1, 1992.

17. Interview with former Mayor Bob Lanier.

18. Jeannine Maughmer, Vicki King interviews.

19. Lanier interview.

20. Caldwell, Crosswell, Lanier and Storemski interviews.

21. John Williams and Tara Parker Hope, "Nuchia Asks Watson to take Assistant Post," *Houston Chronicle,* Feb. 21, 1992.

22. Lanier and Nuchia interviews.

23. Nuchia interview.

24. Ibid.

25. James T. Campbell and Eric Hanson, "Back to the Police Basics/"If We Don't Do It Nobody's Going to Do It," *Houston Chronicle,* Feb. 19, 1992.

26. Claudia Feldman, "Police Chief Nuchia's Philosophy for Policing Houston Rests on Three words: LAW and ORDER," *Houston Chronicle,* Texas Magazine Section, p. 7, Oct. 4, 1992.

27. Hall interview.

28. *Edwards v. City of Houston*; Nuchia, Lanier and Benjamin Hall interviews.

29. HPD Academy Records.

30. Nuchia interview.
31. Nuchia interview; Mike Tolson, "What Price Pursuit? 10 People Have Died as a result of Police Chases this year; both Civilians and Experts are Questioning the City's Pursuit Policy," *Houston Chronicle* Dec. 4,1994.
32. Stephen Johnson, "8 Officers Penalized in Chase/HPD Takes Action on 1994 Incident," *Houston Chronicle*, June 23, 1995.
33. Julie Mason, "'6.8 million Travis building to Office HPD," *Houston Chronicle*, Oct. 13, 1994.

CHAPTER 28

1. Bradford interview.
2. Jodie Jiles interview.
3. Lanier, Bradford interviews
4. "Changes for HPD," *Houston Chronicle*, Jan. 9, 1997.
5. S. K. Bardwell, "A Break for Sergeants," *Houston Chronicle*, Mar. 8, 1997.
6. Interview with former Police Chief Clarence O. "Brad" Bradford.
7. S. K. Bardwell and Lori Rodriguez, "HPD to Collect Profiling Data: Police Chief, Mayor Want to Find Out if Minorities Unfairly Targeted," *Houston Chronicle*, Aug. 12, 1999.
8. S. K. Bardwell, "Plan by HPD Seeks to Curb Racial Profiling, Mayor, Police Chief Will Announce Programs as Urban League Meets," *Houston Chronicle*, Aug. 10, 1999; Bradford interview.
9. Mark Smith, "HPD Writing Fewer Traffic Tickets Under New Data Gathering Policy," *Houston Chronicle*, Oct. 17, 1999; Hans Marticiuc interview.
10. L. T. Hoover, J. A. Bruns, R. Hanser, Y. H. Kang, H. Lyons, J. Moon, S. Roh and L. Zhou, "Racial Profiling Data Analysis, 2002," Sam Houston State University, Police Research Center, 2003; Mike Glenn and Rosanna Ruiz, "Study Finds no Profiling by HPD, Socioeconomic Status, Not Race, is Large Factor in Stops, Analysis Says," *Houston Chronicle* , May 2, 2003, p. 27A.
11. Storemski, Breshears interviews.
12. Breshears interview.
13. Lisa Teachey, S. K. Bardwell, Matt Schwartz, Kristen Mack, "Judge Tosses Bradford Case, Evidence of Perjury Weak," *Houston Chronicle* , Jan. 24, 2003, 1A.
14. Matt Schwartz, Roma Khanna, Peggy O'Hare, "The Bradford Indictment: Case Causes Dismay, Calls for Chief's Resignation," *Houston Chronicle*, Sept. 7, 2002.
15. Kristen Mack, "Chief Briefs Council on HPD Problems: Some Dubious," *Houston Chronicle*, Mar. 6, 2003.

CHAPTER 29

1. Tom Kennedy, "Call It What You Want, the Hans Era was Historic," *Badge and Gun*, Dec. 2007.
2. Marticiuc interview.
3. Hans Marticiuc, "The President's Message," *Badge and Gun*, Feb. 1996, 3.
4. Lanier interview.
5. Mark Clark interview.
6. Tom Kennedy, "Call It What You Want".
7. Ron DeLord interview, Mar. 15, 2012.

8. Craig Varoga interview.
9. Sen. John Whitmire interview, Mar. 4, 2008.
10. Gary Blankinship, Whitmire and Brown interviews.

CHAPTER 30

1. Mayor Bill White interview, May 5, 2008; interview with HPD Chief Harold Hurtt, Jan. 17, 2008.
2. Interview with Charles McClelland, *Badge and Gun*, Dec. 2007.
3. Roma Khanna, "The Taser Effect," *Houston Chronicle*, Jan. 14, 2007.
4. "Texans Player Sues City and Officers Over Use of Taser," *Houston Chronicle*, Nov. 14, 2007.
5. "Fatal HPD Shooting Prompts New Rule, $1.5 Million Payout," *Houston Chronicle*, May 29, 2008.
6. Lise Olsen, "Officer Who Shot Boy Failed Firearms Test," *Houston Chronicle*, Oct. 15, 2007.
7. "Hurtt Calls for Cameras to Catch Traffic Violators," *Houston Chronicle*, Apr. 30, 2004.
8. Hurtt interview, 2008.
9. "City Boosts HPF Cadet Bonus/$12,000 offer gives Houston a lift over Dallas in Recruitment," *Houston Chronicle*, Feb. 21, 2008.
10. "Officer's Pay Tops $172,000," *Houston Chronicle*, Apr. 23, 2006.
11. Matt Stiles, "22 Officers Earned Over $50,000 in OT Last Year/City Controller Checking to See if 80-Hour Rule is Being Violated," *Houston Chronicle*, May 3, 2006.
12. "FEMA Awaits Funding Request," *Houston Chronicle*, Dec. 28, 2005.
13. Hurtt interview, Jan. 17, 2008.
14. Gary Blankinship, Mark Clark interviews, Jan. 15, 2010.
15. Mike Glenn, "Hurtt: Union Survey Clouded by 'Biases': HPD's Chief Criticizes Recent Poll Critical of His Tenure, Asks for Fresh Review," *Houston Chronicle*, July 26, 2006.
16. Clark, Marticiuc and Blankinship interviews.
17. White interview.
18. Ed Kwan and Joel "Sal" Salazar interviews.
19. Anthony Hall interview.

CHAPTER 31

1. Interview with Houston Mayor Annise Parker, Feb. 29, 2012.
2. Interview with Houston Police Chief Charles McClelland, Feb. 21, 2012.
3. Mayor Parker interview.
4. Chief McClelland interview.
5. Ibid.
6. Ibid.
7. Tom Kennedy, "... Grew Up in Patrol," *Badge and Gun*, Jan. 2011, p. 26.
8. Chief McClelland interview.
9. Waynette Chan interview, Feb. 17, 2012.
10. Ibid.
11. Ray Hunt interview, Feb. 8, 2012.
12. Ibid.
13. Ibid.

14. Ibid.

15. Ibid.

16. Bradley Olson, "Data Show Crime Outpaces Officers," *Houston Chronicle*, Aug. 3, 2009, p. A1, A8.

17. Ibid.

18. McClelland interview.

19. James Pinkerton, "Backlog Prompts Lykos to Call for Emergency Lab," *Houston Chronicle*, July 18, 2010.

20. Wendy Siegle, "HPD's Crime Lab Making Improvements but Some Backlogs Still Growing," KUHF Houston Public Radio online, Jan. 13, 2011.

21. See, Bill King, "No Explanation for Drop in Crime Rate," *Houston Chronicle*, Sept. 1, 2011.

22. "Houston Crime Rate Continues Decline," http://www.yourhoustonnews.com, Apr. 24, 2011.

23. Ibid.

24. James Pinkerton, "Odds Now 50-50 an HPD Officer Will Be a Minority," *Houston Chronicle*, Mar. 15, 2010, A1, A6.

25. James Pinkerton, "HPD Considers New Uniforms, Badges, Cars," *Houston Chronicle*, Aug. 13, 2011, B1.

26. Pinkerton, Mar. 15, 2010.

Sources

ARCHIVES

University of Texas Archives, Austin, TX.

Ashbel Smith Papers. Unsigned letter to M.M. Noah, June 27, 1837; Chauncy Goodrich to Ashbel Smith, June 30, 1837; Ashbel Smith to Dr. Lewis, Oct 31, 1837 (typescript).

Augustus C. Allen Papers. Texas State Archives, Austin, Texas.

Littleton Fowler Papers.

James Harper Starr Papers. Memo book 1839–1840 to Feb. 23, 1841, pp. 5–6 (typescript).

Houston Police Department Museum and Archives:

1925 Annual Police Report, Thomas C. Goodson, Superintendent of Police, Vice Investigating Squad, typescript, 1925.

"Arrests Made by Police Department for Violations of Prohibition Law," Chief L. C. Brown Collection, File 84.3.130.

Bacher, Eva Jane File.

Charter of Houston, 1866

Daily Houston Telegraph clippings file, typescript, May 30, Sept. 29, 30, 1868.

Davidson, Terry. *Case Study: Lower Westheimer Neighborhood Oriented Policing Initiative*, Houston Police Department, Mar. 1990, 38 pp.

Defoor, Jerry. *Study of Organizational ad Facility Needs of the Houston Police Department Through the Year 2000*. Dec. 1980.

Dunlap, Al H. "Police Department of Houston, Texas," *The Detective*. Municipal Section, vol. 32, no. 7. Chicago, 1915.

Griffenhagen and Associates. "City of Houston: The Police Department, Report No. 3." Dec. 28, 1939.

Hair, Denny. "The Houston Police: A History and Legacy of the Houston Police Department, 1841–1932." Unpublished manuscript.

Hair, Denny. "The Houston Police: A History and Legacy of the Houston Police Department, 1933–1992." Unpublished manuscript.

Jack Heard Collection.

Houston City Council Minutes, Feb. 1874 through 1875, Book A, microfilm, Accession no. 84.9.

Houston City Directory, 1866

Houston City Directory, 1867–1868

Houston City Directory, 1895

Houston City Directory, 1902–1903

Houston City Directory, 1908–1909

Houston City Directory, 1917

Houston City Directory, 1923–1924

Houston Police Department. "The Personal Scrapbook of James M. Ray, Chief of Police 1910." Accession Number 82.14.1.

Houston Police Museum, Archival File, 82.14.1.

Houston Police Department. "Personal Scrapbook of James Henry Tatum, Senior Captain of Police (1915–1955)," Houston Police Museum, James H. Tatum Collection. Accession no. 82.26.1.

Houston Police Department Rules Manual. Feb. 1973, no. 1766.

Houston Police Department Souvenir Yearbook, 1901, Museum Accession Number 88.2.1.

Houston Police Officers' Union. *Constitution and By-Laws.* Aug. 2005, 22 pp.

Johnny H. Hudgins Collections. Feb. 1941–May 1942 Scrapbook. Accession no. 83.21.1.

Killed in Action Memorial Book.

L. D. Morrison Collection.

Minutes of the 11th District Court (District Clerk's Office, Houston), C (Jan. 1, 1841–May 24, 1842), 152–153. See also B. (Dec 3, 1838–Jan. 7 1841), 170–171.

Ordinances of the City of Houston. City Secretary's Office, Houston, Texas. Vols. 2–5.

Planning and Research Division (HPD). "Official Report by the HPD of the 1967 Riot at Texas Southern University."

Stewart, Ira L, "Outline of Houston Police Department History."

Lonnie V. Streveck Collection. 1941–1942 Scrapbook.

Wycoff, Mary Ann and Timothy N. Oettmeier, "Planning and Implementation Issues for Community Oriented Policing: The Houston Experience." 1996, 82 pp.

Houston Public Library Special Collections:

Annual Message of A. L. Jackson, Mayor of the City of Houston, *Annual Reports of City Officers for the year ending December 31, 1904.*

Annual Mayor's Message and Department Reports, Houston, 1908.

Annual Mayor's Message and Department Reports, Houston, 1910.

Annual Mayor's Message and Department Reports, Houston, 1913.

Charter of the City of Houston and General Ordinances Passed by the City Council from the 31st Day of October 1904, to and including October 31st, 1910. Houston: W. H. Coyle, 1910.

City Council Minutes, Jan. 25, 1866.

Earl Maughmer, Jr. Interview, tape recording, Houston Metropolitan Research Center, 1974.

Mrs. Dilue Harris (Rose) Reminiscences, 1833–38. SC134, Box 14, Folder 6, typescript.

Neal Pickett File Archive, Houston Public Library Texas Manuscript Collection.

Ninth Census of the U.S., Harris County, Texas.

Oscar Holcombe Collection, Houston Metropolitan Research Center, MSS20.

Seventh Census of the U.S., Harris County, Texas.

University of Houston Special Collections:
(George Fuermann Historical Collection)

Box 5, Folder 12–23 City Council Minutes

Box 7, Marshal's Office, folder 6

Box 7, Ordinance Creating the Office of City Scavenger, 1879

Photo Files (box 8–15)

#30 negative of policeman, early 20th c.

#29 inmate in city jail

City County Resolution, 1879

Edwin Bonewitz Collection, MSS 0025, box 4, folder 1

Drafts of Reports by the Police Committee of the Board of Aldermen, Nov. 30, 1872

Minutes of Board of Aldermen, 1879

Sam Houston State University, Newton Gresham Library, Thomason Room Special Collections

Houston Police Vertical File

Ricardo Aldape Guerra File

Interviews:

Bobby Adams, Homicide captain, Sept. 15, 2004

Jim Albright, union and Caldwell history, Aug. 17, 2004

Rusty Alsbrooks, first openly gay officer, Dec. 23, 2004

Phil Archer, Channel 2 reporter (Moody Park Riot), Oct. 9, 2004

Bob Armbruster, HPOU lawyer (Lee & Edwards cases; reviewed my copy Sept. 27, 2007)

John Bales, Sept. 7, 2004

Jo Bankston, one of first women in HPD (Heard chapter and Betsy chapter), Sept. 9, 2004

J. J. Berry, May 23, 2007

Sgt. Jim Binford, longtime Homicide detective, Sept. 29, 2004

Officer Gregg Bisso, HPPU and HPOA chapters, Apr. 30, 2007

Fred Black, early African American officer, June 7, 2004

Albert Blair, early black officer, Aug. 11, 2004

Gary Blankinship, solo and union information, Aug. 6, 2004

Bobby Blaylock, TSU Riot and Carl Hampton shooting, May 10, 2006

Buddy Bond (Pappy's son), interviewed about Pappy's health, June 15, 2006

Clarence Bradford, HPD (Bradford chapters), May 15, 2007

Terry Bratten, academy instructor, Nov. 30, 2004

Joe Breshears, Betsy and Hurtt chapters, Mar. 4, 2008

Tommy Britt, police officer on union history, Aug. 16, 2004

Lee Brown, former Houston Police Chief, Aug. 19, 2004

Chris Burns, HPPU and HPOA history, Oct. 22, 2004

Harry Caldwell, former Houston Police Chief, Sept. 4, 2004

Jack Cato, Sept. 12, 2004

Waynette Chan, Feb. 17, 2012

Mark Clark, union history, Apr. 16, 2004

Mark Clark, Feb. 8, 2012

Hank Coleman, city attorney under Whitmire, Aug. 4, 2005

Jim Conley, academy instructor, Nov. 30, 2004

Art Contreras, Oct. 18, 2004

Bill Coulter, old Post police reporter, Apr. 18, 2004

Floyd Daigle, retired deputy chief, Aug. 3, 2005

Jack Drake, Whitmire aide who found Lee Brown, Oct. 15, 2006

Bill Elkin, former HPOA president, Aug. 4, 2004

Louis Elliott, retired HPD (Torres chapter), Aug. 16, 2005

Craig Ferrell, HPD attorney, Oct. 18, 2007

Nelson Foehner, former sergeant and Caldwell aide on Mar. 23, 2005

Sue Gaines, early policewoman, Sept. 2, 2004

Adrian Garcia, Dec. 15, 2004

Mamie Garcia, Aug. 8, 2005

Anthony Hall, former councilman, Metro head and city attorney, Feb. 26, 2007

Ben Hall, Lanier city attorney, Nov. 29, 2007

Lee Harrington, early GPC leader, Sept. 1, 2004

Homer Harris, Chief Louie Welch's police driver, Dec. 7, 2004

Jack Heard, former Houston Police Chief, Oct. 2, 2004

Ray Hill, gay leader, Sept. 17, 2004

Fred Hofheinz, former Houston Mayor, on Sept. 14, 2004

Ray Hunt, Feb. 8, 2012

Harold Hurtt, former Houston Police Chief, Jan. 17, 2008

David Jones, Whitmire supporter, community activist and KW confident, Oct. 15, 2006

Blair Justice, TSU chapter, author of *Violence in the City*, and for Short years, Feb. 5, 2007

Jim Kelley, retired solo, Aug. 13, 2004

Margaret Landa, Feb. 18, 2002

Victor Landa, Feb. 18, 2002

Bob Lanier, former Houston Mayor, Mar. 7, 2005

Bill Lawson, TSU Riot, June 4, 2007

Richard W. Lee, union matters and the Lee case, Oct. 1, 2004

Steven Lee, Nov. 2009

Edwin Lem, Nov. 2009

Gene Locke, TSU, blacks in HPD, patrol issues, Nov. 10, 2004

Carrol Lynn, former Houston Police Chief, Feb. 15, 2005

Pat Lykos, Apr. 15, 2004

Paul Mabry, Whitmire aide, Apr. 23, 2005

Frank Mancuso, longtime councilman, Apr. 29, 2004

Herman Mar, Nov. 2009

Hans Marticiuc, union matters, Nov. 7, 2007

Bob Martin, retired lieutenant, Aug. 21, 2004

Chester Massey, retired lieutenant, Mar. 15, 2004

Johnny Mata, LULAC leader, Nov. 8, 2004

Jeannine Maughmer Miller, Dec. 10, 2008

Police Chief Charles McClelland, Feb. 21, 2012

Pat McGill, retired sergeant and Buddy's son, Mar. 22, 2005

Mike Mitchell, retired solo officer and founder Assist the Officer, Mar. 11, 2008

Martha Montalva, Dec. 9, 2004

J. C. Mosier, retired sergeant and mayor's driver, Jan. 14, 2004

Wilfred Navarro, June 17, 2004

Ronnie Noskrent, early SWAT, Dec. 8, 2004

Sam Nuchia, former Houston Police Chief, Sept. 11, 2007

Tim Oettmeier, executive assistant chief on NOP, Aug. 5, 2004

Belle Ortega, Aug. 25, 2006

Annise Parker, early gay leader and future Houston mayor, Aug. 14, 2004

Houston Mayor Annise Parker, Feb. 29, 2012

Breck Porter Jr., Feb. 18, 2004

Francis Porter, Feb. 25, 2004

Guadalupe Quintanilla, Apr. 26, 2005

Walter Rankin, former sergeant and do-right officer, Apr. 13, 2004

Dr. Greg Riede, first Psych Services, Nov. 9, 2004

Eli Rivera, Mar. 23, 2005

Anna Russell, city secretary, May 11, 2008

Vince Ryan, former councilman now county attorney, Oct. 27, 2006

Charley Schneider, *Post* police reporter at TSU, Apr. 6, 2004

Joe Schultea, former HPD, Dec. 7, 2004

Volley Schultea, present at TSU Riot, Dec. 7, 2004

June Shane, Oct. 20, 2004

Tommy Shane, Mar. 27, 2009

Jerry Smith, Whitmire city attorney now federal judge, Mar. 14, 2007

Red Smith, oldest living HPD retired officer, Mar. 23, 2004

Lanny Stephenson, former policewoman, Aug. 23, 2004

Dennis Storemski, Oct. 10, 2006

Bob Thomas, HPPU, Sept. 29, 2004

Andy Tobias, prosecutor involved in Moody Riot prosecution, July 5, 2005

Victor Trevino, July 9, 2005

Craig Varoga, Apr. 10, 2008

Sandy Wall, SWAT officer, Jan. 15, 2005

Betsy Watson, former Houston Police Chief, Nov. 12, 2004

Wayne Lawrence, judge

Louie Welch, former Houston Mayor, Sept. 13, 2005

Clarence West, Whitmire agenda director and later city attorney, May 22, 2007

Bill White, former Houston Mayor, May 5, 2008

John Whitmire, state senator and union rep in legislature, Mar. 4, 2008

Kathy Whitmire, Oct. 2, 2006

Clymer Wright, on Herman Short, Mar. 20, 2004

Assistant Chief Wong, Nov. 2009

Les Wunsche, June 29, 2004

Phyllis Wunsche, June 29, 2004

Lily Yep, Nov. 2009

A. V. Young, early black officer and union founder, Sept. 15, 2006

Marvin Zindler, *Houston Post* reporter, Aug. 9, 2007

Nelson Zoch, July 8, 2004

Newspapers and Periodicals:

Badge and Gun

Daily Houston Telegraph

Galveston Daily News

Houston Chronicle

Houston Post

Houston Post-Dispatch

Houston Press

Morning Star

New York Times

St. Louis Republican

Telegraph and Texas Register

Time Magazine

Selected Printed Sources:

Adams, Ephraim Douglass, ed. "British Correspondence Concerning Texas," *Quarterly of the Texas State Historical Society*, 15 (July 1911–April 12, 1911), p. 221.

Ahlfield, Danny Lee. "Fraternalism Gone Awry: The Ku Klux Klan in Houston, 1920–1925." Master's thesis, University of Texas, 1984.

Alexander, Charles C. *Crusade for Conformity: The Ku Klux Klan in Texas, 1920–1930*. Houston: Texas Gulf Coast Historical Association, 1962.

Allen, O.F. *The City of Houston from Wilderness to Wonder*. Temple, Texas, 1936.

Arthur, Dora Fowler, ed. "Jottings from the Old Journal of Littleton Fowler," *Quarterly of the Texas State Historical Association* 2 (July 1898): 79–80.

Barrett, Paul W. and Mary H. Barrett. *Young Brothers Massacre*. Columbia: University of Missouri Press, 1988.

Bartholomew, Ed. *The Houston Story*. Frontier Press, 1951.

Blackburn, Ed, Jr. *Wanted: Historic County Jails of Texas*. College Station: Texas A&M Press, 2006.

Brewer, Victoria E., Kelly Damphousse and Cary D. Adkinson, "The Role of Juveniles in Urban Homicides: The Case of Houston, 1990–1994," *Homicide Studies* 2.3 (Aug. 1998), 321–339.

Brooks, Victoria Lynne. "Crime and Violence in Frontier Houston: A Study of the Criminal District Court of Harris County, 1872–1876." Master's thesis, Rice University, May 1974.

Brown, Richard Maxwell. *Strain of Violence: Historical Studies of American Violence and Vigilantism.* New York: Oxford University Press, 1975.

Bullard, Robert D. *Invisible Houston: The Black Experience in Boom and Bust.* College Station: Texas A&M Press, 1987.

Carleton, Don E. *Red Scare!: Right Wing Hysteria, Fifties Fanaticism and Their Legacy in Texas.* Austin: Texas Monthly Press, 1985.

Carroll, Benajah, ed. *Standard History of Houston, Texas: From a Study of the Original Sources.* Knoxville, Tennessee: H.W. Crew and Company, 1912.

Cartlidge, Ron. *Houdini's Texas Tours 1916 and 1923.* Austin: Ron Cartlidge Publications, 2002.

City of Houston v. J. A. Estes. 35 Tex. Civ. App. 99; 79 S.W. 848; 1904 Tex. App. (retrieved from LEXIS NEXUS, Mar. 19, 2006.)

Curtis, Tom. "New Gang in Town." *Texas Monthly* (Sept. 1977), 83–89, 156, 158–159.

Davie, Flora Agatha. "The Early History of Houston, Texas, 1836–1845," Master's thesis, University of Texas, Aug. 1940.

Dewey, Jim. "William E. Murphy, Deputy Chief of the Houston Police Department, Killed While Seated in a Restaurant." Master's Thesis, University of Houston-Downtown, May 2005.

Dittman, Ralph E. *Allen's Landing: The Authentic Story of the Founding of Houston.* Houston: A. C. and J. K. Allen Publishing, 1986.

Dulaney, W. Marvin. *Black Police in America.* Bloomington: Indiana University Press, 1996.

Dulaney, W. Marvin. "The Texas Negro Peace Officers' Association: The Origins of Black Police Unionism." *The Houston Review* 12:2 (1990), 59–78.

Friedland, Martin L. *The Death of Old Man Rice: A True Story of Criminal Justice in America.* New York: New York University Press, 1994.

Friedman, Lawrence M. *Crime and Punishment in American History.* New York: Basic Books, 1993.

Frost, H. Gordon and Jenkins, John H. *"I'm Frank Hamer": The Life of a Texas Peace Officer*. Austin: Pemberton, 1968.

Fuermann, George. *Houston: The Once and Future City*. Garden City, New York: Doubleday, 1971.

Fuermann, George. *Houston: Land of the Big Rich, Story of a Fabulous City*. New York: Doubleday, 1951.

Fuermann, George. *Reluctant Empire: The Mind of Texas*. New York: Doubleday, 1957.

Garcia, Maria-Cristina. "Manuel Crespo." *Handbook of Texas Online*.

Gardenier, Hugh and Martha Gardinier. *The Ice Box Murders*. Redbud Publishing, 2003

Garvin, Richard M. and Edmond G. Addeo. *The Midnight Special: The Legend of Leadbelly*. Bernard Geis Associates, 1971.

Goldfield, David R. *Cotton Fields and Skyscrapers: Southern City and Region, 1607–1980*. Baton Rouge: Louisiana State University Press, 1980.

Graber, H. W. *A Terry Texas Ranger, 1861–1865: The Life Record of H. W. Graber. 62 Years in Texas*. Dallas: Privately Printed, 1916.

Greene, Casey. "Guardians Against Change: The Ku Klux Klan in Houston and Harris County, 1920–1925." *The Houston Review* 10.1 (1988), 3–20.

Gurasich, Marj. *History of the Harris County Sheriff's Office, 1837–1983*. Harris County Sheriff's Deputies' Association, 1983.

Gurwell, John K. *Mass Murder in Houston*. Houston: Cordovan Press, 1974.

Hadden, Sally E. *Slave Patrols: Law and Violence in Virginia and the Carolinas*. Cambridge: Harvard University Press, 2001.

Haley, James L. *Texas: From the Frontier to Spindletop*. New York: St. Martin's Press, 1985.

Harris, Jack, Jack McGrew and Paul Huhndorff. *The Fault Does Not Lie with Your Set: The First Forty Years of Houston Television*. Austin: Eakin Press, 1989.

Hatley, Allen G. *Texas Constables: A Frontier Heritage*. Lubbock: Texas Tech University Press, 1999.

Haynes, Robert V. *A Night of Violence: The Houston Race Riot of 1917*. Baton Rouge: Louisiana State University Press, 1976.

Hogan, William Ransom. "Rampant Individualism in the Republic of Texas," *Southwestern Historical Quarterly* 44 (Apr. 1941), 454–480.

Hogan, William Ransom. *The Texas Republic: A Social and Economic History*. Austin: University of Texas Press, 1969.

Hooten, Charles. *St. Louis' Isle, or Texiana; with Additional Observations of the United States and Canada*. London: Simmonds and Ward, 1847.

Houston: A History and Guide. Houston: Anson Jones Press, 1942.

Houston Police Officers' Union, www.hpou.org/history.

Houston Police Online, www.ci.houston.tx.us/department/police/museum.

Houstoun, Matilda Charlotte. *Texas and the Gulf of Mexico; or, Yachting in the New World*. Vol. 2. London: John Murray, 1844.

International Association of Chiefs of Police, 1916.

Jackson, Kenneth T. *The Ku Klux Klan in the City, 1915–1930*. New York: Oxford University Press, 1967.

Jackson, Mary Susan. "The People of Houston in the 1850s." PhD diss., Indiana University, Dec. 1974.

Johnston, Marguerite. *Houston, the Unknown City, 1836–1946*. College Station: Texas A&M Press, 1991.

Justice, Blair. *Violence in the City*. Fort Worth: Texas Christian University Press, 1969.

Katz, Donald. *The Valley of the Fallen and other Places*. New York: Random House, 2001.

Kennedy, David M. "Perspectives on Policing" in *The Strategic Management of Police Resources*. National Institute of Justice, 1993.

Kilgore, Linda Elaine. "The Ku Klux Klan and the Press in Texas, 1920–1927." Master's thesis, The University of Texas, Austin, Texas.

King, Joseph. "Police Strikes of 1918 and 1919 in the United Kingdom and Boston and Their Effects." PhD diss., City University of New York, 1999.

Kreneck, Thomas H. *Mexican American Odyssey: Felix Tijerina, Entrepreneur and Civic leader, 1905–1965*. College Station: Texas A&M University Press, 2001.

Lubbock, Francis R. *Six Decades in Texas*. Edited by C. W. Rains. Austin: Ben C. Jones, 1900.

Lundsgaarde, Henry P. *Murder in Space City: A Cultural Analysis of Houston Homicide Patterns*. New York: Oxford University Press.

Mackey, Thomas C. *Red Lights Out: A Legal History of Prostitution, Disorderly 99 Houses, and Vice Districts, 1870–1917*. New York: Garland, 1987.

Mackey, Thomas C. "Thelma Denton and Associates: Houston's Red Light Reservation and a Question of Jim Crow." *Houston Review* 14.3 (1992), 139–152.

Maillard, N. Doran. *The History of the Republic of Texas.* 1842.

Marchiafava, Louis J. *The Houston Police: 1878–1948.* Houston: Rice University Studies, 1977.

Martin, Robert L. *HPD: What Went Wrong and Why: Houston Police Department Problems in the 70s and 80s.* Outskirts Press, 2009.

McAshan, Marie P. *A Houston Legacy: On the Corner of Main and Texas.* Houston: Hutchins House, 1985.

McComb, David G. *Houston, The Bayou City.* 1969. Reprint, Austin: University of Texas Press, 1981.

Meed, Douglas V. *Texas Ranger Johnny Klevenhagen.* Austin: Eakin, 2000.

Merseburger, Marion. "A Political History of Houston, Texas, during the Reconstruction

Period as Recorded by the Press: 1868–1873," Master's thesis, Rice University, May 1950.

Miller, Ray. *Ray Miller's Houston.* Austin: Capitol Printing, 1983.

Moore, Mark H. *Creating Public Value.* Replica Books, 1997.

Nanfria, Linda J. "The Houston Police Department," in *1983 Houston Police Department Yearbook.* Delmar Company, 1983.

Olsen, Jack. *The Man With the Candy: The Story of the Houston Mass Murders.* New York: Simon and Schuster, 1974.

O'Quinn, Trueman E. and Jenny Lind Porter. *Time to Write: How William Sidney Porter Became O'Henry.* Austin: Eakin Press, 1986.

Owens, Nora Estelle. "Presidential Reconstruction in Texas: A Case Study." PhD diss., Auburn University, June 18, 1983.

Pate, Anthony M, Mary Ann Wycoff, Wesley G. Skogan and Lawrence W. Sherman. *Reducing Fear of Crime in Newark and Houston, a Summary Report.* Washington D.C.: Police Foundation, 1986.

Prassel, Richard. *The Western Peace Officer.* Norman: University of Oklahoma Press, 1981.

Richard W. Lee, et al., v. The City of Houston. Supreme Court of Texas, Mar. 6, 1991, *807 South Western Reporter*, 2nd Series, 290–303.

Richard W. Lee, et al., v. The Honorable Dan Downey. Supreme Court of Texas, Oct. 7, 1992, *842 South Western Reporter*, 2nd Series, 646–655.

Roemer, Ferdinand. *Texas, With Particular Reference to German Immigration and the Physical Appearance of the Country* (better known as *Roemer's Texas*). Translated by Oswald Mueller. 1935. Reprint, San Antonio: Standard Printing Company, 1983.

Rosario, F. Arturo. *"Pobre Raza!": Violence, Justice and Mobilization Among Mexico Lindo Immigrants, 1900–1936*. Austin: University of Texas Press, 1999.

Roth, Mitchel P. *Crime and Punishment: A History of the Criminal Justice System*. Thomson-Wadsworth, 2005.

Roth, Mitchel P. *Historical Dictionary of Law Enforcement*. Westport: Greenwood, 2001.

Rousey, Dennis C. *Policing the Southern City: New Orleans, 1805–1889*. Baton Rouge: Louisiana State University Press, 1996.

Rudwick, Elliott M. *The Unequal Badge: Negro Policemen in the South*. Atlanta: Southern Regional Council, 1962.

Schuler, Edgar A. "Houston Race Riot, 1917." *Journal of Negro History* (1944), 300–338.

Sheridan, Francis Cynric. *Galveston Island or, A Few Months off the Coast of Texas: The Journal of Francis C. Sheridan, 1839–1840*. Edited by Willis Winslow Pratt. Austin: University of Texas Press, 1954.

Sibley, Marilyn M. *Travelers in Texas, 1761–1860*. Austin: University of Texas Press, 1967.

Siegel, Stanley E. *Houston: A Chronicle of the Supercity on the Bayou*. Windsor Publications, 1983.

Silverthorne, Elizabeth. *Ashbel Smith of Texas: Pioneer, Patriot, Statesman, 1805–1886*. College Station: Texas A&M Press, 1982.

Smith, C. Calvin. "The Houston Riot of 1917, Revisited." *The Houston Review* 13.2 (1992), 85–102.

Steen, Ralph W. *Twentieth Century Texas: An Economic and Social History*. Austin: Steck Company, 1942.

Talley, W. Bryan. "Turbulence in the Republic of Texas." Master's thesis, Sam Houston State University, Aug. 1969.

Texas in 1837: An Anonymous Contemporary Narrative. Edited by Andrew Forest Muir. Austin: University of Texas Press, 1958.

Thompson, Thomas. *Blood and Money*. Garden City: Doubleday, 1976.

Titterington, Victoria B, and Barry P. Abbott, "Space City Revisited: Patterns of Legal Outcomes in Houston Homicide." *Violence and Victims* 19.1 (Feb. 2004), 83–95.

Tucker, Lee. *Houston: A Sesquicentennial Commemorative.* 1986.

Walker, May. *The History of Black Police Officers in the Houston Police Department.* Houston: Houston Police Department, 1988.

Wallis, Jonnie Lockhart and Hill, Laurence L. *Sixty Years on the Brazos: The Life and Letters of Dr. John Washington Lockhart, 1824–1900.* Waco: Texian Press, facsimile reprint, 1967.

Watson, Dwight. *Race and the Houston Police Department, 1930–1990, A Change Did Come.* College Station: Texas A&M Press, 2005.

Waide, C. D. "When Psychology Failed." *Houston Gargoyle* 1 (May 15, 1928), 5–6; (May 22), 5–6; (May 29), 10–11; (June 5), 11–12; (June 12), 10–11.

Weiss, Harold J., Jr. "Western Lawmen: Image and Reality." *Journal of the West* 24.1 (Jan. 1985), 23–32.

Wheeler, Kenneth W. *To Wear a City's Crown: The Beginnings of Urban Growth in Texas, 1836–1865.* Cambridge: Harvard University Press, 1968.

"When Carrie Nation Came to Houston." www.houstonarchitecture.com/haif/topic/402-when-carrie-nation-came-to-Houston.

Wintz, Cary D. "Blacks" in *The Ethnic Groups of Houston.* Edited by Fred R. Von der Mehden. Houston: Rice University, 1984, 9–40.

Wolfe, Charles and Kip Lornell. *The Life and Legend of Leadbelly.* New York: Harper Collins, 1994.

Works Progress Administration, 1942.

Writers' Program of the Works Project Administration in the State of Texas. *Houston, a History and Guide.* Houston: Anson Jones Press, 1942.

Young, S. O. *A Thumbnail History of the City of Houston Texas, From Its Founding in 1836 to the Year 1912.* Houston, 1912.

Young, S. O. *True Stories of Old Houston and Houstonians: Historical and Personal Sketches.* Galveston: Oscar Springer, 1913.

Zoch, Nelson J. *Fallen Heroes of the Bayou City.* Dallas: Taylor, 2007.

Index

Foley, C., 17
Fonville, R. H., 153
Forrest, Martin T., 42
Fraternal Order of Police (FOP), 48, 102
Frazier, George, 18
"Free State of Galveston," 83
Friendly fire incidents, 211
Fuentes, Pete, 304
Fuermann, George, 178
Fultz, Larry W., 162–163, 180, 240

G

Galveston, 19, 22, 26, 27, 28, 63, 83
Galveston Hurricane, 45; and HPD, 46, 66
Galveston Police Department, 62
Gambill, James T., 110
Gambling Rackets, 12, 114, 144, 149, 187, 188
Gamewell System, 58
Gangs, 134
Garcia, Adrian, 310, 311
Garcia, J. J., 296
Garcia, Mamie, 293, 294, 297
Garcia, Sylvia, 300
Garnett, Ken, 221–222
Gay community and HPD, 317–318, 356, 357, 399
G.I. Bill, 237, 238
Gillett, Rev. Charles, 12
Gonzalez, Johnny, 307
Goodson, Tom C., 65, 80, 84, 103, 147
"Goo Goo Eyes," 51, 52, 59
Gottlieb, Dick, 223
Graber, H.W., 20
Grant, Ulysses S., 36
Gray, Stockey, 237, 242
Gray, William Fairfax, 9
Green, Alexander, 282
Green, Doyle, 249
Greene, Carl, 86

R